A HISTORY OF AMERICAN LITERATURE SINCE 1870

BY

FRED LEWIS PATTEE

Professor of the English Language and Literature in the Pennsylvania
State College.   Author of "A History of American Literature,"
"The Poems of Philip Freneau," "The Foundations of
English Literature," etc.

COOPER SQUARE PUBLISHERS, INC.

NEW YORK

1968

TO DARTMOUTH COLLEGE
AND THE DARTMOUTH MEN
OF THE EIGHTIES, STU-
DENTS AND PROFESSORS,
AMONG WHOM I FIRST
AWOKE TO THE MEANING
OF LITERATURE AND OF
LIFE, THIS BOOK IS IN-
SCRIBED WITH FULL HEART.

PREFACE

American literature in the larger sense of the term began with Irving, and, if we count *The Sketch Book* as the beginning, the centennial year of its birth is yet four years hence. It has been a custom, especially among the writers of text-books, to divide this century into periods, and all have agreed at one point: in the mid-thirties undoubtedly there began a new and distinct literary movement. The names given to this new age, which corresponded in a general way with the Victorian Era in England, have been various. It has been called the Age of Emerson, the Transcendental Period, the National Period, the Central Period. National it certainly was not, but among the other names there is little choice. Just as with the Victorian Era in England, not much has been said as to when the period ended. There has been no official closing, though it has been long evident that all the forces that brought it about have long since expended themselves and that a distinctively new period has not only begun but has already quite run its course.

It has been our object to determine this new period and to study its distinguishing characteristics. We have divided the literary history of the century into three periods, denominating them as the Knickerbocker Period, the New England Period, and the National Period, and we have made the last to begin shortly after the close of the Civil War with those new forces and new ideals and broadened views that grew out of that mighty struggle.

The field is a new one: no other book and no chapter of a book has ever attempted to handle it as a unit. It is an important one: it is our first really national period, all-American, autochthonic. It was not until after the war that our writers ceased to imitate and looked to their own land for material and inspiration. The amount of its literary product has been amazing. There have been single years in which have been turned out more volumes than were produced during all of the Knickerbocker Period. The quality of this output has been uniformly high. In 1902 a writer in *Harper's Weekly* while reviewing a book by Stockton dared even to say: "He belonged to that great period between 1870 and 1890 which is as yet the greatest in our literary history, whatever the greatness of any future time may be." The statement is strong, but it is true. Despite Lowell's statement, it was not until after the Civil War that America achieved in any degree her literary independence. One can say of the period what one may not say of earlier periods, that the great mass of its writings could have been produced no-where else but in the United States. They are redolent of the new spirit of America: they are American literature.

In our study of this new national period we have considered only those authors who did their first distinctive work before 1892. Of that large group of writers born after the beginning of the period and borne into their work by forces that had little connection with the great primal impulses that came from the Civil War and the expansion period that followed, we have said nothing. We have given the names of a few of them at the close of chapter 17, but their work does not concern our study. We have limited ourselves also by centering our attention upon the three literary forms, poetry, fiction, and the essay. History we have neglected largely for the reasons given at the opening of chapter 18, and the drama for the reason that before 1892 there was produced no American drama of any literary value.

We would express here our thanks to the many librarians and assistants who have coöperated toward the making of the book possible, and especially would we tender our thanks to Professor R. W. Conover of the Kansas Agricultural College who helped to prepare the index.

F. L. P.

State College, Pennsylvania,
July 31, 1915.

CONTENTS

A HISTORY OF
AMERICAN LITERATURE
SINCE 1870

A HISTORY OF
AMERICAN LITERATURE
SINCE 1870

CHAPTER I

THE SECOND DISCOVERY OF AMERICA

I

We are beginning to realize that the Civil War marks a dividing line in American history as sharp and definitive as that
burned across French history by the Revolution.   That the South
had been vastly affected by the war was manifest from the first.
The widespread destruction of property, the collapse of the labor
system, and the fall of the social régime founded on negro slavery,
had been so dramatic and so revolutionary in their results that
they had created everywhere a feeling that the ultimate effects
of the war were confined to the conquered territory.   Grady's
phrase, ''the new South,'' and later the phrase, ''the end of an
era,'' passing everywhere current, served to strengthen the impression.   That the North had been equally affected, that there
also an old régime had perished and a new era been inaugurated,
was not so quickly realized.   The change there had been un-
dramatic; it had been devoid of all those picturesque accompani-
ments that had been so romantic and even sensational in the
South; but with the perspective of half a century we can see now
that it had been no less thoroughgoing and revolutionary.

The first effect of the war had come from the sudden shifting
of vast numbers of the population from a position of productive-
ness to one of dependence.   A people who knew only peace and
who were totally untrained even in the idea of war were called
upon suddenly to furnish one of the largest armies of modern

times and to fight to an end the most bitterly contested conflict
of a century. First and last, upwards of two millions of men,
the most of them citizen volunteers, drawn all of them from the
most efficient productive class, were mustered into the federal
service alone. It changed in a moment the entire equilibrium of
American industrial life. This great unproductive army had to
be fed and clothed and armed and kept in an enormously waste-
ful occupation. But the farms and the mills and the great transportation systems had been drained of laborers to supply men
for the regiments. The wheatfields had no harvesters; the Mississippi, the great commercial outlet of the West, had been closed
by the war, and the railroads were insufficient to handle the
burden.

The grappling with this mighty problem wrought a change in
the North that was a revolution in itself. The lack of laborers in
the harvest fields of the Middle West called for machinery, and
the reaper and the mowing machine for the first time sprang into
widespread use; the strain upon the railroads brought increased
energy and efficiency and capital to bear upon the problem of
transportation, and it was swiftly solved. Great meat-packing
houses arose to meet the new conditions; shoes had to be sent to
the front in enormous numbers and to produce them a new and
marvelous machine was brought into use; clothing in hitherto
unheard-of quantities must be manufactured and sent speedily,
and to make it Howe's sewing machine was evolved. It was a
period of giant tasks thrust suddenly upon a people seemingly un-
prepared. The vision of the country became all at once enlarged.
Companies were organized for colossal undertakings. Values
and wealth arose by leaps and bounds. Nothing seemed impossible.

The war educated America. It educated first the millions of
men who were enrolled in the armies. With few exceptions the
soldiers were boys who had never before left their native neighborhoods. From the provincial little round of the farm or the
shop, all in a moment they plunged into regions that to them
were veritable foreign lands to live in a world of excitement and
stress, with ever-shifting scenes and ever-deepening responsibilities, for three and four and even five years. Whole armies of
young men came from the remote hills of New England. Massachusetts alone sent 159,000. The diffident country lad was

trained harshly in the roughest of classrooms. He was forced to measure himself with men.

The whole nation was in the classroom of war. The imperious call for leaders of every grade and in all ranks of activity developed everywhere out of raw material captains of men, engineers, organizers, business directors, financiers, inventors, directors of activities, on a scale before undreamed of in America. It was a college course in which were developed efficiency and self-reliance and wideness of vision and courage and restless activity, and it produced a most remarkable generation of men.

The armies in the field and those other armies that handled the railroads and the mills and the finances and supplies, were sons all of them of a race that had been doubly picked in the generations before, for only the bravest and most virile in body and soul had dared to break from their old-world surroundings and plunge into the untracked West, and only the fittest of these had survived the rigors of pioneer days. And the war schooled this remnant and widened their vision and ground out of them the provincialism that had held them so long to narrow horizons. It was not until 1865 that Emerson could write, "We shall not again disparage America now we have seen what men it will bear." But the chief difference between these men and the early men that had so filled him with apprehension in the thirties and the forties, was in the schooling which had come from the five years of tension when the very life of the nation was in danger.

The disbanding of the armies was followed by a period of restlessness such as America had never before known. The whole population was restless. "War," says Emerson, "passes the power of all chemical solvents, breaking up the old adhesions and allowing the atoms of society to take a new order." The war had set in motion mighty forces that did not stop when peace was declared. Men who had been trained by the war for the organizing and directing of vast activities turned quickly to new fields of effort. The railroads, which had been vastly enlarged and enriched by the war, pushed everywhere now with marvelous rapidity; great industries, like the new oil industry, sprang into wealth and power. The West, lying vast and unbroken almost from the farther bank of the Mississippi, burst into eager life, and the tide of migration which even before the war had turned strongly toward this empire of the plains quickly became a flood.

Railroads were pushed along the wild trails and over the Rocky Mountains. The first transcontinental road was completed in 1868. The great buffalo herds were exterminated in the late sixties and early seventies; millions of acres of rich land were preëmpted and turned over to agriculture; the greatest wheat and corn belts the world has ever known were brought into production almost in a moment; bridges were flung over rivers and cañons; vast cities of the plain arose as by magic. Everywhere a new thrill was in the air. The Civil War had shaken America into eager, restless life. Mark Twain, who was a part of it all, could say in later days: "The eight years in America from 1860 to 1868 uprooted institutions that were centuries old, changed the politics of a people, transformed the social life of half the country, and wrought so profoundly upon the entire national character that the influence cannot be measured short of two or three generations." [1]

To-day we can begin to see the effect which the mighty exodus that followed the war had upon the East. It was little short of revolution. New England had taken the leading place in precipitating the struggle between the States, and she had done it for conscience' sake, and now, though she had won all she had asked, by a curious turn of fate she was repaid for her moral stand by the loss of her leadership and later almost of her identity, for the westward movement that followed the war was in New England a veritable exodus. There had always been emigration from the older States and it had gradually increased during the gold rush period and the Kansas-Nebraska excitement, but the tide had never been large enough to excite apprehension. Now, however, all in a moment the stream became a torrent which took away, as does all emigration from older lands, the most active and fearless and progressive spirits. Whole districts of farming land were deserted with all their buildings and improvements. New Hampshire in 1860 had a population of 326,073; in 1870 the population had shrunk to 318,300, and that despite the fact that all the cities and manufacturing towns in the State had grown greatly during the ten years, the increase consisting almost wholly of foreigners. According to Sanborn, "more than a million acres cultivated in 1850 had gone back to pasturage

[1] *The Gilded Age,* uniform edition, 200.

and woodland in 1900.''[2] All growth since the war has been confined to the cities and the larger manufacturing towns, and this growth and the supplying of the deficit caused by the emigration of the old stock have come from an ever-increasing influx of foreigners. Boston has all but lost its old identity. In Massachusetts in 1900 nearly one-half of the population was born of foreign parentage. New England in a single generation lost its scepter of power in the North, and that scepter gradually has been moving toward the new West.

II

But the change wrought by the war was far more than a rise of new activities and a shifting of population. A totally new America grew from the ashes of the great conflict. In 1860, North and South alike were provincial and self-conscious. New York City was an enormously overgrown village, and Boston and Philadelphia and Charleston were almost as individual and as unlike one another as they had been in the days of the Revolution. There had been nothing to fuse the sections together and to bring them to a common vision. The drama of the settlement had been fierce and piteous, but it had been a great series of local episodes. The Revolution had not been a melting pot that could fuse all the sections into a unity. The war which had begun in New England had drifted southward and each battle, especially toward the end, had been largely a local affair. Until 1860, there had been no passion fierce enough to stir to the very center of their lives all of the people, to melt them into a homogeneous mass, and to pour them forth into the mold of a new individual soul among the nations. The emphasis after 1870 was not upon the State but upon the *Nation*. As early as 1867 a writer in the *North American Review* declared that, ''The influence of our recent war in developing the 'National Sentiment' of the people can hardly be overestimated.''[3] Now there came national banks, national securities, a national railroad, a national college system,—everywhere a widening horizon. Provincialism was dying in every part of the land.

Until 1860, America had been full of the discordant individuality of youth. Its characteristics, all of them, had been char-

2 Sanborn's *New Hampshire*, 317.
3 *North American Review*, 104:301.

acteristics of that turbulent, unsettled period before character had hardened into its final form. From 1820 to 1860 the nation was adolescent. In everything at least that concerned its intellectual life it was imitative and dependent. It was in its awkward era, and like every youth was uncouth and sensitive and self-conscious. It asked eagerly of every foreign visitor, "And what do you think of us?" and when the answer, as in the case of Moore or Marryat or Dickens, was critical, it flew into a passion. It was sentimental to silliness. As late as 1875 the editor of *Scribner's* declared that a large number of all the manuscripts submitted to publishing houses and periodicals were declined because of their sentimentality, and most of the published literature of the time, he added, has "a vast deal of sentimentality sugared through it." That was in 1875; a few years before that date Griswold had published his *Female Poets of America,* and there had flourished the *Token,* the *Forget-Me-Not,* and the *Amaranth.* Adolescence is always sad:

> And I think as I sit alone,
>   While the night wind is falling around,
> Of a cold white gleaming stone
>   And a long, lone, grassy mound.

The age had sighed and wept over *Charlotte Temple,* a romance which went through edition after edition, and which, according to Higginson, had a greater number of readers even in 1870 than any single one of the Waverley Novels.

But even as it sighed over its *Charlotte Temple* and its *Rosebud* and its *Lamplighter,* it longed for better things. It had caught a glimpse, through Irving and Willis and Longfellow and others, of the culture of older lands. America had entered its first reading age. In 1844 Emerson spoke of "our immense reading and that reading chiefly confined to the productions of the English press." In its eagerness for culture it enlarged its area of books and absorbed edition after edition of translations from the German and Spanish and French. It established everywhere the lyceum, and for a generation America sat like an eager school-girl at the feet of masters—Emerson and Beecher and Taylor and Curtis and Phillips and Gough.

But adolescent youth is the period, too, of spiritual awakenings, of religious strugglings, and of the questioning and testing of all that is established. For a period America doubted all things. It read dangerous and unusual books—Fourier, St. Simon, Swedenborg, Jouffroy, Cousin. It challenged the dogmas of the Church. It worked over for itself all the fundamentals of religion. A reviewer in the first volume of *Scribner's* remarks of the fall books that, as usual, theology has the best of it. "Our poets write theology, our novels are theological . . . even our statesmen cannot write without treating theology." [4] The forties and fifties struggled with sensitive conscience over the great problems of right and wrong, of altruism and selfish ambition. The age was full of dreams; it longed to right the wrongs of the weak and the oppressed; to go forth as champions of freedom and abstract right; and at last it fought it out with agony and sweat of blood in the midnight when the stars had hid themselves seemingly forever.

The Civil War was the *Sturm und Drang* of adolescent America, the Gethsemane through which every earnest young life must pass ere he find his soul. He fails to understand the spirit of our land who misses this great fact: America discovered itself while fighting with itself in a struggle for things that are not material at all, but are spiritual and eternal. The difference between the America of 1850 and that of 1870 is the difference between the youth of sixteen and the man of thirty. Before the war the bands of America had played "Annie Laurie" and "Drink to Me only with Thine Eyes"; after the war they played "Rally round the Flag" and "Mine Eyes have Seen the Glory of the Coming of the Lord."

III

The effect of the war upon American literature has been variously estimated. Stedman has been quoted often: "The Civil War was a general absorbent at the crisis when a second group of poets began to form. The conflict not only checked the rise of a new school, but was followed by a time of languor in which the songs of Apollo seemed trivial to those who had listened to the shout of Mars." [5] It was Richardson's opinion that "little that was notable was added to the literature of the country by

[4] *Scribner's Monthly*, i: 220.
[5] *Poets of America*, 437.

the Civil War of 1861. . . . The creative powers of our best authors seemed somewhat benumbed, though books and readers multiplied between 1861 and 1865."[6]   And Greenough White dismisses the matter with the remark that "after the war, Bryant, Longfellow, and Taylor, as if their power of original production was exhausted, turned to translation."[7]

All this lacks perspective.   Stedman views the matter from the true mid-century standpoint.   Poetry to Stedman and Stoddard and Hayne and Aldrich and Taylor was an esoteric, beautiful thing to be worshiped and followed for itself alone like a goddess, a being from another sphere than ours, to devote one's soul to, "like the lady of Shalott," to quote Stevenson, "peering into a mirror with her back turned on all the bustle and glamour of reality."   Keats had been the father of this group of poets which had been broken in upon rudely by the war, and it had been the message of Keats that life with its wretchedness and commonplaceness and struggle was to be escaped from by means of Poesy:

> Away! away! for I will fly to thee,
> Not charioted by Bacchus and his pards,
> But on the viewless wings of Poesy.

But poetry is the voice of life; it is not an avenue by which to escape from life's problems.   The poet springs from his times and voices his era because he must.   If his era smothers him, then so much the less poet he.   No war can check the rise of a new school of poets if the soul of that new age is one to be expressed in poetry.

What Stedman and the others failed to see was the new American soul which had been created by the war and which the new school, trained in the old conceptions of poetry, was powerless to voice.   If the creative powers of the leading authors were numbed, if Bryant and Longfellow and Taylor felt that their power of original production was exhausted and so turned to translation, it was because they felt themselves powerless to take wing in the new atmosphere.

The North before the war had been aristocratic in its intellectual life, just as the South had been aristocratic in its social régime.   Literature and oratory and scholarship had been accom-

[6] *Primer of American Literature*, revised edition, 77.
[7] *Philosophy of American Literature*, 65.

plishments of the few.   J. G. Holland estimated in 1870 that the
lecturers in the widespread lyceum system when it was at its
highest point, "those men who made the platform popular and
useful and apparently indispensable, did not number more than
twenty-five." The whole New England period was dominated
by a handful of men.   The Saturday Club, which contained the
most of them, had, according to Barrett Wendell, twenty-six members "all typical Boston gentlemen of the Renaissance." Howells characterizes it as a "real aristocracy of intellect.   To say
Prescott, Motley, Parkman, Lowell, Norton, Higginson, Dana,
Emerson, Channing, was to say patrician in the truest and often
the best sense, if not the largest." It is significant that these
were all Harvard men.   The period was dominated by college
men.   In addition to the names mentioned by Howells, there
might be added from the New England colleges, Webster, Ticknor, Everett, Bancroft, Hawthorne, Longfellow, Holmes, Parker,
Clarke, Phillips, Sumner, Thoreau, Parsons, and Hale.   Excepting Poe, who for a time was a student at the University of Virginia and at West Point, and Whittier, who was self-educated,
and two women, Margaret Fuller and Mrs. Stowe, who lived in
the period when colleges were open only for men, the list contains
all the leading authors of the mid-period in America.

With few exceptions these names come from what Holmes de-
nominates "the Brahmin caste of New England," a term which
he uses to distinguish them from what he called "the homespun
class"—"a few chosen families against the great multitude."
"Their family names are always on some college catalogue or
other." From 1830 to 1870 the creation of literature was very
little in the hands of the masses; it was in the hands of these
scholars, of this small and provincial "aristocracy of intellect."
Holmes, who gloried in the fact that he lived in Boston, "the hub
of the universe," on Beacon Street, "the sunny street that holds
the sifted few," may be taken as a type of this aristocracy.   It
was a period of the limited circle of producers, and of mutual
admiration within the circumference of that circle.   Each member of the group took himself with great seriousness and was
taken at his own valuation by the others.   When the new democratic, after-the-war America, in the person of Mark Twain,
came into the circle and in the true Western style made free with
sacred personalities, he was received with frozen silence.

The school, on the whole, stood aloof from the civil and religious activities of its period. With the exception of Whittier, who was not a Brahmin, the larger figures of the era took interest in the great issues of their generation only when these issues had been forced into the field of their emotions. They were bookish men, and they were prone to look not into their hearts or into the heart of their epoch, but into their libraries. In 1856, when America was smoldering with what so soon was to burst out into a maelstrom of fire, Longfellow wrote in his journal, "Dined with Agassiz to meet Emerson and others. I was amused and annoyed to see how soon the conversation drifted off into politics. It was not till after dinner in the library that we got upon anything really interesting." [8] The houses of the Brahmins had only eastern windows. The souls of the whole school lived in the old lands of culture, and they visited these lands as often as they could, and, returning, brought back whole libraries of books which they eagerly translated. Even Lowell, the most democratic American of the group, save Whittier, wrote from Paris in 1873, "In certain ways this side is more agreeable to my tastes than the other." And again the next year he wrote from Florence: "America is too busy, too troubled about many things, and Martha is only good to make puddings."

Howells in his novel, *A Woman's Reason,* has given us a view of this American worship of Europe during this period. Says Lord Rainford, who has been only in Boston and Newport: "I find your people—your best people, I suppose they are—very nice, very intelligent, very pleasant—only talk about Europe. They talk about London, and about Paris, and about Rome; there seems to be quite a passion for Italy; but they don't seem interested in their own country. I can't make it out. . . . They always seem to have been reading the *Fortnightly,* and the *Saturday Review,* and the *Spectator,* and the *Revue des Deux Mondes,* and the last French and English books. It's very odd."

Europe colors the whole epoch. Following Irving's *Sketch Book,* a small library was written by eager souls to whom Europe was a wonderland and a dream. Longfellow's *Outre Mer* and *Hyperion,* Tuckerman's *Italian Sketch Book,* Willis's *Pencillings by the Way,* Cooper's *Gleanings in Europe,* Sanderson's *Sketches of Paris,* Sprague's *Letters from Europe,* Colton's *Four Years in*

[8] Longfellow's *Henry Wadsworth Longfellow,* ii: 308.

Great Britain, Taylor's *Views Afoot,* Bryant's *Letters of a Traveller,* Curtis's *Nile Notes of a Howadji,* Greeley's *Glances at Europe,* Mrs. Stowe's *Sunny Memories of Foreign Lands,* Norton's *Notes of Travel and Study in Italy,* Hawthorne's *Our Old Home,* Calvert's *Scenes and Thoughts in Europe,* and, after the war, Howells's *Venetian Life,* and Hay's *Castilian Days* are only the better-known books of the list. "Our people," complained Emerson, "have their intellectual culture from one country and their duties from another," and it was so until after the Civil War had given to America a vision of her own self. *Innocents Abroad* was the first American book about Europe that stood squarely on its own feet and told what it saw without sentimentality or romantic colorings or yieldings to the conventional. After *Innocents Abroad* there were no more rhapsodies of Europe.

America was a new land with a new message and new problems and a new hope for mankind—a hope as great as that which had fired the imagination of Europe during the years of the French Revolution, yet American writers of the mid-century were content to look into their books and echo worn old themes of other lands. The Holmes who in his youth had written *Old Ironsides* was content now with *vers de société,*

> I'm a florist in verse, and what *would* people say
> If I came to a banquet without my bouquet?

And with the thrill and rush of a new nation all about him, Stoddard could sit in his study turning out pretty Herrick-like trifles like this:

> Why are red roses red?
> For roses once were white,
> Because the loving nightingales
>   Sang on their thorns all night—
> Sang till the blood they shed
> Had dyed the roses red.

It was a period when both Europe and America were too much dominated by what Boyesen called "the parlor poet," "who stands aloof from life, retiring into the close-curtained privacy of his study to ponder upon some abstract, bloodless, and sexless theme for the edification of a *blasé,* over-refined public with nerves that can no longer relish the soul-stirring passions and emotions of a healthy and active humanity.'' In Europe, the reaction from this type of work came with Millet, the peasant painter of France, with Tolstoy and the Russian realists, with Balzac and Flaubert in France, with Hardy in England, with Ibsen and Björnson in Norway, workers with whom art was life itself.

America especially had been given to softness and sentimentalism. During the mid-century era, the period of Longfellow, the lusty new nation, which was developing a new hope for all mankind, had asked for bread and it had been given all too often ''lucent syrops tinct with cinnamon.'' The oratory had been eloquent, sometimes grandiloquent. The prose, great areas of it, had been affected, embellished with a certain florid youngmanishness, a honey-gathering of phrases even to the point of bad taste, as when Lowell wrote of Milton: ''A true Attic bee, he made boot on every lip where there was a taste of truly classic honey.'' It was the time when ornateness of figure and poeticalness of diction were regarded as essentials of style.

To understand what the Civil War destroyed and what it created, at least in the field of prose style, one should read the two orations delivered at the dedication of the Gettysburg battlefield. Here was the moment of transition between the old American literature and the new. Everett, the eloquent voice of New England, correct, polished, fervid, massing perfect periods to a climax, scholarly, sonorous of diction, studied of movement, finished, left the platform after his long effort, satisfied. The eyes of the few who could judge of oratory as a finished work of art had been upon him and he had stood the test. Then had come for a single moment the Man of the West, the plain man of the people, retiring, ungainly, untrained in the smooth school of art, voicing in simple words a simple message, wrung not from books but from the depths of a soul deeply stirred, and now, fifty years later, the oration of Everett can be found only by reference librarians, while the message of Lincoln is declaimed by every school-boy.

The half-century since the war has stood for the rise of nationalism and of populism, not in the narrower political meanings of these words, but in the generic sense. The older group of writers had been narrowly provincial. Hawthorne wrote to Bridge shortly before the war: ''At present we have no country. . . . The States are too various and too extended to form really one country. New England is really as large a lump of earth as my heart can take in.'' [9]   The war shook America awake, it destroyed sectionalism, and revealed the nation to itself. It was satisfied no longer with theatrical effects without real feeling. After the tremendous reality of the war, it demanded genuineness and the truth of life. A new spirit—social, dramatic, intense—took the place of the old dreaming and sentiment and sadness. The people had awakened. The intellectual life of the nation no longer was to be in the hands of the aristocratic, scholarly few. Even while the war was in progress a bill had passed Congress appropriating vast areas of the public lands for the establishment in every State of a college for the people ''to promote the liberal and practical education of the industrial classes in the several pursuits and professions of life,'' and it is significant that Lincoln, the first great President of the people, signed the bill.

IV

The chief output of the new era was in the form of realistic fiction. America, shaken from narrow sectionalism and contemplation of Europe, woke up and discovered America. In a kind of astonishment she wandered from section to section of her own land, discovering everywhere peoples and manners and languages that were as strange to her even as foreign lands. Mark Twain and Harte and Miller opened to view the wild regions and wilder society of early California and the Sierra Nevadas; Eggleston pictured the primitive settlements of Indiana; Cable told the romance of the Creoles and of the picturesque descendants of the Acadians on the bayous of Louisiana; Page and Harris and F. H. Smith and others caught a vision of the romance of the old South; Allen told of Kentucky life; Miss French of the dwellers in the canebrakes of Arkansas; and Miss Murfree of a strange people in the Great Smoky Mountains of Tennessee. In twenty years every isolated neighborhood in America had had its chronicler and photographer.

The spirit of the New America was realistic. There had been dreaming and moonlight and mystery enough; now it wanted concrete reality. ''Give us the people as they actually are.

9 Woodberry's *Hawthorne*, 281.

Give us their talk as they actually talk it," and the result was the age of dialect—dialect poetry, dialect fiction, dialect even to coarseness and profanity. The old school in the East stood aghast before what they termed this "Neo-Americanism," this coarse "new literature of the people." Holland in 1872 found "Truthful James" "deadly wearisome." He hoped that the poet had "found, as his readers have, sufficient amusement in the 'Heathen Chinee' and the 'Society upon the Stanislaus' and is ready for more serious work." From this wearisome stuff he then turned to review in highest terms Stoddard's *Book of the East,* a land which Stoddard had never visited save in dreams.

The reviewer of Maurice Thompson's *Hoosier Mosaics* four years later speaks of the author as a promising acquisition to "the invading Goths from over the mountains." Stedman viewed the new tide with depression of soul. In a letter to Taylor in 1873 he says:

> *Lars* is a poem that will *last,* though not in the wretched, immediate *fashion* of this demoralized American period. Cultured as are Hay and Harte, they are almost equally responsible with "Josh Billings" and the *Danbury News* man for the present *horrible* degeneracy of the public taste—that is, the taste of the present generation of book-buyers. I feel that this is not the complaint of a superannuated Roger de Coverley nor Colonel Newcome, for I am in the prime and vigor of active, noonday life, and at work right here in the metropolis. It is a clear-headed, wide-awake statement of a disgraceful fact. With it all I acknowledge, the demand for good books also increases and such works as Paine's *Septembre,* etc., have a large standard sale. But in poetry readers have tired of the past and don't see clearly how to shape a future; and so content themselves with going to some "Cave" or "Hole in the Wall" and applauding slang and nonsense, spiced with smut and profanity.[10]

This is an extreme statement of the conditions, but it was written by the most alert and clear-eyed critic of the period, one who, even while he deplored the conditions, was wise enough to recognize the strength of the movement and to ally himself with it. "Get hold of a dramatic American theme," he counsels Taylor, "merely for policy's sake. The people want Neo-Americanism; we must adopt their system and elevate it." Wise advice indeed, but Taylor had his own ideals. After the failure of *The Masque of the Gods* he wrote Aldrich: "If this public

10 *Life and Letters of E. C. Stedman,* i: 477.

won't accept my better work, I must wait till a new one grows up. . . . I will go on trying to do intrinsically good things, and will not yield a hair's breadth for the sake of conciliating an ignorant public." [11]

V

The exploiting of new and strange regions, with their rough manners, their coarse humor, and their uncouth dialects, brought to the front the new, hard-fought, and hard-defended literary method called realism. For a generation the word was on every critic's pen both in America and abroad. No two seemed perfectly to agree what the term really meant, or what writers were to be classed as realists and what as romanticists. It is becoming clearer now: it was simply the new, young, vigorous tide which had set in against the decadent, dreamy softness that had ruled the mid years of the century.

The whole history of literature is but the story of an alternating current. A new, young school of innovators arises to declare the old forms lifeless and outworn. Wordsworth at the opening of the nineteenth century had protested against unreality and false sentiment—"a dressy literature, an exaggerated literature" as Bagehot expressed it—and he started the romantic revolt by proposing in his poems "to choose incidents and situations from common life, and to relate or describe them, throughout, as far as was possible in a selection of language really used by men." Revolt always has begun with the cry "back to nature"; it is always the work of young men who have no reverence for the long-standing and the conventional; and it is always looked upon with horror by the older generations. Jeffrey, in reviewing the *Lyrical Ballads,* said that the "Ode on Intimations of Immortality" was "beyond doubt the most illegible and unintelligible part of the publication. We can pretend to give no analysis or explanation of it." At last the revolt triumphs, and as the years go on its ideas in turn are hardened into rules of art. Then suddenly another group of daring young souls arises, and, setting its back upon the old, blazes out a new pathway toward what it considers to be truth and nature and art. This new school of revolt from the old and outworn we

[11] *Life and Letters of Bayard Taylor,* ii: 588.

call always the new romantic movement. It is only the new generation pressing upon the old, and demanding a fresh statement of life in terms of truth to present conditions.

In America, and indeed in Europe as well, the early seventies called for this new statement of art. No more *Hyperions*, no more conceits and mere prettinesses, no more fine phrasing, no more castles in Spain, but life real and true, naked in its absolute faithfulness to facts. It was a revolt. If we call the age of Longfellow a romantic period, then this revolt of the seventies was a *new* romanticism, for romanticism always in broadest sense is a revolution against orthodoxy, against the old which has been so long established that it has lost its first vitality and become an obedience to the letter rather than to the spirit.

The new movement seemed to the Brahmins of the older school a veritable renaissance of vulgarity. Even Lowell, who had written the *Biglow Papers*, cried out against it. The new literature from the West and the South was the work of what Holmes had called "the homespun class," "the great multitude." It was written, almost all of it, by authors from no college. They had been educated at the printer's case, on the farm, in the mines, and along the frontiers. As compared with the roll of the Brahmins the list is significant: Whitman, Warner, Helen Jackson, Stockton, Shaw, Clemens, Piatt, Thaxter, Howells, Eggleston, Burroughs, F. H. Smith, Hay, Harte, Miller, Cable, Gilder, Allen, Harris, Jewett, Wilkins, Murfree, Riley, Page, Russell. The whole school thrilled with the new life of America, and they wrote often without models save as they took life itself as their model. Coarse and uncouth some parts of their work might be, but teeming it always was with the freshness, the vitality, and the vigor of a new soil and a newly awakened nation.

VI

The new period began in the early seventies. The years of the war and the years immediately following it were fallow so far as significant literary output was concerned. "Literature is at a standstill in America, paralyzed by the Civil War," wrote Stedman in 1864, and at a later time he added, "For ten years the new generation read nothing but newspapers." The old group was still producing voluminously, but their work was done.

They had been borne into an era in which they could have no part, and they contented themselves with reëchoings of the old music and with translations. In 1871 *The London School Board Chronicle* could declare that, "The most gifted of American singers are not great as creators of home-bred poetry, but as translators," and then add without reservation that the best translations in the English language had been made in America. It was the statement of a literal fact. Within a single period of six years, from 1867 to 1872, there appeared Longfellow's *Divina Commedia*, C. E. Norton's *Vita Nuova*, T. W. Parsons' *Inferno*, Bryant's *Iliad* and *Odyssey*, Taylor's *Faust* and C. P. Cranch's *Æneid*.

It was the period of swan songs. Emerson's *Terminus* came in 1866; *Last Poems* of the Cary sisters, Longfellow's *Aftermath* and Whittier's *Hazel Blossoms* appeared in 1874; and Holmes's *The Iron Gate* was published in 1880. Lowell, the youngest of the group, alone seemed to have been awakened by the war. His real message to America, the national odes and the essays on Democracy which will make his name permanent in literature, came after 1865, and so falls into the new period.

The decade from 1868 is in every respect the most vital and significant one in the history of America. The tremendous strides which were then made in the settlement of the West, the enormous increase of railroads and steamships and telegraphs, the organization of nation-wide corporations like those dealing with petroleum and steel and coal—all these we have already mentioned. America had thrown aside its provincialism and had become a great neighborhood, and in 1876 North, South, East, and West gathered in a great family jubilee. *Scribner's Monthly* in 1875 commented feelingly upon the fact:

All the West is coming East. . . . The Southern States will be similarly moved. . . . There will be a tremendous shaking up of the people, a great going to and fro in the land. . . . The nation is to be brought together as it has never been brought before during its history. In one hundred years of intense industry and marvelous development we have been so busy that we never have been able to look one another in the face, except four terrible years of Civil War. . . . This year around the old family altar at Philadelphia we expect to meet and embrace as brothers.[12]

[12] *Scribner's Monthly*, xi: 432.

The Centennial quickened in every way the national life. It gave for the first time the feeling of unity, the realization that the vast West, the new South, and the uncouth frontier were a vital part of the family of the States. Lowell, so much of whose early heart and soul had been given to Europe, discovered America in this same Centennial year. In Cincinnati he was profoundly impressed with the "wonderful richness and comfort of the country and with the distinctive Americanism that is molding into one type of feature and habits so many races that had widely diverged from the same original stock. . . . These immense spaces tremulous with the young grain, trophies of individual, or at any rate unorganized, courage and energy, of the people and not of dynasties, were to me inexpressibly impressive and even touching. . . . The men who have done and are doing these things know how things should be done. . . . It was very interesting, also, to meet men from Kansas and Nevada and California, and to see how manly and intelligent they were, and especially what large heads they had. They had not the manners of Vere de Vere, perhaps, but they had an independence and self-respect which are the prime element of fine bearing." [13] A little of a certain Brahmin condescension toward Westerners there may be here, but on the whole it rings true. The East was discovering the West and was respecting it.

And now all of a sudden this Neo-Americanism burst forth into literature. There is a similarity almost startling between the thirties that saw the outburst of the mid-century school and the vital seventies that arose in reaction against it. The first era had started with Emerson's glorification of the American scholar, the second had glorified the man of action. The earlier period was speculative, sermonic, dithyrambic, eloquent; the new America which now arose was cold, dispassionate, scientific, tolerant. Both had arisen in storm and doubt and in protest against the old. Both touched the people, the earlier era through the sentiments, the later through the analytical and the dramatic faculties. In the thirties had arisen *Godey's Lady's Book;* in the seventies *Scribner's Monthly.*

So far as literature was concerned the era may be said really to have commenced in 1869 with *Innocents Abroad,* the first book from which there breathed the new wild spirit of revolt. In

[13] Norton's *Letters of James Russell Lowell,* ii: 169.

1870 came Harte's *Luck of Roaring Camp,* thrilling with the new strange life of the gold coast and the Sierra Nevada, and Warner's *My Summer in a Garden,* a transition book fresh and delightful. Then in 1871 had begun the deluge: Burroughs's *Wake-Robin,* with its new gospel of nature; Eggleston's *Hoosier Schoolmaster,* fresh with uncouth humor and the strangeness of the frontier; Harte's *East and West Poems;* Hay's *Pike County Ballads,* crude poems from the heart of the people; Howells's first novel, *Their Wedding Journey,* a careful analysis of actual social conditions; Miller's *Songs of the Sierras;* Carleton's *Poems;* King's *Mountaineering in the Sierra Nevada,* a book of travel glorifying not Europe but a picturesque section of America; and the completed version of Leland's *Hans Breitmann's Ballads,* a book which had waited fourteen years for a publisher who had the courage to bring it out. In 1873 came Celia Thaxter's *Poems,* Aldrich's *Majorie Daw,* H. H.'s *Saxe Holm Stories,* Wallace's *Fair God* and O'Reilly's *Songs of the Southern Seas;* in 1875 James's *Passionate Pilgrim,* Thompson's *Hoosier Mosaics,* Gilder's *The New Day,* Lanier's *Poems,* Catherwood's *A Woman in Armor,* Woolson's *Castle Nowhere* and Irwin Russell's first poem in *Scribner's;* in 1877 Burnett's *That Lass o' Lowrie's* and Jewett's *Deephaven;* in 1878 Craddock's *The Dancing Party at Harrison's Cove* in the *Atlantic Monthly,* Richard M. Johnston's *Life of Stephens;* in 1879 Cable's *Old Creole Days,* Tourgee's *Figs and Thistles,* Stockton's *Rudder Grange,* and John Muir's *Studies in the Sierras,* in *Scribner's.* All the elements of the new era had appeared before 1880.

The old traditions were breaking. In 1874 the editorial chair of the *Atlantic Monthly,* the exclusive organ of the old New England régime, was given to a Westerner. In 1873 came the resurgence of Whitman. The earlier school had ignored him, or had tolerated him because of Emerson, but now with the new discovery of America he also was discovered, and hailed as a pioneer. The new school of revolt in England—Rossetti, Swinburne, Symonds—declared him a real voice, free and individual, the voice of all the people. Thoreau also came into his true place. His own generation had misunderstood him, compared him with Emerson, and neglected him. Only two of his books had been published during his lifetime and one of these had sold fewer than three hundred copies. Now he too was discovered. In the words of Burroughs, "His fame has increased steadily since his death in 1862, as it was bound to do. It was little more than in the bud at that time, and its full leaf and flowering are not yet."

VII

The new age was to express itself in prose. The poetry of the earlier period, soft and lilting and romantic, no longer satisfied. It was effeminate in tone and subject, and the new West, virile and awake, defined a poet, as Wordsworth had defined him in 1815, as "a man speaking to men." America, in the sturdy vigor of manhood, wrestling with fierce realities, had passed the age of dreaming. It had now to deal with social problems, with plans on a vast scale for the bettering of human conditions, with the organization of cities and schools and systems of government. It was a busy, headlong, multitudinous age. Poetry, to interest it, must be sharp and incisive and winged with a message. It must be lyrical in length and spirit, and it must ring true. If it deal with social themes it must be perfect in characterization and touched with genuine pathos, like the folk songs of Riley and Drummond, or the *vers de société* of Bunner and Eugene Field. If it touch national themes, it must be strong and trumpet clear, like the odes of Lowell and Lanier. It must not spring from the far off and the forgot but from the life of the day and the hour, as sprung Whitman's Lincoln elegies, Joaquin Miller's "Columbus," and Stedman's war lyrics. Not many have there been who have brought message and thrill, but there have been enough to save the age from the taunt that it was a period without poets.

In a broad sense, no age has ever had more of poetry, for the message and the vision and thrill, which in older times came through epic and lyric and drama, have in the latter days come in full measure through the prose form which we call the novel. As a form it has been brought to highest perfection. It has been found to have scope enough to exercise the highest powers of a great poet, and allow him to sound all the depths and shallows of human life. It has been the preacher of the age, the theater, the minstrel, and the social student, the prophet and seer and reformer. It has been more than the epic of democracy; it has been horn-book as well and shepherd's calendar. It has been the literary form peculiarly fitted for a restless, observant, scientific age.

The influence of Dickens, who died in 1870, the opening year of the period, cannot be lightly passed over. It had been his task in the middle years of the century to democratise literature, and to create a reading public as Addison had done a century earlier, but Addison's public was London, the London that breakfasted late and went to the coffee house. Dickens created a reading public out of those who had never read books before, and the greater part of it was in America. His social novels with their break from all the conventions of fiction, their bold, free characterization, their dialect and their rollicking humor and their plentiful sentiment, were peculiarly fitted for appreciation in the new after-the-war atmosphere of the new land. Harte freely acknowledged his debt to him and at his death laid a "spray of Western pine" on his grave. The grotesque characters of the Dickens novels were not more grotesque than the actual inhabitants of the wild mining towns of the Sierras or the isolated mountain hamlets of the South, or of many out-of-the-way districts even in New England. The great revival of interest in Dickens brought about by his death precipitated the first wave of local color novels—the earliest work of Harte and Eggleston and Stockton and the author of *Cape Cod Folks*.

This first wave of Dickens-inspired work, however, soon expended itself, and it was followed by another wave of fiction even more significant. In the first process of rediscovering America, Harte, perhaps, or Clemens, or Cable, stumbled upon a tremendous fact which was destined to add real classics to American literature: America was full of border lands where the old régime had yielded to the new, and where indeed there was a true atmosphere of romance. The result was a type of fiction that was neither romantic nor realistic, but a blending of both methods, a romanticism of atmosphere and a realism of truth to the actual conditions and characters involved.

This condition worked itself out in a literary form that is seen now to be the most distinctive product of the period. The era may as truly be called the era of the short story as the Elizabethan period may be called the era of the drama and the early eighteenth century the era of the prose essay. The local color school which exploited the new-found nooks and corners of the West and

South did its work almost wholly by means of this highly wrought and concentrated literary form. Not half a dozen novelists of the period have worked exclusively in the novel and romance forms of the mid-century type. A group of writers, including Harte, Clemens, Cable, Mrs. Cooke, Miss Jewett, Mrs. Wilkins-Freeman, Miss Brown, Miss Murfree, Harris, R. M. Johnston, Page, Stockton, Bierce, Garland, Miss King, Miss French, Miss Woolson, Deming, Bunner, Aldrich, have together created what is perhaps the best body of short stories in any language.

The period at its end tended to become journalistic. The enormous demand for fiction by the magazines and by the more ephemeral journals produced a great mass of hastily written and often ill considered work, but on the whole the literary quality of the fiction of the whole period, especially the short stories, has been high. Never has there been in any era so vast a flood of books and reading, and it may also be said that never before has there been so high an average of literary workmanship.

CHAPTER II

American literature from the first has been rich in humor. The incongruities of the new world—the picturesque gathering of peoples like the Puritans, the Indians, the cavaliers, the Dutch, the negroes and the later immigrants; the makeshifts of the frontier, the vastness and the richness of the land, the leveling effects of democracy, the freedom of life, and the independence of spirit —all have tended to produce a laughing people. The first really American book, Irving's *Knickerbocker's History of New York,* was a broadly humorous production. The mid period of the nineteenth century was remarkably rich in humor. One has only to mention Paulding and Holmes and Saxe and Lowell and Seba Smith and B. P. Shillaber. Yet despite these names and dozens of others almost equally deserving, it must be acknowledged that until the Civil War period opened there had been no school of distinctly American humorists, original and nation-wide. The production had been sporadic and provincial, and it had been read by small circles. The most of it could be traced to older prototypes: Hood, Thackeray, Lamb, Douglas Jerrold, Dickens. The humor of America, "new birth of our new soil," had been discovered, but as yet it had had no national recognition and no great representative.

As late as 1866, a reviewer of "Artemus Ward" in the *North American Review,* published then in Boston, complained that humor in America had been a local product and that it had been largely imitative. It was time, he declared, for a new school of humorists who should be original in their methods and national in their scope. "They must not aim at copying anything; they should take a new form. . . . Let them seek to embody the wit and humor of all parts of the country, not only of one city where their paper is published; let them force Portland to disgorge her Jack Downings and New York her Orpheus C. Kerrs, for the benefit of all. Let them form a nucleus which will draw to itself all the waggery and wit of America."[1] It was the call of the new national spirit, and as if in reply there arose the new school—uncolleged for the most part, untrained by books, fresh, joyous, extravagant in its bursting young life—the first voice of the new era.

The group was born during the thirties and early forties, that second seedtime of American literature. Their birth dates fall within a period of ten years:

1833. David Ross Locke, "Petroleum V. Nasby."
1834. Charles Farrar Browne, "Artemus Ward."
1834. Charles Henry Webb, "John Paul."
1835. Samuel Langhorne Clemens, "Mark Twain."
1836. Robert Henry Newell, "Orpheus C. Kerr."
1839. Melvin DeLancy Landon, "Eli Perkins."
1841. Thomas Nast.
1841. Charles Heber Clark, "Max Adler."
1841. James Montgomery Bailey, "The Danbury News Man."
1841. Alexander Edwin Sweet.
1842. Charles Bertrand Lewis, "M. Quad."

To the school also belonged several who were born outside of this magic ten years. There were Henry Wheeler Shaw, "Josh Billings," born in 1818; and Charles Henry Smith, "Bill Arp," born in 1823. At least three younger members must not be omitted: Robert Jones Burdette, 1844; Edgar Wilson Nye, "Bill Nye," 1850; and Opie Read, 1852.

I

In a broad way the school was a product of the Civil War. American humor had been an evolution of slow growth, and the war precipitated it. The election of Lincoln in 1860 was the beginning. Here was a man of the new West who had worked on flatboats on the Ohio, who had served as a soldier in a backwoods troop, who had ridden for years on a Western circuit, and in rough and ready political campaigns had withstood the heckling of men who had fought barehanded with the frontier and had won. The saddest man in American history, he stands as

[1] Vol. 102:586.

one of the greatest of American humorists. His laughter rings through the whole period of the war, man of sorrows though he was, and it was the Western laughter heard until now only along the great rivers and the frontier and the gold coast of the Pacific. He had learned it from contact with elemental men, men who passed for precisely what they were, men who were measured solely by the iron rule of what they could do; self-reliant men, healthy, huge-bodied, deep-lunged men to whom life was a joy. The humor that he brought to the East was nothing new in America, but the significant thing is that for the first time it was placed in the limelight. A peculiar combination it was, half shrewd wisdom, "hoss sense," as "Josh Billings" called it, the rest characterization which exposed as with a knife-cut the inner life as well as the outer, whimsical overstatement and understatement, droll incongruities told with all seriousness, and an irreverence born of the all-leveling democracy of the frontier.

"It was Lincoln's opinion that the finest wit and humor, the best jokes and anecdotes, emanated from the lower orders of the country people," [2] and in this judgment he pointed out the very heart of the new literature that was germinating about him. Such life is genuine; it rests upon the foundations of nature itself. Lincoln, like the man of the new West that he was, delighted not so much in books as in actual contact with life. "Riding the circuit for many years and stopping at country taverns where were gathered the lawyers, jurymen, witnesses, and clients, they would sit up all night narrating to each other their life adventures; and the things which happened to an original people, in a new country, surrounded by novel conditions, and told with the descriptive power and exaggeration which characterized such men, supplied him with an exhaustless fund of anecdotes which could be made applicable for enforcing or refuting an argument better than all the invented stories of the world." [3]

It was the new humor of the West for the first time shown to the whole world. Lincoln, the man of the West, had met the polished East in the person of Douglas and had triumphed through very genuineness, and now he stood in the limelight of the Presidency, transacting the nation's business with anec-

2 Lamon's *Life of Abraham Lincoln*, 480.
3 Chauncey M. Depew, quoted in Hapgood's *Abraham Lincoln*, 118.

dotes from the frontier circuits, meeting hostile critics with shrewd border philosophy, and reading aloud with unction, while battles were raging or election returns were in doubt, from "Artemus Ward," or "Petroleum Vesuvius Nasby," or *The Flush Times of Alabama and Mississippi*—favorites of his because they too were genuine, excerpts not from books but from life itself.

II

Glimpses there already had been of the new humor of the West. George W. Harris (1814–1868), steamboat captain on the Tennessee River, had created that true child of the West, "Sut Lovengood"; Augustus B. Longstreet (1790–1870) in *Georgia Scenes* had drawn inimitable sketches of the rude life of his region; and Joseph G. Baldwin (1815–1864), like Lincoln, himself a lawyer who had learned much on his frontier circuit, in his *Flush Times* had traced the evolution of a country barrister in a manner that even now, despite its echoes of Dickens, makes the book a notable one.

But the greatest of them all, the real father of the new school of humorists, the man who gave the East the first glimpse of the California type of humor, was George Horatio Derby (1823–1861), whose sketches over the signature "John Phœnix" began to appear in the early fifties. Undoubtedly it would amaze Derby could he return and read of himself as the father of the later school of humor. With him literary comedy was simply a means now and then of relaxation from the burdens of a strenuous profession. He had been graduated from West Point in 1846, had fought in the Mexican War, and later as an engineer had been entrusted by the government with important surveys and explorations in the far West and later in Florida, where he died at the age of thirty-eight of sunstroke. He was burdened all his life with heavy responsibilities and exacting demands upon his energies. He had little time for books, and his writings, what few he produced, were the result wholly of his own observations upon the picturesque life that he found about him in the West.

In his *Phœnixiana,* published in 1855, we find nearly all of the elements that were to be used by the new school of humorists. First, there is the solemn protestation of truthfulness followed

by the story that on the face of it is impossible. "If the son
of the reader . . . should look confidingly into his parent's face,
and inquire—'Is that true, Papa?' reply, oh, reader, unhesitatingly—'My son, it is.' " To make the story still more plausible he quotes "Truthful James." He may then proceed with a
story like this:

He glanced over the first column [of Phœnix's *Pictorial*] when he
was observed to grow black in the face. A bystander hastened to seize
him by the collar, but it was too late. Exploding with mirth, he was
scattered into a thousand fragments, one of which striking him probably inflicting some fatal injury, as he immediately expired, having
barely time to remove his hat, and say in a feeble voice, "Give this to
Phoenix." A large black tooth lies on the table before us, driven
through the side of the office with fearful violence at the time of the
explosion. We have enclosed it to his widow with a letter of con-
dolence.

"*Truthful James*"—we think of Bret Harte, and we think of
him again after passages like this: "An old villain with a bald
head and spectacles punched me in the abdomen; I lost my
breath, closed my eyes, and remembered nothing further."
Derby was the first conspicuous writer to use grotesque exaggerations deliberately and freely as a provocative of laughter.
Irving and many others had made use of it, but in *Phœnixiana*
it amounts to a mannerism. He tells the most astonishing im-
possibilities and then naïvely adds: "It is possible that the circumstances may have become slightly exaggerated. Of course,
there can be no doubt of the truth of the main incidents." In
true California style he makes use often of specific exaggeration. Two men trip over a rope in the dark "and then followed
what, if published, would make two closely printed royal octavo
pages of profanity." So popular was the Phœnix *Herald* that
"we have now seven hundred and eighty-two Indians employed
night and day in mixing adobe for the type molds."
The second characteristic of Derby's humor was its irreverence.
To him nothing was sacred. The first practical joker, he averred,
was Judas Iscariot: he *sold* his Master. Arcturus, he observed,
was a star "which many years since a person named Job was
asked if he could guide, and he acknowledged he could n't do it."
"David was a Jew—hence, the 'Harp of David' was a Jew's-
harp."

He delights in the device of euphemistic statement used so freely by later humorists. The father of Joseph Bowers, he explains, was engaged in business as a malefactor in western New York, but was annoyed greatly by the prejudices of the bigoted settlers. He emigrated suddenly, however, with such precipitation in fact that "he took nothing with him of his large property but a single shirt, which he happened to have about him at the time he formed his resolution." Finally he "ended his career of usefulness by falling from a cart in which he had been standing, addressing a numerous audience, and in which fall he unfortunately broke his neck."

He abounds in true Yankee aphorisms—"when a man is going down, everybody lends him a kick," "Where impudence is wit, 't is folly to reply." He uses unexpected comparisons and whimsical *non sequiturs:* he sails on "a Napa steam packet of four cat-power"; "the wind blew," he declared, "like well-watered roses." R. W. Emerson, he was informed, while traveling in upper Norway, "on the 21st of June, 1836, distinctly saw the sun in all its majesty shining at midnight!—in fact, all night. Emerson is not what you would call a superstitious man, by any means—but, he left."

It was Derby who wrote the first Pike County ballad. "Suddenly we hear approaching a train from Pike County, consisting of seven families, with forty-six wagons, each drawn by thirteen oxen." Elsewhere he has described the typical "Pike": "His hair is light, not a 'sable silvered,' but a *yeller,* gilded; you can see some of it sticking out of the top of his hat; his costume is the national costume of Arkansas, coat, waistcoat, and pantaloons of homespun cloth, dyed a brownish yellow, with a decoction of the bitter barked butternut—a pleasing alliteration; his countenance presents a determined, combined with a sanctimonious expression." "Now rises o'er the plains in mellifluous accents, the grand Pike County Chorus:

> Oh, we 'll soon be thar
> In the land of gold,
> Through the forest old,
> O'er the mounting cold,
> With spirits bold—
> Oh, we come, we come,
> And we 'll soon be thar.
>   Gee up, Bolly! whoo, up, whoo haw!

Not much was added to Western humor after Derby. Mark Twain's earliest manner had much in it that smacks of "Phœnix." The chapters entitled, "Phœnix Takes an Affectionate Leave of San Francisco," "Phœnix is on the Sea," and "Phœnix in San Diego" might have been taken from *Roughing It*. Just as truly the chapters, "Inauguration of the New Collector" and "Return of the Collector," "Thrilling and Frantic Excitement Among Office Seekers" might have been written by Orpheus C. Kerr. Yet despite such similarities, the later school did not necessarily filch from "Phœnix": they learned their art as he had learned it from contact with the new West. All drew from the same model.

III

For the new humor, which was to be the first product of the new period in American literature, was Western humor of the "John Phœnix" type. It came from three great seed places: the Mississippi and its rivers, the California coast, and, later, the camps of the Civil War. It was the humor of the gatherings of men under primitive conditions. It was often crude and coarse. It was elemental and boisterous and often profane. To the older school of poets and scholars in the East it seemed, as it began to fill all the papers and creep even into the standard magazines, like a veritable renaissance of vulgarity. "The worlds before and after the Deluge were not more different than our republics of letters before and after the war," [4] wrote Stedman to William Winter in 1873, and the same year he wrote to Taylor in Europe, "The whole country, owing to *contagion* of our American newspaper 'exchange' system, is flooded, deluged, swamped, beneath a muddy tide of slang, vulgarity, inartistic bathers [*sic*], impertinence, and buffoonery that is not wit." [5]

Many of the new humorists had been born in the East, but all of them had been drilled either in the rough school of the West or in the armies during the war. Shaw had been a deckhand on an Ohio River steamer; Browne had been a tramp printer both in the East and the West, and had lived for a time in California; Clemens had been tramp printer, pilot on the Mississippi, and for five years miner and newspaper man on the Western coast;

4 *Life and Letters of E. C. Stedman*, i: 466.
5 *Ibid.*, i: 477.

Webb and Nye and Newell had seen life in California; Locke had edited country papers in northern Ohio, and C. H. Smith, Landon, Bailey, Sweet, Lewis, and Burdette had been soldiers in the Civil War. All of them had been thrown together with men under circumstances that had stripped them and the life about them of all the veneer of convention and class distinction.

One thing the group had in common: they were newspaper men; most of them had worked at the case; all of them at one time or another were connected with the press. The new humor was scattered by the newspapers that after the war spread themselves in incredible numbers over America. The exchange system, complained of by Stedman, became nation wide. The good things of one paper were seized upon by the others and sown broadcast. Humorous departments became more and more common, until staid old papers like the *Boston Advertiser* had yielded to the popular demand. The alarm voiced by Stedman in his letter to Taylor was taken up by the more conservative magazines. The humor of to-day is written for the multitude, complained the ponderous old *North American Review,* "that uncounted host which reads for its romance *The Ledger* and *The Pirate of the Gulf.* Common schools make us a nation of readers. But common schools, alas! do little to inculcate taste or discrimination in the choice of reading. The mass of the community has a coarse digestion. . . . It likes horse-laughs." [6] But it is useless to combat the spirit of the age.

The wave rolled on until it reached its height in the mid seventies. From journals with an incidental humorous column there had arisen the newspaper that was quoted everywhere and enormously subscribed for solely because of the funny man in charge. The *Danbury News,* the local paper of a small Connecticut city, swelled its subscription list to 40,000 because of its editor Bailey. The vogue of such a paper was not long. At different periods there arose and flourished and declined "Nasby's" *Toledo Blade,* "Lickshingle's" *Oil City Derrick,* Burdette's *Burlington Hawkeye,* "M. Quad's" *Detroit Free Press,* Peck's *Sun,* Sweet's *Texas Siftings,* Read's *Arkansaw Traveller,* and many others.

The greater part of this newspaper humor was as fleeting as the flying leaves upon which it was printed. It has disappeared

6 Vol. 102:588.

never to be regathered. Even the small proportion of it that was put by its authors into book form has fared little better. From all the host of literary comedians that so shook the period with laughter not over four have taken anything even approaching a permanent place. These four are Browne, Locke, Nast, and Shaw.

IV

Charles Farrar Browne, "Artemus Ward," the first of the group to gain recognition, was born of Puritan ancestry in Waterville, Maine, in 1834. Forced by the death of his father in 1847 to rely upon his own efforts for support, he became a typesetter on the Skowhegan *Clarion*, and later, after a wandering career from office to office, served for three years in Boston as a compositor for Snow and Wilder, the publishers of *Mrs. Partington's Carpet Bag*. His connection with Shillaber, the editor of this paper, turned his mind to humorous composition, but it was not until after his second wander period in the South and West that he discovered the real bent of his powers. His career as a humorist may be said to have begun in 1857, when, after two years at Toledo, Ohio, he was called to the local editorship of the Cleveland *Plain-Dealer* and given freedom to inject into the dry news columns all the life and fun that he chose. He began now to write articles purporting to describe the struggles and experiences of one "Artemus Ward," an itinerant showman who was as full of homely wisdom and experience as he was lacking in book learning and refinement. The letters instantly struck a popular chord; they were copied widely. After serving three years on the *Plain-Dealer* their author was called to New York to become the editor of the brilliant but ill-starred comic magazine, *Vanity Fair*. The following year, 1861, he began to lecture, and in 1863 and 1864 he made a six-months' lecture tour of the Pacific Coast. The free, picturesque life of the new cities and the wild camps delighted him. In Virginia City he spent three marvelous weeks with Mark Twain, then a reporter on the local paper. Returning across the Plains, he visited the Mormons. The trip was the graduate course of the young humorist. Not until after his California training was he completely in command of his art. Then in 1866 at the height of his powers he went to London, where his success was instant and unprecedented. He was made an editor of *Punch*, he was discussed in all quarters, and his lectures night by night were attended by crowds. But the end was near. He died of quick consumption March 6, 1867.

The secret of Browne's success as a humorist lay, first of all, in the droll personality of the man. It was the opinion of Haweis, who heard him in London, that his "bursts of quaint humor could only live at all in that subtle atmosphere which Artemus Ward's presence created, and in which alone he was able to operate." [7] He made use of all the humorous devices of his favorite, John Phœnix, and to them he added what may be called the American manner of delivering humor: the setting forth with perfect gravity and even mournfulness his most telling jokes and then the assuming of a surprised or even a grieved expression when the audience laughed.

Furthermore, to Phœnix's devices he added cacography, the device of deliberate misspelling so much used by later humorists. He seems to have adopted it spontaneously as a matter of course. He was to take the character of an ignorant showman and naturally he must write as such a man would write. The misspelling of "Artemus Ward" has character in it. In his hands it becomes an art, and an art that helps make vivid the personality of the old showman. "Artemus Ward" is not a mere Dickens gargoyle: he is alive. Witness this:

If you say anything about my show say my snaiks is as harmliss as the new born Babe.

In the Brite Lexington of yooth, thar aint no sich word as fale.

"Too troo, too troo!" I answered; "it's a scanderlis fact."

He is not at all consistent in his spelling; he is as prodigal as nature and as careless. The mere uninspired cacographist misspells every word that it is possible to misspell, but Browne picks only key words. His art is displayed as much in the words he does not change as in those with which he makes free. He coins new words with telling effect. Of his wife he observes: "As a flap-jackist she has no equal. She wears the belt." And he makes free with older words in a way that is peculiarly his own: "Why this thusness."

The third element he added to the humor of Phœnix was a

[7] Haweis's *American Humorists*, 122.

naïve drollery, a whimsical incongruity, that was peculiar to himself. He caught it from no one, and he imparted it to no one. It can be described only as "Artemus Ward." It lives even apart from his presence in much of the writing that he has left behind him. It is as useless to try to analyze it as it were to describe the odor of apples. One can only quote examples, as for instance this from his adventure "Among the Free Lovers":

The exsentric female then clutched me frantically by the arm and hollered:

"You air mine, O you air mine!"

"Scacely," I sed, endeverin to git loose from her. But she clung to me and sed:

"You air my Affinerty!"

"What upon arth is that?" I shouted.

"Dost thou not know?"

"No, I dostent!"

"Listin man & I'll tell ye!" sed the strange female; "for years I hav yearned for thee. I knowd thou wast in the world sumwhares, tho I did n't know whare. My hart sed he would cum and I took courage. He *has* cum—he's here—you air him—you air my Affinerty! O 't is too mutch! too mutch!" and she sobbed agin.

"Yes," I anserd, "I think it is a darn sight too mutch!"

"Hast thou not yearned for me?" she yelled, ringin her hands like a female play acter.

"Not a yearn!" I bellerd at the top of my voice, throwin her away from me.

Whatever we may think of the quality of this, we must agree that it is original. If there is any trace of a prototype it is Dickens. The characters and the situation are heightened to grotesqueness, yet one must be abnormally keen in palate to detect any Dickens flavor in the style. It is "Artemus Ward" and only "Artemus Ward." All that he wrote he drew from life itself and from American life. It is as redolent of the new world as the bison or the Indian. He wrote only what had passed under his eye and he wrote only of persons. Unlike Mark Twain, he could cross the continent in the wild days of '64 and see nothing apparently but humanity.

The world of Charles Farrar Browne was the child's world of wonder. He was a case, as it were, of arrested development, a fragment of the myth-making age brought into the nineteenth century. His "Artemus Ward" was a latter-day knight-errant traveling from adventure to adventure. The world to him, even as to a child, was full of strange, half mythical beings: Shakers, Spiritualists, Octoroons, Free Lovers, Mormons, Champions of Woman's Rights, Office Seekers, "Seseshers," Princes, and heirs to Empires. The hero is tempted, imposed upon, assaulted, but he always comes out first best and turns with copious advice which is always moral and sensible and appropriate. To the woman who had claimed him as her affinity he speaks thus:

I'm a lawabiding man, and bleeve in good, old-fashioned institutions. I am marrid & my orfsprings resemble me, if I am a showman! I think your Affinity bizniss is cussed noncents, besides bein outrajusly wicked. Why don't you behave desunt like other folks? Go to work and earn a honist livin and not stay round here in this lazy, shiftless way, pizenin the moral atmosphere with your pestifrous idees! You wimin folks go back to your lawful husbands, if you've got any, and take orf them skanderlous gownds and trowsis, and dress respectful like other wimin. You men folks, cut orf them pirattercal wiskers, burn up them infurnel pamplits, put sum weskuts on, go to work choppin wood, splittin fence rales, or tillin the sile. I pored 4th. my indignashun in this way till I got out of breth, when I stopt.

This is not "Artemus Ward" talking; it is Charles Farrar Browne, and it is Browne who rebukes the Shakers, the Spiritualists, the Committee from the Woman's Rights Association, and the office-seekers about Lincoln, who gives advice to the Prince of Wales and Prince Napoleon, who stands by the flag when the mob destroys his show down among the "Seseshers," and who later addresses the draft rioters at Baldwinsville. Browne was indeed a moral showman. Every page of his work is free from profanity and vulgarity. He is never cheap, never tawdry, never unkind to anything save immorality and snobbishness. His New England ancestry and breeding may be felt in all he wrote. At heart he was a reformer. He once wrote: "Humorous writers have always done the most toward helping virtue on its pilgrimage, and the truth has found more aid from them than from all the grave polemists and solid writers that have ever spoken or written."

Beneath his kindly, whimsical exterior there was a spirit that could be blown into an indignation as fierce even as Mark Twain's. While he was local editor of the *Plain-Dealer* he burst out one day in this fiery editorial:

A writer in the Philadelphia *Ledger* has discovered that Edgar A. Poe was not a man of genius. We take it for granted that the writer has never read Poe. His lot in life was hard enough, God knows, and it is a pity the oyster-house critics, snobs, flunkeys, and literary nincompoops can't stop snarling over his grave. The biography of Poe by Griswold—which production for fiendish malignity is probably unequaled in the history of letters—should, it would seem, have sufficed. No stone marks the spot where poor Poe sleeps, and no friendly hand strews flowers upon his grave in summer-time, but countless thousands, all over the world, will read and admire his wildly beautiful pages until the end of time.[8]

This knightly spirit led him to warfare upon everything that was merely sentimental or insincere. He burlesqued the gushing love songs of the period, advertising in his program to render at appropriate intervals "Dearest, Whenest Thou Slumberest Dostest Thou Dreamest of Me?" and "Dear Mother, I 've Come Home to Die by Request." He burlesqued the sensational novels of the day in *Roberto, the Rover*, and *Moses, the Sassy*. Only once did he ever read the *Ledger*, he avers, and that was after his first experience with New England rum:

> On takin the secund glass I was seezed with a desire to break winders, & arter imbibin the third glass I knockt a small boy down, pickt his pocket of a New York *Ledger*, and wildly commenced readin Sylvanus Kobb's last Tail.

He is still read and still republished. There is a perennial charm about his work that raises it above the times that produced it, and that promises to make it permanent. His originality, his unfailing animal spirits which came of the abounding life of the new America, his quaint characterization which has added a new figure to the gallery of fiction, his Americanism, his vein of kindliness and pathos that underlies all that he wrote, his indignation at snobbery and all in the life of his day that was not genuine and pure, and finally the exquisite pathos of his later years, all combine to make him remembered.

V

Among the literary progeny of "Artemus Ward" the most noteworthy, perhaps, was "Petroleum V. Nasby," who became so familiar a figure during the war. The creator of this unique character was David Ross Locke, a native of the State of New

---

[8] Quoted by Ruthrauff in "Artemus Ward at Cleveland," *Scribner's Monthly*, 16:784.

York, and, like Browne, a wandering printer from early boyhood. When the "Artemus Ward" letters began to appear in the Cleveland *Plain-Dealer,* Locke was editor of the Bucyrus *Journal,* a few miles to the westward. Their success spurred him to imitation, but it was not until the firing upon Fort Sumter that he succeeded at all in attracting attention. Wingert's Corners, a small hamlet in Crawford County, Ohio, had petitioned the legislature to remove all negroes from the State. There was a humorous element in such a proposition from such a source. Why not give the bellicose little community an appropriate spokesman, a sort of "copperhead" "Artemus Ward," and have him declare it totally free and independent of the State? The result was a letter in the Findlay *Jeffersonian,* of which Locke was then the editor, dated "Wingert's Corners, March the 21, 1861," and signed "Petroleum V. Nasby." The "Nasby Letters" had begun. The little Ohio hamlet soon proved too small a field for the redoubtable Democrat, and to give free play to his love of slavery and untaxed whisky, his hatred of "niggers" and his self-seeking disloyalty, he was removed to "Confedrit X Roads (wich is in the Stait of Kentucky)," from which imaginary center letters continued to flow during the war and the reconstruction era that followed.

No humorist ever struck a more popular chord. The letters were republished week by week by the entire Northern press, and they were looked for by the reading public as eagerly as if they were reports of battles. The soldiers in the Federal armies read them with gusto, and Lincoln and Chase considered them a real source of strength to the Union cause.

Like most political satires, however, the letters do not wear well. They were too much colored by their times. To-day the atmosphere of prejudice in which they were written has vanished, and the most telling hits and timely jokes raise no smile. A generation has arisen which must have foot-notes if it is to read the letters. We wonder now what it was that could have so captivated the first readers.

"Nasby" has little of "Artemus Ward's" whimsical drollery; indeed, the old Democrat resembles the showman, his prototype, only in his rusticity, his ignorance of culture, and his defiance of the laws of spelling. One is Launcelot Gobbo, the other is Touchstone; one is a mere clown, the other a true humorist, as

genuine as life itself is genuine. It is the duty of the clown to
be a buffoon, to imitate and to come to grief. He essays all the
parts of the acrobats only to roll ignominiously in the dust. Then
to the amazement of the beholders he makes a leap that surpasses
them all. ''Nasby'' at one time or another enters every sphere
of the political life of his day and generally with small glory to
himself. Through ''influence'' he becomes postmaster of ''Confedrit X Roads,'' and through ''influence'' he loses his position.

The die is cast! The guilloteen hez fallen! I am no longer postmaster at Confedrit X Roads, wich is in the stait uv Kentucky. The
place that knowd me wunst will know me no more forever; the paper
wich Deekin Pogram takes will be handed out by a nigger; a nigger
will hev the openin uv letters addressed to parties residin hereabouts
containin remittances; a nigger will have the riflin uv letters adrest to
lottery managers and extractin the sweets therfrom; a nigger will be—
but I could n't dwell upon the disgustin theme no longer.

This is mere clownishness, and yet no type of humor could have
been more acceptable to the time that read it. The Revolutionary War had had its ''McFingal,'' who loudly preached Toryism and as a reward was beaten about and even tarred and feathered. Periods of strife and prejudice always demand a clown,
one who concentrates in a single personality the evils of the time.
''Nasby'' stands for blatant copperheadism, just as ''McFingal''
stands for Toryism, and as a result he delighted the multitude.
His schemes and ideas and adventures were all exaggerated, and
the persons he dealt with, like President Johnson and his circle,
were heightened to the point of caricature. Magnified fifty diameters, the evil or the evil personage, like all things seen under
the magnifying glass, becomes grotesque and startling. The people at first laugh and then they cry out, ''Away with this thing;
it is unendurable.''

Refinement is not to be expected in political satires that came
hot from a period of prejudice and war, but the coarseness of the
''Nasby'' letters goes beyond the bounds of toleration even in
such writings. They smack of the coarseness of the armies of
the period. They reek with whisky until one can almost smell
it as one turns the pages. The uncouth spelling simply adds to
the coarseness; it adds nothing to the reality of the characterization. There is an impression constantly that the writer is straining for comic effect. He who is capable of such diction as,

"They can swear to each other's loyalty, which will reduce the cost of evidence to a mere nominal sum," would hardly be guilty of such spellings as "yeelded," "pekoolyer," and "vayloo," the last standing for "value."

The effect of the letters in forming sentiment in the North at critical periods was doubtless considerable, but such statements as the much-quoted one of George S. Boutwell at Cooper Union that the fall of the Confederacy was due to "three forces—the army, the navy, and the Nasby letters"—must be taken with caution as too much colored by the enthusiastic atmosphere in which it was spoken. Their enormous vogue, however, no one can question. East and West became one as they perused the remorseless logic of these patriotic satires. Strange as it may seem to-day, great numbers of the earlier readers had not a suspicion that "Nasby" of "Confedrit X Roads" was not as real a person even as "Jeff" Davis. According to Major Pond, "one meeting of the 'faithful' framed a resolution commending the fidelity to Democratic principles shown in the Nasby letters, but urging Mr. Nasby, for the sake of policy, not to be so outspoken." [9] In the presence of such testimony criticism must be silent. Realism can have no greater triumph than that.

VI

Periods of prejudice and passion tend always to develop satirists. The Civil War produced a whole school of them. There was "Bill Arp," the "Nasby" of the South, philosopher and optimist, who did so much to relieve Southern gloom during the reconstruction era; there was "Orpheus C. Kerr," who made ludicrous the office-seeking mania of the times; and, greatest of them all, including even "Nasby," there was Thomas Nast, who worked not with pen but with pencil.

No sketch of American humor can ignore Nast. His art was constructive and compelling. It led the public; it created a new humorous atmosphere, one distinctively original and distinctively American. Nast was the father of American caricature. It was he who first made effective the topical cartoon for a leader; who first portrayed an individual by some single trait or peculiarity of apparel; and who first made use of symbolic animals in carica-

[9] Memories of the Lyceum.

ture, as the Tammany tiger, the Democratic jackass, and the
Republican elephant—all three of them creations of Nast. His
work is peculiarly significant. He created a new reading public.
Even the illiterate could read the cartoons during the war period
and the Tweed ring days, and it was their reading that put an
end to the evils portrayed. General Grant when asked, ''Who is
the foremost figure in civil life developed by the Rebellion?''
replied instantly, ''I think Thomas Nast. He did as much as
any one man to preserve the Union and bring the war to an
end.'' [10]

VII

In all the humorous writings of the period there was a deep
undercurrent of wisdom. Ever since the days of Franklin, the
typical American has been a maker of aphorisms quaintly expressed. The man who for years has wrestled with Nature on
frontier or farm has evolved a philosophy of his own. American
life has tended to produce unique individualities: ''Sam
Slicks,'' ''Natty Bumppos,'' ''Pudd'nhead Wilsons,'' ''David
Harums,'' and ''Silas Laphams,''—men rich in self-gained wisdom, who talk in aphorisms like Lincoln's, ''Don't swap horses
when you are crossing a stream.''

There has been evolved what may be called the American type
of aphorism—the concentrated bit of wisdom, old it may be, but
expressed in such a quaint and striking way as to bring surprise
and laughter. The humor may come from the homeliness of the
expression, or the unusual nature of the compared terms, or the
ludicrous image brought suddenly to the mind. Examples are
easily found: ''Flattery is like kolone water, tew be smelt of,
but not swallowed''; ''It is better to be a young June bug than
an old bird of paradise''; ''The man who blows his own trumpet
generally plays a solo''; and ''A reasonable amount of fleas is
good fer a dog—keeps him from broodin' over bein' a dog.''

The leader of the latter-day proverbialists was Henry Wheeler
Shaw, a native of Massachusetts, a student for a time at Hamilton
College, and then for twenty years a deckhand, farmer, and
auctioneer in Ohio. He was forty before he began to write.
His ''Essay on the Mule,'' 1859, found no favor. Rewritten the
next year in phonetic spelling and submitted to a New York paper

[10] Paine's *Thomas Nast: His Period and His Pictures.*

as "A Essa on the Muel, bi Josh Billings," it became quickly
famous. The people of the early seventies wanted local color.
the tang, as it were, of wild fruit,—life, fresh, genuine, and first-
hand. They gave a languid approval to Holmes's *Poet of the
Breakfast Table*, but bought enormous editions of *Josh Billings'
Farmers' Allmanax*. The edition of 1870 sold 90,000 copies in
three months; that of 1871 sold no fewer than 127,000.

The humor of "Josh Billings" is confined to his aphorisms.
In his longer writings and indeed in his lectures, as we read
them to-day, he is flat and insufferable. He has little of the
high spirits and zest and lightness of "Phœnix" and "Ward":
he began his humorous work too late in life for such effects; but
he surpasses them all in seriousness and moral poise. That the
times demanded misspelling and clownishness is to be deplored,
for Shaw was a philosopher, broad and sane; how broad and sane
one can see best in *Uncle Esek's Wisdom*, a column contributed
for years to the *Century Magazine*, and, at the request of J. G.
Holland, printed in ordinary spelling.

"With me everything must be put in two or three lines," he
once declared, but his two or three lines are always as compressed as if written by Emerson. He deals for the most part
with the moral side of life with a common sense as sane as Franklin's. So wide was the field of his work that one may find quotations from him on nearly every question that is concerned with
conduct. His stamp is on all he wrote. One may quote from
him at random and be sure of wisdom:

The best cure for rheumatism is to thank the Lord it ain't the gout.
Building air castles is a harmless business as long as you don't at-
tempt to live in them.
Politeness haz won more viktorys than logick ever haz.
Jealousy is simply another name for self-love.
Faith was given to man to lengthen out his reason.
What the moral army needs just now is more rank and file and fewer
brigadier generals.

VIII

The great tide of comic writings became fast and furious in
the seventies. In 1872 no fewer than nine comic papers were
established in New York alone: *The Brickbat, The Cartoon,
Frank Leslie's Budget of Fun, The Jolly Joker, Nick-nax, Mer-
ryman's Monthly, The Moon, The Phunny Fellow, The Thistle,*

and perhaps others. Some died after the first issue, some persisted longer. Every year saw its own crop of comics rise, flourish and die. In 1877 *Puck* was established, the first really successful comic paper in America; in 1881 appeared *Judge;* and in 1883 *Life,* the first to succeed without politics. Very little of all this humorous product can be called literature; the greater part of it already has passed into oblivion; yet for all that the movement that produced it cannot be neglected by one who would study the period. The outburst of humor in the sixties and the seventies was indeed significant. Poor though the product may have been, it was American in background and spirit, and it was drawn from no models save life itself. For the first time America had a national literature in the broad sense of the word, original and colored by its own soil. The work of every one in the school was grounded in sincerity. The worker saw with his own eyes and he looked only for truth. He attacked sentimentality and gush and all that was affected and insincere. Born of the great moral awakening of the war, the humor had in it the Cervantes spirit. Nast, for instance, in his later years declared, "I have never allowed myself to attack anything I did not believe in my soul to be wrong and deserving of the worst fate that could befall it." The words are significant. The laughter of the period was not the mere crackling of thorns under a pot, not a mere fusillade of quips and puns; there was depth in it and purpose. It swept away weakness and wrongs. It purged America and brought sanity and health of soul. From the work of the humorists followed the second accomplishment of the period: those careful studies in prose and verse of real life in the various sections of America.

BIBLIOGRAPHY [11]

GEORGE HORATIO DERBY. (1823–1861.) *Phœnixiana, or Sketches and Burlesques by John Phœnix,* N. Y. 1855; *The Squibob Papers,* N. Y. 1859; *Phœnixiana, or Sketches and Burlesques by John Phœnix.* Introduction by John Kendrick Bangs. Illustrated by Kemble. N. Y. 1903.

CHARLES FARRAR BROWNE. (1834–1867.) *Artemus Ward, His Book.* N. Y. 1862; *Artemus Ward, His Travels.* 1. Miscellaneous. 2. Among the

[11] No attempt has been made to make the bibliographies in this volume exhaustive or to transcribe title pages.

Mormons, N. Y. 1865; *Betsey Jane Ward. Hur Book of Goaks.* N. Y. 1866; *Artemus Ward in London and Other Papers.* N. Y. 1867; *Artemus Ward's Panorama as Exhibited in Egyptian Hall, London.* Edited by his executors, T. W. Robertson and E. P. Hingston. N. Y. 1869; *The Genial Showman,* London, 1870; *Artemus Ward, His Works Complete,* with a biographical sketch by M. D. Landon. N. Y. 1875; *The Complete Works of Artemus Ward.* London. 1910.

DAVID ROSS LOCKE. (1833–1888.) *Divers Views, Opinions, and Prophecies of Yours Trooly, Petroleum V. Nasby.* 1865; *Nasby Papers.* With an Introduction by G. A. Sala. London. 1866; *Swingin' Round the Cirkle. By Petroleum V. Nasby. His Ideas of Men, Politics, and Things, During 1866.* Illustrated by Thomas Nast. Boston. 1867; *Ekkoes from Kentucky. By Petroleum V. Nasby.* Illustrated by Thomas Nast. Boston. 1868; *The Struggles (Social, Financial, and Political) of Petroleum V. Nasby.* With an Introduction by Charles Sumner. Illustrated by Thomas Nast. Boston. 1872; *Nasby in Exile.* Toledo. 1882.

THOMAS NAST. (1840–1902.) *Thomas Nast. His Period and His Pictures.* By Albert Bigelow Paine. 1904; *Life and Letters of Thomas Nast,* Albert Bigelow Paine, 1910.

HENRY WHEELER SHAW. *Josh Billings: His Sayings.* New York. 1865; *Josh Billings on Ice and Other Things.* N. Y. 1868; *Josh Billings' Farmers' Allmanax for the Year 1870.* N. Y. 1870; *Old Probabilities; Contained in One Volume. Farmers' Allmanax 1870–1880.* N. Y. 1879; *Josh Billings' Old Farmers' Allmanax, 1870–1879.* N. Y. 1902; *Complete Comic Writings of Josh Billings* with biographical introduction. Illustrated by Thomas Nast. N. Y.; *Life of Henry W. Shaw,* by F. S. Smith. 1883.

CHAPTER III

With Mark Twain, American literature became for the first time really national. He was the first man of letters of any distinction to be born west of the Mississippi. He spent his boyhood and young manhood near the heart of the continent, along the great river during the vital era when it was the boundary line between known and unknown America, and when it resounded from end to end with the shouts and the confusion of the first great migration from the East; he lived for six thrilling years in the camps and the boom towns and the excited cities of Nevada and California; and then, at thirty-one, a raw product of the raw West, he turned his face to the Atlantic Coast, married a rare soul from one of the refined families of New York State, and settled down to a literary career in New England, with books and culture and trips abroad, until in his old age Oxford University could confer upon him—"Tom Sawyer," whose schooling in the ragged river town had ended before he was twelve—the degree that had come to America only as borne by two or three of the Brahmins of New England. Only America, and America at a certain period, could produce a paradox like that.

Mark Twain interpreted the West from the standpoint of a native. The group of humorists who had first brought to the East the Western spirit and the new laughter had all of them been reared in the older sections. John Phœnix and Artemus Ward and Josh Billings were born in New England, and Nasby and many of the others were natives of New York State. All of them in late boyhood had gone West as to a wonderland and had breathed the new atmosphere as something strange and exhilarating, but Mark Twain was native born. He was himself a part of the West; he removed from it so as to see it in true perspective, and so became its best interpreter. Hawthorne had once expressed a wish to see some part of America "where the damned shadow of Europe has never fallen." Mark Twain spent his life until he was thirty in such unshadowed places. When he wrote he wrote without a thought of other writings; it was as if the West itself was dictating its autobiography.

I

The father of Mark Twain, John Clemens, a dreamer and an idealist, had left Virginia with his young wife early in the twenties to join the restless tide that even then was setting strongly westward. Their first settlement was at Gainsborough, Tennessee, where was born their first son, Orion, but they remained there not long. Indeed, like all emigrants of their type, they remained nowhere long. During the next ten or eleven years five other children were born to them at four different stations along the line of their westward progress. When the fifth child arrived, to be christened Samuel Langhorne, they were living at Florida, Missouri, a squalid little hamlet fifty miles west of the Mississippi. That was November 30, 1835. Four years later they made what proved to be their last move, settling at Hannibal, Missouri, a small river town about a hundred miles above St. Louis. Here it was that the future Mark Twain spent the next fourteen years, those formative years between four and eighteen that determine so greatly the bent of the later life.

The Hannibal of the forties and the fifties was hardly a town one would pick deliberately for the education of a great man of letters. It lay just a few miles above the northern line of Pike County—that Pike County, Missouri, that gave name to the shiftless, hand-to-mouth, ague-shaken type of humanity later to be celebrated so widely as the Pike. Hannibal was not a Pike community, but it was typically southwestern in its somnolent, slave-holding, care-free atmosphere. The one thing that forever rescued it from the commonplace was the River, the tremendous Mississippi, source of endless dreams and romance. Mark Twain has given us a picture, perfect as an etching, of this river and the little town that nestled beside it:

After all these years I can picture that old time to myself now, just as it was then: the white town drowsing in the sunshine of a summer's morning; the streets empty, or pretty nearly so; one or two clerks sitting in front of the Water Street stores, with their splint-bottomed chairs tilted back against the wall, chins on breast, hats slouched over their faces, asleep—with shingle shavings enough around to show what broke them down; a sow and a litter of pigs loafing along the sidewalk, doing a good business in water-melon rinds and seeds; two or three lonely little freight piles scattered around the "levee"; a pile of "skids" on the slope of the stone-paved wharf, and the fragrant town drunkard asleep in the shadow of them; two or three wood flats at the head of the wharf, but nobody to listen to the peaceful lapping of the wavelets against them; the great Mississippi, the majestic, the magnificent Mississippi, rolling its mile-wide tide along, shining in the sun; the dense forest away on the other side; the "point" above the town, and the "point" below, bounding the river glimpse and turning it into a sort of sea, and withal a very still and brilliant and lonely one. Presently a film of dark smoke appears above one of these remote "points"; instantly a negro drayman, famous for his quick eye and prodigious voice, lifts up the cry, "S-t-e-a-m boat a-comin'!" and the scene changes! The town drunkard stirs, the clerks wake up, a furious clatter of drays follows, every house and store pours out a human contribution, and all in a twinkling the dead town is alive and moving. Drays, carts, men, boys, all go hurrying to a common center, the wharf. Assembled there, the people fasten their eyes upon the coming boat as upon a wonder they are seeing for the first time. . . . The furnace doors are open and the fires glaring bravely; the upper decks are black with passengers; the captain stands by the big bell, calm, imposing, the envy of all; great volumes of the blackest smoke are rolling and tumbling out of the chimneys—a husbanded grandeur created with a bit of pitch pine just before arriving at a town; the crew are grouped on the forecastle; the broad stage is run far out over the port bow, and an envied deck-hand stands picturesquely on the end of it with a coil of rope in his hand; the pent steam is screaming through the gage-cocks; the captain lifts his hand, a bell rings, the wheels stop; then they turn back, churning the water to foam, and the steamer is at rest. Then such a scramble as there is to get aboard, and to get ashore, and to take in freight, and to discharge freight, all at one and the same time; and such a yelling and cursing as the mates facilitate it all with! Ten minutes later the steamer is under way again, with no flag on the jack-staff and no black smoke issuing from the chimneys. After ten more minutes the town is dead again, and the town drunkard asleep by the skids once more.[1]

It was the romance of this river, the vastness and the mystery of it, the great unknown world which lay beyond those "points" where all things disappeared, that made of the boy a restless soul, a dreamer and an idealist—that made of him in-

[1] *Old Times on the Mississippi*, Chap. I.

deed the Mark Twain of the later years. His books nowhere
rise into the pure serene of literature unless touched at some
point by this magic stream that flowed so marvelously through
his boyhood. The two discoverers of the Mississippi were De
Soto and Mark Twain.

The first crisis in the boy's life came in his twelfth year, when
the death of his father sent him as an apprentice to a country
newspaper office, that most practical and most exacting of all
training schools for youth. Two years on the Missouri *Courier,*
four years on the Hannibal *Journal,* then the restlessness of his
clan sent him wandering into the East even as it had sent Artemus Ward and Nasby into the West. For fifteen months he
served as compositor in New York City and Philadelphia, then
a great homesickness for the river came upon him. From boyhood it had been his dream to be the pilot of a Mississippi steamboat; all other professions seemed flat and lifeless compared
with that satisfying and boundless field of action; and it is not
strange that in April, 1857, we find him installed as Horace
Bixby's ''cub'' at the beginning of a new career.

During the next four years he gave himself heart and soul to
the almost superhuman task of committing to memory every
sandbar and point and landmark in twelve hundred miles of a
shifting, treacherous river. The difficulties he has explained
fully in his book. It was a college course of four years, and
no man ever had a better one. To quote his own words:

In that brief, sharp schooling I got personally and familiarly acquainted with all the different types of human nature that are to be
found in fiction, biography, or history. When I find a well-drawn
character in fiction or biography, I generally take a warm personal
interest in him, for the reason that I have known him before—met him
on the river.[2]

It taught him far more than this. The pilot of a great Mississippi boat was a man with peculiar responsibilities. The lives
of the passengers and the safety of the cargo were absolutely
in his hands. His authority was above even the captain's. Only
picked men of courage and judgment with a self-reliance that
never wavered in any crisis were fit material for pilots. To
quote Horace Bixby, the most noted of them all:

2 Paine, *Mark Twain, a Biography,* i: 128.

There were no signal lights along the shore in those days, and no searchlights on the vessels; everything was blind, and on a dark, misty night in a river full of snags and shifting sand-bars and changing shores, a pilot's judgment had to be founded on *absolute certainty*.[3]

Under such conditions men were valued only for what they actually could do. There was no entrance into the inner circle of masters of the river save through genuineness and real efficiency. Sentimentalizing and boasting and sham died instantly in that stern atmosphere. To live for four years in daily contact with such men taught one coarseness of speech and an appalling fluency in the use of profanity, but it taught one at the same time to look with supreme contempt upon inefficiency and pretense.

The "cub" became at length a pilot, to be entrusted after a time with some of the finest boats on the river. He became very efficient in his hard-learned profession so conspicuously so that he won the commendation even of Bixby, who could say in later years, "Sam Clemens never had an accident either as a steersman or as a pilot, except once when he got aground for a few hours in the *bagasse* (cane) smoke, with no damage to any one."[4] But the war put a sudden end to the piloting. The river was closed, and in April, 1861, he went reluctantly back to Hannibal. "I loved the profession far better than any I have ever followed since," he declared in his later years, "and I took a measureless pride in it." It is very possible that but for the war and the change which it wrought upon the river, Mark Twain might have passed his whole life as a Mississippi pilot.

II

After a few weeks in a self-recruited troop that fell to pieces before it could join the Confederate army, the late pilot, now twenty-six years old, started by stage coach across the Plains with his brother Orion, who had just been appointed secretary to the new Governor of Nevada. It was Mark Twain's entry upon what, in college terms, may be called his graduate course. It was six years long and it covered one of the most picturesque eras in the history of Western America.

3 Paine, *Mark Twain, a Biography*, i: 146.
4 *Ibid.*, i: 155.

For a few restive months he remained at Carson City as his brother's assistant, then in characteristic fashion he broke away to join the excited tide of gold seekers that was surging through all the mountains of Nevada. During the next year he lived in mining camps with prospectors and eager claim-holders. Luck, however, seemed against him; at least it promised him little as a miner, and when the Virginia City *Enterprise,* to which he had contributed letters, offered him a position on its staff of reporters, he jumped at the opportunity.

Now for two years he lived at the very heart of the mining regions of the West, in Virginia City, the home of the Comstock lode, then at its highest boom. Everything about him—the newness and rawness of things, the peculiar social conditions, the atmosphère of recklessness and excitement, the money that flowed everywhere in fabulous quantities—everything was unique. Even the situation of the city was remarkable. Hingston, who visited it with Artemus Ward while Mark Twain was still a member of the *Enterprise* staff, speaks of it as "perched up on the side of Mt. Davidson some five or six thousand feet above sea level, with a magnificent view before us of the desert. . . . Nothing but arid rocks and sandy plains sprinkled with sage brush. No village for full two hundred miles, and any number of the worst type of Indians—the Goshoots—agreeably besprinkling the path." [5] Artemus Ward estimated its population at twelve thousand. He was impressed by its wildness, "its splendid streets paved with silver ore," "its unadulterated cussedness," its vigilance committee "which hangs the more vicious of the pestiferous crowd," and its fabulous output of silver which is "melted down into bricks the size of common house bricks, then loaded into huge wagons, each drawn by eight and twelve mules, and sent off to San Francisco." [6]

It was indeed a strange area of life that passed before the young Mississippi pilot. For two winters he was sent down to report the new legislature of the just-organized territory, and it was while engaged in this picturesque gala task that he sent back his letters signed for the first time Mark Twain. That was the winter of 1863. It was time now for him to seek a wider field. Accordingly, the following May he went down

[5] *Artemus Ward, His Travels.*
[6] Paine's *Mark Twain,* i: 260.

to San Francisco, where at length he found employment on the *Morning Call*.

Now for the first time the young reporter found himself in a literary atmosphere. Poets and sketch-writers and humorists were everywhere. There was at least one flourishing literary journal, the *Golden Era*, and its luxuriously appointed office was the literary center of the Pacific Coast. "Joaquin Miller recalls from an old diary, kept by him then, having seen Adah Isaacs Menken, Prentice Mulford, Bret Harte, Charles Warren Stoddard, Fitzhugh Ludlow, Mark Twain, Orpheus C. Kerr, Artemus Ward, Gilbert Densmore, W. S. Kendall, and Mrs. Hitchcock assembled there at one time." [7] Charles Henry Webb was just starting a literary weekly, the *Californian*, and when, a year later, Bret Harte was made its editor, Mark Twain was added to the contributing staff. It was the real beginning of his literary career. He received now helpful criticism. In a letter written in after years to Thomas Bailey Aldrich he says:

Bret Harte trimmed and trained and schooled me patiently until he changed me from an awkward utterer of coarse grotesqueness to a writer of paragraphs and chapters that have found a certain favor in the eyes of even some of the very decentest people in the land.[8]

To the *Californian* and the *Era* he now contributed that series of sketches which later was drawn upon for material for his first published book. But the old restlessness was upon him again. He struck out into the Tuolumne Hills with Jim Gillis as a pocket miner and for months lived as he could in shacks and camps, panning between drenching showers worthless gravel, expecting every moment to find gold. He found no gold, but he found what was infinitely richer. In later years in a letter to Gillis he wrote:

It makes my heart ache yet to call to mind some of those days. Still it should n't, for right in the depths of their poverty and their pocket-hunting vagabondage lay the germ of my coming good fortune. You remember the one gleam of jollity that shot across our dismal sojourn in the rain and mud of Angel's Camp—I mean that day we sat around the tavern and heard that chap tell about the frog and how they filled him with shot. And you remember how we quoted from the yarn and laughed over it out there on the hillside while you and dear old Stoker

[7] Paine's *Mark Twain*, i: 260.
[8] Greenslet's *Thomas Bailey Aldrich*, 98.

panned and washed. I jotted the story down in my note-book that day, and would have been glad to get ten or fifteen dollars for it—I was just that blind. But then we were so hard up. I published that story, and it became widely known in America, India, China, England, and the reputation it made for me has paid me thousands and thousands of dollars since.[9]

The publication in New York, May 1, 1867, of *The Celebrated Jumping Frog of Calaveras County and Other Sketches* and the delivery a week later by the author of *The Jumping Frog* of a lecture on the Sandwich Islands marks the end of the period of preparation in Mark Twain's life. A new American author had arrived.

III

Send this Mississippi pilot, printer, adventurer, miner in rough camps of the Sierras, to Paris, Italy, Constantinople, and the Holy Land, and what will be his impressions? For an answer we must read *The Innocents Abroad.* It will be no *Outre Mer,* we are certain of that, and no *Pencillings by the Way.* Before a line of it was written an atmosphere had been created unique in American literature, for where, save in the California of 1867, was there ever optimism, nay, romanticism, that could reply instantly to the young reporter who asked to be sent on a Don Quixote pilgrimage to Europe and the Orient, "Go. Twelve hundred and fifty dollars will be paid for you before the vessel sails, and your only instructions are that you will continue to write at such times and from such places as you deem proper, and in the same style that heretofore secured you the favor of the readers of the *Alta California*"?

It was not to be a tour of Europe, as Longfellow and Willis and Taylor had made it, the pilgrimage of a devotee to holy shrines; it was to be a great picnic with sixty-seven in the picnic party. Moreover, the recorder of it was bound by his instructions to report it in the style that had won him California fame. It was to be a Western book, written by a Westerner from the Western standpoint, but this does not imply that his Western readers expected an illiterate production full of coarseness and rude wit. California had produced a school of poets and romancers; she had serious literary journals, and she was proud

⁹ Paine's *Mark Twain*, i: 393.

of them. The letters, if California was to set her stamp of approval upon them, must have literary charm; they must have, moreover, freshness and originality; and they must sparkle with that spirit of humor which already had begun to be recognized as a native product.

We open the book and linger a moment over the preface:

Notwithstanding it is only the record of a picnic, it has a purpose, which is, to suggest to the reader how *he* would be likely to see Europe and the East if he looked at them with his own eyes instead of the eyes of those who traveled in those countries before him. I make small pretence of showing any one how he *ought* to look at objects of interest beyond the sea—other books do that, and therefore, even if I were competent to do it, there is no need.

I offer no apologies for any departures from the usual style of travel-writing that may be charged against me—for I think I have seen with impartial eyes, and I am sure I have written at least honestly, whether wisely or not.

Let us read the book straight through. We are impressed with the fact that, despite the supposition of its first readers, it is not primarily a humorous work. It is a genuine book of travels. It is first of all an honest record, even as its author averred. In the second place it is the book of a young man, a young man on a lark and full of the highest spirits. The world is good—it is a good show, though it is full of absurdities and of humbugs that should be exposed. The old stock jokes of the grand tour—the lack of soap, the charge for candles, the meeting of supposed foreigners who break unexpectedly into the best of English, and all the well-known others—were new to the public then and they came with freshness. Then it is the book of one who saw, even as he claimed, with his own eyes. This genuine American, with his training on the river and the wild frontier where men and things are what they *are*, no more and no less, will be impressed only with genuineness. He will describe things precisely as he sees them. Gibraltar ''is pushed out into the sea on the end of a flat, narrow strip of land, and is suggestive of a 'gob' of mud on the end of a shingle''; of the Coliseum: ''everybody recognizes at once that 'looped and windowed' bandbox with a side bitten out''; and of a famous river: ''It is popular to admire the Arno. It is a great historical creek with four feet in the channel and some scows floating around. It would be a very passable river if they would pump some water

into it." That was not written for a joke: it was the way the
Arno honestly impressed the former Mississippi pilot.
He is not always critical. Genuineness and real worth never
fail to impress him. Often he stands before a landscape, a city,
a cathedral, as enthusiastic as any of the older school of travelers. The book is full of vivid descriptions, some of them almost
poetic in their spirit and diction. But things must be what they
pretend to be, or they will disgust him. Everywhere there is
scorn for the mere echoer of the enthusiasm of others. He will
not gush over an unworthy thing even if he knows the whole
world has gushed over it. Da Vinci's "Last Supper," painted
on a dilapidated wall and stained and scarred and dimmed, may
once have been beautiful, he admits, but it is not so now. The
pilgrims who stand before it "able to speak only in catchy ejaculations of rapture" fill him with wrath. "How can they see
what is not visible?" The work of the old masters fills him
always with indignation. They painted not Hebrews in their
scriptural pieces, but Italians. "Their nauseous adulation of
princely patrons was more prominent to me and claimed my
attention more than the charms of color." "Raphael pictured
such infernal villains as Catherine and Marie de Medicis seated
in heaven conversing familiarly with the Virgin Mary and the
angels (to say nothing of higher personages), and yet my friends
abuse me because I am a little prejudiced against the old masters."

Here we have a note that was to become more and more emphatic in Mark Twain's work with every year he lived: his indignation at oppression and insincerity. The cathedrals of Italy
lost their beauty for him when he saw the misery of the population. He stood before the Grand Duomo of Florence. "Like
all other men I fell down and worshiped it, but when the filthy
beggars swarmed around me the contrast was too striking, too
suggestive, and I said 'O sons of classic Italy, *is* the spirit of
enterprise, of self-reliance, of noble endeavor, utterly dead
within ye? Curse your indolent worthlessness, why don't you
rob your church?' Three hundred happy, comfortable priests
are employed in that cathedral."

Everywhere he strikes out at sentimentality. When he learns
how Abelard deliberately sacrificed Héloïse to his own selfish
ideals, he bursts out: "The tons of sentiment I have wasted

on that unprincipled humbug in my ignorance! I shall throttle down my emotions hereafter, about this sort of people, until I have read them up and know whether they are entitled to any tearful attentions or not.'' He is eager to see a French ''grissette,'' but having seen one, bursts out in true Artemus Ward fashion: ''Aroint thee, wench! I sorrow for the vagabond student of the Latin Quarter now, even more than formerly I envied him. Thus topples to the earth another idol of my infancy.'' The story of Petrarch's love for Laura only fills him with pity for the outrageously treated ''Mr. Laura,'' the unknown husband of the heroine, who bore the burden but got none of the glory, and when they tell the thrilling legend of the old medieval castle, he makes only the comment, ''Splendid legend—splendid lie—drive on!''

It was a blow at the whole school of American travel writers; it marked the passing of an era. Bret Harte in the first volume of the *Overland Monthly* (1868), was the first to outline the Western standpoint:

The days of sentimental journeyings are over. The dear old book of travel . . . is a thing of the past. Sentimental musings on foreign scenes are just now restricted to the private diaries of young and impressible ladies and clergymen with affections of the bronchial tubes. . . . A race of good humored, engaging iconoclasts seem to have precipitated themselves upon the old altars of mankind, and like their predecessors of the eighth century, have paid particular attention to the holy church. Mr. Howells has slashed one or two sacred pictorial canvasses with his polished rapier; Mr. Swift has made one or two neat long shots with a rifled Parrott, and Mr. Mark Twain has used brickbats on stained glass windows with damaging effect. And those gentlemen have certainly brought down a heap of rubbish.[10]

It was the voice of the new West and of the new era. With *The Innocents Abroad* begins the new period in American literature. The book is full of the new after-the-war Americanism that did its own thinking, that saw with its own eyes, that put a halo upon nothing save genuineness and substantial worth. It must not be forgotten that America even in the new seventies was still mawkish with sentimentality. The very year *The Innocents Abroad* appeared, *Gates Ajar* sold twenty editions. Mark Twain came into the age like the Goths into Rome. Stand on the solid earth, he cried. Look with your own eyes. Wor-

10 *Overland Monthly,* i: 101.

ship nothing but truth and genuineness. Europe is no better than America. Como is beautiful, but it is not so beautiful as Tahoe. Why this eternal glorification of things simply and solely because it is the conventional thing to glorify them? "The critic," he wrote in later years to Andrew Lang, "has actually imposed upon the world the superstition that a painting by Raphael is more valuable to the civilizations of the earth than is a chromo; and the august opera more than the hurdy gurdy and the villagers' singing society; and the Latin classics than Kipling's far-reaching bugle note; and Jonathan Edwards than the Salvation Army." [11] The new American democracy was speaking. To the man who for four years had learned in the school of Horace Bixby there was no high and no low save as measured, not by appearances or by tradition, but by intrinsic worth.

IV

It has been customary in libraries to place the earlier works of Mark Twain on the same shelf as those of Artemus Ward and Josh Billings. To the thousands who laughed at him as he lectured from year to year he was a mere maker of fun. The public that bought such enormous editions of *The Innocents Abroad* and *Roughing It* bought them as books to laugh over. What shall we say to-day of Mark Twain's humor? A generation has arisen to whom he is but a tradition and a set of books; what is the verdict of this generation?

First of all, it is necessary that we examine the man himself. Nature seems to have forced him into the ranks of the comedians. From his mother he inherited a drawl that was inexpressibly funny; he had a laughable personality, and a laughable angle from which he looked at life. He could no more help provoking mirth than he could help being himself. Moreover, he had been thrown during his formative years into a veritable training school for humorists. On the river and in the mines and the raw towns and cities of the West, he had lived in a gale of high spirits, of loud laughter, of practical jokes, and droll stories that had gone the rough round of the boats or the camps. His humor, therefore, was an echo of the laughter of elemental men who have been flung into conditions full of incongruities

11 Paine's *Mark Twain*, ii: 894.

and strange contrasts. It is the humor of exaggeration run wild, of youthful high spirits, of rough practical jokes, of understatement, of irreverence, and gross absurdity.

But the personality of Mark Twain no longer can give life to his humor; the atmosphere in which it first appeared has gone forever; the man himself is becoming a mere legend, shadowy and more and more distorted; his humor must be judged now like that of Cervantes and Shakespeare, apart from author and times. How does it stand the test? Not at all well. There are the high spirits of the new West in it—that element has not evaporated—and there is in it a personal touch, a drollery that was his individual contribution to humor. There was a certain drawl in his pen as well as in his tongue. It is this alone that saves much of his humorous work from flatness. Concerning *The Jumping Frog*, for instance, Haweis asks in true British way, "What, I should like to know, is the fun of saying that a frog who has been caused to swallow a quantity of shot cannot jump so high as he could before?" The answer is that there is no fun save in the way the story is told; in other words, save in the incomparable drawl of Mark Twain's pen. One can only illustrate:

The feller . . . give it back to Smiley, and says, very deliberate, "Well, I don't see no pints about that frog that's any better'n any other frog."

"May be you don't," Smiley says. "May be you understand frogs, and may be you don't understand 'em; may be you've had experience, and may be you ain't, only a amature, as it were. Any ways I've got *my* opinion, and I'll risk forty dollars that he can out-jump any frog in Calaveras county."

And the feller studied a minute, and then says, kinder sad like, "Well, I'm only a stranger here, and I ain't got no frog; but if I had a frog, I'd bet you!"

Or take this episode from *The Innocents Abroad* where he tells of his sensations one night as a boy upon awakening and finding the body of a murdered man on the floor of his room:

I went away from there. I do not say that I went away in any sort of a hurry, but I simply went—that is sufficient. I went out at the window, and I carried the sash along with me. I did not need the sash, but it was handier to take it than it was to leave it, and so I took it. I was not scared, but I was considerably agitated.

All this and the hundreds of pages like it in *The Innocents Abroad* and *Roughing It* and the later books is excellent drollery, but had Mark Twain written nothing else than this he would be as dead now as an author as even "Doesticks." His drollery is best in the work that lies nearest to the source of his first inspiration. As the Western days faded from his memory, his comedy became more and more forced, until it could reach at last the inane flatness of *Adam's Diary* and flatter still, *Eve's Diary*.

The humor that lives, however, is not drollery; it must be embodied in a humorous character like Falstaff, for instance, or Don Quixote. The most of Mark Twain's fun comes from exaggerated situations with no attempt at characterization, and therein lies his weakness as a humorist. Huckleberry Finn and Colonel Sellers come the nearest to being humorous creations, but Huckleberry Finn is but a bit of *genre*, the eternal bad boy in a Pike County costume, and Colonel Sellers is but a preliminary study toward a character, a shadowy figure that we feel constantly to be on the point of jumping into greatness without ever actually arriving. Narrowly as he may have missed the mark in these two characters, Mark Twain cannot be classed with the great humorists.

V

There are three Mark Twains: there is Mark Twain, the droll comedian, who wrote for the masses and made them laugh; there is Mark Twain, the indignant protester, who arose ever and anon to true eloquence in his denunciation of tyranny and pretense; and there is Mark Twain, the romancer, who in his boyhood had dreamed by the great river and who later caught the romance of a period in American life. The masterpiece of the first is *The Jumping Frog*, of the second *The Man that Corrupted Hadleyburg*, and of the third *Life on the Mississippi* and *Roughing It*.

It is this third Mark Twain that still lives and that will continue to live in American literature. He saw with distinctness a unique area of American life. As the brief and picturesque era faded away he caught the sunset glory of it and embodied it in romance—the steamboat days on the river in the slavery era, the old régime in the South, the barbarism of the Plains,

the great buffalo herds, the wild camps in the gold fields of
Nevada and California. In half a dozen books: *Roughing It,
Life on the Mississippi, The Gilded Age* (a few chapters of it),
Tom Sawyer, Huckleberry Finn, Pudd'nhead Wilson, he has
done work that can never be done again. The world that these
books depict has vanished as completely as the Bagdad of Haroun
al Raschid. Not only has he told the story of this vanished
world, illustrating it with descriptions and characterizations that
are like Flemish portraits, but he has caught and held the spirit
of it, and he has thrown over it all the nameless glow of romance.
It is as golden a land that he leads us through as any we may find
in Scott, and yet it was drawn from the life with painstaking
care. Scott and Bulwer and Cooper angered Mark Twain.
They were careless of facts, they were sentimental, they mis-
interpreted the spirit of the times they depicted and the men
and women who lived in them, but these six books of Mark Twain
may be placed among the source books of American history. Nowhere else can one catch so truly certain phases of the spirit of
the mid-nineteenth century West. Over every page of them may
be written those words from the preface of *The Innocents
Abroad,* ''I am sure I have written at least honestly, whether
wisely or not.''

The books are six chapters of autobiography. *Tom Sawyer*
and *Huckleberry Finn* are recollections of that boyhood by the
river after so long a time had elapsed that the day-dreams and
boyish imaginings were recorded as real happenings; *Life on
the Mississippi* records that romantic adventure of his young
manhood as he recalled it in later days when the old piloting
era had vanished like a dream of boyhood; *The Gilded Age,* a book
of glorious fragments, has in it his uncle James Lampton drawn
from life and renamed Colonel Sellers; *Roughing It* bubbles
over with the joy and the high spirits and the excitement of those
marvelous days when the author and the West were young together; and *Pudd'nhead Wilson* gives the tragedy of slavery
as it passed before his boyish eyes. These books and *The Innocents Abroad* are Mark Twain's contribution to the library of
American classics. The rest of his enormously large output,
despite brilliant passages here and there, does not greatly
matter.

They are not artistic books. The author had little skill in

construction. He excelled in brilliant dashes, not in long-continued effort. He was his own Colonel Sellers, restless, idealistic, Quixotic. What he did he did with his whole soul without restraint or sense of proportion. There is in all he wrote a lack of refinement, kept at a minimum, to be sure, by his wife, who for years was his editor and severest critic, but likely at any moment to crop out. His books, all of them, are monotones, a running series of episodes and descriptions all of the same value, never reaching dramatic climax. The episodes themselves, however, are told with graphic intensity; some of them are gems well-nigh perfect. Here is a picture of the famous pony express of the Plains:

The pony-rider was usually a little bit of a man, brimful of spirit and endurance. No matter what time of the day or night his watch came on, and no matter whether it was winter or summer, raining, snowing, hailing, or sleeting, or whether his "beat" was a level straight road or a crazy trail over mountain crags and precipices, or whether it led through peaceful regions that swarmed with hostile Indians, he must be always ready to leap into the saddle and be off like the wind. He rode fifty miles without stopping, by daylight, moonlight, starlight, or through the blackness of darkness—just as it happened. He rode a splendid horse that was born for a racer and fed and lodged like a gentleman; kept him at his utmost speed for ten miles, and then, as he came crashing up to the station where stood two men holding fast a fresh, impatient steed, the transfer of rider and mailbag was made in the twinkling of an eye, and away flew the eager pair and were out of sight before the spectator could hardly get the ghost of a look.

We had had a consuming desire, from the beginning, to see a pony-rider, but somehow or other all that had passed us and all that met us managed to streak by in the night, and so we heard only a whiz and a hail, and the swift phantom of the desert was gone before we could get our heads out of the windows. But now we were expecting one along every moment, and we would see him in broad daylight. Presently the driver exclaims:

"Here he comes!"

Every neck is stretched further, and every eye strained wider. Away across the endless dead level of the prairie a black speck appears against the sky, and it is plain that it moves. Well, I should think so! In a second or two it becomes a horse and rider, rising and falling, rising and falling—sweeping toward us nearer and nearer—growing more and more distinct, more and more sharply defined—nearer and still nearer, and the flutter of the hoofs comes faintly to the ear— another instant a whoop and a hurrah from our upper deck, a wave of the rider's hand, but no reply, and man and horse burst past our excited faces, and go winging away like a belated fragment of a storm.

The steamboat race and the explosion in chapter four of *The Gilded Age* have few equals in any language for mere picturing power. He deals largely with the out-of-doors. His canvases are bounded only by the horizon: the Mississippi, the great Plains, the Rocky Mountains, Mono Lake, the Alkali Deserts, and the Sierras—he has handled a continent. Only Joaquin Miller and John Muir have used canvases as vast. Huckleberry Finn's floating journey down the river on his raft has in it something of the spirit of *The Odyssey* and *Pilgrim's Progress* and *Don Quixote*. Had Mark Twain's constructive skill and his ability to trace the growth of a human soul been equal to his picturing power, his Defoe-like command of detail and situation, and his mastery of phrase and of narrative, he might have said the last word in American fiction. He was a product of his section and of his education. College and university would have made of him an artist like Holmes, brilliant, refined, and messageless. It would have robbed him of the very fountain-head of his power. It was his to work not from books but from life itself, to teach truth and genuineness of life, to turn the eyes of America from the romance of Europe to her own romantic past.

VI

If Artemus Ward is Touchstone, Mark Twain is Lear's Fool. He was a knightly soul, sensitive and serious, a nineteenth-century knight errant who would protect the weak of the whole world and right their wrongs. The genuineness and honesty that had been ground into his soul on the river and in the mines where a man was a man only when he could show true manliness, were a part of his knightly equipment. When financial disaster came to him, as it had come to Scott, through no fault of his own, he refused to repudiate the debt as he might have done with no discredit to himself, and, though old age was upon him, he set out to earn by his own efforts the whole enormous amount. And he discharged the debt to the full. He had, moreover, the true knight's soul of romance. The *Morte d'Arthur* and the chronicles of Joan of Arc, his favorite reading, contained the atmosphere that he loved. He fain would have given his generation ''pure literature,'' but they bade him back to his cap and bells. Richardson, as late as 1886, classed him with the purveyors of "rude and clownish merriment" and advised him to "make hay while the sun shines." [12]

So he jested and capered while his heart was heavy with personal sorrows that came thick upon him as the years went by, and with the baseness and weakness and misery of humanity as the spectacle passed under his keen observation. Yet in it all he was true to himself. That sentence in the preface tells the whole story: "I have written at least honestly." His own generation bought his books for the fun in them; their children are finding now that their fathers bought not, as they supposed, clownish ephemerae, but true literature, the classics of the period.

And yet—strange paradox!—it was the cap and bells that made Mark Twain and that hastened the coming of the new period in American literature. The cap and bells it was that made him known in every hamlet and in every household of America, north and south and east and west, and in all lands across all oceans. Only Cooper and Mrs. Stowe of all our American authors are known so widely. This popularity it was that gave wings to the first all-American literature and that inspired a new school of American writers. After Mark Twain American literature was no longer confined to Boston and its environs; it was as wide as the continent itself.

BIBLIOGRAPHY

MARK TWAIN. (1835–1910.) *The Celebrated Jumping Frog of Calaveras County and Other Sketches,* 1867; *The Innocents Abroad,* 1869; *Roughing It,* 1872; *The Gilded Age* (with C. D. Warner), 1873; *Old Times on the Mississippi* (*Atlantic Monthly*), 1875; *Tom Sawyer,* 1876; *Life on the Mississippi,* in book form, 1882; *Huckleberry Finn,* 1884; *A Connecticut Yankee in King Arthur's Court,* 1889; *Pudd'nhead Wilson,* 1894; *Personal Recollections of Joan of Arc,* 1896; *Following the Equator,* 1897; *Christian Science,* 1907; Writings of Mark Twain, 25 vols., 1910; *My Mark Twain,* by W. D. Howells, 1911; *Mark Twain, a Biography,* by Albert Bigelow Paine, 1912.

[12] *American Literature,* i: 396, 521.

CHAPTER IV

BRET HARTE

In his *Chronological Outlines of American Literature,* Whitcomb mentions only thirteen American novels published during the seven years before 1870: Taylor's *Hannah Thurston, John Godfrey's Fortunes,* and *Story of Kennett;* Trowbridge's *The Three Scouts;* Donald G. Mitchell's *Doctor Johns;* Holmes's *The Guardian Angel;* Lanier's *Tiger-Lilies,* the transition novel of the decade as we shall see later in our study of Lanier; Louisa M. Alcott's *Little Women;* Beecher's *Norwood;* Elizabeth Stuart Phelps's *The Gates Ajar;* Higginson's *Malbone;* Aldrich's *Story of a Bad Boy;* and Mrs. Stowe's *Oldtown Folks.* To study the list is to realize the condition of American fiction during the sixties. It lacked incisiveness and construction and definite color; it droned and it preached.

Before pronouncing the decade the feeblest period in American fiction since the early twenties of the century, let us examine the most lauded novel written in America between 1860 and 1870, *Elsie Venner* (1861). Strictly speaking, it is not a novel at all: it is another Autocrat volume, chatty, discursive, brilliant. The Brahmins, sons and grandsons of ministers, might enter the law, medicine, teaching, literature, the lyceum lecture field—they never ceased to preach. New England for two centuries was a vast pulpit and American literature during a whole period was written on sermon paper. "The real aim of the story," the Autocrat naïvely observes in his preface, "was to test the doctrine of 'original sin' and human responsibility." He is in no hurry, however. We read four chapters before we learn even the heroine's name. A novel can reasonably be expected to center about its title character: Elsie Venner speaks seventeen times during the story, and eleven of these utterances are delivered from her death-bed at the close of the book. There is no growth in character, no gradual moving of events to a culmination, no clear picture even of the central figure. Elsie is a mere case: the book, so far as she is concerned, is the record of a clinic. But even the clinic is not suffered to move uninterruptedly. Digressions are as frequent as even in the Autocrat papers. A widow is introduced for no apparent reason, studied for a chapter, and then dropped from the narrative. We never feel like one who has lost himself for a time in the life of another in a new world under new skies; we feel rather like one who is being personally conducted through New England by a skilful guide. Note this partial prospectus of what he has to show: Newburyport, Portsmouth, Portland, caste in New England, rural schools, Northampton and Mt. Holyoke, mountain vegetation, rattlesnakes in Massachusetts, the New England mansion house, school compositions, the old type of meeting house, varieties of school girls, the old-time India merchant, oysters in New England, hired help, colonial chimneys, young ladies' seminaries, the hemlock tree. The topics are interesting ones and they are brilliantly treated, often at length, but in a novel, even one written by Dr. Holmes, such things are "lumber." The novel is typical of the fiction of the era. It is discursive, loosely constructed, vague in its characterization, and lacking in cumulative force.

It is significant that the magazines of the period had very little use for the native product. Between 1864 and 1870, *Harper's Magazine* alone published no fewer than ten long serials by English novelists: *Denis Duval* by Thackeray; *The Small House at Allington* by Trollope; *Our Mutual Friend* by Dickens; *The Unkind Word, Woman's Kingdom,* and *A Brave Lady* by Dinah Mulock Craik; *Armadale* by Wilkie Collins; *My Enemy's Daughter* by Justin M'Carthy; *Anteros* by the Author of *Guy Livingstone* [G. A. Lawrence]; and *Anne Furness* by the Author of *Mabel's Progress* [Mrs. T. A. Trollope]. Even the *Atlantic Monthly* left its New England group of producers to publish Charles Reade's *Griffith Gaunt* in twelve instalments. In 1871 *Scribner's Monthly* began the prospectus of its second volume with this announcement:

Our contributors are among the best who write in the English language. George MacDonald—"the best of living story-writers"—will continue his beautiful story, entitled *Wilfred Cumbermede,* throughout the volume. We have the refusal of all Hans Christian Andersen's stories at the hand of his best translator, Mr. Horace E. Scudder. We have engaged the pen of Miss Thackeray, now regarded as the finest story-writer among the gifted women of Great Britain—not even excepting George Eliot. Mrs. Oliphant has written especially for us an exquisitely characteristic story, etc.

The feebleness of the period was understood even at the time. Charles Eliot Norton wrote Lowell in 1874: ''There is not much in the magazine [Atlantic] that is likely to be read twice save by its writers, and this is what the great public likes. There must be a revival of letters in America, if literature as an art is not to become extinct. You should hear Godkin express himself in private on this topic.'' [1]

No wonder that the book-reviewer of *Harper's Magazine* for May, 1870, with nothing better before him than *Miss Van Kortland,* Anonymous; *Hedged In,* by Miss Phelps; and *Askaros Kassis,* by DeLeon, should have begun his review, ''We are so weary of depending on England, France, and Germany for fiction, and so hungry for some genuine American romance, that we are not inclined to read very critically the three characteristic American novels which lie on our table.'' No wonder that when Harte's *The Luck of Roaring Camp* in the *Overland Monthly* was read in the *Atlantic* office, Fields sent by return mail a request ''upon the most flattering terms'' for another story like it, and that the same mail brought also papers and reviews ''welcoming the little foundling of California literature with an enthusiasm that half frightened its author.'' [2]

The new American fiction began with Bret Harte.

I

To turn from Mark Twain to Bret Harte is like turning from the great river on a summer night, fragrant and star-lit, to the glamour and unreality of the city theater. No contrast could be more striking. Francis Brett Harte, born August 25, 1839, was preëminently a man of the East and preëminently also a man of the city. He was born at Albany, New York, he spent his childhood in Providence, Rhode Island, in Philadelphia, in Lowell, Massachusetts, in Boston and other places, and the formative years between nine and eighteen he passed in Brooklyn

[1] *Letters of Charles Eliot Norton,* ii: 36.
[2] Harte. Introduction to the *Collected Works.*

and New York City. He lived all his young life in an atmosphere of culture. His father, a Union College man, a scholar, and a teacher who knew French and Spanish and Italian, Latin and Greek, had accumulated a large and well-selected library in which the boy, frail and sensitive, too frail in his early years to attend school, spent much of his childhood, reading Shakespeare and Froissart at six and Charles Dickens at seven. His mother, a woman of culture, directed his reading, and criticized with discernment his earliest attempts at poetry. It was the training school for a poet, a Bryant or a Longfellow, who should look to the older art for models and be inspired with the dream that had sent Irving and Willis and Taylor as pilgrims to the holy lands of literature across the sea.

The turning point in Harte's life came in 1854, when he was in his fifteenth year. His biographer, Merwin, tells the story:

In 1853 his mother [who had been a widow for nine years] went to California with a party of relatives and friends, in order to make her home there with her elder son, Henry. She had intended to take with her the other two children, Margaret and Francis Brett; but as the daughter was in school, she left the two behind for a few months, and they followed in February, 1854. They traveled by the Nicaragua route, and after a long, tiresome, but uneventful journey, landed safely in San Francisco.[3]

The mother must have remarried shortly after her arrival in California, for two sentences later on the biographer records that "They went the next morning to Oakland across the Bay, where their mother and her second husband, Colonel Andrew Williams, were living."

The young poet had been transplanted into new and strange soil and he took root slowly. During the next year, making his home with his mother at Oakland, he attempted to teach school and then to serve as an apothecary's assistant, but he made little headway in either profession. His heart was far away from the rough, new land that he had entered. He wrote poems and stories and sketches and sent them to the Eastern magazines; he read interminably, and dreamed of literature just as Aldrich and Timrod and Hayne and Stedman and Stoddard were even then dreaming of it on the other side of the continent.

[3] *Life of Bret Harte,* 17.

The next two years of his life, despite the efforts of his biographers, are vague and conjectural. It was his wander period. He began as tutor in a private family in Humboldt County, then, according to Charles Warren Stoddard, "he was an express messenger in the mountains when the office was the target of every lawless rifle in the territory; he was glutted with adventurous experiences." [4] Not for long, however. He seems to have spent the rest of the two years—prosaic anticlimax!— as a type-setter on the *Humboldt Times* and the *Northern California,* as a teacher in the town of Union, and as a drug clerk. That he ever was a miner is gravely to be doubted. He had small taste for roughing it and little sympathy with the typical California life of the times. He was a poet, rather, a man of the city, a reader of romance, how wide and attentive a reader we may judge from *Condensed Novels* which he soon after began to contribute to the San Francisco press.

The events in his life during the next fourteen years in San Francisco are quickly summarized. For the greater part of it he was connected with the *Golden Era,* first as a type-setter and later as an editor and contributor. In 1862 he was married. Two years later he was appointed Secretary of the California Mint, an office that allowed him abundant time for literary work. He was connected with Webb's brilliant and short-lived *Californian,* first as contributor and later as editor, and in 1868, when the *Overland Monthly,* which was to be the *Atlantic* of Western America, was founded, he was made the editor. *The Luck of Roaring Camp* in the second number and *Plain Language from Truthful James* in the September, 1870, number, brought him a popularity that in suddenness and extent had had no precedent in America, save in the case of Mrs. Stowe and *Uncle Tom's Cabin.* The enormous applause intoxicated him; California became too narrow and provincial; and in 1871 he left it, joyous as one who is returning home after long exile.

II

If we may trust Harte's own statement, made, it must be remembered, in the retrospect of later years, he set out deliberately to add a new province to American literature. During

4 *Exits and Entrances,* 241.

the period between 1862 and 1867, he wrote, according to his own statement, *"The Society upon the Stanislaus* and *The Story of M'liss*—the first a dialectical poem, the second a California romance—his first efforts toward indicating a peculiarly characteristic Western American literature. He would like to offer these facts as evidence of his very early, half-boyish, but very enthusiastic belief in such a possibility—a belief which never deserted him, and which, a few years later, from the better known pages of the *Overland Monthly*, he was able to demonstrate to a larger and more cosmopolitan audience in the story of *The Luck of Roaring Camp,* and the poem of *The Heathen Chinee."* [5]

But the poem and the romance were not his first efforts toward a peculiarly characteristic Western American literature. His first vision of the literary possibilities of the region had been inspired by Irving, and he wrote in the *Sketch Book* manner during the greater part of his seventeen years upon the Pacific Coast. Behind the California of the gold and the excitement lay three hundred years of an old Spanish civilization. What Irving had done for the Hudson why could he not do for the Mission lands and the Spanish occupation, "that glorious Indian summer of California history, around which so much poetical haze still lingers—that bland, indolent autumn of Spanish rule, so soon to be followed by the wintry storms of Mexican independence and the reviving springs of American conquest"? [6]   It was a vision worthy of a Hawthorne. That it possessed him for years and was abandoned with reluctance is evident to one who examines his early work.

He voiced it in *The Angelus, Heard at the Mission Dolores, 1868,* in the same volume of the *Overland Monthly* that contained *The Luck of Roaring Camp:*

>   Borne on the swell of your long waves receding,
>   I touch the further Past—
>   I see the dying glow of Spanish glory,
>   The sunset dream and last.
>
>   Before me rise the dome-shaped Mission towers;
>   The white Presidio;
>   The swart commander in his leathern jerkin,
>   The priest in stole of snow.

[5] Harte's General Introduction to his Works.
[6] *The Right Eye of the Commander.*

Once more I see Portata's cross uplifting
Above the setting sun;
And past the headland, northward, slowly drifting
The freighted galleon.

It must not be forgotten that his *Legend of Monte del Diablo,* a careful Irvingesque romance, appeared in the *Atlantic Monthly* as early as 1863. During the same period he wrote *The Right Eye of the Commander, The Legend of Devil's Point, The Adventure of Padre Viventio,* and many short pieces, enough, indeed, to make up a volume the size of *The Sketch Book.* Despite its echoes of Irving, it is significant work. Harte was the first to catch sight of a whole vast field of American romance. Again and again he recurs to it in his later poetry and prose; notably in *Concepcion de Arguello* and its prose version on page 191 of the first volume of the *Overland Monthly, A Convert of the Mission, The Story of a Mine, In the Carquinez Woods,* and in *Gabriel Conroy,* that chaotic book which has in it the materials for the greatest of American romances. Whenever he touches this old Spanish land he throws over it the mellow Washington Irving glow that had so thrilled him in his earlier years, and he writes with power. The Spanish part of *Gabriel Conroy* is exquisite; its atmosphere is faultless:

If there was a spot on the earth which the usual dead monotony of the California seasons seemed a perfectly consistent and natural expression, that spot was the ancient and time-honored *pueblo* and Mission of the blessed St. Anthony. The changeless, cloudless, expressionless skies of the summer seemed to symbolize that aristocratic conservatism which expelled all innovation and was its distinguishing mark. . . .

As he drew rein in the court-yard of the first large *adobe* dwelling, and received the grave welcome of a strange but kindly face, he saw around him everywhere the past unchanged. The sun shone as brightly and fiercely on the long red tiles of the low roofs, that looked as if they had been thatched with longitudinal slips of cinnamon, even as it had shone for the last hundred years; the gaunt wolf-like dogs ran out and barked at him as their fathers and mothers had barked at the preceding stranger of twenty years before. There were the few wild, half-broken mustangs tethered by strong riatas before the veranda of the long low *Fonda,* with the sunlight glittering on their silver trappings; there were the broad, blank expanses of whitewashed *adobe* wall, as barren and guiltless of record as the uneventful days, as monotonous and expressionless as the staring sky above; there were the white, dome-shaped towers of the Mission rising above the green of olives and pear trees, twisted, gnarled and knotted with the rheumatism of age.

. . . The steamers that crept slowly up the darkening coast line were something remote, unreal, and phantasmal; since the Philippine galleon had left its bleached and broken ribs in the sand in 1640, no vessel had, in the memory of man, dropped anchor in the open roadstead below the curving Point of Pines.

Meager and fragmentary as these Spanish sketches are, they nevertheless opened the way for a new school of American romance.

III

Harte's first story with other than a legendary theme was *M'liss*, written for the *Golden Era* sometime before 1867. For the student of his literary art it is the most important of all his writings, especially important because of the revision which he made of it later after he had evolved his final manner. It is transition work. The backgrounds are traced in with Irving-like care; the character of the schoolmaster is done with artistic restraint and certainty of touch. M'liss is exquisitely handled. There is nothing better in all his work than this study of the fiery, jealous little heart of the neglected child. It is not neces-.sarily a California story; it could have happened as well even in New England. It is not *genre* work, not mere exploiting of local oddities; it is worked out in life itself, and it strikes the universal human chord that brings it into the realm of true art.

But even in the earlier version of the story there are false notes. The names of the characters strike us as unusual: M'liss, McSnagley, Morpher, Clytemnestra, Kerg, Aristides, Cellerstina. We feel that the author is straining for the unusual; and we feel it more when the Rev. Joshua McSnagley comes upon the scene:

The reverend gentleman was glad to see him. Moreover, he observed that the master was looking "peartish," and hoped he had got over the "neuralgy" and "rheumatiz." He himself had been troubled with the dumb "ager" since last conference. But he had learned tø "rastle and pray." Pausing a moment to enable the master to write his certain method of curing the dumb "ager" upon the book and volume of his brain, Mr. McSnagley proceeded to inquire after Sister Morpher. "She is an adornment to Christewanity, and has a likely growin' young family," added Mr. McSnagley.

Somehow it does not ring .true. The author is thinking of the effect he hopes to produce. He must fill his reader with wonder. "A saintly Raphael-face, with blond beard and soft blue eyes, belonging to the biggest scamp in the diggings, turned toward the child and whispered, 'Stick to it, M'liss.' " That sentence is the key to the author's later manner. "Life in California is a paradox," he seems everywhere to say, "just look at this."

The transition from F. B. Harte the poet and romancer to Bret Harte the paradox maker and showman came through Dickens. It was the Dickens era in America. The great novelist had made his second tour of the country between November, 1867, and April, 1868, and his journeyings had been a triumphal progress. All classes everywhere were reading his books, and great numbers knew them literally by heart. Dickens wrote home from Washington, "Mr. Secretary Staunton (War Minister) was here. . . . He is acquainted with the minutest details of my books. Give him a passage anywhere and he will instantly cap it and go on with the context. . . . Never went to sleep at night without first reading something from my books which were always with him." [7] The same could have been said of Harte himself. Says Pemberton, "His knowledge of his [Dickens's] books was unrivaled. . . . He could have passed Charles Calverley's famous Pickwick Examination Paper with honors." [8] Everybody knew his Dickens; for a generation men could not speak of the man with moderation. Even a critic like Moncure D. Conway could say of *Oliver Twist* and *The Old Curiosity Shop:* "To this day I cannot help suspecting the sanity of any one who does not concede that they are the two best novels ever written." [9] The death of Dickens in 1870 let loose all over America a flood of eulogy and increased enormously the already great sales of his books.

The art of Dickens was peculiar. He had found in the lower strata of the population of London, that vast settling pool of Great Britain, a society made up of many sharply individualized personalities, abnormalities in body and soul, results of the peculiar inflexible characteristics of the English race and their hard and fast social distinctions. From fragments of this lower London Dickens built him a world of his own and peopled it with com-

7 *Letters of Charles Dickens*, 667.
8 *The Life of Bret Harte*, 166.
9 *Harper's Magazine*, 41:610.

posite creations such as one finds nowhere save in the folklore of a primitive people—creatures as strange as their names, Quilp, Scrooge, Cratchit, Squeers, Snagsby. So tremendously did he believe in them, that we believe in them ourselves. So overflowing was he with high spirits and boisterous laughter that before we realize it we have surrendered completely and are living hilariously not in a land of actual men and women, but in the world that never was and never can be save in the books of Dickens. He never analyzed, he never sought the heart of things, or got at all below the surface of his characters; he was content simply to exhibit his marvelous creations with all their ludicrous incongruities, and the show is so entertaining and the showman exhibits it with such zest, such joyous abandon, that we stand like children and lose ourselves in wonder and enjoyment.

We can see now that the time was ripe for a California Dickens. There was a prepared audience—the whole nation was reading the great novelist of the people. California, moreover, was in the fierce light of the gold excitement—anything that came from it would find eager readers. It was a veritable Dickens land, more full of strange types than even the slums of London: Pikes, Greasers, Yankees, Chinese, gamblers, adventurers from all the wild places of the world, desperadoes, soldiers of fortune, restless seekers for excitement and gold. Everything was ready. Harte doubtless blundered into his success; doubtless he did not reason about the matter at all, yet the result remains the same: he came at the precise moment with the precise form of literature that the world was most sure to accept. It came about as the most natural thing in the world. Saturated with Dickens as he had been from his childhood, it is not strange that this motley society and its amazing surroundings should have appealed to him from the objective and the picturesque side; it is not strange that, even as did Dickens, he should have selected types and heightened them and peopled a new world with them; it is not strange that he should have given these types Dickens-like names: Miggles, McCorkle, Culpepper Starbottle, Calhoun Bungstarter, Fagg, Twinkler, Rattler, Mixer, Stubbs, Nibbles. His work is redolent of Dickens. Sometimes we seem to be reading a clever parody after the fashion of the *Condensed Novels,* as for instance this from *The Romance of Madrono Hollow:*

There was not much to hear. The hat was saying to the ribbons that it was a fine night, and remarking generally upon the clear outline of the Sierras against the blue-black sky. The ribbons, it so appeared, had admired this all the way home, and asked the hat if it had ever seen anything half so lovely as the moonlight on the summit? The hat never had; it recalled some lovely nights in the South in Alabama ("in the South in Ahlabahm" was the way the old man had heard it), but then there were other things that made the night seem so pleasant. The ribbons could not possibly conceive what the hat could be thinking about. At this point there was a pause, of which Mr. Folinsbee availed himself to walk very grimly and craunchingly down the gravel walk toward the gate. Then the hat was lifted, and disappeared in the shadow, and Mr. Folinsbee confronted only the half-foolish, half-mischievous, but wholly pretty face of his daughter.

M'liss is full of such echoes. A little later than *M'liss*, when he was required to furnish the *Overland* with a distinctly Californian story, he set about examining his field precisely as Dickens would have done. "What are some of the most unusual phases of this unique epoch?" he asked himself. During a short period women and children were rare in the remote mining districts. What would result if a baby were born in one of the roughest and most masculine of the camps? It is not hard to conjecture how Dickens would have handled the problem; *The Luck of Roaring Camp* is Harte's solution. The situation and the characters are both unique. They would have been impossible in any other place or at any other moment in the world's history. So with all of Harte's later stories: undoubtedly there may have been a Roaring Camp and undoubtedly there were Cherokee Sals and Kentucks, undoubtedly the gold rush developed here and there Jack Hamlins and Tennessees and Uncle Billys and Yuba Bills. The weakness of Harte is that he takes these and peoples California with them. Like Dickens, he selects a few picturesque and grotesque exceptions and makes of them a whole social system.

Harte had nothing of the earnestness and the sincerity of the older master; after a time he outgrew his manner, and evolved a style of his own—compressed, rapid, picturesque; but this early point of view he never changed. He sought ever for the startling and the dramatic and he elaborated the outside of it with care. He studied the map of California for picturesque names, just as Dickens studied the street signs of London. He passed by the common materials of human life to exhibit the strange phenomena of one single accidental moment in a corner of America.

Once he had begun, however, there was no possibility of stopping. The people demanded work like *The Luck of Roaring Camp* and would accept nothing else. It is pathetic to see him during the early years of his great fame, trying to impress upon the reading public that he is a poet after the old definition of the word. The *Atlantic* had paid him $10,000 to write for a year work like *The Luck of Roaring Camp*. He gave four stories, and he gave also five careful poems of the Longfellow-Whittier type. By 1873 he had put forth no fewer than fourteen books, nine of them being poems or collections of his poetry. In vain. The public ordered him back to the mines and camps that even then were as obsolete as the pony express across the Plains.

Despite his biographers, the latter part of his life is full of mystery. After seven years of literary work in New York City, he went in 1878 as consul to Crefeld, Germany. Two years later he was transferred to Glasgow, Scotland, where he remained for five years. The rest of his life he spent in London, writing year after year new books of California stories. He never returned to America; he was estranged from his family; he seemed to wish to sever himself entirely from all that had to do with his earlier life. He died May 5, 1902, and was buried in Frimby churchyard, in Surrey.

IV

A novelist must rise or fall with his characters. What of Harte? First of all we must observe that he makes no attempts at character development. Each personage introduced is the same at the close of the story as at the opening. He has no fully studied character: we have a burning moment, a flashlight glimpse—intense, paradoxical, startling, then no more. We never see the person again. The name may appear in later sketches, but it never designates the same man. Colonel Starbottle is consistent from story to story only in make-up, in stage "business," and the well known "gags"—as, for instance, a succession of phrases qualified by the adjective "blank." "Yuba Bill" is Harte's synonym for stage driver, "Jack Hamlin" for gambler. We have a feeling constantly that the characters are brought in simply to excite wonder. Gabriel Conroy devotes his life for years to the finding of his sister Grace. He leaves his wife to search for her; he can think of nothing else; yet when at length he does find her among the witnesses in a courtroom he takes it as a mere commonplace. A moment later, however, when told that his wife, for whom we know he cares nothing at all, has given birth to a son, he falls headlong in a swoon.

His characters may perhaps be true to facts; he may be able to give the prototype in every case; and yet we are not convinced. The stories told by the college freshman at home during his first Christmas vacation may all be true, and yet they may give a very false idea of college life in its entirety. So it is with Harte. The very year that he landed in California a procession of one thousand children, each child with a flower in his hand, marched one day in San Francisco. The *Luck of Roaring Camp* gives no such impression. In all save the remotest camps there were churches and worshipers, yet who would suspect it from Harte's tales? California has never accepted Harte's picture of its life, just as the South has never accepted *Uncle Tom's Cabin*. It is not fair to picture an era simply by dwelling on its exceptions and its grotesque possibilities. Art must rest upon the whole truth, not upon half truths.

The truth is that the man had no deep and abiding philosophy of life; he had indeed no philosophy at all. In the words of his discerning biographer, Merwin,

There was a want of background, both intellectual and moral, in his nature. He was an observer, not a thinker, and his genius was shown only as he lived in the life of others. Even his poetry is dramatic, not lyric. It was very seldom that Bret Harte, in his tales or elsewhere, advanced any abstract sentiment or idea; he was concerned only with the concrete; and it is noticeable that when he does venture to lay down a general principle, it fails to bear the impress of real conviction. The note of sincerity is wanting.[10]

The fact that his rascals in a crisis often do deeds of sublime heroism must not deceive us, despite the author's protestations of a great moral purpose underlying his work.

Without claiming to be a religious man or a moralist, but simply as an artist, he shall reverently and humbly conform to the rules laid down by a Great Poet who created the parables of the Prodigal Son and the Good Samaritan, whose works have lasted eighteen hundred

[10] *Life of Bret Harte,* 286.

years, and will remain when the present writer and his generation are forgotten. And he is conscious of uttering no original doctrine in this, but of only voicing the beliefs of a few of his literary brethren happily living, and one gloriously dead, who never made proclamation of this from the housetops.[11]

This is insincere to the point of bathos. We feel like saying, "Bah!" Harte makes his villains heroes at the crisis simply to add *finesse* to his tale. He is dealing with paradoxes; he is working for his reader's wonder. If in a moment where pity is expected, woman is harsh and man tender; if the reputed good man is a rascal at the supreme test, and the reputed rascal proves suddenly to be a saint, it adds to the effectiveness of the tale.

Everywhere there is the atmosphere of the theater. The painted backgrounds are marvels of skill. There are vast color effects, and picturesque tableaux. There is a theatric quality about the heroines; we can see the make-up upon their faces. Too often they talk the stagiest of stage talk as in the first parting scene between Grace Conroy and Arthur Poinset. The end is always a drop-curtain effect. Even *Tennessee's Partner* must have its appropriate curtain. We can imagine a double curtain for *The Outcasts of Poker Flat:* the first tableau showing the two dead women in the snow, the second the inscription over the body of Oakhurst, the gambler. Instead of closing the book with a long breath as after looking at a quivering section of human life, we say, "How strange! What brilliant work!" and we feel like clapping our hands for a tableau of all the cast, the spot light, and the quick curtain.

Bret Harte had no real affection for the West; he never again visited it; he never even wrote to the friends he had left there. With Mark Twain it was greatly different. The West to him was home; he loved it; he recorded its deepest life with sympathy. To Harte it was simply a source of literary material. He skimmed its surface and found only the melodramatic and the sensational.

V

And yet after all the real strength of Bret Harte came from his contact with this Western soil. Irving and Dickens and the early models that had so molded him served only to teach him

---

[11] General Introduction to his Works.

his trade; the breath of life in his works all came from the new life of the West. It would be impossible for one to live during seventeen years of his early life in an atmosphere like that of the west coast and not be transformed by it. Taking his work altogether there is in it far more of California than there is of Dickens or of all the others of the older writers. Only a few things of the life of the West seem to have impressed him. He lived fifteen years in San Francisco yet we see almost nothing of that city in his work; the dramatic career of the Vigilantes he touched upon almost not at all. He selected the remote mining camps for his field and yet he seems to have been impressed by very few of the types that were found in them. Only a few of them ring true at every point, Yuba Bill the stage driver is one. We feel that he was drawn by a master who has actually lived with his model. Yuba Bill is the typical man of the region and the period—masterful, self-reliant, full of a humor that is elemental. There is no prolonged study of him. We see him for a tense moment as the stage swings up to the station, and then he is gone. He is as devoid of sentimentality as even Horace Bixby. The company have been shouting "Miggles!" at the dark cabin but have got no reply save from what proves later to have been a parrot:

"Extraordinary echo," said the Judge.
"Extraordinary d—d skunk!" roared the driver contemptuously.
"Come out of that, Miggles, and show yourself. Be a man."
Miggles, however, did not appear.
Yuba Bill hesitated no longer. Taking a heavy stone from the road, he battered down the gate, and with the expressman entered the enclosure. . . .
"Do you know this Miggles?" asked the Judge of Yuba Bill.
"No, nor don't want to," said Bill shortly.
"But, my dear sir," expostulated the Judge, as he thought of the barred gate.
"Lookee here," said Yuba Bill, with fine irony, "had n't you better go back and sit in the coach till yer introduced? I'm going in," and he pushed open the door of the building.

That rings true. If one were obliged to ride at night over a wild, road-agent-infested trail there is no character in all fiction whom we would more gladly have for driver than Yuba Bill. We would like to see more of him than the brief glimpses allowed us by his creator.

The humor in Harte is largely Western humor. There is the true California ring in such conversations, for instance, as those in the earlier pages of *Uncle Jim and Uncle Billy*. It is an atmosphere rather than a series of hits. One finds it in *The Outcasts of Poker Flat*:

A few of the committee had urged hanging him [Oakhurst] as a possible example, and a sure method of reimbursing themselves from his pockets of the sums he had won from them. "It's agin justice," said Jim Wheeler, "to let this yer young man from Roaring Camp—an entire stranger—carry away our money." But a crude sentiment of equity residing in the breasts of those who had been fortunate enough to win from Mr. Oakhurst overruled this narrower local prejudice.

This atmosphere of humor shimmers through all of the stories. There is never uproarious merriment, but there is constant humor. The conjugal troubles of the "old man" in *How Santa Claus Came to Simpson's Bar* are thus touched upon:

His first wife, a delicate, pretty little woman, had suffered keenly and secretly from the jealous suspicions of her husband, until one day he invited the whole Bar to his house to expose her infidelity. On arriving, the party found the shy, *petite* creature quietly engaged in her household duties and retired abashed and discomfited. But the sensitive woman did not easily recover from her shock of this extraordinary outrage. It was with difficulty she regained her equanimity sufficiently to release her lover from the closet in which he was concealed and escape with him. She left a boy of three years to comfort her bereaved husband. The old man's present wife had been his cook. She was large, loyal, and aggressive.

His characters are exceptions and his situations are theatric, yet for all that he cannot be ignored. He caught the spirit of the early mining camps and with it the romantic atmosphere of the old Spanish Colonial civilization that was swept away by the Anglo-Saxon rush for gold. His name cannot fail to go down with the era he recorded, and to identify oneself forever with an era, even though that era be a brief and restricted one, is no small achievement. He is the writer of the epic of the gold rush of the middle century in America, and whatever the quality of that epic may be, it can never be forgotten. He said in 1868:

It may not have been an heroic era; it may have been a hard, ugly, unworked, vulgar and lawless era; but of such are heroes and aristocracies born. Three hundred years, and what a glamor shall hang about it! . . . A thousand years, and a new Virgil sings the American

Æneid with the episode of Jason and the California golden fleece, and the historians tell us it is a myth! Laugh, my pioneer friends, but your great-great-great-great-grandchildren shall weep reverential tears. History, as was said of martyrdom, is "mean in the making" but how heroic it becomes in the perspective of five centuries! [12]

And in many ways his work is really of epic strength. He dealt with elemental men, often with veritable demigods, as Yuba Bill. His canvases are as broad as those even of Mark Twain. His human drama is played before a truly Western background. While Tennessee is being tried for his life, "Above all this, etched on the dark firmament, rose the Sierra, remote and passionless, crowned with remoter passionless stars." At moments of crisis the narrative always moves with power. The wolves and the fire in the story *In the Carquinez Woods* are intensely vivid and lurid in their presentation. The ride from Simpson's Bar is told with the graphic thrill of an eye-witness, and the description of the snow-storm at the opening of *Gabriel Conroy* reminds one of Thomas Hardy.

VI

Finally, Harte was the parent of the modern form of the short story. It was he who started Kipling and Cable and Thomas Nelson Page. Few indeed have surpassed him in the mechanics of this most difficult of arts. According to his own belief, the form is an American product. We can do no better than to quote from his essay on *The Rise of the Short Story*. It traces the evolution of a peculiarly American addition to literature.

But while the American literary imagination was still under the influence of English tradition, an unexpected factor was developing to diminish its power. It was *humor*, of a quality as distinct and original as the country and civilization in which it was developed. It was first noticeable in the anecdote or "story," and, after the fashion of such beginnings, was orally transmitted. It was common in the bar-rooms, the gatherings in the "country store," and finally at public meetings in the mouths of "stump orators." Arguments were clinched and political principles illustrated by "a funny story." It invaded even the camp meeting and pulpit. It at last received the currency of the public press. But wherever met it was so distinctly original and novel, so individual and characteristic, that it was at once known and appreciated abroad as "an American story." Crude at first, it received a literary polish in the press, but its dominant quality remained. It was concise and condense, yet suggestive. It was delightfully extravagant, or a miracle of under-statement. It voiced not only the dialect, but the habits of thought of a people or locality. It gave a new interest to slang. From a paragraph of a dozen lines it grew into half a column, but always retaining its conciseness and felicity of statement. It was a foe to prolixity of any kind; it admitted no fine writing nor affectation of style. It went directly to the point. It was burdened by no conscientiousness; it was often irreverent; it was devoid of all moral responsibility, but it was original! By degrees it developed character with its incident, often, in a few lines, gave a striking photograph of a community or a section, but always reached its conclusion without an unnecessary word. It became—and still exists as—an essential feature of newspaper literature. It was the parent of the American "short story." [13]

Harte has described the genesis of his own art. It sprang from the Western humor and was developed by the circumstances that surrounded him. Many of his short stories are models. They contain not a superfluous word; they handle a single incident with graphic power; they close without moral or comment. The form came as a natural evolution from his limitations and powers. With him the story must of necessity be brief. He who depicts the one good deed in a wicked life must of necessity use a small canvas. At one moment in his career Jack Hamlin or Mother Shipton or Sandy does a truly heroic deed, but the author must not extend his inquiries too far. To make a novel with Mother Shipton as heroine would be intolerable.

Harte was unable to hold himself long to any one effort. Like Byron, he must bring down his quarry at a single spring; he had no patience to pursue it at length. *Gabriel Conroy* is at the same time the best and the worst American novel of the century. It is the best in its wealth of truly American material and in the brilliant passages that strew its pages; it is the worse in that it utterly fails in its construction, and that it builds up its characters wholly from the outside. Its hero, moreover, changes his personality completely three times during the story, and its heroine is first an uneducated Pike maiden of the Southwest, then a Spanish señorita:

Features small, and perfectly modeled; the outline of the small face was a perfect oval, but the complection was of burnished copper. . . . The imperious habit of command; an almost despotic control of a hun-

[13] Pemberton's *Life of Bret Harte*, 298.

dred servants; a certain barbaric contempt for the unlimited revenues at her disposal that prompted the act, became her wonderfully. In her impatience the quick blood glanced through her bronzed cheek, her little slipper tapped the floor imperiously and her eyes flashed in the darkness.

Later we learn that she had been adopted into this Spanish family after her lover had abandoned her in the earlier chapters, and had been given her complexion by means of a vegetable stain. But there is still another lightning change. At the end of the book she becomes a Pike again and weakly marries the unrepentant rascal who earlier had betrayed her. In the words of Artemus Ward, "it is too much." It is not even good melodrama, for in melodrama the villain is punished at the end.

Bret Harte was the artist of impulse, the painter of single burning moments, the flashlight photographer who caught in lurid detail one dramatic episode in the life of a man or a community and left the rest in darkness.

VII

In his later years Harte's backgrounds became less sharp in outline. His methods grew more romantic; his atmospheres more mellow and golden. The old Spanish dream of the days of his early art possessed him again, and he added to his gallery of real creations—M'liss, Yuba Bill, Jack Hamlin, Tennessee's Partner—one that perhaps is the strongest of them all, Enriquez Saltillo, the last of a fading race. Nothing Harte ever did will surpass that creation of his old age. In *Chu Chu, The Devotion of Enriquez,* and *The Passing of Enriquez* we have the fitting close of the work of the romancer of the west coast. For once at least he saw into the heart of a man. Listen to Enriquez as he makes his defense:

Then they say, "Dry up, and sell out"; and the great bankers say, "Name your own price for your stock, and resign." And I say, "There is not gold enough in your bank, in your San Francisco, in the mines of California, that shall buy a Spanish gentleman. When I leave, I leave the stock at my back; I shall take it, nevarre!" Then the banker he say, "And you will go and blab, I suppose?" And then, Pancho, I smile, I pick up my mustache—so! and I say: "Pardon, señor, you haf mistake. The Saltillo haf for three hundred year no stain, no blot upon him. Eet is not now—the last of the race—who shall confess that he haf sit at a board of disgrace and dishonor!" And then it is that the band begin to play, and the animals stand on their hind legs and waltz, and behold, the row he haf begin.

It is the atmosphere of romance, for the mine which had caused all the trouble had been in the family three hundred years and it had become a part of the family itself. When it passed into the hands of the new régime, when his wife, who also was of the new régime, deserted him, then passed Enriquez. The earth that for three hundred years had borne his fathers opened at the earthquake and took him to herself. It was the conception of a true romancer. The work of Bret Harte opened and closed with a vision of romance, a vision worthy even of a Hawthorne.

BIBLIOGRAPHY

BRET HARTE. (1839–1902.) *The Lost Galleon and Other Tales* [Poems], 1867; *Condensed Novels and Other Papers*, 1867; *The Luck of Roaring Camp and Other Sketches*, 1870; *Plain Language from Truthful James*, 1870; *The Pliocene Skull*, 1871; *Poems*, 1871; *East and West Poems*, 1871; *The Heathen Chinee and Other Poems*, 1871; *Poetical Works*, 1872; *Mrs. Skagg's Husbands*, 1873; *M'liss: An Idyl of Red Mountain*, 1873; *Echoes of the Foot-Hills* [Poems], 1875; *Tales of the Argonauts*, 1875; *Gabriel Conroy*, 1876; *Two Men of Sandy Bar*, 1876; *Thankful Blossom*, 1877; *The Story of a Mine*, 1878; *Drift from Two Shores*, 1878; *The Twins of Table Mountain*, 1879; *Works* in five volumes, 1882; *Flip, and Found at Blazing Star*, 1882; *In the Carquinez Woods*, 1884; *On the Frontier*, 1884; *Maruja*, 1885; *By Shore and Sedge*, 1885; *Snow Bound at Eagle's*, 1885; *A Millionaire of Rough-and-Ready*, 1887; *The Crusade of the Excelsior*, 1887; *The Argonauts of North Liberty*, 1888; *A Phyllis of the Sierras*, 1888; *Cressy*, 1889; *The Heritage of Dedlow Marsh*, 1889; *A Waif of the Plains*, 1890; *A Ward of the Golden Gate*, 1890; *A Sappho of Green Springs*, 1891; *Colonel Starbottle's Client*, 1892; *A First Family of Tasajara*, 1892; *Susy: a Story of the Plains*, 1893; *Sally Dows and Other Stories*, 1893; *A Protégé of Jack Hamlin's*, 1894; *The Bell-Ringer of Angel's*, 1894; *In a Hollow of the Hills*, 1895; *Clarence*, 1895; *Barker's Luck*, 1896; *Three Partners*, 1897; *Tales of Trail and Town*, 1898; *Stories in Light and Shadow*, 1898; *Mr. Jack Hamlin's Meditation*, 1899; *From Sandhill to Pine*, 1900; *Under the Redwoods*, 1901; *Openings in the Old Trail*, 1902; *Life of Bret Harte*, by T. Edgar Pemberton, 1903; *Bret Harte*, by Henry W. Boynton, 1905; *The Life of Bret Harte with Some Account of the California Pioneers*, by Henry Childs Merwin, 1911.

CHAPTER V

THE DISCOVERY OF PIKE COUNTY

The new era of vulgarity in literature, complained of by Stedman, came as a revolt against mid-century tendencies. The movement was not confined to America. In the early seventies, as we have seen, Millet and his Breton peasants for a time took possession of French art; Hardy with his Wessex natives caught the ear of England; Björnson made the discovery that in the Scandinavian peasant lay the only survival of the old Norse spirit; and the Russians Tourgenieff and Tolstoy cast aside the old mythology and told with minuteness the life of the peasant and the serf. Everywhere there was a swing toward the wild and unconventional, even toward the coarse and repulsive. The effeminacy of early Tennysonianism, the cloying sweetness of the mid-century annual, Keatsism, *Hyperionism*, Heineism, had culminated in reaction. There was a craving for the acrid tang of uncultivated things in borderlands and fields unsown.

In America had sprung up a group of humorists who had filled the newspapers and magazines of the era with that masculine laughter which was echoing along the Mississippi and the Ohio and the gold camps of the Sierras. They were pioneers; they were looking for incongruities and exaggerations, and quite by accident they discovered a new American type, the Pike,— strange creature to inspire a new literature.

I

America has evolved four types, perhaps five, that are unique, "new birth of our new soil": the Yankee of the Hosea Biglow and Sam Lawson variety; the frontiersman and scout exemplified in Leather Stocking; the Southern "darky" as depicted by Russell, Harris, Page, and others; the circuit rider of the frontier period; and the Pike.

"A Pike," says Bayard Taylor, "in the California dialect, is a native of Missouri, Arkansas, Northern Texas, or Southern Illinois. The first emigrants that came over the plains were from Pike County, Missouri; but as the phrase, 'a Pike County man,' was altogether too long for this short life of ours, it was soon abbreviated into 'a Pike.' Besides, the emigrants from the aforementioned localities belonged evidently to the same *genus,* and the epithet 'Western' was by no means sufficiently descriptive. . . . He is the Anglo-Saxon relapsed into semi-barbarism. He is long, lathy, and sallow; he expectorates vehemently; he takes naturally to whisky; he has the 'shakes' his life long at home, though he generally manages to get rid of them in California; he has little respect for the rights of others; he distrusts men in 'store clothes,' but venerates the memory of Andrew Jackson." [1]

Although he had not yet been named, the Pike had already figured in American literature. George W. Harris had published in 1867 *Sut Lovengood's Yarns,* a true piece of Pike literature; Longstreet had drawn the type with fidelity in *Georgia Scenes,* Baldwin's *Flush Times,* and the sketches of such ephemeral writers as Madison Tensas, Sol Smith, T. W. Lane, T. A. Burke, and J. L. McConnel, the author of *Western Characters,* had drawn the first broad outlines. In all this work he was simply the crude, uncouth Westerner, the antithesis of the man of the East.

The first to discover him in his California phase and to affix to him for the first time in any book of moment the name Pike was "John Phœnix" who in *Phœnixiana* drew, as we have seen, a sketch which has scarcely been improved upon by later writers. It was not until 1871, however, that the name Pike and the peculiar type denoted by the name became at all known to the reading public.

The instant and enormous vogue of Pike literature came almost by accident. Bret Harte late in the sixties had dashed off in a happy moment a humorous account of an attempt made by two California gamblers to fleece an innocent Chinaman who turned out to be anything but innocent. He had entitled the poem "Plain Language from Truthful James" and had thrown it aside as a trifle. Some months later during the last exciting moments before going to press with an edition of the *Overland Monthly* it was discovered that the form was one page short. There was nothing ready but this poem, and with misgivings

[1] *At Home and Abroad,* Second Series, 51.

Harte inserted it. The result was nothing less than amazing. It proved to be the most notable page in the history of the magazine. The poem captured the East completely; it was copied and quoted and laughed at in every corner of the country. It swept through England and beyond. *The Luck of Roaring Camp* and the two or three strong pieces that followed it had given Harte a certain vogue in the East, but now he swiftly became not only a national, but an international figure. The fame of the "Heathen Chinee," as the poem was now called, brought out of obscurity other poems written by Harte during his editorial days, among them "The Society upon the Stanislaus," and it gave wings to other verses that he now wrote in the "Heathen Chinee" meter and stanza—"Dow's Flat" and "Penelope." Quickly there were added "Jim," "Chiquita," "In the Tunnel," and "Cicely," all of them dealing not with the "heathen Chinee" of his first great strike, but with that other picturesque figure of early California, the Pike.

> It was *gold*,—in the quartz,
> And it ran all alike;
> And I reckon five oughts
> Was the worth of that strike;
> And that house with the coopilow's his'n,—which the same
> is n't bad for a Pike.

These poems with others were published in 1871 with the title *East and West Poems.* The Pike County pieces in the volume number altogether seven; John Hay's *Pike County Ballads,* which came out in book form at almost the same moment, numbered six—thirteen rather remarkable poems when one considers the furore that they created and the vast influence they exerted upon their times.

For a decade and more Pike County colored American literature. In 1871 J. G. Holland summed up the situation:

The "Pike" . . . has produced a strange and startling sensation in recent literature. . . . With great celerity he has darted through the columns of our newspapers, the pages of our magazines, while quiet, well-behaved contributors have stood one side and let him have his own wild way. And it began to seem, at one time, as if the ordinary, decent virtues of civilized society could stand no chance in comparison with the picturesque heroism of this savage in dialect.[2]

[2] *Scribner's Monthly,* 2:430.

Much of Harte's fiction deals with this type. Save for Yuba Bill, who was evidently a Northerner, the New Orleans gamblers like Oakhurst and Jack Hamlin, and the Spanish and Mexican natives, his characters were prevailingly Pikes. The dialect in all of his work is dominated by this Southwestern element. In *The New Assistant at the Pine Clearing School,* for instance, the leader of the strike discourses like this: "We ain't hankerin' much for grammar and dictionary hogwash, and we don't want no Boston parts o' speech rung in on us the first thing in the mo'nin'. We ain't Boston—We're Pike County—we are." Tennessee's Partner was a Pike, and Uncle Jim and Uncle Billy, and Kentuck and Sandy—glorified to be sure and transformed by California and the society of the mines, but none the less Pikes.

Following Harte and Hay came the outburst of local color fiction. *The Hoosier Schoolmaster, Cape Cod Folks, Sam Lawson's Fireside Stories, Hoosier Mosaics, Deephaven, Old Creole Days, In the Tennessee Mountains* were but the beginning. For two decades and more American fiction ran to the study of local types and peculiar dialect. The movement was not confined to prose. The Pike County balladry was continued by Sidney Lanier and Irwin Russell with their songs and ballads of the negro quarters, Will Carleton with his farm ballads, James Whitcomb Riley with his Hoosier studies, Drummond with his tales of the "Habitant" of the Canadian frontier, and by Eugene Field, Sam Walter Foss, Holman F. Day, and scores of others down to Robert W. Service, the depicter of the Yukon and the types of the later gold rush.

II

Whether the Pike County balladry began with Bret Harte or with John Hay, is a question at present unsettled. Mark Twain was positive that Hay was the pioneer. His statement is important:

"It was contemporaneously supposed," he wrote after Hay's death, "that the *Pike County Ballads* were inspired or provoked by the Pike County balladry of Bret Harte, and they were first accepted as imitations or parodies. They were not written later, they were written (and printed in newspapers) earlier. Mr. Hay told me this himself— in 1870 or '71, I should say. I believe—indeed, I am quite sure—that he added that the newspapers referred to were obscure western back-

woods journals and that the ballads were not widely copied. Also he
said this: That by and by, when Harte's ballads began to sweep the
country, the noise woke his (Hay's) buried waifs and they rose and
walked." [3]

To this testimony may be added Howells's belief that Hay's
ballads were prior to Harte's and that "a comparative study will
reveal their priority," [4] and the statement of W. E. Norris, a
schoolmate of the poet, that "the ballads appeared as fugitive
pieces in the newspapers, as I remember, and the attention they
attracted induced the author to compile them with others in
book form." [5]

A comparative study of the poems certainly reveals the fact
that one set was influenced by the other. "Cicely" and "Little
Breeches" have very much in common. They are in the same
meter, and in one place they have practically identical lines:

But I takes mine straight without sugar, and that's what's the matter of me.—*Cicely.*

I want a chaw of terbacker,
    And that's what's the matter with me.
                              —*Little Breeches.*

There are similarities in others of the poems:

Don't know Flynn,—
Flynn of Virginia,—
Long as he's been 'yar?
Look 'ee here, stranger,
Whar *hev* you been?   —*In the Tunnel.*

Whar have you been for the last three year,
That you have n't heard folks tell
How Jimmy Bludso passed in his checks
The night of the *Prairie Belle?*   —*Jim Bludso.*

It must be confessed that a study of the ballads and of the
other poetical works of the two poets leaves one with the impression that Harte was first in the field. Hay's six Pike County
ballads stand isolated among his poems. Everything he wrote
before them and after them is in an utterly different key. One
feels as he reads him straight through—the earlier lyrics, *Cas-*

---

[3] *Harper's Weekly*, 49:530.
[4] *North American Review*, 181:343.
[5] *Century Magazine*, 78:444.

tilian Days, the later lyrics, *The Bread-winners, The Life of Lincoln*—that these poems came from an impulse, that they must have been thrown off in quick succession all at one time in answer to some sudden impression. One feels, therefore, more like trusting a contemporary biographical sketch than the unsupported impressions of contemporaries thirty years after the event. A sketch of John Hay, written by Clarence King in April, 1874, records that when Hay returned from Spain in 1870

All the world was reading Mr. Bret Harte's "Heathen Chinee" and Mr. Hay did what all the world was doing. . . . He read all the poems, but "Chiquita" and "Cicely," which gave him particular pleasure, puzzled him and set him to thinking. . . . He saw how infinitely nobler and better than nature they were, but, having been born and brought up as a Pike himself, he saw that they were not nature. He wrote "Little Breeches" for his own amusement—at least we have heard this is his account of the matter—to see how a genuine Western feeling expressed in genuine Western language, would impress Western people. . . . The ballads were written within a few days of each other: two of them in a single evening.[6]

This seems all the more reasonable after we have considered Hay's earlier poetic ideals. He had been born into a refined home in the middle West, the son of a doctor and a New England mother, and he had grown up amid books and intellectual ideals. At the age of thirteen he had been sent to his uncle in Pike County, Illinois, to attend a private school which proved to be of such excellent quality that three years later he was prepared to enter the Sophomore class at Brown. His life at Providence awakened within him new ideals. He was invited into the literary circle of the little city where he came to know Mrs. Whitman, whose life at one time had touched that of Poe, and more significant still, Nora Perry, the poet, a kindred soul. Graduating at nineteen, the poet of his class, he went back to Warsaw, the little Mississippi River town of his boyhood, dreaming the dreams of a poet. But the outlook for the young dreamer was a depressing one. "I am removed to a colder mental atmosphere," he wrote to Miss Perry. In the West, "I find only a dreary waste of heartless materialism, where great and heroic qualities may indeed bully their way up into the glare, but the flowers of

6 *Scribner's Monthly,* 7:736.

existence inevitably droop and wither." [7]   He wrote much poetry
during this early period—translations of Heine, Longfellow-
like poems of beauty, and stirring lyrics to Miss Perry, who kept
alive his poetic dreams with letters and poems, among them her
"After the Ball" which she had shown him before it appeared
in the *Atlantic*. No Pike County notes in this period: he was
filled with the vision that even then was inspiring the little
transition school of poets struggling along the old paths: Stedman, Stoddard, Aldrich, Hayne, Sill, and the others.

But there was no place in the young West for such dreams.
He burned much of the poetry he had written and set out sternly
to study law in his uncle's office. "I feel that Illinois and Rhode
Island are entirely antipathetic," he confessed to Miss Perry.
Within him he felt the fires even of genius, he wrote, "but when
you reflect how unsuitable such sentiments are to the busy life
of the Mississippi Valley, you may imagine then what an over-
hauling I must receive—at my own hands too. There is, as yet,
no room in the West for a genius." [8]

No more poetry. He turned from it out of sheer sense of
duty and began with the law. But he was to be no lawyer. In
his uncle's office in Springfield he came into intimate contact
with Lincoln, and before his law studies had matured at all, he
found himself in Washington, the assistant secretary of the new
President. Poetry now was out of the question. The war took
his every moment, and after the war there was diplomatic
service abroad, at Paris, at Vienna, at Madrid. The literary
product of this latter period is as far from Pike work as
Rhode Island was from Illinois. One may find it in the section
of his poems headed "Wanderlieder"—beautiful lyrics of the
Longfellow type—"Sunrise in the Place de la Concorde," "The
Monks of Basle," "Ernst of Edelsheim," and the like. He
brought with him too when he returned in 1870 his Spanish
Sketch Book, Castilian Days, the work of a poet, golden atmos-
phered, vivid, delightful. In the five years that followed on the
Tribune staff he wrote for the magazines his best poems. He was
a lyrist with a pen of gold, impassioned at times and impetuous:

7 *A Poet in Exile. Early Letters of John Hay.* Caroline Ticknor, 18.
8 *Ibid.,* 24.

> Roll on, O shining sun,
> To the far seas,
> Bring down, ye shades of eve,
> The soft, salt breeze!
> Shine out, O stars, and light
> My darling's pathway bright,
> As through the summer night
> She comes to me.

And this entitled "Lacrimas":

> God send me tears!
> Loose the fierce band that binds my tired brain,
> Give me the melting heart of other years,
> And let me weep again!
>
> .   .   .   .
>
> We pray in vain!
> The sullen sky flings down its blaze of brass;
> The joys of life are scorched and withery pass:
> I shall not weep again.

Strange company indeed for the Pike County poems. Hay himself was silent about the ballads; he seemed reluctant to talk about them; in later days we know he viewed them with regret.

With Harte the problem is simpler. He wrote from the first all varieties of humorous verse: broad farce like the "Ballad of the Emeu" and the "California Madrigal"; rollicking parodies like "The Tale of a Pony," "The Willows. After Edgar A. Poe," and "The Lost Tails of Miletus"; extravaganzas like "The Stage-Driver's Story" and "To the Pliocene Skull." His Pike verses are in full accord with the greater part of all he wrote both in verse and prose. They are precisely what we should expect from the author of the California Pike tales. That he was in one small part of his work an echo of Hay is exceedingly unlikely. If the *Pike County Ballads* were, as Mark Twain averred, first published in "obscure Western backwoods journals" before "The Heathen Chinee" had appeared, the chances that Harte saw them are so small that it is hardly worth taking the time to consider them, especially when it is further averred that they "were not widely copied." At present the advantage is all with Harte; at present he may be hailed as the father of the Pike balladry and so of the realistic school of poetry in America. The question is not closed, however, nor will it be until the letters and journals of John Hay have been finally given to the world.

III

But even though the *Pike County Ballads* were not the first in the field, even though they were suggested by Harte's work, they were none the less valuable and influential. Hay wrote them from full experience. They rang true at every point as Harte's sometimes did not. Their author had lived from his third until his thirteenth year in full view of the Mississippi River; like Mark Twain he had played about the steamboat wharf, picking up the river slang and hearing the rude stories of the pilots and the deck hands. Warsaw, moreover, was on the trail of the Western immigration, a place where all the border types might be studied. Later, in Pittsfield, the county seat of Pike County, he saw the Pike at home untouched by contact with others—the Golyers, the Frys, the Shelbys, and all the other drinkers of "whisky-skins."

Hay has painted a picture not only of a few highly individualized types; he has drawn as well a background of conditions. He has made permanent one brief phase of middle Western history. It was this element of truth to nature—absolute realism—that gave the poems their vogue and that assured them permanence. Harte's ballads were read as something new and astonishing and theatric; they created a sensation, but they did not grip and convince. Hay's ballads were true to the heart of Western life.

The new literature of the period was influenced more by the *Pike County Ballads* than by the *East and West Poems*. The ballads were something new in literature, something certainly not Bostonian, certainly not English—something that could be described only as "Western," fresh, independent, as the Pike himself was new and independent among the types of humanity. John Hay was therefore a pioneer, a creator, a leader. His was one of those rare germinal minds that appear now and then to break into new regions and to scatter seed from which others are to reap the harvest.

IV

In the same remarkable year in which appeared *East and West Poems* and *Pike County Ballads* and so many other notable first volumes, there began in *Hearth and Home* Edward Eggleston's study of early Indiana life, entitled *The Hoosier Schoolmaster*. Crude as the novel is in its plot and hasty as it is in style and finish, it nevertheless must be numbered as the third leading influence upon the literature of the period.

The extent to which it was influenced by Harte cannot be determined. The brother and biographer of the novelist insists that "the quickening influence that led to the writing of the story" was the reading of Taine's *Art in the Netherlands*. He further records that his brother one day said to him:

"I am going to write a three-number story founded upon your experiences at Ricker's Ridge, and call it *The Hoosier Schoolmaster*." Then he set forth his theory of art—that the artist, whether with pen or brush, who would do his best work, must choose his subjects from the life that he knows. He cited the Dutch painters and justified his choice of what seemed an unliterary theme, involving rude characters and a strange dialect perversion, by reference to Lowell's success with *The Biglow Papers*.[9]

If Eggleston was not influenced by Harte, then it is certain that he drew his early inspiration from the same fountain head as Harte did. Both were the literary offspring of Dickens. One cannot read far in *The Hoosier Schoolmaster* without recognizing the manner and spirit of the elder novelist. It is more prominent in his earlier work—in the short story, *The Christmas Club*, which is almost a parody, in the portraits of Shockey and Hawkins and Miranda Means, and in the occasional moralizing and goody-goodiness of tone.

There are few novelists, however, who contain fewer echoes than Eggleston. He was a more original and more accurate writer than Harte. We can trust his backgrounds and his picture of society implicitly at every point. Harte had saturated himself with the fiction of other men; he had made himself an artist through long study of the masters, and he looked at his material always with the eye of an artist. He selected most carefully his viewpoint, his picturesque details, his lights and

---

[9] George Cary Eggleston's *The First of the Hoosiers*, 297.

shadows, and then made his sketch. Eggleston, on the other hand, had made no study of his art. He had read almost no novels, for, as he expressed it, he was "bred 'after the straitest sect of our religion' a Methodist." All he knew of plot construction he had learned from reading the Greek tragedies.

His weakness was his strength. He silenced his conscience, which rebelled against novels, by resolving to write not fiction but truth. He would make a sketch of life as it actually had been lived in Indiana in his boyhood, a sketch that should be as minute in detail and as remorselessly true as a Millet painting. It was not to be a novel; it was to be history. "No man is worthy," he declared in the preface to *The Circuit Rider,* "to be called a novelist who does not endeavor with his whole soul to produce the higher form of history, by writing truly of men as they are, and dispassionately of those forms of life that come within his scope."

When Eggleston, later in his life, abandoned fiction to become a historian, there was no break in his work. He had always been a historian. Unlike Harte, he had embodied in his novels only those things that had been a part of his own life; he had written with loving recollection; he had recorded nothing that was not true. He had sought, moreover, to make his novels an interpretation of social conditions as he had known them and studied them. "What distinguishes them [his novels]," he once wrote, "from other works of fiction is the prominence which they give to social conditions; that the individual characters are here treated to a greater degree than elsewhere as parts of a study of society—as in some sense the logical result of the environment." [10]

Novels like *The End of the World* and *The Circuit Rider* are in reality chapters in the history of the American people. They are realistic studies, by one to the manner born, of an era in our national life that has vanished forever.

V

Edward Eggleston was born in Vevay, Indiana, December 10, 1837. His father, a member of an old Virginia family, after a brilliant course at William and Mary College, had migrated

[10] *Forum,* 10:286.

westward, settled in Indiana, and just as he was making himself
a notable figure in the law and the politics of his State, had
died when his eldest son, Edward, was but nine years old. The
son had inherited both his father's intellectual brilliancy and his
frail physique. Though eager for knowledge, he was able all
through his boyhood to attend school but little, and, though his
father had provided for a college scholarship, the son never
found himself able to take advantage of it. He was largely self-
educated. He studied whenever he could, and by making use
of all his opportunities he was able before he was twenty to
master by himself nearly all of the branches required for a college degree.

His boyhood was a wandering one. After the death of his
father, the family removed to New Albany and later to Madison.
At the age of thirteen he was sent to southern Indiana to live
with an uncle, a large landowner, and it was here in the lowlands
of Decatur County that he had his first chance to study those
primitive Hoosier types that later he was to make permanent in
literature. Still later he lived for a year and a half with his
father's people in Virginia.

Before he was nineteen he had chosen his profession. The
tense Methodist atmosphere in which he had been reared had
had its effect. He would be a preacher, a circuit rider, one of
those tireless latter-day apostles that had formed so picturesque
a part of his boyhood. ''How did he get his theological education? It used to be said that Methodist preachers were educated
by the old ones telling the young ones all they knew; but besides
this oral instruction [he] carried in his saddle bags John Wesley's simple, solid sermons, Charles Wesley's hymns, and a
Bible.'' [11]

Eggleston's saddle bags contained far more than these. He
read Whitfield and Thomas à Kempis, the *Œdipus Tyrannus* in
the Greek, and all the history and biography that he could buy
or borrow. His ''appointment'' was in southeastern Indiana, a
four-weeks' circuit with ten preaching places far apart in the
Ohio River bottoms with their scattering population of malarial
Pikes and their rude border civilization. He began his work
with enthusiasm. He lived with his people; he entered intimately into their affairs; he studied at first hand their habits of

[11] *The Circuit Rider,* Chap. XX.

life and of thought. It was an ideal preparation for a novelist, but the rough life was in no way fitted for his frail physique. After six months he broke down almost completely and was sent into the pine forests of Minnesota to recuperate. For several years he was connected with the Minnesota conference. He held pastorates in St. Paul and other places, but his health still continuing precarious, he at length retired to Chicago as an editor of the *Little Corporal,* a juvenile paper later merged in *St. Nicholas.* This step turned his attention to literature as a profession. From Chicago he was called to Brooklyn to the staff of the *Independent,* of which he later became the editor, and the rest of his life, save for a five years' pastorate in Brooklyn, he devoted to literature.

VI

The Western novels of Edward Eggleston are seven in number. One of them, *The Mystery of Metropolisville,* deals with frontier life in Minnesota, a stirring picture of a vital era; all the others are laid in Indiana or eastern Ohio in that malarial, river-bottom, Pike area that had been familiar to his boyhood. Two of them are historical novels: *The Circuit Rider,* which deals with Indiana life during the early years of the century before the War of 1812, and *The Graysons,* a stirring tale involving Abraham Lincoln, who had lived in the State from 1816 to 1830. *The End of the World* described the Millerite excitement of Eggleston's early boyhood; the others, *The Hoosier Schoolmaster, Roxy,* and *The Hoosier Schoolboy,* were studies of sections of life that he had known intimately. One other novel he wrote, *The Faith Doctor,* the scene of which is laid in New York, and many short stories and juveniles.

The atmosphere and the characters of these Western stories strike us as strangely unreal and exaggerated to-day. In his short story, *The Gunpowder Plot,* Eggleston complained that "whenever one writes with photographic exactness of frontier life he is accused of inventing improbable things." It seems indeed like a world peopled by Dickens, these strange phantasmagoria, "these sharp contrasts of corn-shuckings and camp-meetings, of wild revels followed by wild revivals; these contrasts of highwayman and preacher; this *mélange* of picturesque simplicity, grotesque humor, and savage ferocity, of abandoned wickedness and austere piety.'' [12] But grotesque and unreal as it is, it is nevertheless a true picture of the West in which Lincoln spent his boyhood. Every detail and every personage in all the novels had an exact counterpart somewhere in that stirring era.

The novelist, however, is not content with a mere graphic picture. He is a philosopher. *The Circuit Rider,* for instance, the most valuable study in the series, brings home to the reader the truth of the author's dictum that ''Methodism was to the West what Puritanism was to New England.'' ''In a true picture of this life,'' he adds, ''neither the Indian nor the hunter is the center-piece, but the circuit rider. More than any one else, the early circuit preachers brought order out of this chaos. In no other class was the real heroic element so finely displayed.''

The figure of the circuit rider as he strides through the book, thundering the ''Old Homeric epithets of early Methodism, exploding them like bomb-shells—'you are hair-hung and breeze-shaken over hell,' '' has almost an epic quality. ''Magruder was a short stout man, with wide shoulders, powerful arms, shaggy brows, and bristling black hair. He read the hymns two lines at a time, and led the singing himself. He prayed with the utmost sincerity, but in a voice that shook the cabin windows and gave the simple people a deeper reverence for the dreadfulness of the preacher's message.''

It was his business to preach once or twice a day and three times on the Sabbath in a parish that had no western bounds. He talked of nothing but of sin and wrath and judgment to come. His arrival in the settlement cast over everything an atmosphere of awe. He aroused violent antagonisms. The rough element banded together to destroy his influence. They threatened him with death if he entered certain territory, but he never hesitated. He could fight as well as he could pray. They would fall broken and bruised before his savage onslaught and later fall in agony of repentance before his fiery preaching. His sermons came winged with power.

He hit right and left. The excitable crowd swayed with consternation, as in a rapid and vehement utterance, he denounced their sins, with the particularity of one who had been familiar with them all his life. . . . Slowly the people pressed forward off the fences. All at once there was a loud bellowing cry from some one who had fallen

12 Preface to *The Circuit Rider.*

prostrate outside the fence, and who began to cry aloud as if the portals of an endless perdition were yawning in his face. . . . This outburst of agony was fuel to the flames, and the excitement now spread to all parts of the audience. . . . Captain Lumsden . . . started for his horse and was seized with that curious nervous affection which originated in these religious excitements and disappeared with them. He jerked violently—his jerking only adding to his excitement.

Eggleston has caught with vividness the spirit of this heroic age and brought it to us so that it actually lives again. The members of the conference at Hickory Ridge have gathered to hear the bishop read the appointments for the year:

The brethren, still in sublime ignorance of their destiny, sang fervently that fiery hymn of Charles Wesley's:

> Jesus, the name high over all,
> In hell or earth or sky,
> Angels and men before him fall,
> And devils fear and fly.

And when they reached the last stanzas there was the ring of soldiers ready for battle in their martial voices. That some of them would die from exposure, malaria, or accident during the next year was probable. Tears came to their eyes, and they involuntarily began to grasp the hands of those who stood next to them as they approached the climax of the hymn. . . .

> Happy if with my latest breath
> I may but gasp His name,
> Preach Him to all, and cry in death,
> " Behold, behold the Lamb! "

Then, with suffused eyes, they resumed their seats, and the venerable Asbury, with calmness and a voice faltering with age, made them a brief address:

"General Wolfe," said the British Admiralty, "will you go and take Quebec?" "I 'll do it or die," he replied. Here the bishop paused, looked round about upon them, and added, with a voice full of emotion, "He went and did both. We send you first to take the country allotted to you. We want only men who are determined to do it or die! Some of you, dear brethren, will do both. If you fall, let us hear that you fell like Methodist preachers at your post, face to the foe, and the shout of victory on your lips!"

The effect of this speech was beyond description. There were sobs, and cries of "Amen," "God grant it," "Hallelujah!" from every part of the old log church. Every man was ready for the hardest place, if he must.

With the circuit rider Eggleston undoubtedly added another type to the gallery of American fiction.

VII

The novels of Eggleston have not the compression, the finish, the finesse of Harte's. Some of his works, notably *The Hoosier Schoolmaster*, were written at full speed with the press clattering behind the author. Often there is to the style a mawkish Sunday-school juvenile flavor. There is often a lack of art, of distinction, of constructive skill. But there are compensations even for such grave defects. There is a vividness of characterization and of description that can be compared even with that of Dickens; there is the ability to sketch a scene that clings to the memory in all its details. The trial scene in *The Graysons* is not surpassed for vividness and narrative power in any novel of the period. And, finally, there is a realism in background and atmosphere that makes the novels real sources of history.

The influence of Eggleston's work was enormous. He helped to create a new reading public, a public made up of those who, like himself, had had scruples against novel reading. He was an influence in the creating of a new and healthy realism in America. What Hay was to the new school of local color poets, Eggleston was to the new school of novelists. Harte was a romanticist; Eggleston was a realist. From Harte came the first conception of a new and powerful literature of the West. Eggleston was the directing hand that turned the current of this new literature into the channel of realism.

BIBLIOGRAPHY

JOHN HAY. (1838–1905.) *The Pike County Ballads and Other Pieces,* (167 pages), 1871; *Jim Bludso of the Prairie Belle, and Little Breeches,* illustrated by Eytinge (23 pages), 1871; *Castilian Days,* 1871; *The Bread-winners,* 1883; *Poems by John Hay,* 1890 and 1899; *A Poet in Exile: Early letters of John Hay.* Edited by Caroline Ticknor, 1910.

EDWARD EGGLESTON. (1837–1902.) *Mr. Blake's Walking-Stick,* 1870; *The Hoosier Schoolmaster,* 1871; *The End of the World,* 1872; *The Mystery of Metropolisville,* 1873; *The Circuit Rider,* 1874; *The Schoolmaster's Stories,* 1874; *Roxy,* 1878; *The Hoosier Schoolboy,* 1883; *Queer Stories,* 1884; *The Graysons,* 1888; *The Faith Doctor,* 1891; *Duffels* (short stories), 1893; *The First of the Hoosiers,* by George Cary Eggleston, 1903.

CHAPTER VI

The work of Harte and even of Hay is the work of an on-looker rather than a sharer. One feels that both were studying their picturesque surroundings objectively for the sake of "copy"; but Joaquin Miller, like Mark Twain, may be said to have emerged from the materials he worked in. He could write in his later years, "My poems are literally my autobiography." "If you care to read further of my life, making allowance for poetic license, you will find these [poems] literally true." In some ways he is a more significant figure than either Harte or Hay. No American writer, not even Thoreau or Whitman, has ever been more uniquely individual, and none, not even Mark Twain, has woven into his writings more things that are peculiarly American, or has worked with a more thorough first-hand knowledge of the picturesque elements that went into the making of the new West. He is the poet of the American west-ward march, the poet of "the great American desert," the poet preëminently of the mountain ranges from Alaska to Nicaragua as John Muir is their prose interpreter.

I

The life of Miller is a series of foot-notes to his poems. He was born on the line of the westward march. In the valuable autobiographical preface to the Bear edition of his poems he writes: "My cradle was a covered wagon, pointed west. I was born in a covered wagon, I am told, at or about the time it crossed the line dividing Indiana from Ohio." That was in 1841, and the name given him was Cincinnatus Hiner Miller. His parents, like those of Mark Twain, were of that restless generation that could abide nowhere long, but must press ever on and on west-ward. His mother's people had migrated from the Yadkin River country in North Carolina with the Boones, "devoted Quakers in

search of a newer land''; his grandfather Miller was a Scotch-
man, a restless pioneer who had fallen at Fort Meigs, leaving a
family of small children to come up as they could in the wilderness. One of them, the father of the poet, picked up in a varied
career along the border certain elements of book learning that
enabled him to teach school in the settlement towns of Ohio and
Indiana.

The boy's earliest memories were of the frontier with its land
clearing, its Indian neighbors, and its primitive hardships.
Schooling he received at the hands of his father. The first book
that he could remember was Frémont's *Explorations*, read aloud
to the family by the father until all knew it literally by heart,
maps and all. Lured by its enthusiastic descriptions and by reports of a former pupil who had gone to Oregon and by the new
act of Congress which gave to every homesteader six hundred and
forty acres of land free, on March 17, 1852, with ''two big heavily
laden wagons, with eight yoke of oxen to each, a carriage and two
horses for mother and baby sister, and a single horse for the three
boys to ride,'' the family set out across the wild continent of
America. ''The distance,'' he records, ''counting the contours
of often roundabout ways, was quite, or nearly, three thousand
miles. The time was seven months and five days. There were
no bridges, no railroad levels, nothing of the sort. We had only
the road as nature had made it. Many times, at night, after
ascending a stream to find a ford, we could look back and see
our smoldering camp-fires of the day before.''

That heroic journey into the unknown West with its awful
dangers, its romantic strangeness, its patriarchal conditions, its
constant demand for self-dependence, made an indelible impress
on the young lad. It was a journey of Argonauts, one of the
thousands of journeys that made picturesque a whole epoch. He
has described it in some of the most stirring of his poems. All
through his poetry occur stanzas like this:

> What strength! what strife! what rude unrest!
> What shocks! what half-shaped armies met!
> A mighty nation moving West,
> With all its steely sinews set
> Against the living forests. Hear
> The shouts, the shots of pioneer,
> The rending forests, rolling wheels,
> As if some half-checked army reels,

Recoils, redoubles, comes again,
Loud-sounding like a hurricane.

He has described it too in prose that is really stirring. His dedicatory preface to *The Ship in the Desert*, London, 1876, is a poem of the Whitman order. Note a stanza like this:

How dark and deep, how sullen, strong and lionlike the mighty Missouri rolled between his walls of untracked wood and cleft the unknown domain of the middle world before us! Then the frail and buffeted rafts on the river, the women and children huddled together, the shouts of the brawny men as they swam with the bellowing cattle, the cows in the stormy stream eddying, whirling, spinning about, calling to their young, their bright horns shining in the sun. The wild men waiting on the other side; painted savages, leaning on their bows, despising our weakness, opening a way, letting us pass on to the unknown distances, where they said the sun and moon lay down together and brought forth the stars. The long and winding lines of wagons, the graves by the wayside, the women weeping together as they passed on. Then hills, then plains, parched lands like Syria, dust and alkali, cold streams with woods, camps by night, great wood fires in circles, tents in the center like Cæsar's battle camps, painted men that passed like shadows, showers of arrows, the wild beasts howling from the hills.

Two years with his parents on the new Oregon farm, and the lad ran away to the mines. "Go, I must. The wheels of the covered wagon in which I had been born were whirling and whirling, and I must be off." For a time he was cook in a mining camp, but it was work impossible for a boy of thirteen, and soon he was on his wanderings again, first with one Ream, an adventurer, then with Mountain Joe, a trader in half-wild horses. He was drawn into Gibson's fight with the Modocs, was wounded frightfully by an arrow that pierced close to the base of the brain, and later was nursed back to life by a squaw who had adopted him in place of her son who had fallen in the battle. "When the spring came and Mount Shasta stood out white and glorious above the clouds, I hailed him as a brother." And again he stole away and joined another band of Indians. "When the Modocs arose one night and massacred eighteen men, every man in the Pit River Valley, I alone was spared and spared only because I was *Los bobo*, the fool. Then more battles and two more wounds." For a long time his mind was like that of a child. The Indians indeed, as he records, treated him "as if [he] had been newly born to their tribe.".

Soon I was stronger, body and soul. The women gave me gold—
from whence?—and I being a "renegade," descended to San Francisco
and set sail for Boston, but stopped at Nicaragua with Walker. Thence
up the coast to Oregon, when strong enough. I went home, went to
college some, taught school some, studied law at home some; but ever
and ever the lure of the mountains called and called, and I could not
keep my mind on my books. But I could keep my mind on the perils
I had passed. I could write of them, and I did write of them, almost
every day. *The Tale of the Tall Alcalde, Oregonian, Californian, With
Walker in Nicaragua*—I had lived all these and more; and they were
now a part of my existence. . . . Meantime I was admitted to the bar.
Then came the discovery of gold in Idaho, Montana, and so on, and
I was off like a rocket with the rest.

To call Miller illiterate, as many, especially in printing offices
which have handled his copy, have done, is hardly fair. His
father, it must be remembered, was a schoolmaster with the
Scotch reverence for serious books and for education, and the
boy's early schooling was not neglected. To say, on the other
hand, as many, including the poet himself, have said, that he
received a college education, is also to speak without knowledge.
He did complete a course in Columbia University, Eugene,
Oregon, in 1859, but it was an institution in no way connected
with the present University of Oregon. It was, rather, a mission
school maintained by the Methodist Church South, and, according
to Professor Herbert C. Howe of the University of Oregon, "its
instruction was, at its utmost stretch, not enough to carry its
pupils through the first half of a high school course, and most
of its pupils were of grammar grade." It was closed suddenly
early in the Civil-War period because of the active Southern
sympathies of its president, who was himself very nearly the
whole "university." It is significant that at almost the same
time the Eugene *Democratic Register* edited by Miller was suppressed for alleged disloyalty to the Union.

For a period the poet undoubtedly did apply himself with
diligence to books. Of his fellow students at Eugene he has recorded, "I have never since found such determined students
and omnivorous readers. We had all the books and none of the
follies of the great centers." The mania for writing had seized
him early. Assisted by his father, he had recorded the events
of his trip across the plains in a journal afterwards burned with
his parental home in Oregon. "The first thing of mine in print
was the valedictory class poem, 'Columbia College.'" Undoubt-

edly during this period he read widely and eagerly. "My two brothers and my sister were by my side, our home with our parents, and we lived entirely to ourselves, and really often made ourselves ill from too much study. We were all school teachers when not at college."

Living away from the centers of culture, with books as exotic things that came from without, almost as from another world, Miller, like many another isolated soul, grew to maturity with the feeling that something holy lay about the creation of literature and that authors, especially poets, were beings apart from the rest of men. Poetry became to him more than an art: it became a religion. "Poetry," he declared in his first London preface, "is with me a passion which defies reason." It was an honest declaration. During the sixties as express messenger in the Idaho gold fields, as newspaper editor, and judge, he wrote verse continually—"I lived among the stars"—but he preserved of all he wrote only a few rather colorless pieces which he published in 1868 with the title *Specimens*. The next year he issued at Portland, Oregon, *Joaquin et al,* a book of one hundred and twenty-four pages. It was his salute to the literary world. He addressed it "To the Bards of San Francisco Bay," and his address sheds light upon the timid young poet:

> I am as one unlearned, uncouth,
> From country come to join the youth
> Of some sweet town in quest of truth,
>   A skilless Northern Nazarine,
> From whence no good can ever come.
> I stand apart as one that's dumb:
> I hope, I fear, I hasten home,
>   I plunge into my wilds again.

He followed his book down to what was to him the glorious city of art and of soul that would welcome him with rapture, for was he too not a bard? Says Charles W. Stoddard, "Never had a breezier bit of human nature dawned upon me this side of the South Seas than that poet of the Sierra when he came to San Francisco in 1870." [1]

But the great Western city, as did New York a few months later, went on totally unaware of his advent. The bards even of San Francisco Bay did not come to the borders of the town to

[1] *Exits and Entrances,* 223.

welcome the new genius. They seemed unaware of his presence. Harte was inclined to be sarcastic, but finally allowed the *Overland Monthly* to say a word of faint praise for the young poet, despite what it termed his "pawing and curvetting." "His passion," it declared in a review written probably by Ina Coolbrith, "is truthful and his figures flow rather from his perception than his sentiment." But that was all. He considered himself persecuted. His associates in the law had made fun of the legal term in the title of his book, had hailed him as "Joaquin" Miller, and had treated him as a joke. "I was so unpopular that when I asked a place on the Supreme Bench at the Convention, I was derisively told: 'Better stick to poetry.' Three months later, September 1, 1870, I was kneeling at the grave of Burns. I really expected to die there in the land of my fathers." He would support himself as Irving had supported himself with his pen. He sought cheap quarters in the great city and began to write. February 1, 1871, he recorded in his diary: "I have nearly given up this journal to get out a book. I wanted to publish a great drama called 'Oregonian,' but finally wrote an easy-going little thing which I called 'Arazonian,' and put the two together and called the little book *Pacific Poems*. It has been ready for the printer a long time."

He took the manuscript from publisher to publisher until, as he declares, every house in London had rejected it. His reception by Murray shows the general estimate of poetry by London publishers in the early seventies:

He held his head to one side, flipped the leaves, looked in, jerked his head back, looked in again, twisted his head like a giraffe, and then lifted his long finger:

"Aye, now, don't you know poetry won't do? Poetry won't do, don't you know?"

"But will you not read it, please?"

"No, no, no. No use, no use, don't you know?"

Then in desperation he printed a part of it at his own expense under the title *Pacific Poems* and sent out copies broadcast to the press. Never was venture so unpromising crowned with results so startling. The little book was hailed everywhere as something remarkable. The *St. James Gazette* declared that the poem "Arazonian"—that was Miller's early spelling of the word—was by Browning. The new author was traced to his miserable lodgings and made a lion of, and before the year was over the whole original manuscript of *Pacific Poems* had been brought out in a beautiful edition with the title *Songs of the Sierras.* Its author's real name did not appear upon the title page. The poems were by "Joaquin Miller," a name destined completely to supersede the more legal patronymic. "The third poem in my first London book," he explains, "was called 'California,' but it was called 'Joaquin' in the Oregon book. And it was from this that I was, in derision, called 'Joaquin.' I kept the name and the poem, too, till both were at least respected." [2]

Few American books have been received by the English press, or any press for that matter, with such unanimous enthusiasm. Miller was the literary discovery of the year. The *London Times* declared the book the "most remarkable utterance America has yet given"; the *Evening Standard* called it poetry "the most original and powerful." The pre-Raphaelite brotherhood counted its author as one of their own number, and gave him a dinner. Browning hailed him as an equal, and the press everywhere celebrated him as "the Oregon Byron." The reason for it all can be explained best, perhaps, in words that W. M. Rossetti used in his long review of the poet in the *London Academy:* "Picturesque things picturesquely put . . . indicating strange, outlandish, and romantic experiences." The same words might have been used by a reviewer of Byron's first Eastern romance on that earlier morning when he too had awakened to find himself famous. The book, moreover, was felt to be the promise of stronger things to come. "It is a book," continued Rossetti, "through whose veins the blood pulsates with an abounding rush, while gorgeous subtropical suns, resplendent moons, and abashing majesties of mountain form ring round the gladiatorial human life."

II

Of Miller's subsequent career, his picturesque travels, his log cabin life in Washington, D. C., his Klondike experiences and the like, it is not necessary to speak. There was always an element of the sensational about his doings and his equipment. To the majority of men he was a *poseur* and even a mountebank.

2 *Songs of the Sierras*, Bear edition, 133.

At times indeed it was hard for even his friends to take him with seriousness. How was one, for instance, to approach in serious mood *As It Was in the Beginning,* 1903, a book twelve inches by five, printed on coarse manila wrapping stock, bound in thin yellow paper, and having on the cover an enormous stork holding in his bill President Roosevelt as an infant? Those who were closest to him, however, are unanimous in declaring that all this eccentricity was but the man himself, the expression of his own peculiar individuality, and that he was great enough to rise above the conventionalities of life and be himself. C. W. Stoddard, who of all men, perhaps, knew him most intimately in his earlier period, maintained that

People who knew him wondered but little at his pose, his Spanish mantle and sombrero, his fits of abstraction or absorption, his old-school courtly air in the presence of women—even the humblest of the sex. He was thought eccentric to the last degree, a bundle of affectations, a crank—even a freak. Now I who have known Joaquin Miller as intimately as any man could know him, know that these mannerisms are natural to him; they have developed naturally; they are his second nature.[3]

Hamlin Garland, Charles F. Lummis, and many others who have known the poet intimately have spoken in the same way. His mannerisms and his eccentric point of view arose from the isolation in which his formative years were passed, his ignorance of life, his long association with highly individualized men in the mines and the camps and the mountains, and his intimate knowledge of the picturesque Spanish life of Mexico and Central America. His education had been peculiar, even unique. "All that I am," he declares in *My Own Story,*[4] "or ever hope to be I owe them [the Indians]. I owe no white man anything at all." He had never been a boy, he was utterly without sense of humor, and he had a native temperament aside from all this, that was all his own—need we say more?

[3] *Exits and Entrances,* 231.
[4] "My *Life Among the Modocs, Unwritten History, Paquita, My Life Among the Indians, My Own Story,* or whatever other name enterprising or piratical publishers, Europe or America, may have chosen to give the one prose book Mulford and I put out in London during the Modoc War."—Bear edition, iv: 169.

III

When one approaches the poetry of Joaquin Miller, one is at first confused by the lavishness of it, the strength, and then swiftly the dreary weakness of it. It is like his own landscapes, abounding in vast barrens and flats, with here and there glimpses of glittering peaks and vast ranges, and now and then oases full of marvelous revel of color and strange birds and tropic flowers. Three-fourths of all he wrote is lifeless and worthless, but the other quarter is to American poetry what the Rockies are to the American landscape. Few poets have so needed an editor with courage to reject and judgment to arrange. Miller himself has edited his poems with barbarous savageness. He has not hesitated to lop off entire cantos, to butcher out the whole trunk of a poem, leaving only straggling and unrelated branches, to add to work in his early manner stanzas after his later ideals, and to revamp and destroy and cast utterly away after a fashion that has few precedents. He has done the work with a broad-ax when a lancet was needed. His editings are valuable, indeed, only in the new prose matter that he has added as foot-note and introduction.

The key to Miller's poetry is an aphorism from his own pen: "We must, in some sort, live what we write if what we write is to live." The parts of his work that undoubtedly will live are those poems that deal most closely with the material from which he sprang and of which his early life was molded. He is the poet of the frontier and of the great mid-century exodus across the Plains. Poems like "The Heroes of Oregon," and "Exodus for Oregon," are a part of the national history. They thrill at every point with reality and life.

> The Plains! the shouting drivers at the wheel;
> The crash of leather whips; the crush and roll
> Of wheels; the groan of yokes and grinding steel
> And iron chain, and lo! at last the whole
> Vast line, that reach'd as if to touch the goal,
> Began to stretch and stream away and wind
> Toward the west, as if with one control;
> Then hope loom'd fair, and home lay far behind;
> Before, the boundless plain, and fiercest of their kind.

And again

> Then dust arose, a long dim line like smoke
> From out of riven earth. The wheels went groaning by,
> Ten thousand feet in harness and in yoke,
> They tore the ways of ashen alkali,
> And desert winds blew sudden, swift and dry.
> The dust! it sat upon and fill'd the train!
> It seemed to fret and fill the very sky.
> Lo! dust upon the beasts, the tent, the plain,
> And dust, alas! on breasts that rose not up again.

Pictures of the Plains, the Indian camp, the mine, the mountain, the herd, the trail, are to be found scattered everywhere in his work. One finds them in the most unlikely places—diamonds embedded often in whole acres of clay. In so unpromising a book as *As It Was in the Beginning* with its grotesque introduction explaining in characteristic mixed metaphor that ''When, like a sentinel on his watch tower, the President, with his divine audacity and San Juan valor, voiced the real heart of the Americans against 'race suicide,' I hastened to do my part, in my own way, ill or well, in holding up his hands on the firing line'' —even in this book one finds sudden flashes of truest poetry. He is describing winter on the Yukon. About him are an eager band of gold-seekers ready to press north:

> The siege of Troy knew scarce such men;
> The cowards had not voyaged then,
> The weak had died upon the way.

He describes with realism the horrors and the beauties of the Arctic night, then at last the rising of the sun after the long darkness:

> Then glad earth shook her raiment wide,
> As some proud woman satisfied,
> Tiptoed exultant, till her form,
> A queen above some battle storm,
> Blazed with the glory, the delight
> Of battle with the hosts of night.
> And night was broken, light at last
> Lay on the Yukon. Night had past.

In passages like these the imagination of the poet breaks out for a moment like the moon from dark clouds, but all too often it is *only* for a moment.

He is the poet preëminently of the mountains of the Northwest. The spell of them was on him as it was on John Muir. At times in their presence he bursts into the very ecstasy of

poetry; sonorous rhapsodies and invocations in which he reaches
his greatest heights:

> Sierras, and eternal tents
> Of snow that flash o'er battlements
> Of mountains! My land of the sun,
> Am I not true? have I not done
> All things for thine, for thee alone,
> O sun-land, sea-land thou mine own?

There is a sweep and vastness about him at his best that one
finds in no other American poet. No cameo cutting for him, no
little panels, no parlor decorations and friezes. His canvas is
all out of doors and as broad as the continent itself:

> Oh, heart of the world's heart! West! my West!
> Look up! look out! There are fields of kine,
> There are clover-fields that are red as wine;
> And a world of kine in the fields take rest,
> And ruminate in the shade of the trees
> That are white with blossoms or brown with bees.
> There are emerald seas of corn and cane;
> There are cotton fields like a foamy main,
> To the far-off South where the sun was born.

The wild freedom of the Western air beats and surges in his
lines:

> Room! room to turn round in, to breathe and be free,
> To grow to be giant, to sail as at sea
> With the speed of the wind on a steed with his mane
> To the wind, without pathway or route or a rein.
> Room! room to be free where the white border'd sea
> Blows a kiss to a brother as boundless as he;
> Where the buffalo come like a cloud on the plain,
> Pouring on like the tide of a storm-driven main,
> And the lodge of the hunter to friend or to foe
> Offers rest; and unquestion'd you come or you go.
> My plains of America! Seas of wild lands!
> From a land in the seas in a raiment of foam,
> That has reached to a stranger the welcome of home,
> I turn to you, lean to you, lift you my hands.

Or again this magnificent apostrophe to the Missouri River:

> Hoar sire of hot, sweet Cuban seas,
>   Gray father of the continent,
> Fierce fashioner of destinies,
>   Of states thou hast upreared or rent,

> Thou know'st no limit; seas turn back
>   Bent, broken from the shaggy shore;
> But thou, in thy resistless track,
>   Art lord and master evermore.
> Missouri, surge and sing and sweep!
> Missouri, master of the deep,
> From snow-reared Rockies to the sea
> Sweep on, sweep on eternally!

And grandest of all, the poem that has all America in it and the American soul, perhaps the grandest single poem of the period, "Columbus":

> Behind him lay the gray Azores,
>   Behind the Gates of Hercules;
> Before him not the ghost of shores;
>   Before him only shoreless seas.
> The good mate said: "Now must we pray,
>   For lo! the very stars are gone,
> Brave Adm'r'l speak; what shall I say?"
>   "Why, say: 'Sail on! sail on! and on!'"

In his enthusiasm for the mountains and the American landscape Miller was thoroughly sincere. Despite all his posturing and his fantastic costumes he was a truly great soul, and he spoke from his heart when he said in 1909: "But pity, pity, that men should so foolishly waste time with either me or mine when I have led them to the mighty heart of majestic Shasta. Why yonder, lone as God and white as the great white throne, there looms against the sapphire upper seas a mountain peak that props the very porch of heaven; and yet they bother with and want to torment a poor mote of dust that sinks in the grasses at their feet."[5]

IV

This leads us to the second phase of Miller's personality: he was a philosopher, a ponderer upon the deeper things of the spirit. He had inherited with his Scotch blood a religious strain, and a large section of his poetry deals with regions far indeed from his Sierras. He has written much upon the common fundamentals of humanity: religion, love, honor, courage, truth, and the like. In his "Vale! America," written in Italy during his second European sojourn, he could say,

[5] Bear edition, ii: 91.

I have lived from within and not from without,

And again

Could I but return to my woods once more,
And dwell in their depths as I have dwelt,
Kneel in their mosses as I have knelt,
Sit where the cool white rivers run,
Away from the world and half hid from the sun,
Hear winds in the wood of my storm-torn shore,
To tread where only the red man trod,
To say no word, but listen to God!
Glad to the heart with listening—
It seems to me that I then could sing,
And sing as never sung man before.

There was within him indeed something of the recluse and the hermit. No one of the period, not even Muir or Burroughs, approached Nature with more of worship. He would live with her and make her central in every point of his life. In his later years he built him a cabin on the heights above San Francisco Bay with a tremendous outlook of sea and mountain and sky, and lived there the rest of his life.

I know a grassy slope above the sea,
The utmost limit of the westmost land.
In savage, gnarl'd, and antique majesty
The great trees belt about the place, and stand
In guard, with mailed limb and lifted hand,
Against the cold approaching civic pride.
The foamy brooklets seaward leap; the bland
Still air is fresh with touch of wood and tide,
And peace, eternal peace, possesses, wild and wide.

He became more and more solitary, more and more of a mystic as the years went on. Even from the first, as Rossetti pointed out, there is an almost oriental pantheism in him. It came perhaps from his Indian training. "Some curious specimens," Rossetti observed, "might be culled of the fervid interfusion of external nature and the human soul in his descriptive passages. The great factors of the natural world—the sea, the mountains, the sun, moon, and stars—become personalities, animated with an intense life and dominant possession."

But Miller was by no means a satyr, as many have pictured him, delighting in wildness for the mere sake of wildness. He overflowed with humanity. No man was ever more sensitive or

more genuinely sympathetic. In his later years he sat above
the tumult a prophet and seer, and commented and advised
and warned. Great areas of his poetry have nothing to do with
the West, nothing at all with the manner and the material that
are so naturally associated with his name. For decades his voice
was heard wherever there was oppression or national wrong.
He wrote sonorous lyrics for the Indians, the Boers, the Russian
Jews; he wrote the ringing ''Cuba Libre'' which was read by
the Baroness de Bazus in the leading American cities before the
Spanish war; he championed the cause of woman; and everywhere he took the side of the weaker against the strong. In this
he resembles Mark Twain, that other prophet of the era. The
freedom of the new West was in both of them, the true American
''hatred of tyranny intense.'' He was won always by gentleness
and beauty: he wrote a *Life of Christ*, he wrote *The City Beautiful*, and *Songs of the Soul*.

But almost all that he wrote in this pet field of his endeavor
perished with its day. Of it all there is no single poem that
may be called distinctive. He moralizes, he preaches, he champions the weak, but he says nothing new, nothing compelling.
He is not a singer of the soul: he is the maker of resounding
addresses to the peaks and the plains and the sea; the poet of
the westward march of a people; the poet of elemental men in
elemental surroundings—pioneers amid the vastness of the uttermost West.

V

It is easy to find defects in Miller's work. Even the sophomore
can point out his indebtedness to Byron and to Swinburne—

The wine-dark wave with its foam of wool—

his Byronic heroes and overdrawn heroines; his diction excessive
in alliteration and adjectives; his barbarous profusion of color;
his overworking of the word ''tawney''; his inability to tell a
story; his wordiness and ramblings; his lack of distinctness and
dramatic power. One sweeps away the whole of this, however,
when one admits that three quarters of all that Miller wrote
should be thrown away before criticism begins.

The very faults of the poet serve as arguments that he *was* a poet—a poet born, not a poet made from study of other poets. He was not classic: he was romantic—a poet who surrendered himself to the music within him and did not care. "To me," he declared in his defense of poesy, "the savage of the plains or the negro of the South is a truer poet than the scholar of Oxford. They may have been alike born with a love of the beautiful, but the scholar, shut up within the gloomy walls, with his eyes to a dusty book, has forgotten the face of Nature and learned only the art of utterance." [6] This is one of the keys to the new era that opened in the seventies. It explains the new laughter of the West, it explains the Pike balladry, it explains the new burst of democratic fiction, the studies of lowly life in obscure environments. "To these poets," he continues; "these lovers of the beautiful; these silent thinkers; these mighty mountaineers, far away from the rush and roar of commerce; these men who have room and strength and the divine audacity to think and act for themselves—to these men who dare to have heart and enthusiasm, who love the beautiful world that the Creator made for them, I look for the leaven of our loaf."

Miller comes nearer to Mark Twain than to any other writer, unless it be John Muir. True, he is wholly without humor, true he had never been a boy, and in his mother's words had "never played, never had playthings, never wanted them"; yet notwithstanding this the two men are to be classed together. Both are the recorders of a vanished era of which they were a part; both emerged from the material which they used; both wrote notable prose—Miller's *Life Among the Modocs* and his other autobiographic picturings rank with *Life on the Mississippi;* both worked with certainty in one of the great romantic areas of human history. There is in the poems of Miller, despite all their crudity, a sense of adventure, of glorious richness, of activity in the open air, that is all his own. His Byronism and his Swinburneism were but externals, details of manner: the song and the atmosphere about it were his own, spun out of his own observation and colored by his own unique personality.

His own definition of poetry determines his place among the poets and explains his message: "To me a poem must be a picture," and it must, he further declared, be drawn always from Nature by one who has seen and who knows. "The art of poetry

6 *The Independent*, June, 1879.

is found in books; the inspiration of poetry is found only in Nature. This book, the book of Nature, I studied in the wilderness like a monk for many years." The test of poetry, he maintained, is the persistence with which it clings in the memory, not the words but the picture. Judged by this standard, *Songs of the Sierras,* which is a succession of gorgeous pictures that cling in the imagination, must rank high.

It was his ideal to draw his generation away from their pursuit of gold and their slavery in the artificial round of the cities, their worship of European culture, European architecture, European books, and show them the beauties of their own land, the glories of the life out of doors, the heroism and sacrifice of the pioneers who made possible the later period.

"Grateful that I was born in an age of active and mighty enterprise, and exulting, even as a lad, in the primitive glory of nature, wild woods, wild birds, wild beasts, I began, as my parents pushed west through the wilderness, to make beauty and grandeur the god of my idolatry, even before I yet knew the use of words. To give expression to this love and adoration, to lead others to see grandeur, good, glory in all things animate or inanimate, rational or irrational, was my early and has ever been my one aspiration."

He would be the prophet of a new era. To the bards who are to come he flings out the challenge: "The Old World has been written, written fully and bravely and well. . . . Go forth in the sun, away into the wilds, or contentedly lay aside your aspirations of song. Now, mark you distinctly, I am not writing for nor of the poets of the Old World or the Atlantic seaboard. They have their work and their way of work. My notes are for the songless Alaskas, Canadas, Californias, the Aztec lands and the Argentines that patiently await their coming prophets." [7]

VI

The treatment of Miller by his own countrymen has never been so laudatory as that accorded him by other lands, notably England, but his complaint that his own people neglected him is groundless. All the leading magazines—the *Atlantic, Scribner's,* the *Independent,* and the rest—opened their columns to

[7] Bear Edition, iii: 33.

him freely. That reviews of his work and critical estimates of him generally were more caustic on this side the Atlantic came undoubtedly from the fact that the critic who was to review him approached his book always in a spirit of irritation at the British insistence that an American book to be worth the reading must be redolent of the wild and the uncouth, must deal with Indians, and buffaloes, and the various extremes of democracy. Miller has been the chief victim of this controversy—a controversy, indeed, which was waged through the whole period. The eccentricities of the man and his ignorance and his picturesque crudeness, set over against the extravagant claims of British writers, aroused prejudices that blinded the American critic to the poet's real worth.

On the whole the English have been right. Not that American literature to be of value must be shaggy and ignorant, a thing only of Pikes and slang and dialect. It means rather that the new period which opened in the seventies demanded genuineness, reality, things as they are, studies from life rather than studies from books; that it demanded not the reëchoing of outworn ideals and measures from other lands, but the spirit of America, of the new Western world, of the new soul of the new republic. And what poet has caught more of this fresh new America than the singer of the Sierras, the singer of the great American deserts, and the northern Yukon?

BIBLIOGRAPHY

JOAQUIN MILLER. (1841–1913.) *Specimens*, 1868; *Joaquin et al*, 1869; *Pacific Poems*, 1870; *Songs of the Sierras*, 1871; *Songs of the Sunlands*, 1873; *Unwritten History: Life Amongst the Modocs* (with Percival Mulford), 1874; *The Ship in the Desert*, 1875; *First Families of the Sierras*, 1875; *Songs of the Desert*, 1875; *The One Fair Woman*, 1876; *The Baroness of New York*, 1877; *Songs of Italy*, 1878; *The Danites in the Sierras*, 1881; *Shadows of Shasta*, 1881; *Poems, Complete Edition*, 1882; *Forty-nine: a California Drama*, 1882; *'49: or, the Gold-seekers of the Sierras*, 1884; *Memorie and Rime*, 1884; *The Destruction of Gotham*, 1886; *Songs of the Mexican Seas*, 1887; *In Classic Shades and Other Poems*, 1890; *The Building of the City Beautiful, a Poetic Romance*, 1893; *Songs of the Soul*, 1896; *Chants for the Boer*, 1900; *True Bear Stories*, 1900; *As It Was in the Beginning*, 1903; *Light: a Narrative Poem*, 1907; *Joaquin Miller's Poetry*, Bear Edition, 1909.

CHAPTER VII

THE TRANSITION POETS

The second generation of poets in America, those later singers born during the vital thirties in which had appeared the earliest books of the older school, began its work during the decade before the Civil War. It was not a group that had been launched, as were the earlier poets of the century, by a spiritual and moral cataclysm, or by a new strong tide in the national life. It was a school of deliberate art, the inevitable classical school which follows ever upon the heels of the creative epoch.

It came as a natural product of mid-century conditions. America, hungry for culture, had fed upon the romantic pabulum furnished so abundantly in the thirties and the forties. It looked away from the garish daylight of the new land of its birth into the delicious twilight of the lands across the sea, with their ruins and their legends and their old romance.

We have seen how it was an age of sugared epithet, of adolescent sadness and longing, of sentiment even to sentimentality. Its dreams were centered in the East, in that old world over which there hung the glamour of romance. "I hungrily read," writes Bayard Taylor of this epoch in his life, "all European books of travel, and my imagination clothed foreign countries with a splendid atmosphere of poetry and art. . . . Italy! and Greece! the wild enthusiasm with which I should tread those lands, and view the shrines 'where young Romance and Love like sister pilgrims turn'; the glorious emotions of my soul, and the inspiration I should draw from them, which I now partly feel. How my heart leaps at the sound of:

> Woods that wave on Delphi's steep,
> Isles that gem the Ægean deep.

The isles of Greece! hallowed by Homer and Milton and Byron! My words are cold and tame compared with my burning thoughts." [1]

[1] *Life and Letters of Bayard Taylor,* i: 35.

The increasing tide of translations that marked the thirties and the forties, the new editions of English and continental poets—Shelley, Keats, Heine; the early books of the Victorians—Elizabeth Barrett Browning, the young Tennyson—came across the sea to these sensitive souls like visitants from another planet. "I had the misfortune," Taylor writes in 1848, "to be intoxicated yesterday—with Tennyson's new poem, 'The Princess.' . . . For the future, for a long time at least, I dare not read Tennyson. His poetry would be the death of mine. His intense perception of beauty haunts me for days, and I cannot drive it from me." [2]

Poetry was a thing to be spoken of with awed lips like love or the deeper longings of the soul. It was an ethereal thing apart from the prose of life; it was beauty, melody, divinest art —a thing broken into harshly by the daily round, a thing to be stolen away to in golden hours, as Stoddard and Taylor stole away on Saturday nights to read their poets and their own poems, and to lose themselves in a more glorious world. "My favorite poet was Keats, and his was Shelley, and we pretended to believe that the souls of these poets had returned to earth in our bodies. My worship of my master was restricted to a silent imitation of his diction; my comrade's worship of his master took the form of an ode to Shelley. . . . It is followed in the volume before me by an airy lyric on 'Sicilian Wine,' which was written out of his head, as the children say, for he had no Sicilian wine, nor, indeed, wine of any other vintage." [3]

It explains the weakness of the whole school. All too often did these young poets of the second generation write from out their heads rather than their hearts. They were practitioners of the poetic art rather than eager workers in the stuff that is human life. They were inspired not by their times and the actual life that touched elbows with theirs in their toil from day to day; they were inspired by other singers. Poetry they wove from poetry; words from words. Song begotten from other song perishes with its singer. To endure, poetry must come from "that inexpressible aching feeling of the heart"—from the impact of life upon life; it must thrill with the deepest emotions of its creator's soul as he looks beyond his books and all the

[2] *Life and Letters of Bayard Taylor*, 1:119.
[3] R. H. Stoddard in *The Atlantic Monthly*, February, 1879.

printed words of others into the yearning, struggling world of men.

I

The members of this second generation of poets fall into two distinct groups: first, those who caught not at all the new note that came into American life and American literature after the war, and so, like the survivors of the earlier school, went on to the end only echoing and reëchoing the earlier music; and, secondly, those transitional poets who yielded to the change of times and retuned their instruments to the new key. Of the first group four only may be mentioned: Thomas Buchanan Read (1822–1872), George Henry Boker (1823–1890), Bayard Taylor (1825–1878), and Richard Henry Stoddard (1825–1903). None of these may be called a poet of the transition; none of these, not even Taylor, caught the new spirit of recreated America; none of them added to poetry any notes that have influenced the song or the life or the spirit of later years. They were poets of beauty without a message, and they caught no new vision of beauty.

The work of the group began early, only a few years later than that of the major singers. Taylor's *Ximena* appeared in 1844; Boker's *Lesson of Life* and Read's *Poems* in 1847; and Stoddard's *Footprints* in 1849. By 1870 they had settled into their final manner. It was theirs to strike the last notes, ineffective and all too often decadent, of that mid-century music that had begun with Bryant and Poe, with Emerson and Whittier, with Willis and Longfellow.

II

We may pause a moment with Taylor. His personality in the early seventies undoubtedly was more potent in America than that of any other poet. His was the leading poetic voice of the Centennial of 1876, that great national gathering that marks in a way the birth of the new American spirit.

But Taylor was not at all an original force. His power lay in his picturesque personality. His Macaulay-like memory charged with enormous store of literature from all lands and at instant command; his bluff and hearty manner; and the atmosphere of romance which surrounded him, made him a marked man wherever he went. He appealed to the imagination of adolescent America. Like Byron, he had traveled far in the mysterious East; there was the sensuousness and dreaminess of the Orient about him; he had "ripened," as he expressed it, "in the suns of many lands."

The weakness of Taylor was the weakness of Stoddard, of Aldrich, of the early Stedman, of all the poets of beauty. They had drunk like the young Tennyson of the fatal draft of Keats. To them beauty concerned itself with the mere externals of sense. Keats is the poet of rich interiors, of costly hangings, and embroidered garments. To read him is to come into the presence of rare wines, of opiates that lap one in long forgetfulness, of softly whispering flutes and viols, of rare tables heaped with luscious dainties brought from far, of all the golden East can bring of luxury of furnishings and beauty of form and color. "A thing of beauty," he sings, "is a joy forever," but beauty to Keats is only that which brings delight to the senses. Of beauty of the soul he knows nothing. His women are Greek goddesses: nothing more. In Keats, and later in his disciples, Taylor and Stoddard and Aldrich, we never come face to face with souls in conflict for eternal principles. Shelley looked at life about him and reacted upon it. He showed us Prometheus bound to the rock for refusal to yield to tyrannic law, and then liberated by the new soul of human love. He believed that he had a vision of a new heaven and earth with Reason as its god and Love its supreme soul, and he beat out his life in eagerness to bring men into this new heaven in the clouds. Keats reacted upon nothing save the material which he found in books: translations from the Greek, Spenser, Shakespeare, that earlier adolescent dreamer Marlowe, Milton, Coleridge. With the exception of hints from "Christabel" which we find worked into "The Eve of St. Agnes" and "Lamia," Keats never got nearer his own century than Milton's day. He turned in disgust from the England about him—that England with its Benthamite individualism, inheritance from the French Revolution, which even then was culminating in all the misery and riot and civil strife that later we find pictured in the novels of Dickens and Kingsley—he turned from it to the world of merely sensuous delight, where selfishly he might swoon away in a dream of beauty.

Taylor and Stoddard and the early Aldrich reacted not at all

on the America that so sadly needed them. They added sentiment to the music of Keats and dreamed of the Orient with its
life of sensuous surfeit:

> The Poet came to the land of the East
> When spring was in the air:
> The Earth was dressed for a wedding feast,
> So young she seemed and fair;
> And the Poet knew the land of the East—
> His soul was native there.
>
> .   .   .   .   .   .
>
> And further sang the Nightingale:
> *Your* bower not distant lies.
> I hear the sound of a Persian lute
> From the jasmined window rise,
> And, twin-bright stars, through the lattice bars,
> I saw the Sultana's eyes.
>
> The Poet said: I will here abide,
> In the Sun's unclouded door;
> Here are the wells of all delight
> On the lost Arcadian shore:
> Here is the light on sea and land,
> And the dream deceives no more.

"Taylor, Boker, Stoddard, Read, Story, and their allies," confessed Stedman in his later years, "wrote poetry for the sheer
love of it. They did much beautiful work, with a cosmopolitan
and artistic bent, making it a part of the varied industry of men
of letters; in fact, they were creating a civic Arcadia of their
own." [4]

But in making this civic Arcadia of their own they deliberately
neglected the opportunity of reacting upon the actual civic life
of their own land in their own and later times. They lived in
one of the great germinal periods in the history of the race and
they deliberately chose to create a little Arcadia of their own.

No man of the century, save Lowell, was given the opportunity
to react upon the new world of America at a critical moment
such as was given to Taylor at the Centennial in 1876. Subject
and occasion there were worthy of a Milton. A new America had
arisen from the ashes of the war, eager and impetuous. A new
era had begun whose glories we of a later century are just beginning to realize. Who was to voice that era? The land needed

[4] *An American Anthology.* Introduction, xxvi.

a poet, a seer, a prophet, and in Taylor it had only a dreamer of beauty, gorgeous of epithet, musical, sensuous. "The National Ode," when we think of what the occasion demanded, must be classed as one of the greatest failures in the history of American literature. Freneau's "The Rising Glory of America," written in 1772, is an incomparably better ode. There are no lines in Taylor's poem to grip the heart and send the blood into quicker beat; there are no magnificent climaxes as in Lowell's odes:

> Virginia gave us this imperial man.

> Mother of States and undiminished men,
> Thou gavest us a country giving him.

> New birth of our new soil, the first American.

There is excessive tinkling of rimes; there is forcing of measures that could have come only of haste; there is lack of incisiveness and of distinctive poetic phrases that cling in the memory and become current coin; there is lack of vision and of message. The poet of beauty was unequal to his task. There was needed a prophet and a creative soul, and the lack of such a leader at the critical moment accounts in part perhaps for the poetic leanness of the period that was to come.

III

The poets of the second group, the transition poets, for the most part were born during the thirties. Like Taylor and Stoddard, they were poets of beauty who read other poets with eagerness and wrote with deliberation. Their early volumes are full of exquisitely finished work modeled upon Theocritus and Heine, upon Keats and Shelley. They reacted but little upon the life about them; they railed upon America as crude and raw, a land without adequate art, and were content to fly away into the world of beauty and forget.

Then suddenly the war crashed in their ears. For the first time they caught a vision of life, of their country, of themselves, and for the first time they burst into real song. "For eight years," wrote the young Stedman in 1861, "I have cared *nothing* for politics—have been disgusted with American life and doings. Now for the first time I am proud of my country and my grand heroic brethren. The greatness of the crisis, the Homeric grandeur of the contest, surrounds and elevates us all. . . . Henceforth the sentimental and poetic will fuse with the intellectual to dignify and elevate the race.''⁵

Edmund Clarence Stedman was of old New England stock. He had inherited with his blood what Howells termed, in words that might have emanated from Dr. Holmes himself, ''the quality of Boston, the honor and passion of literature.'' He was born in Hartford, Connecticut, October 8, 1833. Bereft of his father when he was but two years of age, and later, when he was a mere child, forced to leave his mother and live with an uncle who could little supply the place that only father and mother can fill in a boy's life, he grew into a headstrong, moody youth who resented control. He was a mere lad of fifteen when he entered Yale, the youngest member indeed of his class, and his rustication two years later was only a natural result. Boyishness and high spirits and impetuous independence of soul are not crimes, however, and the college in later years was glad to confer upon him his degree.

Returning to Norwich, the home of his uncle, he pursued for a time the study of law. Later he connected himself with the local newspaper, and in 1853, at the age of twenty, he was married. Two years later, he left newspaper work to become the New York representative of a firm which was to engage in the manufacture and sale of clocks. Accordingly in the summer of 1855 he took up for the first time his residence in the city that was to be so closely connected with the rest of his life.

The clock factory made haste to burn and Stedman again was out of employment, this time in the great wilderness of New York. For a time he was a real estate and commission broker, later he was a clerk in a railroad office. Still later he attracted wide attention with his ephemeral poem ''The Diamond Wedding,'' and on the strength of this work became a correspondent of the *Tribune.* In 1861 he went to the front as war correspondent of the Washington *World,* and his letters during the early years of the struggle were surpassed by those of no other correspondent. In 1862 he was given a position in the office of the Attorney-General and a year later he began his career as a broker in Wall Street, a career that was to hold him in its grip for the rest of his life.

⁵ *Life and Letters of Edmund Clarence Stedman,* i: 242.

Pan and Wall Street are far from synonymous. There was poetry in Stedman's soul; there were within him creative powers that he felt were able to place him among the masters if he could but command time to study his art. He worshiped beauty and he was compelled to keep his eye upon the stock-ticker. He read Keats and Tennyson, Moschus and Theocritus, but it was always after the freshness of his day had been given to the excitement of the market place. Time and again he sought to escape, but the pressure of city life was upon him. He had a growing family now and there were no resources save those that came from his office. It was a precarious business in which he engaged; it was founded upon uncertainty; failure might come at any moment through no fault of his own. Several times during his life he was on the brink of ruin. Time and again his health failed him, but he still struggled on. The financial chapter of his biography is one of the most pathetic in literary annals. But through toil and discouragement, amid surroundings fatal to poetic vision, he still kept true to his early literary ideals, and his output when measured either in volumes or in literary merit is remarkable.

The first period of Stedman's poetic life produced little save colorless, passionless lyrics, the echoes of a wide reading in other poets. He went, like all of his clan, to books rather than life. He was early enamoured of the Sicilian idylists. It was a dream that never quite deserted him, to make "a complete, metrical, English version of the idyls of Theocritus, Moschus, and Bion"—an idle dream indeed for a vigorous young poet in a land that needed the breath of a new life. Why dawdle over Theocritus when fields are newly green and youth is calling? Stedman himself seems to have misgivings. "When the job [the collecting of the various texts] was nearly ended, I reflected that one's freshest years should be given to original work, and such excursions might well be deferred to the pleasures of old age. My time seemed to have been wasted." [6]

During this earlier period poetry was to him an artistic thing to be judged coldly from the standpoint of art and beauty. He worked with extreme care upon his lines. For a time he considered that he had reached his highest level in "Alcetryon," and he waited eagerly for the world to discover it. William Winter, his fellow poet of beauty, hailed it as "not unworthy of the

[6] *Life and Letters of Edmund Clarence Stedman*, i: 384.

greatest living poet, Tennyson"; Professor Hadley of Yale pronounced it "one of the most successful modern-antiques that I have ever seen." Then Lowell, with one of his flashes of insight, told the whole truth: "I don't believe in these modern antiques —no, not in Landor, not in Swinburne, not in any of 'em. They are all wrong. It is like writing Latin verses—the material you work in is dead." It was the voice of an oracle to the young poet. Twenty-three years later he wrote of his chagrin when Lowell had praised his volume in the *North American Review* and had said nothing of his *pièce de résistance* "Alectryon." "Finally I hinted as much to him. He at once said that it was my 'best piece of work,' but no 'addition to poetic literature,' since we already have enough masterpieces of that kind—from Landor's *Hamadryad* and Tennyson's *Œnone* down to the latest effort by Swinburne or Mr. Fields. . . . Upon reflection, I thought Lowell right. A new land calls for new song." [7]

The episode is a most significant one. It marks the passing of a whole poetic school.

To the war period that followed this era in the poet's life belong the deepest notes of Stedman's song. In his *Alice of Monmouth,* he is no longer the mere poet of beauty, he is the interpreter of the thrill, the sacrifice, the soul of the great war. The poem has the bite of life in it. "The Cavalry Song" thrills with the very soul of battle:

> Dash on beneath the smoking dome,
>   Through level lightnings gallop nearer!
> One look to Heaven! no thoughts of home:
>   The guidons that we bear are dearer.
>   Charg-e!
> Cling! Clang! forward all!
> Heaven help those whose horses fall!
>   Cut left and right!

The poem "Wanted—a Man" written in the despondent autumn of 1862, came not from books, but hot from a man's heart:

> Give us a man of God's own mold,
>   Born to marshal his fellow men;
> One whose fame is not bought or sold
>   At the stroke of a politician's pen;
> Give us the man of thousands ten,

[7] *Life and Letters of Edmund Clarence Stedman,* i: 372.

Fit to do as well as to plan;
Give us a rallying-cry, and then,
Abraham Lincoln, give us a MAN!

O, we will follow him to the death,
Where the foeman's fiercest columns are!
O, we will use our latest breath,
Cheering for every sacred star!
His to marshal us high and far;
Ours to battle, as patriots can
When a Hero leads the Holy War!—
Abraham Lincoln, give us a MAN!

Poems like this will not die. They are a part of the deeper history of America. They are worth more than ships or guns or battlements. Only a few notes like this did Stedman strike. Once again its deep note rang in "The Hand of Lincoln":

Lo, as I gaze, that statured man,
Built up from yon large hand, appears:
A type that Nature wills to plan
But once in all a people's years.

What better than this voiceless cast
To tell of such a one as he,
Since through its living semblance passed
The thought that bade a race be free!

Another deep note he struck in that war period that so shook him, a note called forth by personal bereavement and put into immortal form in "The Undiscovered Country," a song that was to be sung at the funerals of his wife and his sons, and later at his own:

Could we but know
The land that ends our dark, uncertain travel,
Where lie those happier hills and meadows low—
Ah, if beyond the spirit's inmost cavil,
Aught of that Country could we surely know,
Who would not go?

Aside from a handful of spontaneous love songs—"At Twilight," "Autumn Song," "Stanzas for Music," "Song from a Drama," "Creole Love Song"—nothing else of Stedman's poetic work greatly matters. He is a lyrist who struck a few true notes, a half dozen perhaps—thin indeed in volume, but those few immortal.

As the new period progressed, the period in America that had awakened to the full realization that "a new land needs new song," he became gradually silent as a singer and gave himself more and more to prose criticism, a work for which nature had peculiarly endowed him.

IV

In this transition group, poets of external beauty, *Spätromantiker* yet classicists in their reverence for rule and tradition and in their struggle for perfection, the typical figure is Thomas Bailey Aldrich (1836–1907). By birth he was a New Englander, a native of Portsmouth, New Hampshire, where he spent that boyhood which he made classic in the *Story of a Bad Boy*. Three years in New Orleans whither his father had moved for business reasons, years that seem to have made slight impression upon him, and then, his father dying and a college course becoming out of the question, he went with his mother to New York, where he resided for fourteen years, or between 1852 and 1866. It was a period of activity and of contact with many things that were to influence his later life. He held successively the positions of counting-room clerk, junior literary critic on the *Evening Mirror*, sub-editor of the *Home Journal*, literary adviser to Derby and Jackson, and managing editor of the *Illustrated News*. He formed a close friendship with Taylor and Stoddard and Stedman, and he saw something of the Bohemian group that during the late fifties and early sixties made headquarters at Pfaff's celebrated resort, 647 Broadway. Then came his call to Boston as editor of *Every Saturday*, his adoption as a Brahmin, his residence on Beacon Street, and his admission to the inner circle of the *Atlantic Monthly*.

Aldrich's literary life was from first to last a struggle between his Bohemian New York education and his later Brahmin classicism. His first approach to poetry had been through G. P. Morris and Willis on the *Mirror* and the *Journal*. From them it was that he learned the strain of sentimentalism which was to produce such poems as "Mabel, Little Mabel," "Marian, May, and Maud," and "Babie Bell." Then swiftly he had come under the spell of Longfellow's German romance, with its Emma of Ilmenau maidens, its delicious sadness and longing, and its worship of the night—that dreamy old-world atmosphere which had so influenced the mid century. It possessed the young poet completely, so completely that he never freed himself entirely from its spell. Longfellow was his poet master:

> O Poet-soul! O gentle one!
> Thy thought has made my darkness light;
> The solemn voices of the night
> Have filled me with an inner tone.

> I'll drink thy praise in olden wine,
> And in the cloak of fine conceite
> I'll tell thee how my pulses beat,
> How half my being runs to thine.

Then had come the acquaintance with Taylor and Stoddard, and through them the powerful influence of Keats and Tennyson.

To study the evolution of Aldrich as a poet, one need not linger long over *The Bells* (1855), that earliest collection of echoes and immaturities; one will do better to begin with his prose work, *Daisy's Necklace*, published two years later, a book that has a significance out of all proportion to its value. As we read it we are aware for the first time of the fact which was to become more and more evident with every year, that there were two Aldriches: the New York romanticist dreaming over his *Hyperion*, his Keats, his Tennyson, and the Boston classicist, severe with all exuberance, correct, and brilliant. The book is crude, a mere *mélange* of quotations and echoes, fantastic often and sentimental, yet one cannot read a chapter of it without feeling that it was written with all seriousness. When, for example, the young poet speaks of "The Eve of St. Agnes," we know that he speaks from his heart: "I sometimes think that this poem is the most exquisite definition of one phase of poetry in our language. Musical rhythm, imperial words, gorgeous color and luxurious conceit seemed to have culminated in it." But in the Prologue and the Epilogue of the book there is the later Aldrich, the classicist and critic, who warns us that the work is not to be taken seriously: that it is a mere burlesque, an extravaganza.

In his earlier work he is a true member of the New York school. He looks at life and poetry from the same standpoint that Taylor and Stoddard had viewed them in their attic room on those ambrosial nights when they had really lived. Taylor's *Poems of the Orient*, inspired by Shelley's "Lines to an Indian

Air'' and by Tennyson's ''Recollections of the Arabian Nights,'' made a profound impression upon him. Stoddard, who soon was to issue his *Book of the East,* was also to the young poet like one from a rarer world. When in 1858 Aldrich in his twenty-second year issued his gorgeous oriental poem, *The Course of True Love Never Did Run Smooth,* he dedicated it to Stoddard, ''under whose fingers this story would have blossomed into true Arabian roses.'' To his next volume he was to add *Cloth of Gold,* a grouping of sensuous lyrics breathing the soul of ''The Eve of St. Agnes'': ''Tiger Lilies,'' ''The Sultana,'' ''Latakia,'' ''When the Sultan Goes to Ispahan,'' and others. Even as Taylor and Stoddard, he dreamed that his soul was native in the East:

> I must have known
> Life otherwhere in epochs long since fled,
> For in my veins some Orient blood is red,
> And through my thoughts are lotus blossoms blown.

Everywhere in this earlier work sensuous beauty, soft music faintly heard in an atmosphere breathing sandal-wood, and oriental perfume:

> Lavender and spikenard sweet,
> And attars, nedd, and richest musk.

Everywhere rich interiors, banquets fit for Porphyro to spread for Madeline, and, dimly seen in the spice-breathing twilight, the maiden of his dreams:

> The music sang itself to death,
>   The lamps died out in their perfume:
> Abbassa, on a silk divan,
>   Sate in the moonlight of her room.
> Her handmaid loosed her scented hair
>   With lily fingers; from her brow
> Released the diamond, and unlaced
>   The robe that held her bosom's snow;
> Removed the slippers from her feet
>   And led her to an ivory bed.

Had Aldrich persisted in such work, he would have become simply another Stoddard, an echoer of soft sweetness, out of print in the generation following his death. But for Aldrich there was a restraining force. The classicist, the Brahmin, within the sentimental young poet was to be awakened by the greatest of the classicists and the Brahmins, Dr. Holmes, himself. "You must not feed too much on 'apricots and dewberries,'" he wrote in 1863. "There is an exquisite sensuousness that shows through your words and rounds them into voluptuous swells of rhythm as 'invisible fingers of air' lift the diaphanous gauzes. Do not let it run away with you. You love the fragrance of certain words so well that you are in danger of making nosegays when you should write poems. . . . Your tendency to vanilla-flavored adjectives and patchouli-scented participles stifles your strength in cloying euphemisms." [8]

Wise criticism, but the critic said nothing of a deeper and more insidious fault. There was no originality in Aldrich's earlier work. Everywhere it echoed other poetry. Like Taylor and Stoddard, the poet had so saturated himself with the writings of others that unconsciously he imitated. One can illustrate this no better perhaps than by examining a passage which Boynton in a review of the poet cites as beauty of the highest order. It is from the poem "Judith":

> Thy breath upon my cheek is as the air
> Blown from a far-off grove of cynnamon,
> Fairer art thou than is the night's one star;
> Thou makest me a poet with thine eyes.

Beautiful indeed it is, but one cannot help thinking of Keats' "Eve's one star" and Marlowe's:

> Oh, thou art fairer than the evening air
> Clad in the beauty of a thousand stars;
> Brighter art thou than flaming Jupiter.

> .   .   .   .

> Sweet Helen, make me immortal with a kiss.

One has, too, an uneasy feeling that the whole poem would never have been written but for Arnold's "Sohrab and Rustum" and Tennyson's narratives.

Aldrich's later life was a prolonged struggle against the poetic habits of this New York period of his training. The second side of his personality, however, that severe classical spirit which made war with his romantic excesses, more and more possessed him. "I have a way," he wrote in 1900, "of looking at my own verse as

[8] Greenslet's *Thomas Bailey Aldrich*, 64.

if it were written by some man I did n't like very well, and thus I am able to look at it rather impersonally, and to discover when I have fallen into mere 'fine writing,' a fault I am inclined to, while I detest it." [9]

Imitation was his besetting sin. It was his realization of this fact more than anything else that caused him to omit from later editions such wide areas of his earlier work. Of the forty-eight poems in *The Bells* he suffered not one to be reprinted; of his second volume he reprinted only two fragments: "Dressing the Bride" and "Songs from the Persian"; of the forty-seven lyrics in his third volume he admitted only seven into his definitive edition, and of the twenty in his fourth volume he spared but five. Of the vast number of lyrics that he had produced before the edition of 1882 only thirty-three were deemed of enough value to be admitted into his final canon.

It was not alone on account of its lack of finish that this enormous mass of poetical material was condemned. The poet had been born with nothing in particular to say. Nothing had compelled him to write save a dilettante desire to work with beautiful things. His life had known no period of storm and stress from which were to radiate new forces. His poems had been therefore not creations, but exercises to be thrown aside when the mood had passed. Exquisite work it often was, but there was no experience in it, no depth of life, no color of any soil save that of the dream-world of other poets.

The Aldrich of the later years became more and more an artist, a seeker for the perfect, a classicist. "The things that have come down to us," he wrote once to Stedman, "the things that have *lasted*, are perfect in form. I believe many a fine thought has perished being inadequately expressed, and I know that many a light fancy is immortal because of its perfect wording." [10] He defended himself again and again from the charge that he was a mere carver of cherry stones, a maker of exquisite trifles. "Jones's or Smith's lines," he wrote in 1897, " 'to my lady's eye-brow'—which is lovely in every age—will outlast nine-tenths of the noisy verse of our stress and storm period. Smith or Jones who never dreamed of having a Mission, will placidly sweep down

9 Greenslet's *Thomas Bailey Aldrich*, 210.
10 *Ibid.*, 156.

to posterity over the fall of a girl's eyelash, leaving our shrill
didactic singers high and dry on the sands of time." [11]
He has summed it up in his "Funeral of a Minor Poet":

> Beauty alone endures from age to age,
> From age to age endures, handmaid of God,
> Poets who walk with her on earth go hence
> Bearing a talisman.

And again in his poem "Art":

> "Let art be all in all," one time I said
> And straightway stirred the hypercritic gall:
> I said not, "Let technique be all in all,"
> But art—a wider meaning.

His essay on Herrick was in reality an apology for himself:
"It sometimes happens that the light love song, reaching few or
no ears at its first singing, outlasts the seemingly more prosperous
ode which, dealing with some passing phase of thought, social or
political, gains the instant applause of the multitude. . . . His
workmanship places him among the masters. . . . Of passion, in
the deeper sense, Herrick has little or none. Here are no 'tears
from the depth of some divine despair,' no probing into the tragic
heart of man, no insight that goes much further than the pathos
of a cowslip on a maiden's grave."

All this is true so far as it goes, but it must never be forgotten
that beauty is a thing that concerns itself with far more than the
externals of sense. To be of positive value it must deal with the
soul of man and the deeps of human life. A poet now and then
may live because of his lyric to a girl's eyelash, but it is certain
that the greater poets of the race have looked vastly deeper than
this or they never would have survived the years. Unless the
poet sees beyond the eyelash into the soul and the deeps of life,
he will survive his generation only by accident or by circumstance,
a fact that Aldrich himself tacitly admitted in later years by
dropping from the final edition of his poems all lyrics that had
as their theme the merely trivial.

To the early Aldrich, life had been too kind. He had known
nothing of the bitterness of defeat, the losing battle with fate, the
inexorableness of bereavement. He had little sympathy with

[11] Greenslet's *Thomas Bailey Aldrich*, 200.

his times and their problems, and with his countrymen. Like
Longfellow, he lived in his study and his study had only eastern
windows. Herrick, whom he defended as a poet immortal because
of trifles made perfect, can never be charged with this. No singer
ever held more to his own soil and the spirit of his own times.
His poems everywhere are redolent of England, of English
meadows and streams, of English flowers. He is an English poet
and only an English poet. But so far as one may learn from his
earlier work, Aldrich might have lived in England or indeed in
France. From such lyrics as "The Winter Robin" one would
guess that he was English. Surely when he longs for the spring
and the return of the jay we may conclude with certainty that
he was not a New Englander.

During his earlier life he was in America but not of it. Even
the war had little effect upon him. He was inclined to look at
life from the standpoint of the aristocrat. He held himself aloof
from his generation with little of sympathy for the struggling
masses. He was suspicious of democracy: "We shall have
bloody work in this country some of these days," he wrote to
Woodberry in 1894, "when the lazy *canaille* get organized. They
are the spawn of Santerre and Fouquier-Tinville." [12] And again,
"Emerson's mind would have been enriched if he could have had
more terrapin and less fish-ball."

The mighty westward movement in America after the war concerned him not at all. Much in the new literary movement re-
pelled him. He denounced Kipling and declared that he would
have rejected the "Recessional" had it been offered to the
Atlantic. Realism he despised:

> The mighty Zolaistic Movement now
> Engrosses us—a miasmatic breath
> Blown from the slums. We paint life as it is,
> The hideous side of it, with careful pains
> Making a god of the dull Commonplace,
> For have we not the old gods overthrown
> And set up strangest idols?

A poet should be a leader of his generation. He should be in
sympathy with it; he should interpret the nation to itself; he
should have vision and he should be a compeller of visions. It
is not his mission weakly to complain that the old is passing and

12 Greenslet's *Thomas Bailey Aldrich*, 178.

that the new is strange and worthless. The America of the seventies and the eighties was tremendously alive. It was breaking new areas and organizing a new empire in the West; it was lifting up a splendid new hope for all mankind. It needed a poet, and its poets were looking eastward and singing of the fall of my lady's eyelash.

V

The best refutation of Aldrich is furnished by Aldrich himself. The years between 1881 and 1890, the period of his editorship of the *Atlantic Monthly*, were a time of small production, of pause and calm, of ripening, of final adjustment. Following his resignation of the editorship, he began again actively to produce poetry and now for ten or twelve years he worked in contemporary life— in occasional and commemorative odes, monodies and elegies; in studies of the deeper meanings of life; in problems of death and of destiny. The volumes of 1891, 1895, and 1896 contain the soul of all his poetry. From them he omitted practically nothing when at last he made up the definitive edition of his work. The Aldrich of the sixties and the seventies had been trivial, artificial, sentimental; the Aldrich who wrote in the nineties had a purpose: he worked now in the deeps of life; he was in earnest; he had a message. It is significant in view of his oft expressed theories of poetry that when in 1897 Stedman asked him to indicate his best lyrics for publication in the *American Anthology,* he chose these: "Shaw Memorial Ode," "Outward Bound," "Andromeda," "Reminiscence," "The Last Cæsar," "Alice Yeaton's Son," "Unguarded Gates," "A Shadow of the Night," "Monody on Wendell Phillips," "To Hafiz," "Prescience," "Santo Domingo," "Tennyson," "Memory," "Twilight," "Quits"— all but one of them, "Prescience," first published after 1891. There are no "apricots and dewberries" about these masterly lyrics; they deal with no such trivialities as the fall of an eyelash. They thrill with the problems of life and with experience. It was not until this later period that the poet could say to a bereaved friend: "You will recall a poem of mine entitled 'A Shadow of the Night.' There is a passage here and there that might possibly appeal to you"—a severe test, but one that reveals the true poet. What has he for his generation? What has he for the crises of life, inevitably must be asked at last of every poet. His change of ideals he voiced in "Andromeda":

> The smooth-worn coin and threadbare classic phrase
> Of Grecian myths that did beguile my youth
> Beguile me not as in the olden days:
> I think more grace and beauty dwell with truth.

Now in the rich afternoon of his art the poet is no longer content to echo the music of masters. He has awakened to the deeper meanings of life; he is himself a master; he now has something to say, and the years of his apprenticeship have given him a flawless style in which to say it. No other American poet has approached the perfect art of these later lyrics. Who else on this side of the water could have written "The Sisters' Tragedy," with its melody, its finish, its distinction of phrase?

> Both still were young, in life's rich summer yet;
> And one was dark, with tints of violet
> In hair and eye, and one was blonde as she
> Who rose—a second daybreak—from the sea
> Gold tressed and azure-eyed.

And, moreover, in addition to all this it is a quivering section of human life. One reads on and on and then—sharply draws his breath at the rapier thrust of the closing lines.

What a world of distance between the early sensuous poet of the New York school and the seer of the later period who could pen a lyric beginning,

> O short-breathed music, dying on the tongue
> Ere half the mystic canticle be sung!
> O harp of life so speedily unstrung!
> Who, if 't were his to choose, would know again
> The bitter sweetness of the last refrain,
> Its rapture and its pain?

Or this in its flawless perfectness:

> At noon of night, and at the night's pale end,
>   Such things have chanced to me
> As one, by day, would scarcely tell a friend
>   For fear of mockery.
>
> Shadows, you say, mirages of the brain!
>   I know not, faith, not I.
> Is it more strange the dead should walk again
>   Than that the quick should die?

A few of his later sonnets, "Outward Bound," redolent of his early love of the sea, "When to Soft Sleep We Give Ourselves Away," "The Undiscovered Country," "Enamored Architect of Airy Rhyme," and "I Vex Me Not with Brooding on the Years," have hardly been surpassed in American literature.

It was from this later period that Aldrich chose almost all of his poems in that compressed volume which was to be his lasting contribution to poetry, *A Book of Songs and Sonnets*. It is but a fraction of his work, but it is all that will survive the years. He will go down as the most finished poet that America has yet produced; the later Landor, romantic yet severely classical; the maker of trifles that were miracles of art; and finally as the belated singer who awoke in his later years to message and vision and produced with his mastered art a handful of perfect lyrics that rank with the strongest that America has given to song.

BIBLIOGRAPHY

JAMES BAYARD TAYLOR. (1825–1878.) *Ximena; or, the Battle of Sierra Morena, and other Poems*, Philadelphia, 1844; *Rhymes of Travel, Ballads, Lyrics, and Songs*, Boston and London, 1851; *Poems of the Orient*, Boston, 1854; *Poems of Home and Travel*, 1855; *The Poet's Journal*, 1862; *The Picture of St. John, a Poem*, 1866; *Translation of Faust*, 1870–1871; *The Masque of the Gods*, 1872; *Lars: a Pastoral of Norway*, 1873; *The Prophet: a Tragedy*, 1874; *Home Pastorals, Ballads, and Lyrics*, 1875; *The National Ode*, 1876; *Prince Deukalion*, 1878; *Poetical Works*, Household Edition, 1880, 1902; *Life and Letters of Bayard Taylor*, edited by Marie Hansen Taylor and Horace E. Scudder. 2 vols. 1884; *Bayard Taylor*, American Men of Letters Series, A. H. Smyth. 1896; *Life of Bayard Taylor*, R. H. Conwell.

RICHARD HENRY STODDARD. (1825–1903.) *Footprints*, New York, 1849; *Poems*, Boston, 1852; *Songs of Summer*, Boston, 1857; *The King's Bell*, New York, 1862; *Abraham Lincoln: an Horatian Ode*, New York, 1865; *The Book of the East, and Other Poems*, Boston, 1871; *Poems*, New York, 1880; *The Lion's Cub, with Other Verse*, New York, 1890; *Recollections, Personal and Literary*, by Richard Henry Stoddard. Edited by Ripley Hitchcock, New York, 1903.

EDMUND CLARENCE STEDMAN. (1833–1908.) *The Prince's Ball*, New York, 1860; *Poems, Lyrical and Idyllic*, New York, 1860; *The Battle of Bull Run*, New York, 1861; *Alice of Monmouth. An Idyl of the Great War and Other Poems*, New York, 1863; *The Blameless Prince, and Other Poems*, Boston, 1869; *The Poetical Works of Edmund Clarence Stedman*, Boston, 1873; *Favorite Poems*. Vest Pocket Series, 1877; *Hawthorne and Other Poems*, 1877; *Lyrics and Idyls with Other Poems*, London, 1879; *The Poetical Works of Edmund Clarence Stedman*. Household Edition,

1884; *Songs and Ballads*, 1884; *Poems Now First Collected*, 1897; *Mater Coronata*, 1901; *The Poems of Edmund Clarence Stedman*, 1908; *Life and Letters of Edmund Clarence Stedman*. By Laura Stedman and George M. Gould. 2 vols. New York, 1910.

THOMAS BAILEY ALDRICH. (1836–1907.) *The Bells. A Collection of Chimes*, New York, 1855; *Daisy's Necklace and What Came of It. A Literary Episode* [Prose], New York, 1857; *The Course of True Love Never Did Run Smooth*, New York, 1858; *The Ballad of Babie Bell, and Other Poems*, New York, 1859; *Pampinea, and Other Poems*, New York, 1861; *Poems*. With Portrait, New York, 1863; *The Poems of Thomas Bailey Aldrich*, Boston, 1865; *Cloth of Gold, and Other Poems*, 1874; *Flower and Thorn. Later Poems*, 1877; *Friar Jerome's Beautiful Book, and Other Poems*, 1881; *XXXVI Lyrics and XII Sonnets*, 1881; *The Poems of Thomas Bailey Aldrich*. Illustrated by the Paint and Clay Club, 1882; *Mercedes, and Later Lyrics*, 1884; *The Poems of Thomas Bailey Aldrich*. Household Edition, 1885; *Wyndham Towers*, 1890; *The Sisters' Tragedy, with Other Poems, Lyrical and Dramatic*, 1891; *Mercedes. A Drama in Two Acts, as Performed at Palmer's Theatre*, 1894; *Unguarded Gates, and Other Poems*, 1895; *Later Lyrics*, 1896; *Judith and Holofernes, a Poem*, 1896; *The Works of Thomas Bailey Aldrich*, Riverside Edition, 1896; *The Poems of Thomas Bailey Aldrich*. Revised and Complete Household Edition, 1897; *A Book of Songs and Sonnets Selected from the Poems of Thomas Bailey Aldrich*, 1906; *The Life of Thomas Bailey Aldrich*, by Ferris Greenslet, 1908.

CHAPTER VIII

One phase of the new discovery of America following the Civil War—return to reality, insistence upon things as they are—expressed itself in nature study. While the new local color school was ransacking the odd corners of the land for curious types of humanity, these writers were calling attention to the hitherto unnoticed phenomena of fields and meadows and woodlands. Handbooks of birds and trees, nature guides and charts of all varieties were multiplied. Nature study became an art, and it ranged all the way from a fad for dilettantes to a solemn exercise in the public school curriculum.

I

The creator and inspirer and greatest figure of this school of nature writers was Henry David Thoreau. In point of time he was of the mid-century school that gathered about Emerson. He was born in 1817, two years earlier than Lowell, and he died in 1862, the first to break the earlier group, yet in spirit and influence and indeed in everything that makes for the final fixing of an author's place in the literary history of his land, he belongs to the period after 1870.

His own generation rejected Thoreau. They could see in him only an imitator of Emerson and an exploiter of newnesses in an age grown weary of newnesses. They did not condemn him: they ignored him. Of his first book, *A Week on the Concord and Merrimac Rivers*, 1849, printed at Thoreau's expense, only two hundred and nineteen copies had been sold in 1853 when the remainder of the edition was returned to the author. *Walden; or, Life in the Woods* fared somewhat better because of the unique social experiment which it recorded, but not enough better to encourage its author ever to publish another book. After the death of Thoreau, Emerson undertook to give him permanence by editing four or five posthumous volumes made up of his scattered magazine articles and papers, but even this powerful influence could not arouse enthusiasm. The *North American Review,* which in 1854 had devoted seven patronizing lines to *Walden,* took no note of Emerson's editings until the *Letters to Various Persons* appeared in 1865. Then it awoke in anger. To publish the letters of an author is to proclaim that author's importance, and what had Thoreau done save to live as a hermit for two years in the woods? He was a mere eccentric, a "Diogenes in his barrel, reducing his wants to a little sunlight"; one of "the pistillate plants kindled to fruitage by the Emersonian pollen." "It is something eminently fitting that his posthumous works should be offered us by Emerson, for they are strawberries from his own garden." He was an egotist, a poser for effect, a condemner of what he could not himself attain to. "He condemns a world, the hollowness of whose satisfactions he had never had the means of testing." "He had no humor"; "he had little active imagination"; "he was not by nature an observer." "He turns commonplaces end for end, and fancies it makes something new of them." His nature study was only "one more symptom of the general liver complaint." "I look upon a great deal of the modern sentimentalism about Nature as a mark of disease."

The review was from no less a pen than Lowell's and it carried conviction. Its author spread it widely by republishing it in *My Study Windows,* 1871, and including it in his collected works. It was the voice of Thoreau's generation, and to England at least it seems to have been the final word. Stevenson after reading the essay was emboldened to sum up the man in one word, a "skulker." The effect was almost equally strong in America. During the period from 1868 to 1881, not one of the author's volumes was republished in a new edition. When in 1870 Thomas Wentworth Higginson, his foremost champion in the dark period, had attempted to secure the manuscript journal for possible publication, he was met by Judge Hoar, the latter-day guardian of Concord, with the question: "Why should any one wish to have Thoreau's journal printed?"

That was the attitude of the seventies. Then had come the slow revival of the eighties. At the beginning of the decade H. G. O. Blake, into whose hands Thoreau's papers had fallen, began to publish extracts from the journals grouped according to days and seasons: *Early Spring in Massachusetts,* 1881,

Summer, 1884, and *Winter,* 1888. The break came in the nineties. Between 1893 and 1906 were published, in addition to many individual reprints of Thoreau's books, the Riverside edition in ten volumes, the complete journal in fourteen volumes, and the definitive Walden edition in twenty volumes. A Thoreau cult had arisen that hailed him as leader and master. After all the years he had arrived at his own. In the case of no other American has there been so complete and overwhelming a reversal of the verdict of an author's own generation.

Lowell devoted his whole essay to a criticism of Thoreau as a Transcendental theorist and social reformer. To-day it is recognized that fundamentally he was neither of these. His rehabilitation has come solely because of that element condemned by Lowell as a certain "modern sentimentalism about Nature." It is not alone because he was a naturalist that he has lived, or because he loved and lived with Nature: it was because he brought to the study of Nature a new manner, because he created a new nature sentiment, and so added a new field to literature. Instead of having been an imitator of Emerson, he is now seen to have been a positive original force, the most original, perhaps, save Whitman, that has contributed to American literature.

The first fact of importance about Thoreau is the fact that he wrote day after day, seldom a day omitted for years, the 6,811 closely printed pages of his journal, every part done with thoroughness and finish, with no dream that it ever was to be published. It is a fact enormously significant; it reveals to us the naked man; it furnishes a basis for all constructive criticism. "My journal," he wrote November 16, 1850, "should be the record of my love. I would write in it only of the things I love, my affection for an aspect of the world, what I love to think of." And again, "Who keeps a journal is purveyor to the gods." And still again, February 8, 1841, "My journal is that of me which would else spill over and run to waste, gleanings from the field which in action I reap. I must not live for it, but, in it, for the gods. They are my correspondents, to whom daily I send off this sheet, post-paid. I am clerk in their counting house, and at evening transfer the account from day-book to ledger." He was not a poser for effect, for it is impossible for one to pose throughout 6,811 printed pages wrought for no eyes save his own and the gods. His power came rather from the fact that he did not pose; that he wrote spontaneously for the sheer love of the writing. "I think," he declares in one place, "that the one word that will explain the Shakespeare miracle is unconsciousness." The word explains also Thoreau. Again he adds, "There probably has been no more conscious age than the present." The sentence is a key: in a conscious age, a classical age building on books, watchful of conventions and precedents, Thoreau stood true only to himself and Nature. Between him and the school of Taylor and Stoddard there was the whole diameter. He was affected only by the real, by experience, by the testimony of his own soul. "The forcible writer," he wrote February 3, 1852, "stands boldly behind his words with his experience. He does not make books out of books, but he has been *there* in person."

In his nature observations Thoreau was not a scientist. It was not his object to collect endless data for the purpose of arriving at laws and generalizations. He approached Nature rather as a poet. There was in him an innate love for the wild and elemental. He had, moreover, a passion for transcending, or peering beyond, those bounds of ordinary experience and capturing the half-divined secrets that Nature so jealously guards. His attitude was one of perpetual wonder, that wonder of the child which has produced the mythology of the race. Always was he seeking to catch Nature for an instant off her guard. His eyes were on the strain for the unseen, his ears for the unheard.

I was always conscious of sounds in Nature which my ears could not hear, that I caught but a prelude to a strain. She always retreats as I advance. Away behind and behind is she and her meaning. Will not this faith and expectation make itself ears at length? I never saw to the end, nor heard to the end, but the best part was unseen and unheard.—February 21, 1842.

Nature so absorbed him that he lived constantly in an eager, expectant atmosphere. "I am excited by this wonderful air," he writes, "and go, listening for the note of the bluebird or other comer." It was not what he saw in Nature that was important; it was what he felt. "A man has not seen a thing who has not felt it." He took stock of his sensations like a miser. "As I came home through the woods with my string of fish, trailing my pole, it being now quite dark, I caught a glimpse of a woodchuck stealing across my path, and felt a strange thrill of savage delight, and was strongly tempted to seize and devour him raw; not that I was hungry then, except for that wildness which he represented.'' It was by this watchfulness for the elemental, this constant scrutiny of instincts and savage outcroppings, that he sought to master the secret that baffled him. He would keep himself constantly in key, constantly sensitive to every fleeting glimpse of harmony that Nature might vouchsafe him.

Nature stirred him always on the side of the imagination. He loved Indian arrow-heads, for they were fragments of a mysterious past; he loved twilight effects and midnight walks, for the mystery of night challenged him and brought him nearer to the cosmic and the infinite:

I have returned to the woods and . . . spent the hours of midnight fishing from a boat by moonlight, serenaded by owls and foxes, and hearing, from time to time, the creaking note of some unknown bird close at hand. These experiences were very memorable and valuable to me—anchored in forty feet of water, and twenty or thirty rods from the shore . . . communicating by a long flaxen line with mysterious nocturnal fishes which had their dwelling forty feet below, or sometimes dragging sixty feet of line about the pond as I drifted in the gentle night breeze, now and then feeling a slight vibration along it, indicative of some life prowling about its extremity, of dull uncertain blundering purpose there. . . . It was very queer, especially in dark nights, when your thoughts had wandered to vast and cosmogonal themes in other spheres, to feel this faint jerk which came . . . to link you to Nature again.

Burroughs, like most scientists, slept at night. His observations were made by day: there is hardly a night scene in all his works; but Thoreau abounds in night scenes as much even as Novalis or Longfellow. He was at heart a mystic and he viewed Nature always from mystic standpoints. In ''Night and Moonlight'' he writes:

Is not the midnight like Central Africa to most of us? Are we not tempted to explore it—to penetrate to the shores of its lake Tchad, and discover the sources of the Nile, perchance the Mountains of the Moon? Who knows what fertility and beauty, moral and natural, are there to be found? In the Mountains of the Moon, in the Central Africa of the night, there is where all Niles have their hidden heads.

It was to discover these Mountains of the Moon, these mysterious sources of the Nile, forever so far away and yet forever so near, that Thoreau went to Nature. He went not to gather and to classify facts; he went to satisfy his soul. Burroughs is inclined to wonder and even laugh because of the many times he speaks of hearing the voice of unknown birds. To Burroughs the forest contained no unknown birds; to Thoreau the forest was valuable only because it *did* contain unknown birds. His straining for hidden melodies, his striving for deeper meanings, his dreaming of Mountains of the Moon that might become visible at any moment just beyond the horizon—it is in these things that he differs from all other nature writers. He was not a reporter; he was a prophet. "My profession is always to be on the alert, to find God in nature, to know His lurking places, to attend all the oratorios, the operas in nature. Shall I not have words as fresh as my thought? Shall I use any other man's word?"

To him Nature was of value only as it furnished message for humanity. "A fact," he declared, "must be the vehicle of some humanity in order to interest us." He went to Nature for tonic, not for fact; he sought only truth and freedom and spontaneousness of soul. He had no desire to write a botany, or an ornithology; rather would he learn of Nature the fundamentals of human living. "I went into the woods because I wished to live deliberately, to front only the essential facts of life, and see if I could not learn what it had to teach, and not, when I came to die, discover that I had not lived." Burroughs went into the woods to know and to make others to know, Thoreau went in to think and to feel; Burroughs was a naturalist, Thoreau a *super*naturalist.

Thoreau belongs completely to the later period: he is as thoroughly of American soil as even Mark Twain or Lincoln or Whitman. While Longfellow and Lowell, Taylor and Aldrich, and the rest of their school were looking eagerly to Europe, Thoreau was completely engrossed with his own land. "No truer American ever existed than Thoreau," wrote Emerson in his essay. "His preference of his country and condition was genuine, and his aversion from English and European manners and tastes almost reached contempt. . . . He wished to go to Oregon, not to London." It was this new-worldness, this freshness, this originality that made him the man of the new era. He went always to the sources; his work is redolent at every point of American soil. His images, his illustrations, his subject matter, all are American. His style, after he had outgrown an early fondness for Carlyle, is peculiarly his own, wonderfully simple and limpid and individual.   Often it flows like poetry:

> The sun is near setting away beyond Fair Haven.   A bewitching stillness reigns through all the woodland, and over all the snowclad landscape.   Indeed, the winter day in the woods or fields has commonly the stillness of twilight.   The pond is perfectly smooth and full of light.   I hear only the strokes of a lingering woodchopper at a distance and the melodious hooting of an owl.—December 9, 1856.

And what is this but poetry?

> On the morning when the wild geese go over, I, too, feel the migratory instinct strong within me, and anticipate the breaking up of winter.   If I yielded to this impulse, it would surely guide me to summer haunts.   This indefinite restlessness and fluttering on the perch no doubt prophesy the final migration of souls out of nature to a serener summer, in long harrows and waving lines, in the spring weather, over that fair uplands and fertile Elysian meadows, winging their way at evening, and seeking a resting place with loud cackling and uproar.— January 29, 1859.

Thoreau was one of the most tonic forces of the later period. His inspiration and his spirit filled all the later school of Nature writers.   One cannot read him long, especially in his later and more unconscious work, and find oneself unmoved.   He inspires to action, to restlessness of soul.   Take an entry like that of January 7, 1857, made during one of the most tumultuous of New England winter storms: ''It is bitter cold, with a cutting N.W. wind. . . . All animate things are reduced to their lowest terms. This is the fifth day of cold, blowing weather,'' and so on and on till one fairly hears the roaring of the storm.   Yet, despite the blast and the piercing cold, Thoreau goes out for his walk as usual and battles with the elements through miles of snow-smothered wilderness.   ''There is nothing so sanative, so poetic, as a walk in the woods and fields even now, when I meet none abroad for pleasure.   Nothing so inspires me, and excites such serene and profitable thought.''   His battle with the wind and the cold and the wilderness grips us as we read.   We too would rush into the storm and breast it and exult in it; we too would walk with Nature under the open skies, in the broad, wholesome places, and view the problems of life with serene soul.   It is this dynamic element of Thoreau that has given him his following.   He is sincere, he is working from the impulses of his soul, he is genuine. He is not a scientist: he is a poet and a seer. When we walk with Burroughs, we see as with new eyes; when with Thoreau, we feel. With Burroughs we learn of signs and seasons and traits; with Thoreau we find ourselves straining ears to catch the deeper harmonies, the mysterious soul of Nature, that somehow we feel to be intertwined eternally with the soul of man.

II

The transition from Thoreau to John Burroughs was through Thomas Wentworth Higginson. Wilson Flagg (1805–1884) had contributed to the early volumes of the *Atlantic* a series of bird studies Irving-like in atmosphere and sentiment, but he had made little impression. He was too literary, too much the child of the mid century. In his study of the owl, for instance, he could write: "I will not enter into a speculation concerning the nature and origin of those agreeable emotions which are so generally produced by the sight of objects that suggest the ideas of decay and desolation. It is happy for us, that, by the alchemy of poetry, we are able to turn some of our misfortunes into sources of melancholy pleasure, after the poignancy of grief has been assuaged by time," and so on and on till he got to midnight and the owl. It is a literary effort. There is lack of sincerity in it: the author is thinking too exclusively of his reader. The difference between it and a passage from Thoreau is the difference between a reverie in the study and a battle in the woods. Higginson, who followed in the *Atlantic* with "April Days," "The Life of Birds," and the other studies which he issued as *Out-Door Papers* in 1863, avoided the over-literary element on one hand and the over-scientific on the other and so became the first of what may be called the modern school of nature writers.

As we read Higginson's book to-day we find style and method curiously familiar. For the first time in American literature we have that chatty, anecdotal, half-scientific, half-sentimental treatment of out-door things that soon was to become so common. It is difficult to persuade oneself that a paper like "The Life of Birds," for instance, was not written by the Burroughs of the earlier period. *Out-Door Papers* and *Wake-Robin* are pitched in the same key. Who could be positive of the authorship of a fragment like this, were not Higginson's name appended:

To a great extent, birds follow the opening foliage northward, and flee from its fading, south; they must keep near the food on which they live, and secure due shelter for their eggs. Our earliest visitors shrink from trusting the bare trees with their nests; the song-sparrow seeks the ground; the blue-bird finds a box or hole somewhere; the red-wing haunts the marshy thickets, safer in the spring than at any other season; and even the sociable robin prefers a pine-tree to an apple-tree, if resolved to begin housekeeping prematurely. The movements of birds are chiefly timed by the advance of vegetation; and the thing most thoroughly surprising about them is not the general fact of the change of latitude, but their accuracy in hitting the precise locality. That the same cat-bird should find its way back, every spring, to almost the same branch of yonder larch-tree—that is the thing astonishing to me.

The most notable thing, however, about Higginson's out-door papers was their ringing call for a return to reality. It was he who more than any one else created interest in Thoreau; and it was he who first gained attention with the cry, "Back to nature." "The American temperament," he declared, "needs at this moment nothing so much as that wholesome training of semi-rural life which reared Hampden and Cromwell to assume at one grasp the sovereignty of England. . . . The little I have gained from colleges and libraries has certainly not worn so well as the little I learned in childhood of the habits of plant, bird, and insect. . . . Our American life still needs, beyond all things else, the more habitual cultivation of out-door habits. . . . The more bent any man is on action, the more profoundly he needs the calm lessons of Nature to preserve his equilibrium." To the new generation of writers he flung a challenge: "Thoreau camps down by Walden Pond and shows us that absolutely nothing in Nature has ever yet been described—not a bird or a berry of the woods, not a drop of water, not a spicula of ice, nor winter, nor summer, nor sun, nor star." And again, "What do we know, for instance, of the local distribution of our birds? I remember that in my latest conversation with Thoreau last December, he mentioned most remarkable facts in this department, which had fallen under his unerring eyes."

This was published in the *Atlantic*, September, 1862. In May, 1865, as if in answer to the challenge, there appeared in the same magazine John Burroughs's "With the Birds," a paper which he had written two years before. The army life of Higginson and later his humanitarian work in many fields put an end to his out-door writings, but not to his influence.

III

John Burroughs was born on a farm in Roxbury, New York, just below the Otsego County made famous by Cooper and the Leather-stocking Tales. His boyhood until he was seventeen "was mainly occupied," to quote his own words, "with farm work in the summer, and with a little study, offset by much hunting and trapping of wild animals in winter." One must study this boyhood if one is to understand the man's work:

> From childhood I was familiar with the homely facts of the barn, and of cattle and horses; the sugar-making in the maple woods in early spring; the work of the corn-field, hay-field, potato-field; the delicious fall months with their pigeon and squirrel shootings; threshing of buckwheat, gathering of apples, and burning of fallows; in short, everything that smacked of, and led to, the open air and its exhilarations. I belonged, as I may say, to them; and my substance and taste, as they grew, assimilated them as truly as my body did its food. I loved a few books much; but I loved Nature, in all those material examples and subtle expressions, with a love passing all the books of the world.[1]

Of schooling he had little. "I was born," he once wrote, "of and among people who neither read books nor cared for them, and my closest associations since have been alien to literature and art." The usual winter term in his native district, a year or two in academy courses after he was seventeen—that was the extent of his formal education. At twenty he was married, at twenty-seven, after having drifted about as a school teacher, he settled at Washington in a position in the Treasury Department that held him closely for nine years.

It was a period of self-discipline. His intellectual life had been awakened by Emerson, and he had followed him into wide fields. He read enormously, he studied languages, he trained himself with models of English style. His love of the country, legacy of the boyhood which he never outgrew, impelled him to a systematic study of ornithology. Birds were his avocation, his enthusiasm; by and by they were to become his vocation.

In 1861, when he was twenty-four, he came for the first time in contact with *Leaves of Grass,* and it aroused him like a vision.

[1] *Notes on Walt Whitman,* 1867.

It produced the impression upon me in my moral consciousness that actual Nature did in her material forms and shows; . . . I shall never forget the strange delight I had from the following passage, as we sat there on the sunlit border of an autumn forest:

I lie abstracted, and hear beautiful tales of things, and the reasons of things;
They are so beautiful, I nudge myself to listen.
I cannot say to any person what I hear—I cannot say it to myself—it is very wonderful;
It is no small matter, this round and delicious globe, moving so exactly in its orbit forever and ever, without one jolt, or the untruth of a single second;
I do not think it was made in six days, nor in ten thousand years, nor in ten billions of years;
Nor planned and built one thing after another, as an architect plans and builds a house.

It was the touch that he needed. There was in him a strain of wildness even as in Thoreau, an almost feminine shrinking from the crowd, a thinking of Nature as something apart from man, a retreat and an antidote; Whitman added the human element, the sympathetic touch, the sense of the value of man.

Burroughs's first work appeared that same year in the New York *Leader,* a series of papers under the heading "From the Back Country"—crude things compared with Higginson's polished work, yet filled with a genuineness and a freshness that were notable. All of his earlier sketches were the work of a careful observer who wrote from sheer love of Nature. Moreover, they were the work of a dreamer and a poet. As the years took him farther from that marvelous boyhood, the light upon it grew softer and more golden. He dreamed of it in the spring when the bluebird called and the high-hole; he dreamed of it on his walks in the city suburbs when the swallows greeted him and the warblers. His *Atlantic* paper "With the Birds," now the first chapter of his published works, begins with the sentence, now suppressed, "Not in the spirit of exact science, but rather with the freedom of love and old acquaintance, would I celebrate some of the minstrels of the field and forest." And years later, when he wrote the general introduction to his works, he could say:

My first book, *Wake-Robin,* was written while I was a government clerk in Washington. It enabled me to live over again the days I had passed with the birds and in the scenes of my youth. I wrote the

book sitting at a desk in front of an iron wall. I was keeper of a
vault in which many millions of bank notes were stored. During my
long periods of leisure I took refuge in my pen. How my mind reacted from the iron wall in front of me and sought solace in memories
of the birds and of summer fields and woods! Most of the chapters
of *Winter Sunshine* were written at the same desk. The sunshine there
referred to is of a richer quality than is found in New York and
New England.

That was the secret of the early work of John Burroughs:
to him Nature was a part of his boyhood, with boyhood's light
upon it. He dreamed of her when the city homesickness was
upon him and when he wrote of her he wrote from a full heart.
He felt every line of it; the light that plays over it is indeed
of "richer quality" than is found over any actual hills. A
part of his early popularity came undoubtedly from the
sentiment which he freely mingled with his studies of field and
woodland.

There is something almost pathetic in the fact that the birds remain
forever the same. You grow old, your friends die or remove to distant
lands, events sweep on and all things are changed. Yet there in your
garden or orchard are the birds of your boyhood, the same notes, the
same calls, and, to all intents and purposes, the identical birds endowed
with perennial youth. The swallows, that built so far out of your
reach beneath the eaves of your father's barn, the same ones now squeak
and chatter beneath the eaves of your barn. The warblers and shy
wood birds you pursued with such glee ever so many summers ago,
and whose names you taught to some beloved youth who now, perchance, sleeps amid his native hills, no marks of time or change cling
to them; and when you walk out to the strange woods, there they
are, mocking you with their ever renewed and joyous youth. The call
of the high-holes, the whistle of the quail, the strong piercing note of
the meadow lark, the drumming of the grouse—how these sounds ignore the years, and strike on the ear with the melody of that springtime when the world was young, and life was all holiday and romance.[2]

The twenty years following his first *Atlantic* paper were the
years of his professional life. He left his clerkship at Washington in 1873 to become a national bank inspector, and until 1884,
when he finally retired to rural life, he was busy with his duties
as receiver of broken banks, examiner of accounts, and financial
expert. During the two decades he published his most distinctive

[2] *Birds and Poets.* "A Bird Melody."

nature volumes: *Wake-Robin, Winter Sunshine, Birds and Poets, Locusts and Wild Honey,* and *Pepacton,* a small output for a man between the years of twenty-six and forty-six, yet one that is significant. Not a page of it had been written in haste, not a page that his later hand had found it necessary to revise. The primal freshness of youth is upon the books; they are as full of vitality and sweetness as a spring morning. Doubtless they are all the better for being the enthusiasms of hours stolen from a dry profession. It is tonic to read them. They are never at fault either in fact or in influence; they are the work of a trained observer, a scientist indeed, yet one who has gone to Nature like a priest to the holy of holies with the glow in his heart and the light on his face.

During the following decade, or, more exactly, the period between 1884 and 1894, he added four more books, three of them, *Fresh Fields, Signs and Seasons,* and *Riverby,* devoted to Nature, though with more and more of the coldly scientific spirit. These with the five earlier volumes stand alone as Burroughs's contribution to the field that he has made peculiarly his own. They contain his freshest and most spontaneous work.

To read these volumes is like going out ourselves into the forest with an expert guide who sees everything and who has at his command an unlimited store of anecdote and chatty reminiscence of birds and animals and even plants. To Burroughs, Nature was sufficient in herself. He loved her for the feelings she could arouse within him, for the recollections she could stir of the springtime of his life, for the beauty and the harmony that everywhere he found, and for the elemental laws that he saw on all sides at work and that stirred his curiosity. He had no desire to study Nature to secure evidences of a governing personality. He would draw no moral and offer no solutions of the problem of good and evil. Of the fortunes of the spirit of man he cared but little; as for himself, serene, he would fold his hands and wait. He was no mystic like Thoreau, listening for higher harmonies and peering eagerly beyond every headland to discover perchance the sources of the Nile. Upon him there was no necessity save to observe, to record, to discover new phenomena, to enlarge the store of facts, to walk flat-footed upon the material earth and observe the working of the physical mechanics about him and to teach others to observe them and to enjoy them.   To appreciate the difference between Burroughs and Thoreau one has but to read them side by side.   For instance, on March 21, 1853, Thoreau makes this entry:

As I was rising this crowning road, just beyond the old lime kiln, there leaked into my open ear the first peep of a hyla from some far pool . . . a note or two which scarcely rends the air, does no violence to the zephyr, but yet leaks through all obstacles and far over the downs to the ear of the listening naturalist, as it were the first faint cry of the new-born year, notwithstanding the notes of birds.   Where so long I have heard the prattling and moaning of the wind, what means this tenser, far-piercing sound?

Burroughs writes of the same subject in this way:

From what fact or event shall we really date the beginning of spring?   The little piping frogs usually furnish a good starting point. One spring I heard the first note on the 6th of April; the next on the 27th of February; but in reality the latter season was only about two weeks earlier than the former. . . . The little piper will sometimes climb a bullrush to which he clings like a sailor to a mast, and send forth his shrill call.   There is a Southern species, heard when you have reached the Potomac, whose note is far more harsh and crackling.   To stand on the verge of a swamp vocal with these, pains and stuns the ear.

Then in a foot-note:

The Southern species is called the green hyla.   I have since heard them in my neighborhood on the Hudson.

Never was there writer who kept his feet more firmly on solid earth.   He takes nothing for granted; he is satisfied only with the testimony of the senses, and his own senses.   Everything— example, allusion, figure of speech, subject and predicate—comes from him in the concrete.   Everything is specific, localized, dated.   He was in accord with his era that demanded only reality.   It is the task of the writer, he declared, "to pierce through our callousness and indifference and give us fresh impressions of things as they really are."

How permanent is such work?   How valuable is it?   Is Nature then a thing simply to be observed and classified and reduced to formulæ?   To determine the average day on which the bluebird comes, or the wild geese fly, or the hyla calls, is there virtue in that?   To Burroughs, Nature was a thing to be observed accurately for new facts to add to the known.   Of Thoreau he wrote: "Ten years of persistent spying and inspecting of Nature and no new thing found out." Do we ask of the poet and the seer simply for mere new material phenomena found out to add to our science? The supreme test that must come at last to all literature is the question: How much of human life is there in it? How much "Thus saith the Lord"? Who seeks for material things with eyes, however keen, and dreams of no sources of the Nile, no vision that may come perchance from supernatural power latent in bird and leaf and tendril, is a scientist, however charming he make his subject or however sympathetic be his attitude. Judged by such a standard, Burroughs falls short, far short of a place with the highest. He must decrease, while Thoreau increases. He must be placed at last among the scientists who have added facts and laws, while Thoreau is seated with the poets and the prophets.

But though he be thus without vision and without message, save as an invitation to come to material Nature and learn to observe is a message, Burroughs has a charm of manner and a picturesqueness of material that are to be found in few other writers of the period. His power lies in his simplicity and his sincerity. He is more familiar with his reader than Thoreau. He is never literary, never affected; he talks in the most natural way in the world; he tells story after story in the most artless way of homely little happenings that have passed under his own eye, and so charming is his talk that we surrender ourselves like children to listen as long as he will. When we read Thoreau we are always conscious of Thoreau. His epithets, his distinction of phrase, his sudden glimpses, his unexpected turns and climaxes, his humor, for in spite of Lowell's dictum, he is full of humor, keep us constantly in the presence of literature; but with Burroughs we are conscious of nothing save the birds and the season and the fields. We are walking with a delightful companion who knows everything and who points out new wonders at every step.

The poetry of Burroughs faded more and more from his work with every book, and the spirit of the scientist, of the trained observer impatient of everything not demonstrable by the senses, grew upon him, until at length it took full control and expressed itself as criticism, as scientific controversy, and as philosophical discussion. *Riverby*, 1894, with its prefatory note stating that the volume was "probably my last collection of out-of-door papers," marks the point of division between the two periods. If we follow the Riverside edition, at present [1914] the definitive canon, eight books preceded *Riverby* and eight followed it. The groups are not homogeneous; it is not to be gathered that on a certain date Burroughs abandoned one form of essay and devoted himself exclusively to another, but it is true that the work of his last period is prevailingly scientific and critical. His *Indoor Studies,* 1889, *Whitman, a Study,* and *Literary Values* are as distinctively works of literary criticism as Arnold's *Essays in Criticism;* his *Light of Day* discusses religion from the standpoint of the scientist; his *Ways of Nature* is scientific controversy; and his *Time and Change* and *The Summit of the Years* are philosophy.

It is in this second period that Burroughs has done his most distinctive work, though not perhaps his most spontaneous and delightful. By temperament and training he is a critic, a scientific critic, an analyzer and comparer. Only men of positive character, original forces, attract him: Emerson and Whitman, and later Wordsworth, Carlyle, and Arnold, men who molded the intellectual life of their age. His first published book had been a critical study, *Notes on Walt Whitman,* 1867, a work the most wonderful in many ways of his whole output. It came at a critical moment, in those pregnant closing years of the sixties, and it struck clear and full the note of the new period. Burroughs's later studies of Whitman are more finished and more mature than this never-republished volume, but they lack its clarion quality. It is more than a defense and an explanation of Whitman: it is a call to higher levels in literature and art, a call for a new definition of poetry, a condemnation of that softness and honey sweetness of song that had lured to weakness poets like Taylor and Stoddard. Poetry henceforth must be more than mere beauty for beauty's sake: it must have a message; it must come burning from a man's soul; it must thrill with human life.

And it is here that Burroughs stands as a dominating figure. He was the first of American critics to insist without compromise that poetry is poetry only when it is the voice of life—genuine, spontaneous, inevitable. "How rare," he complained in later years, "are real poems—poems that spring from real feeling, a

real throb of emotion, and not from a mere surface itching for expression.'' This has been the key to all his criticism: literature is
life, the voicing of a man's soul. Moreover, it is a voicing of the
national life, the expression of a nation's soul:

All the great imaginative writers of our century have felt, more
or less, the stir and fever of the century, and have been its priests and
prophets. The lesser poets have not felt these things. Had Poe been
greater or broader he would have felt them, so would Longfellow.
Neither went deep enough to touch the formative currents of our
social or religious or national life. In the past the great artist has
always been at ease in Zion; in our own day only the lesser artists
are at ease, unless we except Whitman, a man of unshaken faith, who
is absolutely optimistic, and whose joy and serenity come from the
breadth of his vision and the depth and universality of his sympathies.[3]

The literary criticism of Burroughs—four volumes of it in
the final edition, or nearly one-fourth of his whole output—may
be classed with the sanest and most illuminating critical work in
American literature. Lowell's criticism, brilliant as it is at
times, is overloaded with learning. He belongs to the school of
the early reviewers, ponderous and discursive. He makes use of
one-third of his space in his essay on Thoreau before he even
alludes to Thoreau. He is self-conscious, and self-satisfied; he
poses before his reader and enjoys the sensation caused by his
brilliant hit after hit. Stedman, too, is often more literary
than scientific. Often he uses epithet and phrase that have
nothing to commend them save their prettiness, their affectation of the odd or the antique. He is an appreciator of literature rather than critic in the modern sense. Burroughs, however, is always simple and direct. He is a scientific critic who
compares and classifies and seeks causes and effects. He works
not on the surface but always in the deeper currents and always
with the positive forces, those writers who have turned the direction of the literature and the thinking of their generation. In
marked contrast with Stedman, he can place Longfellow and
Landor among the minor singers: ''Their sympathies were
mainly outside their country and their times.'' He demands
that the poet have a message for his age. He says of Emerson:
''Emerson is a power because he partakes of a great spiritual
and intellectual movement of his times; he is unequivocally of
to-day and New England.''

[3] *Literary Values,* "Poetry and National Life," 184.

Burroughs's nature essays, charming as they are and full as they are of a delightful personality, will be superseded by others as careful and as charming; Burroughs's criticism was the voice of an era, and it will stand with the era. It was in his later years that he put forth his real message.

IV

John Burroughs is the historian of a small area; he has the home instinct, the hereditary farmer's love for his own fields and woods, and the haunts of his childhood. He is contemplative, tranquil, unassertive. John Muir was restless, fervid, Scotch by temperament as by birth, the very opposite of Burroughs. He was telescopic, not microscopic; his units were glaciers and Yosemites, Sierras and Gardens of the Gods.

The childhood of Muir was broken at eleven by the migration of his family from their native Scotland to the wilderness of Wisconsin, near the Fox River. After a boyhood in what literally was a new world to him, he started on his wanderings. By accident he found himself in the University of Wisconsin, where he studied for four years, the first author of note to be connected with the new state college movement, the democratizing of education. He pursued no regular course, but devoted himself to chemistry, botany, and other natural sciences that interested him, and then, to quote his own words, "wandered away on a glorious botanical and geological excursion, which has lasted nearly fifty years and is not yet completed, always happy and free, poor and rich, without thought of a diploma, of making a name, urged on and on through endless, inspiring, Godful beauty."

First he went to Florida, walking all the way, and sleeping on the ground wherever night overtook him; then he crossed to Cuba, with visions of South America and the Amazon beyond; but malarial fever, caused by sleeping on swampy ground, turned him away from the tropics toward California, where he arrived in 1868. The tremendous scenery of this west coast, those American Alps edging a continent from the Sierras to the Alaskan glaciers, so gripped his imagination and held him that he forgot everything save to look and wonder and worship. For years he explored the region, living months at a time in the forests of the

Yosemite, in the wild Alpine gardens and glacial meadows of the Sierra, in passes and cañons, moving as far north as Alaska, where he was the first to see the great glacier now called by his name, sleeping where night overtook him, disdaining blanket or shelter, and returning to civilization only when driven by necessity. After years of such wandering he became as familiar with the mighty region, the tremendous western wall of a continent, as Thoreau was with Concord or Burroughs was with the banks of the Pepacton.

Unlike Burroughs, Muir sent down no roots during his earlier formative period; he was a man without a country, anchored to no past, a soul unsatisfied, restless, bursting eagerly into untrodden areas, as hungry of heart as Thoreau, but with none of Thoreau's provincialism and transcendental theories. In 1869 in the Big Tuolumne Meadows he was told of a marvelous, but dangerous, region beyond, and his account of the episode illumines him as with a flash-light:

Recognizing the unsatisfiable longings of my Scotch Highland instincts, he threw out some hints concerning Bloody Cañon, and advised me to explore it. "I have never seen it myself," he said, "for I never was so unfortunate as to pass that way. But I have heard many a strange story about it, and I warrant you will at least find it wild enough." Next day I made up a bundle of bread, tied my note-book to my belt, and strode away in the bracing air, full of eager, indefinite hope.

His first out-of-doors article, a paper on the Yosemite glaciers, was published in the New York *Tribune* in 1871. Later he contributed to the *Overland Monthly,* to *Harper's,* and *Scribner's Monthly* articles that have in them an atmosphere unique in literature. What sweep and freedom, what vastness of scale, what abysses and gulfs, what wildernesses of peaks. It is like sweeping over a continent in a balloon. One is ever in the vast places: one thrills with the author's own excitement:

How boundless the day seems as we revel in these storm-beaten sky-gardens amidst so vast a congregation of onlooking mountains. . . . From garden to garden, ridge to ridge, I drifted enchanted, now on my knees gazing into the face of a daisy, now climbing again and again among the purple and azure flowers of the hemlocks, now down among the treasuries of the snow, or gazing afar over domes and peaks, lakes and woods, and the billowy glaciated fields of the upper Tuolumne, and trying to sketch them. In the midst of such beauty, pierced with its rays, one's body is all a tingling palate. Who would n't be a mountaineer! Up here all the world's prizes seem nothing.—July 26, 1869.

I chose a camping ground on the brink of one of the lakes, where a thicket of hemlock spruce sheltered me from the night wind. Then after making a tin cupful of tea, I sat by my campfire reflecting on the grandeur and significance of the glacial records I had seen. As the night advanced, the mighty rock-walls of my mountain mansion seemed to come nearer, while the starry sky in glorious brightness stretched across like a ceiling from wall to wall, and fitted closely down into all the spiky irregularities of the summits. Then, after a long fireside rest, and a glance at my note-book, I cut a few leafy branches for a bed, and fell into the clear, death-like sleep of the mountaineer.

No pain here, no dull empty hours, no fear of the past, no fear of the future. These blessed mountains are so compactly filled with God's beauty, no petty personal hope or experience has room to be. . . . Perched like a fly on this Yosemite dome, I gaze and sketch and bask, oftentimes settling down into dumb admiration without definite hope of ever learning much, yet with the longing, unresisting effort that lies at the door of hope, humbly prostrate before the vast display of God's power, and eager to offer self-denial and renunciation with eternal toil to learn any lesson in the divine manuscript.—July 20, 1869.

To read Muir is to be in the presence not of a tranquil, chatty companion like Burroughs, who saunters leisurely along the spring meadows listening for the birds just arrived the night before and comparing the dates of the hyla's first cry; it is rather to be with a tempestuous soul whose units are storms and mountain ranges and mighty glacial moraines, who strides excitedly along the bare tops of ragged peaks and rejoices in their vastness and awfulness, who cries, "Come with me along the glaciers and see God making landscapes!" One gets at the heart of Muir in an episode like this, the description of a terrific storm in the Yuba region in December, 1874:

The force of the gale was such that the most steadfast monarch of them all rocked down to its roots with a motion plainly perceptible when one leaned against it. Nature was holding high festival, and every fiber of the most rigid giants thrilled with glad excitement. I drifted on through the midst of this passionate music and motion across many a glen, from ridge to ridge; often falling in the lee of a rock for shelter, or to gaze and listen. Even when the glad anthem had swelled to its highest pitch, I could distinctly hear the varying tones of individual trees—spruce, and fir, and pine, and leafless oak.

. . . Toward midday, after a long, tingling scramble through copses of hazel and ceanothus, I gained the summit of the highest ridge in the neighborhood; and then it occurred to me that it would be a fine thing to climb one of the trees to obtain a wider outlook and get my ear close to the Æolian music of its topmost needles. . . . Being accustomed to climb trees in making botanical studies, I experienced no difficulty in reaching the top of this one, and never before did I enjoy so noble an exhilaration of motion. The slender tops fairly flapped and swished in the passionate torrent, bending and swirling backward and forward, round and round, tracing indescribable combinations of vertical and horizontal curves, while I clung with muscles firm braced, like a bobolink on a reed.

He had more humor than Burroughs, more even than Thoreau, a sly Scotch drollery that was never boisterous, never cynical. In the Bloody Cañon he meets the Mono Indians and finds little in them that is romantic:

The dirt on their faces was fairly stratified and seemed so ancient in some places and so undisturbed as almost to possess a geological significance. The older faces were, moreover, strangely blurred and divided into sections by furrows that looked like cleavage joints, suggesting exposure in a castaway condition on the mountains for ages. Viewed at a little distance they appeared as mere dirt specks on the landscape.

Like Thoreau, he was a mystic and a poet. He inherited mysticism with his Scotch blood as he inherited wildness and the love of freedom. He was not a mere naturalist, a mere scientist bent only on facts and laws: he was a searcher after God, even as Thoreau. As one reads him, one feels one's soul expanding, one's horizons widening, one's hands reaching out for the infinite. The message of Muir is compelling and eager:

Next to the light of the dawn on high mountain-tops, the alpenglow is the most impressive of all the terrestrial manifestations of God; . . . stay on this good fire mountain and spend the night among the stars. Watch their glorious bloom until dawn, and get one more baptism of light. Then, with fresh heart, go down to your work, and whatever your fate, under whatever ignorance or knowledge you may afterwards chance to suffer, you will remember these fine, wild views, and look back with joy.

And again after his joyous study of the water ouzel, a prose lyric, rapturous and infectious, he cries:

And so I might go on, writing words, words, words; but to what purpose? Go see him and love him, and through him as through a window look into Nature's warm heart.

The output of Muir, especially of books, has been small. To one who cares nothing for money and who is indifferent to fame, it is hard to offer inducements. He wrote only to please himself; he would not be commanded or bribed or begged, for why should one write words when the Sierras are in bloom and the winds are calling in the upper peaks? The public at large knows little of him, compared with what it knows of Burroughs or even of Thoreau. His influence, therefore, has been small. Though he had published many magazine articles, it was not until 1894 that he published *The Mountains of California,* his first book. *Our National Parks* came in 1901, and *My First Summer in the Sierra* in 1911. The last is Muir's journal, kept on the spot, full of the thrill and the freshness of the original day. If it be a sample of the journal which we have reason to believe that he kept with Thoreau-like thoroughness almost to the time of his death—he died in December, 1914—the best work of John Muir may even yet be in store.

Muir was more gentle than Thoreau or Burroughs, and more sympathetic with everything alive in the wild places which he loved. Unlike Burroughs, he has named the birds without a gun, and, unlike Thoreau, he has refused to kill even fish or rattlesnakes. He could look on even the repulsive lizards of his region, some of them veritable monsters in size and hideousness, with real affection:

Small fellow-mortals, gentle and guileless, they are easily tamed, and have beautiful eyes, expressing the clearest innocence, so that, in spite of prejudices brought from cool, lizardless countries, one must soon learn to like them. Even the horned toad of the plains and foothills, called horrid, is mild and gentle, with charming eyes, and so are the snake-like species found in the underbrush of the lower forests. . . . You will surely learn to like them, not only the bright ones, gorgeous as the rainbow, but the little ones, gray as lichened granite, and scarcely bigger than grasshoppers; and they will teach you that scales may cover as fine a nature as hair or feather or anything tailored.

And there is no more sympathetic, interpretative study among all the work of the nature-writers than his characterization of the Douglas squirrel of the Western mountains:

One never tires of this bright chip of Nature, this brave little voice crying in the wilderness, observing his many works and ways, and listening to his curious language. His musical, piney gossip is savory to the ear as balsam to the palate; and though he has not exactly the gift of song, some of his notes are sweet as those of a linnet—almost flute-like in softness; while others prick and tingle like thistles. He is the mocking-bird of squirrels, pouring forth mixed chatter and song like a perennial fountain, barking like a dog, screaming like a hawk, whistling like blackbirds and sparrows; while in bluff, audacious noisiness he is a jay.

Emerson visited Muir during his trip to the West Coast, climbed the precarious ladder that led to his room in the Yosemite sawmill, and passed a memorable afternoon. "He is more wonderful than Thoreau," he said, and he tried long to induce him to leave the mountains for the East, and to live in the midst of men. But to Muir the leaving of the Yosemite and the Sierra was like leaving God Himself. To him the city was the place of unnatural burdens, of money that dulls and kills the finest things of the soul, of separation from all that is really vital in the life of man.

His style is marked by vividness and fervid power. He makes a scene stand out with sharpness. He is original; there are in his work no traces of other writings save those of the Bible, with which he was saturated, and at rare intervals of Thoreau. Often there is a rhetorical ring to his page, a resonant fullness of tone that can be described only by the word eloquent. In passages describing storm or mountain majesty there is a thrill, an excitement, that are infectious. The prose of John Muir may be summed up as sincere and vigorous, without trace of self-consciousness or of straining for effect. Few writers of any period of American literature have within their work more elements of promise as they go down to the generations to come.

V

Beginning with the late sixties, out-of-door themes more and more took possession of American literature. Burroughs was only one in an increasing throng of writers; he was the best known and most stimulating, and soon, therefore, the leader and inspirer. The mid-nineteenth century had been effeminate in the bulk of its literary product; it had been a thing of indoors and of books: the new after-the-war spirit was masculine even at times to coarseness and brutality. Maurice Thompson (1844–1901), one of the earliest of the new period, perceived the bent of the age with clearness. "We are nothing better than

refined and enlightened savages," he wrote in 1878. "The wild
side of the prism of humanity still offers its pleasures to us. . . .
Sport, by which is meant pleasant physical and mental exercise combined—play in the best sense—is a requirement of this
wild element, this glossed over heathen side of our being, and
the bow is its natural implement." [4]   It was the apology of the
old school for the new era of sport. Thompson would direct
these heathen energies toward archery, since it was a sport that
appealed to the imagination and that took its devotees into the
forests and the swamps, but there was no directing of the resurg-
ing forces. Baseball and football sprang up in the seventies and
grew swiftly into hitherto unheard-of proportions. Yachting,
camping, mountaineering, summer tramping in the woods and
the borders of civilization swiftly became popular. The Adirondacks and the Maine forests and the White Mountains sprang
into new prominence. As early as 1869 Stedman had complained
that *The Blameless Prince* lay almost dead on the shelves while
such books as Murray's *Adventures in the Wilderness* sold enormously. For a time indeed W. H. H. Murray—"Adirondack
Murray"—did vie even with Bonner's *Ledger* in popularity.
He threw about the wilderness an alluring, half romantic atmosphere that appealed to the popular imagination and sent
forth, eager and compelling, what in later days came to be known
as "the call of the wild." His books have not lasted. There
is about them a declamatory, artificial element that sprang too
often from the intellect rather than the heart. Charles Dudley
Warner in his *In the Wilderness*, 1878, and William H. Gibson
in such books as *Camp Life in the Woods*, sympathetically illustrated by their author, were far more sincere and wholesome.
Everywhere for a decade or more there was appeal for a return
to the natural and the free, to the open-air games of the old
English days, to hunting and trapping and camping—a masculine, red-blooded resurgence of the savage, a return to the wild.
The earlier phase of the period may be said to have culminated
in 1882 with the founding of *Outing*, a magazine devoted wholly
to activities in the open air.

The later eighties and the nineties are the period of the bird
books. C. C. Abbott's *A Naturalist's Rambles About Home*,
1884; Olive Thorne Miller's *Bird Ways*, 1885; Bradford Tor-

[4] *The Witchery of Archery*, 1878.

rey's *Birds in the Bush,* 1885; and Florence Merriam Bailey's *Birds Through an Opera Glass,* 1889, may be taken as representative. Bird life and bird ways for a period became a fad; enthusiastic observers sprang up everywhere; scientific treatises and check lists and identification guides like Chapman's *Handbook of Birds of Eastern North America,* began to appear in numbers. What the novelists of locality were doing for the unusual human types in isolated corners of the land, the nature writers were doing for the birds.

Of all the later mass of Nature writings, however, very little is possessed of literary distinction. Very largely it is journalistic in style and scientific in spirit. Only one out of the later group, Bradford Torrey, compels attention. Beyond a doubt it is already safe to place him next in order after Burroughs and Muir. He is more of an artist than Burroughs, and he is more literary and finished than Muir. In his attitude toward Nature he is like Thoreau—sensitive, sympathetic, reverent. It was he who edited the journals of Thoreau in their final form, and it was he also who after that experience wrote what is undoubtedly the most discriminating study that has yet been made of the great mystic naturalist.

BIBLIOGRAPHY

JOHN BURROUGHS. (1837———.) *Notes on Walt Whitman, as Poet and Person,* New York, 1867; *Wake-Robin,* 1871; *Winter Sunshine,* 1875; *Birds and Poets,* 1877; *Locusts and Wild Honey,* 1879; *Pepacton,* 1881; *Fresh Fields,* 1884; *Signs and Seasons,* 1886; *Indoor Studies,* 1889; *Riverby,* 1894; *Whitman, a Study,* 1896; *The Light of Day,* 1900; *Literary Values,* 1904; *Far and Near,* 1904; *Ways of Nature,* 1905; *Leaf and Tendril,* 1908; *Time and Change,* 1912; *The Summit of the Years,* 1913; *Our Friend John Burroughs.* By Clara Barrus. 1914.

JOHN MUIR. (1838–1914.) "Studies in the Sierras," a series of papers in *Scribner's Monthly,* 1878; *The Mountains of California,* 1894; *Our National Parks,* 1901; *Stickeen, the Story of a Dog,* 1909; *My First Summer in the Sierra,* 1911; *The Story of My Boyhood and Youth,* 1913; *Letters to a Friend,* 1915.

WILLIAM HAMILTON GIBSON. (1850–1896.) *Camp Life in the Woods and the Tricks of Trapping and Trap-Making,* 1876; *Pastoral Days, or Memories of a New England Year,* 1882; *Highways and Byways, or Saunterings in New England,* 1883; *Happy Hunting Grounds, a Tribute to the Woods and Fields,* 1886; *Strolls by Starlight and Sunshine,* 1890; *Sharp Eyes,* 1891; *Our Edible Toadstools and Mushrooms,* 1895.

CHARLES CONRAD ABBOTT. (1843———.) *The Stone Age in New Jersey,*

1876; *Primitive Industry*, 1881; *A Naturalist's Rambles About Home*, 1884; *Upland and Meadow*, 1886; *Wasteland Wanderings*, 1887; *Days out of Doors*, 1889; *Outings at Odd Times*, 1890; *Recent Rambles*, 1892; *Outings in a Tree-Top*, 1894; *The Birds About Us*, 1894; *Notes of the Night*, 1895; *Birdland Echoes*, 1896; *The Freedom of the Fields*, 1898; *Clear Skies and Cloudy*, 1899; *In Nature's Realm*, 1900.

"OLIVE THORNE MILLER"—HARRIET MANN MILLER. (1831——.) *Little Folks in Feathers and Fur*, 1879; *Queer Pets at Marcy's*, 1880; *Bird Ways*, 1885; *In Nesting Time*, 1888; *Four Handed Folk*, 1890; *Little Brothers of the Air*, 1890; *Bird-Lover in the West*, 1894; *Upon the Tree Tops*, 1896; *The First Book of Birds*, 1899; *True Bird Stories*, 1903; *With the Birds in Maine*, 1904; and others.

BRADFORD TORREY. (1843–1912.) *Birds in the Bush*, 1885; *A Rambler's Lease*, 1889; *The Foot-Path Way*, 1892; *A Florida Sketch-Book*, 1894; *Spring Notes from Tennessee*, 1896; *A World of Green Hills*, 1898; *Every-Day Birds*, 1900; *Footing It in Franconia*, 1900; *The Clerk of the Woods*, 1903; *Nature's Invitation*, 1904; *Friends on the Shelf*, 1906.

FLORENCE MERRIAM BAILEY. (1863——.) *Birds Through an Opera Glass*, 1889; *My Summer in a Mormon Village*, 1895; *A Birding on a Bronco*, 1896; *Birds of Village and Field*, 1898; *Handbook of Birds of Western United States*, 1902.

FRANK BOLLES. (1856–1894.) *Land of the Lingering Snow*, 1891; *At the North of Bearcamp Water: Chronicles of a Stroller in New England from July to December*, 1893; *From Blomidon to Smoky*, 1895.

CHAPTER IX

Whitman and Thoreau stand as the two prophets of the mid century, both of them offspring of the Transcendental movement, pushing its theories to their logical end, both of them voices in the wilderness crying to deaf or angry ears, both of them unheeded until a new generation had arisen to whom they had become but names and books. Thoreau was born in 1817; Whitman in 1819, the year of Lowell, Story, Parsons, Herman Melville, J. G. Holland, Julia Ward Howe, and E. P. Whipple, and of the Victorians, Kingsley, Ruskin, George Eliot, and Arthur Hugh Clough. Whitman published *Leaves of Grass,* his first significant volume, in 1855, the year of *Hiawatha,* of *Maud,* and of Arnold's *Poems.* He issued it again in 1856 and again in 1860—a strange nondescript book rendered all the more strange by the fact, thoroughly advertised in the second edition, that it had won from Emerson the words: ''I find it the most extraordinary piece of wit and wisdom that America has yet contributed. . . . I greet you at the beginning of a great career.'' But even the compelling name of Emerson could not sell the book; little notice, in fact, was taken of it save as a few voices expressed horror and anger; and when in 1862 Whitman became lost in the confusion of the war, he had made not so much impression upon America as had Thoreau at the time of his death that same year. Until well into the seventies Walt Whitman seemed only a curious phenomenon in an age grown accustomed to curious phenomena.

The antecedents and the early training of Whitman were far from literary. He came from a race of Long Island farmers who had adhered to one spot for generations. No American was ever more completely a product of our own soil.

My tongue, every atom of my blood, formed from this soil, this air,
Born here of parents born here,
From parents the same, and their parents' parents the same.

They were crude, vigorous plowmen, unbookish and elemental.

The father was the first to break from the soil and the ancestral environment, but he left it only to become a laborer on buildings in the neighboring city of Brooklyn.

The boyhood of Whitman was passed in the city, though with long vacations in the home of his grandparents on Long Island. His schooling was brief and desultory. He left the schools at twelve to become office boy for a lawyer and from that time on he drifted aimlessly from one thing to another, serving for brief periods as doctor's clerk, compositor in a country printing office, school teacher in various localities, editor and proprietor of a rural weekly, stump speaker in the campaign of 1840, editor of various small journals, contributor of Hawthornesque stories and sketches to papers and magazines, writer of a melodramatic novel, and in 1846 editor of the Brooklyn *Daily Eagle*. But he could hold to nothing long. In 1848 he was induced by a stranger who had taken a fancy to him to go to New Orleans as editor of the *Crescent* newspaper, but within a year he was back again in New York, where for the next few years he maintained a half-loafing, half-working connection with several papers and periodicals.

It was during this period that he made himself so thoroughly familiar with the middle and lower strata of New York City life. He spent hours of every day riding on Broadway vehicles and on Fulton ferry boats and making himself boon companion of all he met. He knew the city as Muir knew the peaks and mountain gardens of the Sierra, and he took the same delight in discovering a new specimen of humanity on a boat or an omnibus that Muir might take in finding a new plant on an Alaska glacier.

I knew all the drivers then, Broadway Jack, Dressmaker, Balky Bill, George Storms, Old Eliphant, his brother, Young Eliphant (who came afterward), Tippy, Pop Rice, Big Frank, Yellow Joe, Pete Callahan, Patsey Dee, and dozens more; for there were hundreds. They had immense qualities, largely animal—eating, drinking, women—great personal pride, in their way—perhaps a few slouches here and there, but I should have trusted the general run of them, in their simple good will and honor, under all circumstances.[1]

Almost daily, later ('50 to '60), I cross'd on the boats, often up in the pilot-houses where I could get a full sweep, absorbing shows, ac-

[1] *Specimen Days.*

companiments, surroundings. What oceanic currents, eddies, under-
neath—the great tides of humanity also, with ever-shifting movements.
Indeed, I have always had a passion for ferries; to me they afford
inimitable, streaming, never-failing, living poems. The river and bay
scenery, all about New York island, any time of a fine day—hurrying,
splashing sea-tides—the changing panorama of steamers, all sizes.
. . . My old pilot friends, the Balsirs, Johnny Cole, Ira Smith, William White, and my young ferry friend, Tom Gere—how well I remember them all.[2]

I find in this visit to New York, and the daily contact and rapport
with its myriad people, on the scale of the oceans and tides the best,
most effective medicine my soul has yet partaken—the grandest physical habitat and surroundings of land and water the globe affords.[1]

The earlier Whitman is a man *par excellence* of the city as
Muir is of the mountains and Thoreau of the woods.

I

A jungle of writings has sprung up about Whitman; as many
as four biographies of him have appeared in a single year, yet
aside from two or three careful studies, like those of Perry and
Carpenter, no really scholarly or unbiased work has been issued.
Before the last word can be spoken of the poet there must be an
adequate text with variorum readings and chronological arrange-
ment. The present definitive edition is a chaos, almost useless
for purposes of study. New and old are mixed indiscrim-
inatingly. The "Chants Democratic," for instance, of the earlier
editions have been dismembered and scattered from end to end
of the book. All of the older poems were in constant state of
revision from edition to edition, until now patches from every
period of the poet's life may be found on many of them. Large
sections of the earlier editions were omitted, enough indeed at
one time and another to make up a volume. The fact is important, since the material rejected by a poet at different stages in
his evolution often tells much concerning his art.

There is, moreover, a strange dearth of biographical material
at critical points in Whitman's life, notably during that formative period preceding the first issue of *Leaves of Grass*. In his
later years he talked of his own experiences and aims and ideals
with the utmost freedom; through Traubel, his Boswell, he put

[2] *Specimen Days.*

himself on record with minuteness; his poetic work is all autobiographical; and almost all of his editions are prefaced by long
explanations and defenses, yet of the really significant periods of
his life we know little. A crude man of the people, a Broadway
rough, as he described himself, who has been writing very ordinary poems and stories and editorials—how ordinary we can
easily judge, for very many of them have been preserved—
suddenly brings out a book of poems as unlike any earlier work
of his or any previous work of his nation or language as an issue
of the *Amaranth* or the *Gem* would be unlike the book of *Amos*.
What brought about this remarkable climax? Was it the result of an evolution within the poet's soul, an evolution extend-
ing over a period of years? Did it come as a sudden inspiration
or as a deliberate consummation after a study of models? We
do not know. There are no contemporary letters, no transition
poems, no testimony of any friend to whom the poet laid bare his
soul. At one period we have verses like these:

> We are all docile dough-faces,
>   They knead us with the fist,
> They, the dashing Southern lords,
>   We labor as they list;
> For them we speak—or hold our tongues,
>   For them we turn and twist.

Then suddenly without warning we have this:

> Free, fresh, savage,
> Fluent, luxuriant, self-content, fond of persons and places,
> Fond of fish-shape Paumanok, where I was born,
> Fond of the sea—lusty-begotten and various,
> Boy of the Mannahatta, the city of ships, my city,
>   .   .   .   .
> Solitary, singing in the West, I strike up for a new world.

That is the problem of Walt Whitman, a problem the most
baffling and the most fascinating in the later range of American
literature.

II

There can be little doubt that the primal impulse in the creation of *Leaves of Grass* came from the intellectual and moral un-
rest of the thirties and the forties. Whitman caught late, perhaps latest of all the writers of the period, the Transcendental

spirit that had so unsettled America and the rest of the world
as well. "What a fertility of projects for the salvation of the
world!" Emerson had cried in 1844. Who "will ever forget what
was somewhat vaguely called the 'Transcendental Movement' of
thirty years ago"? Lowell had asked in 1865. "Apparently
set astir by Carlyle's essays on the 'Signs of the Times,' and on
'History,' the final and more immediate impulse seemed to be
given by 'Sartor Resartus.' At least the republication in Boston of that wonderful Abraham à Sancta Clara sermon on Falstaff's text of the miserable forked radish gave the signal for
a sudden mental and moral mutiny. . . . The nameless eagle of
the tree Ygdrasil was about to set at last, and wild-eyed enthusi-
asts rushed from all sides, eager to thrust under the mystic
bird that chalk egg from which the newer and fairer creation
was to be hatched in due time." [3] Whitman was a product of
this ferment. He took its exaggerations and its wild dreams as
solemn fact. He read Emerson and adopted his philosophy
literally and completely: "Whoso would be a man must be a
nonconformist." "He who would gather immortal palms must
not be hindered by the name of goodness." "Insist on yourself; never imitate." "Welcome evermore to gods and men is
the self-helping man. For him all doors are flung wide; him all
tongues greet, all honors crown, all eyes follow with desire. Our
love goes out to him." "Trust thyself; every heart vibrates to
that iron string." "With consistency a great soul has simply
nothing to do," and so on and on.

All criticism of Whitman must begin with the fact that he
was uneducated even to ignorance. He felt rather than
thought. Of the intellectual life in the broader sense—science,
analysis, patient investigation—he knew nothing. When he read
he read tumultuously, without horizon, using his emotions and
his half conceptions as interpreters. A parallel may be drawn
between him and that other typical product of the era, Mrs.
Eddy, the founder of the Christian Science cult. Both were
mystics, almost pathologically so; both were electric with the urge
of physical health; both were acted upon by the transcendental
spirit of the era; both were utterly without humor; and both in
all seriousness set about to establish a new conception of religion.

[3] Works, i: 361.

I too, following many, and followed by many, inaugurate a Religion.

To Whitman the religious leader of an era was its poet. He would broaden the conception of the Poet until he made of him the leader and the savior of his age.

The maker of poems settles justice, reality, immortality,
His insight and power encircle things and the human race,
He is the glory and extract, thus far, of things, and of the human race.
The singers do not beget—only THE POET begets,
The singers are welcomed, understood, appear often enough—but rare
    has the day been, likewise the spot, of the birth of the maker of
    poems,
Not every century, or every five centuries, has contained such a day,
    for all its names.

With assurance really sublime he announced himself as this poet of the new era, this new prophet of the ages:

Bearded, sunburnt, gray-necked, forbidding, I have arrived
To be wrestled with.

I know perfectly well my own egotism,
I know my omnivorous words, and I cannot say any less,
And would fetch you, whoever you are, flush with myself.

He hails as comrade and fellow savior even Him who was crucified:

We few, equals, indifferent of lands, indifferent of times,
We, inclosers of all continents, all castes—allower of all theologies,
Compassionaters, perceivers, rapport of men,
We walk silent among disputes and assertions, but reject not the dis-
    puters, nor anything that is asserted,
We hear the bawling and din—we are reached at by divisions, jeal-
    ousies, recriminations on every side,
They close peremptorily upon us to surround us, my comrade,
Yet we walk unheld, free, the whole earth over, journeying up and
    down, till we make our ineffaceable mark upon time and the di-
    verse eras,
Till we saturate time and eras, that the men and women of races, ages
    to come, may prove brethren and lovers as we are.

He too would give his life to the lowly and the oppressed; he too would eat with publicans and sinners; he too would raise the sick and the dying:

To any one dying—thither I speed, and twist the knob of the door,
Turn the bed-clothes toward the foot of the bed,

Let the physician and the priest go home.
I seize the descending man, and raise him with resistless will.
O despairer, here is my neck,
By God! you shall not go down! Hang your whole weight upon me.
I dilate you with tremendous breath—I buoy you up,
Every room of the house do I fill with an armed force,
Lovers of me, bafflers of graves.
Sleep! I and they keep guard all night,
Not doubt—not decease shall dare to lay finger upon you,
I have embraced you.

The poetic message of Whitman, the new message that was, as he believed, "to drop in the earth the germs of a greater religion," he summed up himself in the phrase "The greatness of Love and Democracy"—Love meaning comradeship, hearty "hail, fellow, well met" to all men alike; Democracy meaning the equality of all things and all men—*en masse*. He is to be the poet of the East and the West, the North and the South alike; he is to be the poet of all occupations, and of all sorts and conditions of men. He salutes the whole world *in toto* and in detail. A great part of ·*Leaves of Grass* is taken up with enumerations of the universality and the detail of his poetic sympathy. He covers the nation with the accuracy of a gazetteer, and he enumerates its industries and its population, simply that he may announce, "I am the poet of these also."

The appearance of Whitman marks the first positive resurgence of masculinity in mid-century America. He came as the first loud protest against sentimentalism, against Longfellowism, against a prudish drawing-room literature from which all life and masculine coarseness had been refined. Whitman broke into the American drawing-room as a hairy barbarian, uncouth and unsqueamish, a Goth let loose among ladies, a Vandal smashing the bric-à-brac of an over-refined generation. He came in with a sudden leap, unlooked-for, unannounced, in all his nakedness and vulgarity like a primitive man, and proceeded to sound his barbaric yawp over the roofs of the world. He mixed high and low, blab and divinity, because he knew no better. Like the savage that he was he adorned himself with scraps of feathers from his reading—fine words: *libertad, camerado, ma femme, ambulanza, enfans d'Adam;* half understood fragments of modern science; wild figures of speech from the Transcendental dreamers which he took literally and pushed to their logical limit.

And he poured it all out in a mélange without coherence or logical
sequence: poetry and slang, bravado and egotism, trash and divinity and dirt.   At one moment he sings:

Smile, O voluptuous, cool-breathed Earth!
Earth of the slumbering and liquid trees!
Earth of departed sunset! Earth of the mountains, misty-topt!
Earth of the vitreous pour of the full moon, just tinged with blue!
Earth of shine and dark, mottling the tide of the river!
Earth of the limpid gray of clouds, brighter and clearer for my sake!
Far-swooping elbowed Earth! Rich, apple-blossomed Earth!
Smile, for Your Lover comes!

And the next moment be bursts out:

Earth! you seem to look for something at my hands,
Say, old Top-knot! what do you want?

And he does it all honestly, unsmilingly, and ignorantly.   It is
because he had so small a horizon that he seems so to project beyond the horizon.   To understand him one must understand first
his ignorance.

But if he is a savage, he has also the vigor and dash and
abounding health of the savage.   He enters upon his work with
unction and perfect abandonment; his lines shout and rush and
set the blood of his reader thrilling like a series of war whoops.
His first poem, the ''Proto-Leaf,'' is, to say the least, exhilarating.
Read straight through aloud with resonant voice, it arouses in
the reader a strange kind of excitement.   The author of it was
young, in the very tempest of perfect physical health, and he had
all of the youth's eagerness to change the course of things.   His
work is as much a gospel of physical perfection as is *Science and
Health*.   It is full of the impetuous passions of youth.   It is not
the philosophizing of an old savant, or of an observer experienced in life, it is the compelling arrogance of a young man in
full blood, sure of himself, eager to reform the universe.   The
poems indeed are

Health chants—joy chants—robust chants of young men.

The physical as yet is supreme.   Of the higher laws of sacrifice,
of self-effacement, of character that builds its own aristocracy and
draws lines through even the most democratic mass, the poet
knows really nothing.   He may talk, but as yet it is talk without
basis of experience.

The poems are youthful in still another way: they are of the young soil of America; they are American absolutely, in spirit, in color, in outlook. Like Thoreau, Whitman never had all his life long any desire to visit any other land than his own. He was obsessed, intoxicated, with America. He began his reckoning of time with the year 1775 and dated his first book "the year 80 of the States." A large section of his poems is taken up with loving particularization of the land—not of New England and New York alone, but of the whole of it, every nook and corner of it. For the first time America had a poet who was as broad as her whole extent and who could dwell lovingly on every river and mountain and village from Atlantic to Pacific.

Take my leaves, America!
Make welcome for them everywhere, for they are your own offspring.
Surround them, East and West!

He glories in the heroic deeds of America, the sea fight of John Paul Jones, the defense of the Alamo, and his characterization of the various sections of the land thrills one and exhilarates one like a glimpse of the flag. What a spread, continent-wide, free-aired and vast—"Far breath'd land, Arctic braced! Mexican breezed!"—one gets in the crescendo beginning:

O the lands!
Lands scorning invaders! Interlinked, food-yielding lands!

It is the first *all* American thrill in our literature.

The new literary form adopted by Whitman was not a deliberate and studied revolt from the conventional forms of the times: it was rather a discovery of Walt Whitman by himself. Style is the man: the "easily written, loose-fingered chords" of his chant, unrimed, lawless; this was Whitman himself. How he found it or when he found it, matters not greatly. It is possible that he got a hint from his reading of Ossian or of the Bible or of Eastern literature, but we know that at the end it came spontaneously. He was too indolent to elaborate for himself a deliberate metrical system, he was too lawless of soul to be bound by the old prosody. Whatever he wrote must loaf along with perfect freedom, unpolished, haphazard, incoherent. The adjective that best describes his style is *loose*—not logical, rambling, suggestive. His mind saunters everywhither and does not concentrate. In other words, it is an uneducated mind, an unfocused mind, a primitive mind.

The result was that, despite Whitman's freshness and force and stirring Americanism, he made little impression in the decade following the first *Leaves of Grass*. Emerson's commendation of him had been caused by his originality and his uncouth power, but none of the others of the mid-century school could see anything in the poems save vulgarity and egotistic posing. Lowell from first to last viewed him with aversion; Whittier burned the book at once as a nasty thing that had soiled him. The school of Keats and Tennyson, of Longfellow and Willis, ruled American literature with tyrannic power, and it was too early for successful revolution.

III

The Civil War found Whitman young; it left him an old man. There seems to have been no midde-age period in his life. He had matured with slowness; at forty, when he issued the 1860 *Leaves of Grass,* he was in the very prime of youth, the physical still central. There had been no suffering in his life, no grip of experience; he spoke much of the soul, but the soul was still of secondary importance. He wrote to his mother in 1862:

I believe I weigh about two hundred, and as to my face (so scarlet) and my beard and neck, they are terrible to behold. I fancy the reason I am able to do some good in the hospitals among the poor languishing and wounded boys, is that I am so large and well—indeed like a great wild buffalo, with much hair. Many of the soldiers are from the West, and far North, and they take to a man that has not the bleached, shiny and shaven cut of the cities and the East.[3]

The world of the 1860 *Leaves of Grass* is a world as viewed by a perfectly healthy young man, who has had his way to the full. The appeal of it is physiological rather than spiritual. It ends the first period of Whitman's poetical life.

His next book, *Drum-Taps,* came in 1866. Between the two had come the hospital experience of 1862–1865, from which had emerged the Whitman of the later period.

He had been drawn into this hospital experience, as into everything else in his life, almost by accident. It had come to him

4 *The Wound-Dresser.*

after no hard-fought battle with himself; it was the result of no compelling convictions. The war had progressed for a year before it assumed concrete proportions for him. It required the news that his brother was lying desperately wounded at Fredericksburg to move his imagination. When he had arrived at the front and had found his brother in no serious condition after all, he had drifted almost by accident into the misery of the ambulance trains and the hospitals, and before he had realized it, he was in the midst of the army nurses, working as if he had volunteered for the service. And thus he had drifted on to the end of the war, a self-appointed hospital worker, touching and helping thousands of sinking lives.

And he gave during those three years not only his youth but also his health of body. He was weakened at length with malaria and infected with blood poisoning from a wound that he had dressed. Moreover, the experience drained him on the side of his emotions and his nervous vitality until he went home to become at last paralytic and neurotic. The strain upon him he has described with a realism that unnerves one:

I dress the perforated shoulder, the foot with the bullet-wound,
Cleanse the one with a gnawing and putrid gangrene, so sickening, so offensive,
While the attendant stands beside me holding the tray and pail.
I am faithful, I do not give out,
The fractur'd thigh, the knee, the wound in the abdomen,
These and more I dress with impassive hand (yet deep in my breast a fire, a burning flame).

The war allowed Whitman to put into practice all his young manhood's dream of saviorship. It turned him from a preacher into a prophet and a man of action, one who took his earlier message and illustrated it at every point with works. It awakened within him a new ideal of life. He had been dealing heretofore with words:

Words! book-words! What are you?
Words no more, for harken and see,
My song is there in the open air, and I must sing,
With the banner and pennant a-flapping.

No longer does he exult in his mere physical body. Lines like these he now edits from his early editions:

How dare a sick man, or an obedient man, write poems for these States?

Also lines like these:

O to be relieved of distinctions! to make as much of vices as virtues!
O to level occupations and the sexes!   O to bring all to common ground!
    O adhesiveness!
O the pensive aching to be together,—you know not why, and I know
    not why.

He omits everywhere freely now from the early editions, not
from the "Children of Adam," however, though Emerson advised it with earnestness.   The Whitmans were an obstinate race.
"As obstinate as a Whitman," had been a degree of comparison; and here was one of them who had taken a position before
the world and had maintained it in the face of persecution.   Retreat would be impossible; but it is noteworthy that he wrote no
more poems of sex and that he put forth no more of his tall talk
and braggadocio.   Swiftly he had become the poet of the larger
life: the immaterial in man, the soul.

Drum-Taps, 1866, gives us the first glimpse of this new Whitman.   The tremendous poem, "Rise, O Days, from Your Fathom-
less Deeps," marks the transition.   In it he declares that he had,
with hunger of soul, devoured only what earth had given him,
that he had sought to content himself simply with nature and the
material world.

> Yet there with my soul I fed, I fed content, supercilious.

He does not condemn this earlier phase of his development:

'T was well, O soul—'t was a good preparation you gave me,
Now we advance our latest and ampler hunger to fill.
Now we go forth to receive what the earth and the sea never gave us.

Now for the first time he realizes the meaning of Democracy, the
deep inner meaning of Man and America.

Long had I walk'd my cities, my country roads through farms, only
    half satisfied,
One doubt nauseous undulating like a snake, crawl'd on the ground
    before me,
Continually preceding my steps, turning upon me oft, ironically hissing
    low;
The cities I loved so well I abandon'd and left, I sped to the certainties
    suitable to me,
Hungering, hungering, hungering, for primal energies and Nature's
    dauntlessness,
I refresh'd myself with it only, I could relish it only,

I waited the bursting forth of the pent fire—on the water and air I
     waited long;
But now I no longer wait, I am fully satisfied, I am glutted,
I have witness'd the true lightning, I have witness'd my cities electric,
I have lived to behold man burst forth.

It is the same thrill that had aroused Stedman, and made him
proud for the first time of his country. Henceforth the poet will
sing of Men—men not as magnificent bodies, but as triumphant
souls. *Drum-Taps* fairly quivers and sobs and shouts with a new
life. America has risen at last—one feels it in every line. The
book gives more of the actual soul of the great conflict and of the
new spirit that arose from it than any other book ever written.
"Come up from the Fields, Father," tells with simple pathos
that chief tragedy of the war, the death message brought to
parents; "The Wound-Dresser" pictures with a realism almost
terrifying the horrors of the hospitals after a battle; "Beat!
Beat! Drums!" arouses like a bugle call; such sketches as "Cavalry Crossing a Ford," "Bivouac on a Mountain Side," and "A
March in the Ranks Hard-Prest, and the Road Unknown," are
full of the thrill and the excitement of war; and finally the poems
in "Memories of President Lincoln": among them "When
Lilacs Last in the Dooryard Bloom'd," "O Captain! My Captain!" and "Hush'd Be the Camps To-day," come near to the
highest places yet won by elegaic verse in English.

IV

In June, 1865, after he had served for a short time as a clerk
in the Interior Department at Washington, Whitman had been
discharged on the ground that he kept in his desk an indecent
book of which he was the author. As a result of the episode, W.
D. O'Connor, an impetuous young journalist, published in September the same year a pamphlet entitled *The Good Gray Poet*,
defending Whitman as a man incapable of grossness and hailing
him as a new force in American literature. Despite its extravagance and its manifest special pleading, the little book is a notable
one, a document indeed in the history of the new literary period.
It recognized that a new era was opening, one that was to be
original and intensely American.

It [*Leaves of Grass*] is, in the first place, a work purely and entirely
American, autochthonic, sprung from our own soil; no savor of Europe

nor of the past, nor of any other literature in it; a vast carol of our
own land, and of its Present and Future; the strong and haughty psalm
of the Republic. There is not one other book, I care not whose, of
which this can be said. I weigh my words and have considered well.
Every other book by an American author implies, both in form and
substance, I cannot even say the European, but the British mind. The
shadow of Temple Bar and Arthur's Seat lies dark on all our letters.
Intellectually, we are still a dependency of Great Britain, and one word
—colonial—comprehends and stamps our literature. . . . At most, our
best books were but struggling beams; behold in *Leaves of Grass* the
immense and absolute sunrise! It is all our own! The nation is in it!
In form a series of chants, in substance it is an epic of America. It is
distinctly and utterly American. Without model, without imitation,
without reminiscence, it is evolved entirely from our own polity and
popular life.

The defense fell for the most part on deaf ears. It had been
Whitman's dream that the great poet of democracy was to be
the idol of the common people, the poet loved and read even by
the illiterate.

The woodman that takes his ax and jug with him shall take me with
    him all day,
The farm-boy, plowing in the field, feels good at the sound of my voice.

But the common people heard him not gladly: they preferred
Longfellow. The American average man—"en masse"—sees no
poetry in him. Moreover, he has been rejected very largely by
the more educated. It has been his curious experience to be
repudiated by democratic America and to be accepted and hailed
as a prophet by the aristocratic intellectual classes of England
and of Europe generally. Swinburne, W. M. Rossetti, Symonds,
Dowden, Saintsbury, Tennyson, and very many others accepted
him early and at full value, as did also Freiligrath, Schmidt,
and Björnson. A cult early sprang up about him, one composed
largely of mystics, and revolutionists, and reformers in all fields.

In 1871, Whitman issued what unquestionably is his most
notable prose work, *Democratic Vistas*. It is pitched in major
key: it swells O'Connor's piping note into a trumpet blast.
Boldly and radically it called for a new school of literature.
The old is outgrown, it cried; the new is upon us; make ready
for the great tide of Democratic poetry and prose that even now
is sweeping away the old landmarks.

To the new era it was what Emerson's *American Scholar* was

to the period that had opened in the thirties. It was our last great declaration of literary independence. Emerson, the Harvard scholar, last of a long line of intellectual clergymen, had pleaded for the aristocracy of literature, the American scholar, the man thinking his own thoughts, alone, the set-apart man of his generation; Whitman pleaded for the democracy of literature, for an American literature that was the product of the mass, a literature of the people, for the people, and by the people. Emerson had spoken as an oracle: ''What crowded and breathless aisles! What windows clustering with eager heads!'' Whitman was as one crying in the wilderness, uncouth, unheeded save by the few. Emerson was the clarion voice of Harvard; Whitman was the voice of the great movement that so soon was to take away the scepter from Harvard and transfer it upon the strong new learning of the West. His message was clear and it came with Carlyle-like directness:

Literature, strictly considered, has never recognized the People, and, whatever may be said, does not to-day.

Our fundamental want to-day in the United States, with closest, amplest reference to present conditions, and to the future, is of a class, and the clear idea of a class, of native authors, literati, far different, far higher in grade than any yet known, sacerdotal, modern, fit to cope with our occasions, lands, permeating the whole mass of American mentality, taste, belief, breathing into it a new breath of life.

He has this to say of the poets who thus far had voiced America:

Touch'd by the national test, or tried by the standards of democratic personality, they wither to ashes. I say I have not seen a single writer, artist, lecturer, or what-not, that has confronted the voiceless but ever erect and active, pervading, underlying will and typic aspiration of the land, in a spirit kindred to itself. Do you call these genteel little creatures American poets? Do you term that perpetual, pistareen, pastepot work, American art, American drama, taste, verse? I think I hear, echoed as from some mountaintop afar in the west, the scornful laugh of the Genius of these States.

America has not been free. She has echoed books; she has looked too earnestly to the East.

America has yet morally and artistically originated nothing. She seems singularly unaware that the models of persons, books, manners, &c., appropriate for former conditions and for European lands, are but exiles and exotics here.

Our literature must be American in spirit and in background, and only American.

What is the reason our time, our lands, that we see no fresh local courage, sanity, of our own—the Mississippi, stalwart Western men, real mental and physical facts, Southerners, &c., in the body of our literature? especially the poetic part of it. But always instead, a parcel of dandies and ennuyés, dapper little gentlemen from abroad, who flood us with their thin sentiment of parlors, parasols, piano-songs, tinkling rimes, the five-hundredth importation—or whimpering and crying about something, chasing one aborted conceit after another, and forever occupied in dyspeptic amours with dyspeptic women. While, current and novel, the grandest events and revolutions, and stormiest passions of history, are crossing to-day with unparallel'd rapidity and magnificence over the stages of our own and all the continents, offering new materials, opening new vistas, with largest needs, inviting the daring launching forth of conceptions in literature, inspired by them, soaring in highest regions, serving art in its highest.

America demands a poetry that is bold, modern, and all-surrounding and kosmical, as she is herself. It must in no respect ignore science or the modern, but inspire itself with science and the modern. It must bend its vision toward the future, more than the past. Like America, it must extricate itself from even the greatest models of the past, and, while courteous to them, must have entire faith in itself, and the products of its own democratic spirit only.

Faith, very old, now scared away by science, must be restored, brought back by the same power that caused her departure—restored with new sway, deeper, wider, higher than ever. Surely, this universal ennui, this coward fear, this shuddering at death, these low, degrading views, are not always to rule the spirit pervading future society, as it has in the past, and does the present.

The book came winged with a double message: it was a defense and an explanation of Walt Whitman, the poet of democracy, and it was the call for a new era in American literature. In both aspects it was notable, notable as Wordsworth's early prefaces were notable. It was both an effect and a cause. The same impulse that launched it launched also Thoreau and the nature school, Bret Harte and the Pike County balladists, Mark Twain and the vulgarians, Howells and realism, and all the great wave of literature of locality. Its effect and the effect of *Leaves of Grass* that went with it has been a marked one. After these two books there could be no more dilettanteism in art, no more art for mere art's sake, no more imitation and subservience to foreign masters; the time had come for a literature' that was genuine and compelling, one that was American both in message and in spirit.

V

1871 was the culminating year of Whitman's literary life. He was at the fullness of his powers. His final attack of paralysis was as yet a year away. For the exhibition of the American Institute he put the message of *Democratic Vistas* into poetic form—"After All, not to Create Only"—a glorious invitation to the muses to migrate to America:

Placard "Remov'd" and "To Let" on the rocks of your snowy Parnassus,

a perfect hexameter line it will be noted, as also this:

Ended, deceas'd through time, her voice by Castaly's fountain.

And the same year he put forth an enlarged and enriched *Leaves of Grass*, including in it the splendid "Passage to India," celebrating the opening of the Suez Canal, a poem that is larger than the mere geographic bounds of its subject, world-wide as they were, for it is a poem universe-wide, celebrating the triumphs of the human soul.

We too take ship, O soul,
Joyous we too launch out on trackless seas,
Fearless for unknown shores on waves of ecstasy to sail,
Amid the wafting winds (thou pressing me to thee, I thee to me, O soul),
Caroling free, singing our song of God.

Passage to more than India!
Are thy wings plumed indeed for such far flights?
O soul, voyagest thou indeed on voyages like those?
Disportest thou on waters such as those?
Soundest below the Sanscrit and the Vedas?
Then have thy bent unleash'd.

The poems grouped around this splendid outburst, as indeed all the rest of his poems until illness and age began to dim his powers, are pitched in this major key. No poet in any time ever maintained himself longer at such high levels. His poems which he entitled "Whispers of Heavenly Death," are all of the upper air and the glory of the released soul of man. Not even Shelley has more of lyric abandon and pure joy than Whitman in such songs as "Darest Thou Now, O Soul":

> Then we burst forth, we float,
> In Time and Space, O soul, prepared for them,
> Equal, equipt at last (O joy! O fruit of all!) them to fulfil, O soul.

And what deeps and abysses in a lyric like this:

> A noiseless patient spider,
> I mark'd where on a little promontory it stood isolated,
> Mark'd how to explore the vacant vast surrounding,
> If launch'd forth filament, filament, filament, out of itself,
> Ever unreeling them, ever tirelessly speeding them.

> And you, O my soul, where you stand,
> Surrounded, detached, in measureless oceans of space,
> Ceaselessly musing, venturing, throwing, seeking the spheres to con-
>   nect them,
> Till the bridge you will need be form'd, till the ductile anchor hold,
> Till the gossamer thread you fling catch somewhere, O my soul!

And then at last, paralyzed and helpless, his work done, the body he had gloried in slipping away from him, there came that magnificent outburst of faith and optimism that throws a glory over the whole of American poetry, the "Prayer of Columbus":

> My terminus near,
> The clouds already closing in upon me,
> The voyage balk'd, the course disputed, lost,
> I yield my ships to Thee.

> My hands, my limbs grow nerveless,
> My brain feels rack'd, bewildered,
> Let the old timbers part, I will not part,
> I will cling fast to Thee, O God, though the waves
>   buffet me,
> Thee, Thee at least I know.

Sometime the poems of Whitman will be arranged in the order in which he wrote them, and then it will be seen that the poems by which he is chiefly judged—the chants of the body, the long catalogues of things (reduced greatly by the poet in his later editings), the barbaric yawp and the egotism—belong to only one brief period in his literary development; that in his later work he was the poet of the larger life of man, the most positive singer of the human soul in the whole range of English literature. If the earlier Whitman is the singer of a type of democracy that does not exist in America except as an abstract theory, the later Whitman is the singer of the universal heart of man.

The Whitman that will endure emerged from the furnace of the Civil War. In his own words:

Without those three or four years and the experiences they gave, *Leaves of Grass* would not now be existing.[5]

And again,

I know very well that my "Leaves" could not possibly have emerged or been fashion'd or completed, from any other era than the latter half of the nineteenth century, nor any other land than democratic America, and from the absolute triumph of the national Union arms.[6]

He is not always easy reading; he is not always consecutive and logical. He said himself that the key to his style was suggestiveness.

I round and finish little, if anything; and could not, consistently with my scheme. The reader will always have his or her part to do, just as much as I have had mine. I seek less to state or display any theme or thought, and more to bring you, reader, into the atmosphere of the theme or thought—there to pursue your own flight.

He is oracular; he talks darkly, like the priestess in the temple, in snatches and Orphic ejaculations, and we listen with eagerness. Had he been as clear and as consecutive as Longfellow he would not have had at all the vogue that has been his. Somehow he gives the impression constantly to his reader, as he gave it in earlier years to Thoreau, that there is something superhuman about him. He is a misty landscape illuminated by lightning flashes. We feel that we are near lofty mountains; now and then we catch glimpses of a snowy peak, but only for a moment. The fitful roll of the thunder excites us and the flashes sometimes terrify, and the whole effect of the experience is on the side of the feelings. There is little clear vision. Or, perhaps, a better figure: taking his entire work we have the great refuse heap of the universe. He shows it to us with eagerness; nothing disgusts him, nothing disconcerts him. Now he pulls forth a diamond, now a potsherd, and he insists that both are equally valuable. He is joyous at every return of the grappling hook. Are not all together in the heap; shall the diamond say to the potsherd, I am better than thou?

[5] *November Boughs.*
[6] *A Backward Glance o'er Travel'd Roads.*

He was early touched by the nature movement of the mid century. With half a dozen poems he has made himself the leading American poet of the sea. In all of his earlier work there breathes the spirit of the living out-of-doors until he may be ranked with Thoreau and Muir and Burroughs. It was the opinion of Burroughs that "No American poet has studied American nature more closely than Whitman, or is more cautious in his uses of it." He is not the poet of the drawing-room—he is the poet of the vast sweep of the square miles, of the open sky, of the cosmos. "Democracy most of all affiliates with the open air," he contended; "is sunny and hardy and sane only with Nature— just as much as art is." And it was his mission, as he conceived it, "to bring people back from their persistent strayings and sickly abstractions, to the costless average, divine, original concrete."

He is not a scientist with Nature; he does not know enough to be a scientist, and his methods and cast of mind are hopelessly unscientific. He is simply a man who feels.

You must not know too much, or be too precise or scientific about birds and trees and flowers and water craft; a certain free margin, and even vagueness—perhaps ignorance, credulity—helps your enjoyment of these things, and of the sentiment of feather'd, wooded, river, or marine nature generally. I repeat it—don't want to know too exactly, or the reasons why.

Such a paragraph is worth a chapter of analysis, and so also is a poem like this:

When I heard the learn'd astronomer,
When the proofs, the figures, were ranged in columns before me,
When I was shown the charts and diagrams, to add, divide, and measure them,
When I sitting heard the astronomer where he lectured with much applause in the lecture-room,
How soon unaccountable I became tired and sick,
Till rising and gliding out I wander'd off by myself,
In the mystical moist night air, and from time to time,
Look'd up in perfect silence at the stars.

His intellect is not so developed as his emotions. He cannot think; he can feel. And after all is not the essence of all poetry, of all the meanings of life, of the soul, of Nature in its message to man, a thing not of the intellect but of the sensitive spirit of man?

VI

Of Whitman's poetic form there is still much to learn. In its earlier phases there was a sprawliness about it that at times was almost fatal to poetic effects, but he grew more metric with every edition and more and more pruned out the worst of his lines, such for instance as this:

Or, another time, in warm weather, out in a boat, to lift the lobster-
    pots, where they are sunk with heavy stones (I know the buoys).

His lines are not prose, even the worst of them. There is a roll about them, a falling of the voice at stressed intervals, an alternate time-beat, crude at times, violated often, yet nevertheless an obedience to law.

It is impossible for any poet, however lawless and apathetic to rules, to compose year after year without at last falling into a stereotyped habit of manner, and evolving a metric roll that is second nature. That Whitman was not conscious of any metric law within himself goes without saying. He believed that he was as free as the tides of the ocean and the waves that rolled among the rocks—lawless, unconfined.

I have not only not bother'd much about style, form, art, etc., but I confess to more or less apathy (I believe I have sometimes caught myself in decided aversion) toward them throughout, asking nothing of them but negative advantages—that they should never impede me, and never under any circumstances, or for their own purposes only, assume any mastery over me.[7]

But a study of Whitman reveals the fact that certain laws *did* more and more assume mastery over him. With every year the time-beat of his poems grew increasingly hexametric. One may go through his later poems and find on the average a full hex-ameter line on every page. I quote at random:

To the cities and farms I sing as they spread in the sunshine before me.

How shall the young man know the whether and when of his brother?

Behold thy fields and farms, thy far-off woods and mountains.

His ear unconsciously seemed to demand the roll of the dactyl, then a cesura after from five to seven beats, then a closing roll

---

[7] Preface to *Good-by My Fancy.*

longer or shorter as his mood struck him.   The greater number
of his later lines open as if the line was to be a hexameter: "Over
the breast of the spring," "Passing the yellow-spear'd wheat,"
"Passing the apple tree blows," "Coffin that passes through
lakes," and so on and on.

But one can make a broader statement.   The total effect of the
poems after 1870, like the "Song of the Redwood,". for instance,
is hexametric, though few of the lines may be hexameters as they
stand.   One might arrange this song like this:

A California song, | a prophecy and indirection,
A thought impalpable | to breathe as air, a chorus
Of dryads, fading departing, | or hamadryads departing,
A murmuring, fateful giant | voice out of the earth and sky,
Voice of a mighty dying | tree in the redwood forest
Dense.   Farewell my brethren, | Farewell O earth and sky,
Farewell ye neighboring waters, | my time has ended, my term
Has come along the northern coast | just back from the rockbound shore,
And the caves in the saline air | from the sea in the Mendocino
Country with the surge for base | and accompaniment low and hoarse,
With crackling blows of axes | sounding musically driven
By strong arms driven deep | by the sharp tongues of the axes,
There in the redwood forest | dense I heard the mighty
Tree in its death chant chanting.

Crude hexameters these undoubtedly, requiring much wrenching
and eliding at times, yet for all that as one reads them aloud one
cannot escape the impression that the total effect is hexametric.
May it not be that the primal time beat for poetry is the hex-
ameter, and that the prehistoric poets evolved it spontaneously
even as the creator of *Leaves of Grass* evolved it?

VII

To insist that Whitman has had small influence on later poetry
because none of the later poets has made use of his chant is feeble
criticism.   No poet even *can* make use of his verse form without
plagiarism, for his loose-fingered chords and his peculiar time-
beat, his line-lengths, his wrenched hexameters—all this was
Whitman himself.   In all other ways he enormously influenced
his age.   His realism, his concrete pictures, his swing and freedom, his Americanism, his insistence upon message, ethic purpose, absolute fidelity to the here and now rather than to books
of the past—all have been enormously influential.   He is the

central figure of the later period, the voice in the wilderness that hailed its dim morning and the strong singer of its high noon.

BIBLIOGRAPHY

WALT WHITMAN. (1819–1892.) During the lifetime of the poet there were issued ten editions of *Leaves of Grass*, with the following dates: 1855, 1856, 1860, 1867, 1871, 1876, 1881, 1888, 1889, 1891.

Among his other publications were the following: 1866. *Drum-Taps;* 1870. *Passage to India;* 1871. *Democratic Vistas;* 1875. *Memoranda During the War;* 1876. *Specimen Days and Collect;* 1876. *Two Rivulets;* 1888. *November Boughs;* 1891. *Good Bye My Fancy.*

Among the works published after his death the most important are: 1897. *Calamus: a Series of Letters Written During the Years 1868–1880 to a Young Friend.* Edited by R. M. Bucke; 1898. *The Wound Dresser: Letters Written from the Hospitals in Washington During the War of the Rebellion.* Edited by R. M. Bucke; 1904. *Diary in Canada.* Edited by W. S. Kennedy; 1910. Complete Prose Works, 10 vols. with biographical matter by O. L. Triggs, 1902; *Poems,* with biographical introduction by John Burroughs, 1902.

Among the great mass of biographies and studies may be mentioned the following: *The Good Gray Poet,* W. D. O'Connor, 1865; *Notes on Walt Whitman as Poet and Person,* John Burroughs, 1867; *Whitman: a Study,* John Burroughs, 1893; *In Re Walt Whitman,* R. M. Bucke, H. Traubel, and T. B. Harned, 1893; *Walt Whitman, the Man,* T. Donaldson, 1896; *Walt Whitman: a Study,* J. Addington Symonds, 1897; *Walt Whitman (the Camden Sage) as Religious and Moral Teacher: a Study,* W. Norman Guthrie, 1897; *Anne Gilchrist and Walt Whitman,* E. P. Gould, 1900; *Walt Whitman's Poetry,* E. G. Holmes, 1901; *Walt Whitman the Poet of the Wider Selfhood,* M. T. Maynard, 1903; *Walt Whitman,* J. Platt, 1904; *A Life of Walt Whitman,* Henry B. Binns, 1905; *A Vagabond in Literature,* A. Rickett, 1906; *Walt Whitman; His Life and Works,* Bliss Perry, 1906; *Days with Walt Whitman. With Some Notes on His Life and Work,* Edward Carpenter, 1906; *With Walt Whitman in Camden (March 28–July 14, 1880),* Horace Traubel, 1906; *Walt Whitman.* English Men of Letters Series. George Rice Carpenter, 1909; *Approach to Walt Whitman,* C. E. Noyes, 1910; *Democracy and Poetry,* F. B. Gummere, 1911; *Walt Whitman,* Basil de Selincourt, 1914. A bibliography of Whitman's writings is appended to O. L. Triggs's *Selections,* 1898.

CHAPTER X

The nineteenth century both in Europe and America was a period of revolt, of breakings away from tradition, of voices in the wilderness. It was the age of Byron and Shelley, of Carlyle and Tolstoy, of Heine and Hugo. Literature came everywhere as the voice of revolution. It rang with protest—Dickens and George Eliot, Kingsley, Whittier, and Mrs. Stowe; it dreamed of a new social era—Fourier and the sons of Rousseau in France, the Transcendentalists in America; it let itself go in romantic abandon and brought back in a flood feeling and sentiment— the *spätromantiker* and Bulwer-Lytton and Longfellow. Everywhere conviction, intensity, travail of soul.

The school died in the last quarter of the century consumed of its own impetuous spirit, and it left no heirs. A feminine age had come, an age of convention and of retrospect. The romantic gave way to the inevitable classic; the hot passion of revolt to the cool fit of deliberate art. In America, the New England school that had ruled the mid years of the century became reminiscent, fastidious, self-contained, to awake in sudden realization that it no longer was a power, that its own second generation were women led by Aldrich, James, Howells, immigrants from New York and the West. The early leaders, Emerson, Whittier, Lowell, all intensity and conviction, had been replaced by the school of deliberate workmen who had no message for their times, only technique and brilliancy.

I

This reaction from the New England school can be studied nowhere more convincingly than in the personalities and work of Henry James, father and son. The elder James, companion of Carlyle and Emerson and Alcott, disciple and interpreter of Swedenborg and Sandeman, was a typical product of the mid-century school—mystical, intense, concerned with the inner rather than the other aspects of man. ''Henry James was true comfort," Emerson wrote in his diary in 1850; "wise, gentle, polished, with heroic manners and a serenity like the sun." He pursued no profession, but like Alcott devoted his life to philosophy and to literature. He wrote for the few a small handful of books, mostly forgotten now, though he who would read them will find them clothed in a richness of style and a felicity of expression that reminds one of the prose of the greater periods of English literature.[1]

The son of this mid-century genius, Henry James, Jr., cultured, cold, scientific, disciple of Turgenieff, of Flaubert and Daudet, Maupassant and Zola—"grandsons of Balzac"—stands as the type of the "later manner," the new school that wrote without message, that studied with intensity the older models, that talked evermore of its "art."

"We know very little about a talent," this younger James has written in his essay on Stevenson, "till we know where it grew up.". The James family, we know, grew up outside the New England environment, in the State of New York—first at Albany, where the future novelist was born in 1843, then until he was twelve in New York City. But this in reality tells us nothing. The boy grew up in London rather than New York. The father had inherited means that permitted a retired and scholarly life. Following the birth of Henry, his second son, he had taken his family for a year and a half to England, and he had come back, both he and his wife, to quote his son's words, "completely Europeanized." "Had all their talk for its subject, in my infant ears, that happy time?—did it deal only with London and Piccadilly and the Green Park? . . . I saw my parents homesick, as I conceived, for the ancient order."[2] He grew up in the presence of imported books and papers, the smell of whose ink fresh from London and the Strand fed his imagination.

Even his playmates transported him into the old world. It was one Louis De Coppet, a small boy, "straight from the Lake of Geneva," that first really aroused in him "the sense of Europe . . . that pointed prefigurement of the manners of 'Europe,'

[1] James's chief works are *Society the Redeemed Form of Man, Remarks on the Gospels, Moralism and Christianity, The Nature of Evil, Substance and Shadows, The Secret of Swedenborg, What is the State? The Church of Christ, Christianity the Lyric of Creation,* and *Literary Remains,* edited by William James.

[2] *A Small Boy and Others.*

which, inserted wedge-like, if not to say peg-like, into my young
allegiance was to split the tender organ into such unequal halves.
His the toy hammer that drove in the very point of the golden
nail. It was as if there had been a mild magic in that breath,
however scant, of another world.'' [3] While other lads were reading their juveniles, the young James was poring over *Punch*.
''From about 1850 to 1855,'' he writes in his essay on Du
Maurier, speaking of himself in the third person, ''he lived, in
imagination, no small part of the time, in the world represented
by the pencil of Leech. . . . These things were the features of a
world which he longed so to behold that the familiar woodcuts
grew at last as real to him as the furniture of his home.''

II

Such was the early environment of Henry James. Refinement
and rare culture breathed upon his cradle and surrounded his
whole boyhood like an atmosphere. He was kept sheltered from
the world without, as from something coarse and degrading. He
was not allowed to attend the public schools. ''Considering with
much pity our four stout boys,'' the father wrote to Emerson in
1849, ''who have no playroom within doors and import shocking
bad manners from the street, we gravely ponder whether it
would n't be better to go abroad for a few years with them, allowing them to absorb French and German and get such a sensuous
education as they cannot get here.'' [4]

The plan did not mature until 1855 when the boy was twelve.
In the *interim* tutors were employed for his education who in-
structed him with desultory, changing methods, allowing him
always to take apparently the paths of his preference. In these
same paths he seems to have continued during the four years of
his residence abroad with his parents in London, Geneva, Bou-
logne-sur-Mer, and Paris. All harshness he avoided, all sharpness of discipline—mathematics, examinations. He would sit,
boy as he was, only in the places of beauty and refinement. ''The
whole perfect Parisianism I seemed to myself always to have possessed mentally—even if I had but just turned twelve.'' [5]

One does not understand Henry James who neglects this forma-

[3] *A Small Boy and Others.*
[4] *Notes of a Son and Brother.*
[5] *A Small Boy and Others.*

tive period of his life. He returned to America an esthete, a
dreamer, with his heart in the lands of culture, dissatisfied with
the rush and rudeness that were preparing a new world for its
future. He was too frail in health to enter the armies which
soon were recruiting about him for the great war; he had no inclination, because of his father's prejudice, to undertake a college course; he shrank from the usual professions open to young
men of his class. He did for a year attend lectures at the Harvard Law School, but it was with no thought of preparing for a
legal career. He dreamed of literature as a profession. He
would woo the muse, but the muse he would woo "was of course
the muse of prose fiction—never for the briefest hour in my case
the presumable, not to say the presuming, the much-taking-for-
granted muse of rime, with whom I had never had, even in
thought, the faintest flirtation." For this profession he trained
himself as deliberately and as laboriously as if it were the violin
that he was to master, or the great organ. He read industriously,
especially in the French; he resided now in Boston, where his
father at last had settled, now in France, now in Italy. Like
Story, the sculptor, whom in so many ways he resembled, he
would live at the richest centers of his art. Finally, in the late
seventies, he took up his residence permanently abroad to return
only as a rare visitant.

III

Henry James more than any other American author stands for
specialization, for a limited field cultivated intensively and exclusively. Poetry, as he has explained, was no part of his en-
dowment; he never attempted it even at the age when all men
are poets; romance never attracted him. He approached his
chosen field of prose fiction deliberately as a scientist, and prepared himself for it as a man studies medicine. He began as he
ended—more crude in his art to be sure, more conventional, more
youthful in thought and diction, yet not fundamentally different
from his final manner.

His first published work, *The Story of a Year,* which appeared
in the March, 1865, number of the *Atlantic,* at first reading seems
little different from the hundreds of tales of the Civil War that
were appearing everywhere during the period. It is full of a
young man's smartness and literary affectations: "In early May,

two years ago, a young couple I wot of,'' etc. ''Good reader, this
narrative is averse to retrospect,'' etc. And yet the story, despite its youthfulness, contains all the elements that we now associate with the fiction of Henry James. It is first of all a slight
story—not so slight as some of the later work, but nevertheless a
mere episode expanded into a novelette; furthermore, it was written not so much for the displaying of movement of incident as
for the analysis of movements of feeling and the growth of elements of character: ''I have to chronicle,'' he says at one point,
''another silent transition.'' Then too its ending suggests the
French school:

"No, no, no," she almost shrieked, turning about in the path. "I
forbid you to follow me."
But for all that he went in.

We stand uncertain, startled, piqued—then the suggestion
comes surging over us: Perhaps the author means that she married him after all! Could she do it? Did she do it? And then
we find with a thrill of surprise that he has given us the full
answer in his previous analysis of her character. It is finesse, it
is the careful adjustment of parts, it is deliberate art.

There are other characteristics in the story that were to mark
all the work of James. The tale, for instance, leaves us unmoved.
We admire its brilliancy, but at no point does it grip us with its
tragedy or its comedy. The faithlessness of the heroine and the
death of the hero alike leave us cold. We do not care. Sympathy, the sympathy of comprehension, that sympathy that enters into the little world the author has created and for a time
loses itself as if it were actually native there—of this there is
nothing. It is all objective, external phenomena observed and
recorded on a pad—a thing alone of the intellect.

That James should have followed this story with an essay on
''The Novels of George Eliot'' is no mere coincidence. How completely he had saturated himself with all the work of the great
English sibyl, appears on every page. Her faithfulness to her
material, her vivid photographs, her devotion to science which
little by little crushed out her woman's heart, her conception of
the novel as the record of a dissection—the reactions of human
souls under the scalpel and the microscope, her materialism that
refused all testimony save that of the test-tube and the known

reagents, that reduced man to a problem in psychology—all this made its reflex upon the young student. He too became a scientist, taking nothing for granted, stripping himself of all illusions, relegating the ideal, the intuitive, the spiritual to the realm of the outgrown; he too became a taker of notes—"The new school of fiction in France is based very much on the taking of notes," he remarks in his essay on Daudet. "The library of the great Flaubert, of the brothers Goncourt, of Emile Zola, and of the writer of whom I speak, must have been in a large measure a library of memorandum-books." [6] In his earlier work at least, he was George Eliot with the skill and finesse of Maupassant, and he may be summed up with his whole school in the words he has put into the mouth of his own Anastasia Blumenthal: "It was meager," he makes her say of the singing of Adelina Patti, "it was trivial, it lacked soul. You can't be a great artist without a great passion."

IV

During the first period of his literary life, the period that ended somewhere in the early nineties, James took as the subject of his study that vagrom area that lies on the borderland between the old culture of Europe and the new rawness of America. Howells has made much of the longings of certain classes in the older parts of his native land to visit the European cities, and he has pictured more than once their idealizations of foreign things, their retrospections and dreamings. James showed these Americans actually in Europe, their manners as seen against the older background, their crudeness and strength; and in doing so he produced what was widely hailed as the new international novel. There was nothing really new about it. James wrote of Americans in Europe just as Mark Twain wrote of Americans on the Mississippi or in California. As a scientist he must deal only with facts which had passed under his own observation—that was his much-discussed "realism"—and the life that he was most familiar with was the life of the pensions and grand hotels of Rome and Switzerland and Paris and London.

His world in reality was small. He had been reared in a cloister-like atmosphere where he had dreamed of "life" rather than lived it. It is almost pathetic to think of him going up

---

[6] *Partial Portraits*, 1894 ed., 207.

to the Harvard Law School because in a vague way it stood for something which he had missed and longed to feel. "I thought of it under the head of 'life,' " he says. He had played in his childhood with books rather than boys; he had been kept away from his natural playmates because of their "shocking bad manners"; he had never mingled with men in a business or a professional way; he had never married; he stood aloof from life and observed it without being a part of it. Americans he knew chiefly from the specimens he had found in Europe during his long residences; European society he knew as a visitor from without. With nothing was he in sympathy in the full meaning of the word, that sympathy which includes its own self in the group under observation.

For ten years he wrote studies, essays on his masters, George Eliot, Balzac, Daudet, and stories that were not greatly different from these essays—analyses of types, and social conditions, and of the reactions that follow when a unit of one social system is thrust into another. In 1875 he enlarged his area with *Roderick Hudson,* a novel of length, and he followed it with *The American, The Europeans, Daisy Miller,* and others, all of them international in setting. In his later period, the period, say, after 1890, he confined himself to the depicting of society in London, the rapid change toward unconventionality in manners that marked the end of the century. He was so far now from contact with his native land that of necessity he must cease to use it as his source of literary material.

The earlier group of stories center about a comparatively few types. First, there are the young men of the Roland Mallet, Ralph Touchett order, "highly civilized young Americans," he calls them in *Confidence,* "born to an easy fortune and a tranquil destiny"; "men who conceive of life as a fine art." His novels are full of them, creatures of whim who know nothing of the bitterness of struggle, who drift from capital to capital of Europe mindful only of their own comfort, highly sensitive organisms withal, subject to evanescent emotions which they analyze with minuteness, and brilliant at every point when their intellectual powers are called into play. They talk in witty flashes for hours on end and deliver finished lectures at the call of an epigram. They cannot talk without philosophizing or hear a maiden laugh without analysis. They are brilliant all the time. The conversation of Gilbert Osmond and Mrs. Merle fills Isabel with amazement: "They talked extremely well; it struck her almost as a dramatic entertainment, rehearsed in advance." Page after page they talk in a staccato, breathless profusion of wit, epigram, repartee, verbal jewels worthy of Alexander Pope flying at every opening of the lips—is even French culture as brilliant as this? Mr. Brand in *The Europeans* listening to the Baroness Münster, bursts out rapturously at last, "Now I suppose that is what is called conversation, real conversation. It is quite the style we have heard about—the style of Madame de Staël, of Madame Récamier."

Within this narrow circle of Europe-visiting, highly civilized, occupationless men and women, James is at his best. Had he not been reared by Henry James, Senior? Had he not lived his whole life in the charmed circle of the highly civilized? But once outside of this small area he ceases to be convincing. Of the great mass of the American people he knows but little. He has seen them only at a distance.

> As some rich woman, on a winter's morn,
> Eyes through her silken curtains the poor drudge
> Who with numb, blacken'd fingers makes her fire . . .
> And wonders how she lives, and what the thoughts
> Of that poor drudge may be,

so of James when he attempts to portray the great mass of his countrymen. One needs to examine only the case of Christopher Newman in *The American*. Given a man who left home at eight years of age to work in the mills, who at length manufactures wash tubs, then leather, and at last by sheer Yankee impudence and energy makes himself a millionaire at forty. Thrust this man suddenly into the circles of French nobility, place him in the presence of the Countess de Belgrade and ask yourself if he will talk like this:

She is a woman of conventions and proprieties; her world is the world of things immutably decreed. But how she is at home in it, and what a paradise she finds it. She walks about in it as if it were a blooming park, a Garden of Eden; and when she sees "This is genteel," or "This is improper," written on a mile-stone she stops ecstatically, as if she were listening to a nightingale or smelling a rose.

This is not Christopher Newman; this is no American self-made man talking; it is Henry James himself.   Did he realize his mistake when his art was more mature and his judgment more ripe? Collate the changes which he made thirty years later for the final edition of *The American*.   Newman is asked, for instance, if he is visiting Europe for the first time.   According to the earlier version he replies, "Very much so"; according to the latest version, "Quite immensely the first."   Is more proof needed?   All his average Americans—Daisy Miller, Henrietta Stackpole, Casper Goodwood, and the others, fall short in the same way.   Objectively they are true to life.   As a painter of external portraits, as a depicter of tricks of personality, of manners, of all that makes up a perfect external likeness, James is surpassed not even by Howells; but he fails to reach the springs of life.   Howells's Silas Lapham is a living personality; James's Christopher Newman is a lay figure in Yankee costume.   For James knows Americans chiefly as he has studied them in pensions and hotels along the grand tour.   He has not been introduced to them, he has simply watched them—their uneasiness in their new element, their attempts at adjustment, their odd little mistakes; he hears them talk at the tables around him—their ejaculations, their wonder, their enthusiasm, and he jots it all down.   He has no sympathy, he has no feeling, he has no object, save the scientific desire to record phenomena.

This material he weaves into novels—stories, but not stories told with narrative intent, not stories for entertainment or wonder or sensation.   The story is a clinic, a dissection, a psychological seminar.   *What Maisie Knew* is an addition to the literature of child study.   It is as if he had set himself to observe case after case for his brother, William James, to use as materials for psychological generalizations and a final treatise.   The data are often inaccurate because of the observer's personal equation; it does not always conform with the results of our own observing—we wonder, for instance, if he is as far afield in his pictures of the European aristocracy as in those of his average Americans—yet the process is always the same.

Rapidity of movement is foreign to his method; he is not concerned with movement.   On the portrait of one lady he will expend two hundred thousand words.   Basil in *The Bostonians* passes the evening with his Cousin Olive: the call occupies nine chapters; Verena Tarrant calls on Miss Chancellor: it is two chapters before either of them moves or speaks. It transports us back into the eighteenth century to the nine-volume novel. At every step analysis, searchings for the springs of thought and act —philosophizing. Lord Warburton stands before Miss Archer to propose marriage, but before we hear his voice we must analyze minutely his sensations and hers. Her first feeling was alarm. "This alarm was composed of several elements, not all of which were disagreeable; she had spent several days in analyzing them," etc. A review of this analysis fills a page. Then we study the psychology of the lover. First, he wonders why he is about to propose: "He calculated that he had spent about twenty-six hours in her company. He had summed up all this—the perversity of the impulse, the—" etc., etc. A proposal each step and speech of which is followed by a careful clinic to determine the resultant emotion, and a rigid analysis of all the elements that combined to produce that particular shade of emotion and no other, can hardly satisfy the demands of the average modern reader of fiction. It is the province of the novel to produce with verisimilitude an area of human life and to make the reader for a swift period at home in that area; it is not the record of a scientific investigation.

V

James has dealt almost wholly with exceptions and unusual cases. His "Bostonians" are not typical Bostonians at all—it is not too strong to declare that they are abnormalities; his "Europeans" are almost as bad; his characters studied along the grand tour are rare exceptions if we compare them with the great average American type. Of strong, elemental men and women, the personalities shown by novelists like Fielding and Tolstoy and Hardy and Mark Twain, he knows nothing. He is feminine rather than masculine; he is exquisite rather than strong. In his essay on Turgenieff he records that the great Russian was never one of his admirers. "I do not think my stories struck him as quite meat for men."

There is a lack, too, of seriousness: the novels really accomplish nothing. "The manner," according to Turgenieff's opinion, "is more apparent than the matter." Style is preferred to message. There is no humor, no stirring of emotions, nothing pitched above the key of perfect refinement—the reader does not feel and there-

fore does not care.   It is a mere intellectual exercise, a problem
in psychology.

That James himself was aware of this weakness we learn from
his essay on Daudet.   Of Sidonie Chebe he writes, "She is not
felt," and again, "His weakness has been want of acquaintance
with his subject.   He has not *felt* what he has observed."   It is
a judgment that sweeps over the whole fiction of Henry James.
He has never been possessed by his subject or by his characters,
he has never been seized and hurried along by his stories, he has
never told them because they had to be told, he has never written
a single sentence with held breath and beating heart, and as a
result his work can never find for long an audience save the select
few; an audience indeed that at length must become as restricted
as that which now reads the exquisite creations of the elder James,
his father.

There is another element that must be weighed before we can
understand fully the work of this writer, an element that is distinctly classical.   The basis underlying all of this mass of analysis
is self-consciousness.   Never was author more subjective and
more enamoured of his own psychological processes than Henry
James.   Never does he lose sight of himself.   These characters of
his are all of them Henry James.   They slip out of their costumes
at slightest provocation to talk with his tones, to voice his philosophy, to follow his mental processes.   In externals they are true
to model though not always deeply; the hands are the hands of
Christopher Newman, but the voice is the voice of Henry James.

The tendency to self-consciousness has colored everything.
Even his criticism has had its personal basis.   It has consisted
of studies in expatriation: the life of Story, that prototype of
James; the life of Hawthorne, that exposition of the rawness of
America and the unfitness of the new land for the residence of
men of culture; *The American Scene*—that mental analysis
tracing every shade of emotion as he revisits what has become to
him a foreign land.   His literary essays cover largely the experiences of his apprenticeship.   They trace the path of his own
growth in art.   They are strings of brilliants, flashing, often incomparable, but they are not criticism in the highest sense of the
word criticism.   Few men have said such brilliant things about
Balzac, Maupassant, Daudet, Stevenson as James, yet for all that
a critic in the wider sense of the term really he is not.   He lacks

perspective, philosophy, system. He makes epigrams and pithy remarks. The ability to project himself into the standpoint of another, to view with sympathy of comprehension, he did not have. Within his limited range he could measure and the rules of art he could apply with brilliancy, but he could not feel.

Self-study, the pursuit of every fleeting impression, became in the author at last a veritable obsession. In his later books like *Notes of a Son and Brother,* for instance, and *The American Scene,* his finger is constantly upon his own pulse. He seeks the source of his every fleeting emotion. He does not tell us why he did not want to enter Harvard; he tries rather to trace the subtle thread of causation that could have led him not to *want* to want to go. When *A Small Boy and Others* appeared the world cried out, "Is it possible that at last Henry James has revealed himself?" whereas the truth was that few men ever have revealed themselves more. All this endless dissection and analysis and scrutiny of the inner workings is in reality an analysis of Henry James himself. Objective he could not be. He could only stand in his solitude and interpret his own introspections.

And his solitude it has been and his self-contemplation that have evolved his later manner. A consciously wrought-out style like Pater's or Maupassant's comes always as a result of solitude, of self-conscious concentration, of classicism. Eternal contemplation of manner can result only in mannerism more and more, until mannerism becomes the ruling characteristic. Classicism perishes at last of its own refinement.

VI

The evolution of William Dean Howells is a problem vastly different. To place Howells as a leader of those forces of refinement that followed after the New England period is seemingly to ignore the facts of his origin and his early training, for the little river town on the Ohio where he was born in 1837 was as far removed from New England manners and sentiments as was even the Hannibal of Tom Sawyer and Huckleberry Finn. He was reared to despise Yankees as a mean-spirited race, and he spent his childhood and young manhood in close contact with the rough, virile material that was shaping up the great West.

Howells was of the third generation in Ohio, a Westerner of the Westerners. His grandfather, a Welsh manufacturer, "came to this country early in the nineteenth century and settled his family in a log cabin in the Ohio woods, that they might be safe from the sinister influences of the village where he was managing some woolen mills.'' [7] He finally settled down as a druggist and bookseller in a small village, and his son, perhaps from contact with his father's wares, developed a passion for literature—strange acquisition, it would seem, to gain in the wilderness.

It was from this literary father rather than from his mother, who was from the river-faring folk of the region, that the young William Dean Howells was to derive his early love for books. He seems to have been a Henry James, Senior, with Southwestern training and environment and a lack of means that forbade his following the path of his desires. He too was a Swedenborgian and a mystic, and he too, despite unfavorable surroundings, kept in his household a literary atmosphere. Moore's *Lalla Rookh*, Thomson's *Seasons*, Dickens, Scott, Cowper, Burns, he read to his family—poetry the most of it, for ''his own choice was for poetry, and most of our library, which was not given to theology, was given to poetry.'' An unusual character indeed in the headlong, practical West of the mid century! While the mother was about her tasks and the children were shelling peas for dinner, he would sit and tell of Cervantes and the adventures of Don Quixote, transporting the little group into castles in Spain, and creating visions and longings that were to dominate the whole life of his little son. He watched with pleasure the literary tendencies of the boy: ''when I began to show a liking for literature he was eager to guide my choice.''

The father satisfied his literary longings by editing country newspapers and serving as reporter at various times at the State capital during sessions of the legislature. He remained in no place long. With what Howells has called ''the vagarious impulse which is so strong in our craft,'' he removed his family to new fields of labor with surprising regularity. There was little chance for schooling. Almost from infancy the boy was a part of his father's printing office. In *A Boy's Town*, that delightful autobiographic fragment told in the third person, he has given a glimpse of this early period:

My boy was twelve years old by that time and was already a swift

[7] *My Literary Passions*, 4.

compositor, though he was still so small that he had to stand on a chair to reach the case in setting type on Tyler's inaugural message. But what he lacked in stature he made up in gravity of demeanor; and he got the name of "The Old Man" from the printers as soon as he began to come about the office, which he did almost as soon as he could walk. His first attempt in literature, an essay on the vain and disappointing nature of human life, he set up and printed off himself in his sixth or seventh year; and the printing office was in some sort his home, as well as his school, his university. He could no more remember learning to set type than he could remember learning to read.

The autobiographical writings of Howells leave us with the impression of a gentle, contemplative boy given rather to reading and dreaming in a solitary corner than to Mark-Twain-like activities with Tom Sawyers and Huck Finns. Though by birth and rearing he was a complete Westerner of the river section, mingling freely with all its elements, he seems never to have taken root in the region or to have been much influenced by it. He has spoken somewhere of De Quincey as a man "eliminated from his time and place by his single love for books." Howells, like James, was a detached soul. From his earliest youth he was not a resident of Ohio, but a resident of the vaster world of literature. He read enormously and with passion, and from his boyhood he seems—also like Henry James—to have had no dream of other than a literary career. He saw not the headlong West that surged about him but the realms of poetry and romance. "To us who have our lives so largely in books," he wrote in later years, "the material world is always the fable, and the ideal the fact. I walked with my feet on the ground, but my head was in the clouds, as light as any of them. . . . I was living in a time of high political tumult, and I certainly cared very much for the question of slavery which was then filling the minds of men; I felt deeply the shame and wrong of our fugitive slave law; I was stirred by the news from Kansas, where the great struggle between the two great principles in our nationality was beginning in bloodshed; but I cannot pretend that any of these things were more than ripples on the surface of my intense and profound interest in literature." [8]

It is suggestive that his earliest "passions" among the authors were Goldsmith, Irving, and Cervantes, and later Pope, Macaulay, and Curtis—the most of them literary artists and finishers, with

[8] *My Literary Passions.*

grace of style and softness and dreaminess of atmosphere, rather than stormy creators who blazed new trails and crashed into the unknown with lawless power. He taught himself the use of literary English by painstaking imitation of the classics which took his young fancy. His passion for Pope was long continued. When other boys in the schools were shirking their English grammar, Howells week after week and month after month was toiling at imitations of the great master of incisive English, "rubbing and polishing at my wretched verses till they did sometimes take on an effect, which, if it was not like Pope's, was like none of mine." From him "I learned how to choose between words after a study of their fitness." Juveniles and boys' books of adventure he seems never to have known. From the first he was enamoured of the classics, and of the classics best fitted to educate him for the career that was to be his: "my reading from the first was such as to enamour me of clearness, of definiteness."

Never was youth more industrious in his efforts at self-mastery. He wasted not a moment. He discovered Macaulay and read him as most boys read pirate stories. "Of course I reformed my prose style, which had been carefully modeled after that of Goldsmith and Irving, and began to write in the manner of Macaulay, in short, quick sentences and with the prevalent use of brief Anglo-Saxon words." His health began to suffer from his application, but he worked steadily on. He produced quantities of poems and even a novel or two which he either destroyed or consigned to the oblivion of the newspaper upon which he worked. Later he enlarged the field of his literary apprenticeship by securing a position on a Columbus journal, or as he has himself expressed it, he was "for three years a writer of news paragraphs, book notices, and political leaders on a daily paper in an inland city." [9] Then he began to enlarge his literary field by contributing "poems and sketches and criticisms for the *Saturday Press* of New York." [9]

In December, 1859, he issued his first book, *Poems of Two Friends,* a small volume of rather ordinary verses written in conjunction with J. J. Piatt, and a few months later he published a campaign life of Abraham Lincoln, a book more notable for its effect upon its author's fortunes than for any quality it may have had, for it was as a result of it that he was sent in 1861 to Italy

[9] *Literary Friends and Acquaintance.*

for a glorious four years of graduate study, if we may so term it, in Italian literature and language and life.

One cannot dwell too carefully upon these years of Howells's literary apprenticeship. As one reads his published work one finds from the first no immaturities. He burst upon the reading public as a finished writer. When his work first began to appear in the East, the *North American Review* of Boston voiced its astonishment:

> We made occasion to find out something about him, and what we learned served to increase our interest. This delicacy, it appeared, was a product of the rough and ready West, this finish the natural gift of a young man with no advantage of college training, who, passing from the compositor's desk to the editorship of a local newspaper, had been his own faculty of the humanities. But there are some men who are born cultivated.[10]

But Howells was not born cultivated; he achieved cultivation by a process of self-discipline that has few parallels in the history of literature. He is a classicist as James is a classicist. If his style is clear and concise, if he knows as few modern authors the resources of the English tongue, it is because he gave without reserve to the mastering of it all the enthusiasm and time and strength of his youth and young manhood. He was not a genius: he was a man of talent of the Pope-Macaulay order that makes of literature not a thing of inspirations and flashes and visions, but a profession to be learned as one learns the pipe organ after years of practice, as an art demanding an exquisite skill to be gained only by unremitting toil.

VII

The Howells of the earlier period was a poet. Speaking of the winter of 1859–60, which saw the publication of his first volume, he writes: "It seemed to me as if the making and the reading of poetry were to go on forever, and that was to be all there was to it." "Inwardly I was a poet, with no wish to be anything else, unless in a moment of careless affluence I might so far forget myself as to be a novelist."

His reading more and more was in the poets. Heine he read with passion, and Longfellow and Tennyson, and then Heine, evermore Heine. "Nearly ten years afterwards Mr. Lowell

[10] October, 1865.

wrote me about something of mine that he had been reading:
'You must sweat the Heine out of your bones as men do mer-
cury.' '' The seven poems which Lowell accepted and printed
in the *Atlantic* in 1860 and 1861 are redolent of Heine, with
here and there traces of Longfellow. When he came East just
before his appointment to Venice it was as a poet, and a poet
making a pilgrimage to the mother-land of poesy.

New England was to him indeed a land of dreams and romance.
''As the passionate pilgrim from the West,'' to use his own words,
''approached his Holy Land at Boston,'' he felt like putting the
shoes from off his feet. New England was the home of Emerson
and Longfellow and Holmes, of Whittier and Hawthorne and
Lowell, and all the *Atlantic* immortals, and he appreciated it as
Irving and Willis had appreciated old England earlier in the
century, or as Longfellow and Taylor had appreciated the continent of Europe.

Following this passionate pilgrimage with its glimpses of the
New England Brahmins, came the transfer of the young Westerner to Venice, ''the Chief City,'' as he somewhere has termed
it, ''of sentiment and fantasy.'' It was like stepping from the
garish light of to-day into the pages of an old romance. The
duties of his office were light, the salary was fifteen hundred dollars a year, and he was enabled to give, to use his own words,
''nearly four years of nearly uninterrupted leisure'' to a study
of Italian literature and to poetic composition. We may catch
glimpses of what the four years meant to the eager young Westerner in *A Foregone Conclusion* and *A Fearful Responsibility*,
stories that center about an American consul at Venice. The
poetic quality of the period was heightened in the second year
of his official life by his marriage—spring and Venice and a bride
with whom to share them—no wonder that he completed a long
poem in *terza rima,* ''dealing,'' as he has expressed it, ''with a
story of our Civil War in a fashion so remote that no editor
would print it,'' and that he deluged the magazines of two continents with poems and poetic sketches.

For the earlier Howells was a poet—until one realizes it one
fails completely to understand him. He turned from poetry
reluctantly, compelled by the logic of his time and by the fact
that he had no compelling message for his age. He was of the
contemplative, classical school, more at home in the eighteenth

century than in the stormy nineteenth. He published in 1867 *No Love Lost, A Romance of Travel,* in unrimed pentameters, a refined, leisurely poem classical in form and spirit. He issued editions of his poems in 1873 and 1886, and again as late as 1895, but the age refused to regard him as a poet and he was forced into other fields. "My literary life," he observes almost sadly as he reviews his Venetian period, "almost without my willing it, had taken the course of critical observance of books and men in their actuality." [11]

From poetry Howells turned to sketches, a variety of composition which he had cultivated since his boyhood. Irving had been one of his earliest passions, and following Irving had come Ik Marvel and Hawthorne and Curtis—gentle, contemplative writers with the light of poetry upon their work. Even like Irving and Longfellow and Taylor, he would record the strange new world in which he found himself. "I was bursting with the most romantic expectations of life in every way, and I looked at the whole world as material that might be turned into literature." He lived note-book in hand. Everything was new and entrancing, even the talk of servants on the street or the babble of children at their play. It was all so new, so romantic, so removed from the world that he always had known. He would reproduce it in its naked truth for his countrymen; he would turn it all into literature for the magazines of America, and he would republish it at length as a new *Sketch Book.*

Venetian Life belongs on the same shelf as *Outre Mer* and *Views Afoot* and *Castilian Days*—prose sketches with the golden light of youth upon them. *Italian Journeys* is the first and best of a long series of sentimental "bummelings" that its author was to record—delicious ramblings, descriptions, characterizations— realistic studies, we may call them, made by a poet. Nothing that Howells ever wrote has been better than these earlier travel sketches, half poetry, half shrewd observation. In his later travel sketches—*Tuscan Cities, London Films, Certain Delightful English Towns,* and the like—this element grew constantly less and less. Wiser they undoubtedly are, and more scholarly and philosophic, but the freshness and poetic charm of the earlier Howells is not in them. The philosopher has taken the place of the poet.

[11] *My Literary Passions,* 154.

VIII

The first period of Howells's literary life, the period of sketches and prose studies, covers the fifteen years of his connection with the *Atlantic Monthly,* first from 1866 to 1871 as assistant editor, and then from 1871 to 1881 as editor. He had returned from Venice a cosmopolitan and an accomplished Italian scholar. There was no trace of the West upon him; it was as if he had always lived in Boston. His sketches now centered about Cambridge life, just as earlier they had centered upon Italian themes —careful little character studies like "Mrs. Johnson" and "My Doorstep Acquaintance," little sentimental journeys like "A Pedestrian Tour" and "A Day's Pleasure," and chatty talks about himself and his opinions and experiences, something after the manner of Dr. Holmes, a variety of composition in which he was to grow voluminous in later years.

His book reviewing in the *Atlantic* during this period is notable from the fact that almost all of the chief works of the new national period of which he was a part passed under his pen. Freshness and truth and originality never failed to arrest his attention; he was a real force in the directing of the *Atlantic* element of the American reading public toward the rising new school of authors, but aside from this his criticism is in no way significant. His art and his enthusiasm were in his sketches— American sketches now with the light of Europe over them. *Their Wedding Journey* is an American counterpart to *Italian Journeys,* and it is made coherent by introducing a married pair on their bridal tour and describing places and manners as they became acquainted with them. The interest comes not at all from the narrative; it comes from the setting. It is an American sentimental journey over which the author strives to throw the soft light of European romance. Rochester was like Verona; and Quebec—"on what perverse pretext was it not some ancient town of Normandy?"

Sketches, pictures of life, studies of manners, these are the object of the book. The author is not writing to record incidents, for there are few incidents to record. "That which they [the bridal pair] found the most difficult of management," he declares, "was the want of incident for the most part of the time; and I who write their history might also sink under it, but that I am supported by the fact that it is so typical in this respect. I even imagine the ideal reader for whom one writes as yawning over these barren details with the life-like weariness of an actual traveling companion of theirs.''

As a story from the standpoint of Bonner's *New York Ledger,* then in the high tide of its prosperity, it was dreary reading. But it was true in every line, true of background, and true to the facts of human life as Howells saw those facts. ''Ah! poor real life, which I love,'' he exclaims, after a minute sketch of a commercial traveler and some loud-voiced girls on the train, ''can I make others share the delight I share in thy foolish and insipid face?''

But this earlier Howells gives us more than real life: he gives us real life touched with the glow of poetry, for the poet in Howells died a lingering death. It seems as if novel-writing had come to him, as he declares all of his literary life had come, almost without his willing it. It grew gradually and naturally out of his sketch-writing. In his early sketch books he had studied places and ''men in their actuality,'' and he would now make his sketches more comprehensive and bind them with a thread of narrative. A sketch like ''A Day's Outing'' in *Suburban Sketches,* and a ''novel'' like *Their Wedding Journey* differ only in the single element of quantity. *A Chance Acquaintance,* the record of another sentimental journey, with its careful sketches along the St. Lawrence and the Saguenay, and at Quebec, and its *Pride-and-Prejudice*-like study of a typical Bostonian and a Western girl, has more of story than the earlier book, but it is still a sketch book rather than a novel. *Private Theatricals,* his fourth essay at fiction, is so minute a study of a particular summer boarding house and its patrons that it was never allowed to get beyond serial publication, at least one can think of no other reason for its suppression, and *The Undiscovered Country* might be entitled *Sketches Among the Spiritualists and the Shakers.*

The Howells of this earlier period has little of story and little of problem. His object is to present men and manners ''in their actuality.'' *A Foregone Conclusion,* the most idyllic of his novels, in reality is an added chapter to *Venetian Life,* written in the retrospect of later years. The golden light of Venice is over it, a Venice now more mellow and poetic because it is a part of the author's vanishing youth—his *alma mater,* as it were;

more golden every year. The springtime is in every page of it:

> The day was one of those that can come to the world only in early June at Venice. The heaven was without a cloud, but a blue haze made mystery of the horizon where the lagoon and sky met unseen. The breath of the sea bathed in freshness the city at whose feet her tides sparkled and slept. . . . The long garland of vines that festoons all Italy seemed to begin in the neighboring orchards; the meadows waved their long grasses in the sun, and broke in poppies as the sea-waves break in iridescent spray; the poplars marched in stately procession on either side of the straight, white road to Padua, till they vanished in the long perspective.

One loves to linger over this early Howells, despite all his diffuseness and his lack of dramatic power. One knows that there is a fatal weakness in the attempted tragedy of the priest, that the tale does not grip and compel and haunt the soul as such a tale must if it be worth telling at all, that its ending is sprawling and conventional, and yet one cannot but feel that there is in it, as there is in all of the work of this earlier period of the author's life, youth and freshness and beauty—and poetry. These earlier studies are not merely cold observations upon life and society, analysis as of reactions in a test-tube; these are the creations of a young poet, a romancer, a dreamer: the later manner was an artificial acquirement like the taste for olives.

IX

Howells's second literary period begins with the year 1881 when he resigned the editorship of the *Atlantic Monthly* and settled in the country at Belmont to devote all his time to the writing of fiction for the *Century* magazine. During the decade that followed he produced his two strongest works, *A Modern Instance*, and *The Rise of Silas Lapham*, and also *A Woman's Reason, The Minister's Charge, Indian Summer*, and others. He had found his life work. During the earlier period he had been, as it were, experimenting; he had published fifteen books, only five of which were novels, but it was clear now that the five pointed the way he was to go.

He began now with larger canvas and with more sweep and freedom. No more idyllic sketches now: his business was to make studies at full length of American character and American manners. He would do for New England what Jane Austen had done for her narrow little corner of old England. He too had "the exquisite touch," to use the words of Sir Walter Scott, "which renders ordinary commonplace things and characters interesting from the truth of the description and the sentiment." Like her he would bring no message and analyze no passion more intense than the perplexity of a maiden with two lovers; and like her he would deal not with the problems of the soul of man, but with the manners of a small province.

His essay on Henry James in the *Century* of November, 1882, the proclamation of the new Howells, raised a tempest of discussion that did not subside for a decade. "The stories," he declared, "were all told long ago; and now we want to know merely what the novelist thinks about persons and situations." "The art of fiction has become a finer art in our day than it was with Dickens and Thackeray. We could not suffer the confidential attitude of the latter now, nor the mannerism of the former, any more than we could endure the prolixity of Richardson or the coarseness of Fielding. These great men are of the past—they and their methods and interests; even Trollope and Reade are not of the present." And of the new novel—"The moving accident is certainly not its trade; and it prefers to avoid all manner of dire catastrophes." James he classified not as a story-teller, but as a character-painter, and he proceeded to set forth the thesis that "the novelist's main business is to possess his reader with a due conception of his characters and the situations in which they find themselves. If he does more or less than this he equally fails." "It is, after all, what a writer has to say rather than what he has to tell that we care for now-a-days."

But the Howells of the eighties was not ready yet for grounds so advanced when it came to his own work. The romancer within him died hard. "I own," he admitted, "that I like a finished story," and he proceeded to tell finished stories with plots and moving accidents and culminating ends. *A Woman's Reason* is as elaborate in plot and incident as a novel by Mrs. Braddon, and it has as conventional an ending. The heroine, apparently deserted by her lover, is forced to live in a humble boarding house where she is wooed persistently by a member of the English nobility. She is true, however, to her old lover, who after having lived years on a desert island which for a time we are permitted to share with him, returns at last to rescue her, and the marriage crowns the book with gold. *A Modern Instance* and *The Rise of Silas Lapham,* undoubtedly his strongest work, are first of all stories, and to the great majority of all who have ever read them they have been *only* stories. In other words, they have been read for what the author had to tell, and not necessarily for what he has had to say.

He has been careful always that his tales end well, as careful indeed as an E. P. Roe. The ending of *A Foregóne Conclusion* and of *The Minister's Charge* fly in the very face of realism. He is bold in his theories, but in the application of these theories to his own work he has an excess of timidity. Realism should flout the conventionalities; it should have regard only for the facts in the case, affect the reader as they may, but Howells had continually on his mind the readers of the *Atlantic* and the nerves of the "Brahmins." The end of *An Imperative Duty,* for instance, could have come only as a concession to the conventional reader. He allows the woman with the negro blood to marry the man she loves, and then hastens to say that they lived the rest of their lives in Italy, where such matches are not criticized and where the woman passed everywhere as an Italian. It would have been stronger art to have made her rise superior to her selfishness, the soul triumphant over the flesh, and refuse to marry the man, and to do it for the sole compelling reason that she loved him.

The much-discussed realism of the Howells of the eighties was simply a demand for truth, an insistence that all characters and backgrounds be drawn from nature, and that no sequence of events be given that might not happen in the life of the average man. His stories therefore, like James's, move slowly. There is much in them of what is technically called "lumber"—material that is brought in for other reasons than to advance the progress of the story. Every character is minutely described; cravats and waistcoats, hats and watch-charms, dresses and furbelows, are dwelt upon with thoroughness. The author stops the story to describe a carpet, a wardrobe, a peculiarity of gesture. A page is taken up with a description of the heroine's drawing-room, another is given to the view from her window. As a result we get from the reading of the book, in spite of our impatience at its slow movement, a feeling of actuality. Bartley Hubbard and Marcia seem at the end like people we have known; we are sure we should recognize Squire Gaylord even if we met him on Tremont Street. Silas Lapham, the typical self-made American of the era, and his wife and daughters, are speaking likenesses, done with sympathy; for the early years of Howells had enabled him, unlike James, to enter into bourgeois life with comprehension. Everywhere portraits done with a thousand careful touches—New England types largely drawn against a minute background of manners.

It cannot fail that these novels, even like those of Jane Austen, will be valued in years to come as historical documents. As a picture of the externals of the era they portray there is nothing to compare with them. The Boston of the seventies, gone now as completely as the Boston of the Revolution, lives in these pages. Every phase of its external life has been dwelt upon: its underworld and its lodging houses and its transformed country boys in *The Minister's Charge;* the passing of the old Boston of the India trade days and the helplessness of the daughters of the patricians in *A Woman's Reason;* literary and journalistic Boston in *A Modern Instance;* the high and low of Boston society in *The Rise of Silas Lapham;* the entry of woman into the learned professions in *Dr. Breen's Practice,* and so on and on—he has covered the field with the faithfulness of a sociological historian. He is a painter of manners, evermore manners.

As to whether or not he touched the soul of New England as did Rose Terry Cooke, for instance, is another question. His knowledge of the region was an acquirement, not a birthright. The surface of its society, the peculiarities of its manners and its point of view, the unusual traits of its natives, these he saw with the sharpened eyes of an outsider, but he never became so much a part of what he wrote that he could treat it, as Mrs. Wilkins-Freeman treated it, from the heart outward. The thing perhaps that impressed him first and most deeply as he came a stranger into the provincial little area was the so-called New England conscience, "grim aftercrop of Puritanism, that hypochondria of the soul into which the Puritanism of her father's race had sickened in her, and which so often seems to satisfy its crazy claim upon conscience by enforcing some aimless act of self sacrifice." [12] All of his New England characters have this as their humor, using the word in the Ben Jonsonian sense. Novels like *A*

[12] *An Imperative Duty.*

Woman's Reason and *The Minister's Charge* turn upon it. With Hawthorne the thing became a moving power, a tragic center of his art that could move the soul to pity or to terror, but Howells treats it never with the sympathy of comprehension. He never so treats it that we feel it; he never shows us a character possessed by its power until it is driven over the brink of tragedy. It is simply one of the details that make up the portrait of a New Englander, as in *The Lady of the Aroostook,* the maiden cries out at the happy moment when her lover declares himself: " 'Oh, I knew it, I knew it,' cried Lydia. And then, as he caught her to him at last, 'Oh—Oh—are you *sure* it 's right?' " It is an element of manners, a picturesque peculiarity, a "humor."

X

In his first period Howells was poetic and spontaneous, in his second he was deliberate and artistic, in his third he was scientific and ethical. The last period began in a general way at the opening of the nineties with the publication, perhaps, of *A Hazard of New Fortunes.* He had spent another year in Europe, and in 1886 had removed to New York to do editorial work for the Harpers.

Now began what undoubtedly was the most voluminous literary career in the history of American literature. He took charge of the "Easy Chair" in *Harper's Monthly,* writing for it material equivalent to a volume a year, and in addition he poured out novels, books of travel, sketches, reviews, juveniles, autobiographies, comedies, farces, essays, editings, biographies— a mass of material equaled in bulk only by the writings of men like Southey or Dumas. He had learned his art with completeness. The production of clear and precise and brilliant English had become second nature, and he could pour it out steadily and with speed.

His novels more and more now began to conform to his realistic theories. The story sank gradually from prominence, and gradually analysis and scientific purpose took its place. *Annie Kilburn,* 1888, may be taken as the point of transition. The story could be told in a single chapter. There is no love-making, no culminating marriage or engagement, no passion, no crime, no violence greater than the flashing of eyes, no mystery, no climax. It is the afternoon talk of the ladies of a rural parish. For chapter after chapter they babble on, assisted now and then by the doctor or the minister or the lawyer who drops in for a cup of tea. As in the work of James, one may turn a dozen pages and find the same group still refining upon the same theme over the same tea-cups. The object of the author is not progress in events, but progress in characterization and ethical analysis. Through the mouths of these talkers he is discussing the problems of the rural church and the rural community. He attempts to settle nothing finally, but he sets the problem before the reader in all its phases, and the reader may come to his own conclusion.

This novel is typical of all the fiction of the later Howells. Everywhere now problems—moral, social, psychological—problems discussed by means of endless dialogue. *A Hazard of New Fortunes* is almost as long as *Pamela,* and when it is ended there is no logical reason for the ending save that the novelist has used the space allotted to him. Another volume could easily have been added telling of the experiences of the Dreyfooses in Europe. The novelist may stop at any point, for he is not telling a story, he is painting character, and manners and developing a thesis. In *Annie Kilburn* the effect of the sudden ending is disconcerting. It is like the cutting off of a yard of cloth.

Howells had passed under the powerful influence of Tolstoy. "As much as one merely human being can help another," he declares, "I believe that he has helped me; he has not influenced me in esthetics only, but in ethics, too, so that I can never again see life in the way I saw it before I knew him." It is absurd, however, to think that any influence could fundamentally have changed the art of a man like Howells in his fiftieth year. What Tolstoy did for him was to confirm and deepen tendencies in his work that already had become established and to turn his mind from the contemplation exclusively of manners and men in their actuality to problems ethical and social. He gave to him a message and a wider view of art. "What I feel sure is that I can never look at life in the mean and sordid way that I did before I read Tolstoy." "He has been to me that final consciousness, which he speaks of so wisely in his essay on 'Life.'"

As an example of this final Howells we may read *The Landlord of Lion's Head,* or *The Traveler from Altruria,* or *The Quality of Mercy,* which are not so much novels as minute studies of social or moral phases of the times, illustrated by means of a particular case and made clear by voluminous details. Minor characters serve as a chorus as the case proceeds, and the final effect is sermonic rather than novelistic. The poetic and the esthetic have yielded to the ethical and socialistic. In America every art ends at last in a sermon.

XI

The realism of Howells is of the eighteenth-century type rather than the nineteenth. It is classicism, as Henry James's is classicism. His affinity is with Richardson rather than with Zola. He was timid and conscious of his audience. He had approached Boston with too much of reverence; the "tradition of the *Atlantic*" lay heavily upon him during all of his earlier period; the shadow of Lowell was upon his page and he wrote as in his presence; the suggestive words in a review of one of his earlier books by the *North American Review*, final voice of New England refinement, compelled him: "He has the incapacity to be common." Thus his early writings had in them nothing of the Western audacity and newness. A realistic reaction from the romantic school of the early nineteenth century was everywhere —on the Continent, in England, in America—changing literary standards; Howells felt it and yielded to it, but he yielded only as Longfellow would have yielded had he been of his generation, or Holmes, or Lowell. He yielded to a modified realism, a timid and refined realism, a realism that would not offend the sensibilities of Boston, the "Boston," to quote from *A Chance Acquaintance*, "that would rather perish by fire and sword than to be suspected of vulgarity; a critical, fastidious, reluctant Boston, dissatisfied with the rest of the hemisphere." He records scarcely a crime in all his volumes: he has not in his voluminous gallery a woman who ever broke a law more serious than indiscretions at an afternoon tea. As a result there is no remorse, no problems of life in the face of broken law, no decisions that involve life and death and the agony that is sharper than death. In his pages life is an endless comedy where highly conventional and very refined people meet day after day and talk, and dream of Europe, and make love in the leisurely, old-fashioned way, and marry happily in the end the lover of their choice.

He is as tedious as Richardson and at times nearly as voluminous. He uses page after page of *The Lady of the Aroostook* to tell what might have been told in a single sentence. The grandfather and the aunt set the general situation before the reader, then the aunt and the clergymen, then the two passengers, then the passengers and the captain, then the heroine and the cabin boy in six pages, and finally at the very end of the book the heroine and the transplanted New England woman in Venice. Art is "nothing too much." We feel instinctively that the author is making a mountain out of a molehill because he believes his readers will expect him to do it. To Bostonians he believes it would be inexpressibly shocking for a girl to sail for Europe the only woman on board the ship, though she be under the express care of the fatherly old sea captain and though two of the three other passengers are Boston gentlemen. The perturbation of these two model young men, their heroic nerving of themselves to live through the experience, their endless refinings and analyzings of the situation, and all of their subsequent doings are simply Howells's conception of "the quality of Boston."

It is Richardsonism; it is realism of the *Pamela* order; it is a return to the eighteenth century with its reverence for respectability and the conventions, its dread of letting itself go and making scenes, its avoidance of all that would shock the nerves of the refined circle for which it wrote. The kinship of Howells with Richardson indeed is closer even than that between Howells and James. They approach life from the same angle. Both profess to deal with men and manners in their actuality, both would avoid the moving accident and discard from their fictions all that is fantastic or improbable; both would keep closely within the circle of the highly respectable middle-class society of which they were a part; both professed to work with no other than a moral purpose; and both would reveal the inner life of their characters only as the reader might infer it after having read endless descriptions and interminable conversations; and both wrote, as Tennyson termed *Pamela* and *Clarissa*, "great still books" that flow on and on with sluggish current to no particular destination.

Howells is less dramatic than Richardson, yet one may turn pages and chapters of his novels into dramatic form by supplying to the dialogue the names of the speakers. Howells, indeed, acquired a faculty in the construction of sparkling dialogue so brilliant that he exercised it in the production of a surprising number of so-called comedies: *A Counterfeit Presentiment, The Mouse-Trap, The Elevator,* and the like, dramatic in form but essentially novelistic in all things else. His genius was not dramatic. He evolves his characters and situations slowly. The swift rush and culminating plot of the drama are beyond him. His comedies are chapters of dialogue from unwritten novels—studies in character and manners by means of conversations.

Richardson's novels centered about women; they were written *for* women; they were praised first of all for their minute knowledge of the feminine heart. There was indeed in his own nature a feminine element that made him the absolute opposite of a masculine type, for instance like Fielding. Howells also centered his work about women. In one of the earliest reviews of his work is the sentence "his knowledge of women is simply marvelous." Like his earlier prototype, he has expended upon them a world of analysis and dissection and description. With what result? To one who has read all of his fictions straight through there emerges at last from the helpless, fluttering, hesitating, rapturous and dejected, paradoxical, April-hoping, charming throng of his heroines—Mrs. March, Kitty Ellison, Lydia, Marcia, Mrs. Campbell, Mrs. Roberts, Helen Harkness, Florida, Mrs. Lapham and her daughters, Dr. Breen, Clara Kingsbury, Rhoda Aldgate, Annie Kilburn, Mrs. Dreyfoos and the hundred others—there emerges a single woman, the Howells type, as distinct a creature as the Richardson type, and as one compares the two he is startled to find them almost identical. The Richardson feminine is a trembling, innocent, helpless creature pursued by men; the Howells type is the same woman transported into the nineteenth century, inconsequent, temperamental, often bird-like and charming, electric at repartee, pursued by men and fleeing flutteringly from them, yet dependent upon them for her very existence. In all of these fictions there is scarcely a feminine figure, at least in a leading rôle, of whom her sex may be proud. His masculine characters are many of them strong and admirable, even to the minor figures like Mr. Harkness and Captain Butler and Squire Gaylord. He has, perhaps, created two characters—Silas Lapham and Bartly Hubbard—to place beside Natty Bumppo, and Uncle Remus, and Yuba Bill, Sam Lawson, Colonel Sellers, and a few others, as permanent additions to the gallery of American types. But with all his studies of women he has added nothing original, no type that can be accepted as characteristic or admirable.

XII

The art of Howells is essentially of this present world. Of the soul of man and the higher life of his dreams and aspirations he has nothing to tell. He writes of Hawthorne: "In all his books there is the line of thoughts that we think of only in the presence of the mysteries of life and death. It is not his fault that this is not intelligence, that it knots the brow in sore doubt rather than shapes the lips to utterance of the things that can never be said." Howells would ignore such themes. He is of the age of doubt, the classical age, rather than of the age of faith that sees and creates. Lightly he skims over the surface of material things, noting the set of a garment or the shade of a cravat, recording rather than creating, interested in life only as it is affected by manners, sketching with rapid pen characters evolved by a provincial environment, tracing with leisurely thoroughness the love story of a boy and girl, recording the April changes of a maiden's heart, the gossip of an afternoon tea—a feminine task one would suppose, work for a Fanny Burney, a Maria Edgeworth or a Mrs. Gaskell, no work indeed for a great novelist at the dawn of a new period in a new land. While the West, of which his earlier life was a part, was crashing out a new civilization; while the air was electric with the rush and stir of rising cities; while a new star of hope for the nations was rising in the West; while a mighty war of freedom was waging about him and the soul of man was being tried as by fire, Howells, like Clarissa Harlowe, is interested "in her ruffles, in her gloves, her samplers, her aunts and uncles."

And yet even as we class him as a painter of manners we remember that America has no manners in the narrower sense of the term. New England had the nearest approach to manners, yet New England, all must admit, was wholly imitative; she was enamoured of Europe. Howells has another side to his classicism, one utterly wanting in Richardson—he is a satirist of manners, a critic and a reformer. Richardson took English manners as he took the English Constitution and the English language as a matter of course. He never dreamed of changing the order of things; he would only portray it and teach individuals how best to deport themselves under its laws. Howells, after his first awe of New England had subsided, became critical. He would change manners; he would portray them that men by seeing them would learn their ridiculousness—in short, he became, what every classicist must sooner or later become, a satirist—a chafer under the conventions that bind him,—a critic.

Howells then is the rare figure of a lyric poet and a romanticist who deliberately forced himself into classicism as a result of his environment. His earlier works are the record of a transition— enthusiasm, poetic glow, romance, tempered more and more with scientific exactness and coldness and skill. Like James, he learned his profession with infinite toil; like James, he formed himself upon masters and then defended his final position with a summary of the laws of his art. Like James, he schooled himself to distrust the emotions and work wholly from the intellect. The result in the case of both, in the case of all classicists in fact, has been that the reader is touched only in the intellect. One smiles at the flashes of wit; one seldom laughs. No one ever shed a tear over a page either of Howells or James. One admires their skill; one takes a certain pleasure in the lifelikeness of the characters —especially those of Howells—but cold lifelikeness is not the supreme object of art; manners and outward behavior are but a small part of life. Unless the novelist can lay hold of his reader's heart and walk with him with sympathy and conviction he must be content to be ranked at last as a mere showman and not a voice, not a leader, not a prophet.

XIII

Howells, like James, was peculiarly a product of the later nineteenth century and of the wave of democracy in literature that came both to Europe and America as a reflex from the romanticism of Scott and Coleridge and the German *Sturm und Drang*. Had he lived a generation earlier he would have been a poet of the Dr. Holmes type, an Irving, or a George William Curtis. The spirit of the times and a combination of circumstances made of him the leader of the depicters of democracy in America. From the vantage point of the three leading magazines of the period he was enabled to command a wide audience and to exert enormous influence. His beautiful style disarmed criticism and concealed the leanness of his output. Had he been less timid, had he dared like Mark Twain or Whitman to forget the fastidious circle within which he lived, and write with truth and honesty and sincerity the great nation-wide story with its passion, its tragedy, its comedy, its tremendous significance in the history of humanity, he might have led American fiction into fields far broader than those into which it finally settled.

In the process of the new literary discovery of America Howells's part was to discover the prosaic ordinary man of the middle class and to make him tolerable in fiction. He was the leading force in the reaction against the Sylvanus Cobb type of romance that was so powerful in America in the early seventies. He made the new realism respectable. All at once America found that she was full of material for fiction. Hawthorne had taught that the new world was barren of material for the novelist, Cooper had limited American fiction to the period of the settlement and the Revolution; Longfellow and Taylor had turned to romantic Europe. After Howells's minute studies of the New England middle class, every provincial environment in America produced its recorder, and the novel of locality for a time dominated American literature.

In another and more decided way, perhaps, Howells was a potent leader during the period. He has stood for finished art, for perfection of style, for literary finish, for perfect English in an age of slovenliness and slang. No writer of the period has excelled him in accuracy of diction, in brilliancy of expression, in unfailing purity of style. There is an eighteenth-century fastidiousness about every page that he has written.

The tribute of Mark Twain is none too strong: "For forty years his English has been to me a continual delight and astonishment. In the sustained exhibition of certain great qualities—clearness, compression, verbal exactness, and unforced and seemingly unconscious felicity of phrasing—he is, in my belief, without peer in the English-speaking world. *Sustained.* I entrench myself behind that protecting word. There are others who exhibit those qualities as greatly as does he, but only by intervaled distributions of rich moonlight, with stretches of veiled and dimmer landscape between, whereas Howells's moon sails cloudless skies all night and all the nights.''

BIBLIOGRAPHY

HENRY JAMES. (1843-1916.) *Watch and Ward* [in the *Atlantic*], 1871; *A Passionate Pilgrim, Roderick Hudson, Transatlantic Sketches*, 1875; *The American*, 1877; *French Poets and Novelists, The Europeans, Daisy Miller*, 1878; *An International Episode, Life of Hawthorne, A Bundle of Letters, The Madonna of the Future, Confidence*, 1879; *Diary of a Man of Fifty, Washington Square*, 1880; *The Portrait of a Lady*, 1881; *The Siege of London*, 1883; *Portraits of Places, Tales of Three Cities, A Little Tour in France*, 1884; *The Author of Beltraffio*, 1885; *The Bostonians, Princess Casamassima*, 1886; *Partial Portraits, The Aspern Papers, The Reverberator*, 1888; *A London Life*, 1889; *The Tragic Muse*, 1890; *The Lesson of the Master*, 1892; *Terminations*, 1896; *The Spoils of Poynton, What Maisie Knew*, 1897; *In the Cage*, 1898; *The Awkward Age*, 1899; *The Soft Side, The Sacred Font*, 1901; *The Wings of the Dove*, 1902; *The Better Sort, William Wetmore Story and His Friends*, 1903; *The Question of Our Speech, The Lesson of Balzac* [Lectures], 1905; *The American Scene*, 1906; *Italian Hours, Julia Bride, Novels and Tales*, 24 volumes, 1909; *Finer Grain*, 1910; *The Outcry*, 1911; *A Small Boy and Others*, 1912; *Notes of a Son and Brother*, 1913; *Notes on Novelists, with Some Other Notes*, 1914.

WILLIAM DEAN HOWELLS. (1837——.) *Poems of Two Friends*, 1859; *Lives and Speeches of Abraham Lincoln and Hannibal Hamlin* [Hamlin by J. L. Hayes], 1860; *Venetian Life*, 1866; *Italian Journeys*, 1867; *No Love Lost: a Romance of Travel*, 1868; *Suburban Sketches*, 1871; *Their Wedding Journey*, 1872; *A Chance Acquaintance, Poems*, 1873; *A Foregone Conclusion*, 1874; *Amateur Theatricals* [in the *Atlantic*], 1875; *The Parlor Car: Farce*, 1876; *Out of the Question: a Comedy, A Counterfeit Presentiment*, 1877; *The Lady of the Aroostook*, 1879; *The Undiscovered Country*, 1880; *A Fearful Responsibility, and Other Stories, Dr. Breen's Practice: a Novel*, 1881; *A Modern Instance: a Novel*, 1882; *The Sleeping-Car: a Farce, A Woman's Reason: a Novel*, 1883; *The Register: Farce, Three Villages*, 1884; *The Elevator: Farce, The Rise of Silas Lapham, Tuscan Cities*, 1885; *The Garroters: Farce, Indian Summer, The Minister's Charge*, 1886; *Modern Italian Poets: Essays and Versions, April Hopes*, 1887; *A Sea-Change; or, Love's Stowaway: a Lyricated Farce, Annie Kilburn: a Novel*, 1888; *The Mouse-Trap, and Other Farces, A Hazard of New Fortunes: a Novel*, 1889; *The Shadow of a Dream: a Story, A Boy's Town*, 1890; *Criticism and Fiction, The Albany Depot, An Imperative Duty*, 1891; *The Quality of Mercy: a Novel, A Letter of Introduction: Farce, A Little Swiss Sojourn, Christmas Every Day, and Other Stories Told for Children*, 1892; *The World of Chance: a Novel, The Unexpected Guests: a Farce, My Year in a Log Cabin, Evening Dress: Farce, The Coast of Bohemia: a Novel*, 1893; *A Traveler from Altruria: Romance*, 1894; *My Literary Passions, Stops of Various Quills*, 1895; *The Day of Their Wedding: a Novel, A Parting and a Meeting, Impressions and Experiences*, 1896; *A Previous Engagement: Comedy, The Landlord at Lion's Head: a Novel, An Open-Eyed Conspiracy: an Idyl of Saratoga*, 1897; *The Story of a Play: a Novel*, 1898; *Ragged Lady: a Novel, Their Silver*

Wedding Journey, 1899; *Room Forty-five: a Farce, The Smoking Car: a Farce, An Indian Giver: a Comedy, Literary Friends and Acquaintance: a Personal Retrospect of American Authorship*, 1900; *A Pair of Patient Lovers, Heroines of Fiction*, 1901; *The Kentons, The Flight of Pony Baker: a Boy's Town Story, Literature and Life: Studies*, 1902; *Questionable Shapes, Letters Home*, 1903; *The Son of Royal Langbrith: a Novel*, 1904; *Miss Bellard's Inspiration: a Novel, London Films*, 1905; *Certain Delightful English Towns*, 1906; *Through the Eye of a Needle: a Romance, Mulberries in Pay's Garden, Between the Dark and the Daylight*, 1907; *Fennel and Rue: a Novel, Roman Holidays, and Others*, 1908; *The Mother and the Father: Dramatic Passages, Seven English Cities*, 1909; *My Mark Twain: Reminiscences and Criticisms, Imaginary Interviews*, 1910; *Parting Friends: a Farce*, 1911; *Familiar Spanish Travels, New Leaf Mills*, 1913; *The Seen and Unseen at Stratford-on-Avon*, 1914.

CHAPTER XI

The New England school, which had so dominated the mid-nineteenth century, left, as we have seen, no heirs. As the great figures of the "Brahmins" disappeared one by one, vigorous young leaders from without the Boston circle came into their places, but the real succession—the native New England literary generation after Emerson—was feminine. During the decade from 1868 the following books, written by women born, the most of them, in those thirties which had witnessed the beginnings of the earlier group, came from the American press:

1868. *Little Women,* Louisa M. Alcott (1832–1888).
1868. *The Gates Ajar,* Elizabeth Stuart Phelps (1844–1911).
1870. *Verses,* Helen Hunt Jackson (1831–1885).
1872. *Poems,* Celia Thaxter (1836–1894).
1873. *The Saxe Holm Stories,* "Saxe Holm."
1875. *One Summer,* Blanche Willis Howard (1847–1898).
1875. *After the Ball and Other Poems,* Nora Perry (1841–1896).
1877. *Deephaven,* Sarah Orne Jewett (1849–1909).
1878. *The China Hunter's Club,* Annie Trumbull Slosson (1838 ——).

Of the same generation, but earlier or else later in the literary field, were the poets Elizabeth Akers Allen (1832–1911), and Louise Chandler Moulton (1835–1908) ; the essayist Mary Abigail Dodge, "Gail Hamilton" (1838–1896) ; the novelists Rose Terry Cooke (1827–1892), Jane G. Austin (1831–1894), and Harriet Prescott Spofford (1835——) ; and, latest of all to be known, the intense lyrist Emily Dickinson (1830–1886). In the eighties was to come the school of the younger realists, a part of the classical reaction—Alice Brown (1857——), Kate Douglas Wiggin (1859——) and Mary E. Wilkins (1862——), who were to record the later phases of the New England decline.

Outside of the New England environment there was also a notable outburst of feminine literature. In the thirteen years from 1875 appeared the following significant first volumes:

1875. *Castle Nowhere,* Constance Fenimore Woolson (1848–1894).
1875. *A Woman in Armor,* Mary Hartwell Catherwood (1847–1902).
1877. *That Lass o' Lowrie's,* Frances Hodgson Burnett (1849——).
1883. *The Led Horse Claim,* Mary Hallock Foote (1847——).
1884. *In the Tennessee Mountains,* Mary Noailles Murfree (1850——).
1884. *A New Year's Masque,* Edith M. Thomas (1854——).
1886. *The Old Garden and Other Verses,* Margaretta Wade Deland (1857——).
1886. *Monsieur Motte,* Grace King (1852——).
1887. *Knitters in the Sun,* Alice French (1850——).

The wide recognition of the Victorian women, Charlotte Brontë, George Eliot, and Mrs. Browning, and their American contemporaries, Margaret Fuller and Mrs. Stowe, had given the impetus, and the enormous popularity of prose fiction, a literary form peculiarly adapted to feminine treatment, the opportunity. During all the period the work of women dominated to a large degree the literary output.

I

The earliest group to appear was made up of daughters of the Brahmins—Louisa M. Alcott, Elizabeth Stuart Phelps, Rose Hawthorne Lathrop, Helen Hunt Jackson, and others—transition figures who clung to the old New England tradition, yet were touched by the new forces.   The representative figure is Elizabeth Stuart Phelps.   Daughter and granddaughter of theologians and divinity professors, reared in the atmosphere of the Andover theological seminary of the earlier period, she was a daughter of her generation, a perfect sample of the culminating feminine product of two centuries of New England Puritanism—sensitive to the brink of physical collapse, intellectual, disquieted of soul, ridden of conscience, introspective.   We know the type perfectly. Miss Jewett, Mrs. Freeman, Miss Brown, have drawn us scores of these women—the final legatees of Puritanism, daughters of Transcendentalists and abolitionists and religious wranglers.

Literature to this group of women was not only a heritage from the past, from great shadowy masters who were mere names and books, it was a home product in actual process of manufacture about their cradles.   The mother of Elizabeth Stuart Phelps —Elizabeth Stuart—had published in 1851 *Sunny-Side,* a simple story of life in a country parsonage, that had sold one hundred thousand copies in one year.   She had followed it with *A Peep at Number Five,* a book that places her with Mrs. Stowe as a pioneer depicter of New England life, and then, at the very opening of her career, she had died in 1852. "It was impossible to be her daughter and not to write. Rather, I should say, impossible to be *their* daughter and not to have something to say, and a pen to say it." [1] The daughter was publishing at thirteen; at nineteen she was the author of twelve Sunday-school books; [1] at twenty-four she had issued *The Gates Ajar,* which was to go through twenty editions the first year and to be translated into the principal European languages.

Gates Ajar is a significant book, significant beyond its real literary merit. It is a small book, an excited, over-intense book, yet as a document in the history of a period and a confession laying bare for an instant a woman's soul it commands attention. It is not a novel; it is a *journal intime,* an impassioned theological argument, a personal experience written with tears and read with tears by hundreds of thousands. It was the writer herself who had received the telegram telling that a loved one— not a brother as the book infers—had been shot in battle; it was her own life that had almost flickered out as the result of it; and it was she who had tried to square the teachings ingrained into her Puritan intellect with the desolation of her woman's heart.

It was peculiarly a New England book: only a New Englander of the old tradition can understand the full meaning of it, and yet it came at a moment when the whole nation was eager and ready for its message. The war had brought to tens of thousands what it had brought to this New England woman. In every house there was mourning, and the Puritan vision of the after life, unreasonable and lifeless, was inadequate for a nation that had been nourished upon sentimentalism. The heart of the people demanded something warm and sensible and convincing in place of the cold scriptural metaphors and abstractions. The new spirit that had been awakened by the war called for reality and concrete statement everywhere, and it found in the book, which made of heaven another earth—a glorified New England perhaps—with occupation and joys and friendships unchanged, a revelation with which it was in full accord. It brought comfort, for in every line of it was the intensity of conviction, of actual

---

[1] *Chapters from a Life.*

experience. It quivered with sympathy, it breathed reality from every page, and it seemed to break down the barriers until the two worlds were so near together that one might hold his breath to listen. The book, while it undoubtedly helped to prolong the sentimental era in America, nevertheless must be counted among the forces that brought to the new national period its fuller measure of toleration, its demand for reality, its wider sympathy.

All the author's later books bear the same marks of intensity, of subjectivity, of purpose: all of them are outpourings of herself. She is a special pleader shrilling against abuses, as in *Loveliness*, which excoriates vivisection, arguing for causes as in *The Story of Avis* and *Doctor Zay*, which take high ground concerning women, or preaching sermons as in *A Singular Life*, a vision of the ideal pastor and his church. The accumulated Puritanism within her gave to all her work dramatic tension. It is impossible to read her with calmness: one is shocked and grieved and harrowed; one is urged on every page to think, to feel, to rush forth and right some wrong, to condemn some evil or champion some cause.

Her world was largely a subjective one; to write she must be touched strongly on the side of her sympathy, she must have brought vividly into her vision some concrete case. Before she could write "The Tenth of January"—*Atlantic*, 1868—she must spend a month in the atmosphere of the tragedy, not to collect realistic details, but to feel for herself the horror that she would impart. Her aim was sentimental: the whole story centers about the fact that while the ruins of the fallen mill were burning there floated out of the flames the voices of imprisoned girls singing "Shall We Gather at the River?" In its fundamentals her work, all of it, is autobiographic. Womanlike, she denied the fact—"If there be one thing among the possibilities to which a truly civilized career is liable, more than another objectionable to the writer of these words, the creation of autobiography has long been that one,"[2] and yet her books, all of them, have been chapters out of her own spiritual life. She has felt rather than seen, she has pleaded rather than created. Rather than present a rounded picture of the life objectively about her, she has given analyses of her own New England soul.

[2] *Chapters from a Life.*

She yielded, at last, in some degree, to the later tendencies of American literature, and drew with realistic faithfulness characters and characteristics in the little New England world that was hers—*A Madonna of the Tubs, The Supply at St. Agatha's, Jack, the Fisherman*, and a few others, yet even these are something more than stories, something more than pictures and interpretations. In *Jack, the Fisherman*, for instance, the temperance lesson stands out as sharply as if she had taken a text. The artist within her was dominated ever by the preacher; the novelist by the Puritan.

II

Another transition figure, typical of a group of writers and at the same time illustrative of the change that came over the tone of American literature after the war period, is Harriet Prescott Spofford. A country girl, born in a Maine village, educated in the academy of a country town in New Hampshire, compelled early to be the chief support of an invalided father and mother, she turned from the usual employments open to the women of her time—work in the cotton mills and school teaching—to the precarious field of literature. That could mean only story-writing for the family weeklies of the day, for a bourgeois public that demanded sentimental love stories and romance. Success made her ambitious. She applied herself to the study of fiction—American, English, French. How wide was her reading one may learn from her essays later published in the *Atlantic*, "The Author of 'Charles Auchester'" and "Charles Reade." The new realism which was beginning to be felt as a force in fiction, she flouted with indignation:—"he never with Chinese accuracy, gives us gossiping drivel that reduces life to the dregs of the commonplace." Rather would she emulate the popular novelist Elizabeth Sheppard: "At his, Disraeli's, torch she lit her fires, over his stories she dreamed, his 'Contarini Fleming' she declared to be the touchstone of all romantic truth."[3] The essay reveals the author like a flash-light. She too dreamed over Disraeli and the early Bulwer-Lytton, over Charlotte Brontë and Poe, over George Sand and French romance until at last when she submitted her first story to the *Atlantic*, "In a Cellar," Lowell for a time feared that it was a translation.

[3] *Atlantic*, June, 1862.

Other American women have had imaginations as lawless and as gorgeously rich as Harriet Prescott Spofford's; Augusta J. Evans Wilson, for instance, whose *St. Elmo* (1866) sold enormously even to the end of the new period, but no other American woman of the century was able to combine with her imaginings and her riotous colorings a real distinction of style. When in the fifth volume of the *Atlantic* appeared "The Amber Gods," judicious readers everywhere cried out in astonishment. Robert Browning and others in England praised it extravagantly. A new star had arisen, a novelist with a style that was French in its brilliancy and condensation, and oriental in its richness and color.

The Amber Gods fails of being a masterpiece by a margin so small that it exasperates, and it fails at precisely the point where most of the mid-century fiction failed. In atmosphere and style it is brilliant, so brilliant indeed that it has been appraised more highly than it deserves. Moreover, the *motif*, as one gathers it from the earlier pages, is worthy of a Hawthorne. The amber beads have upon them an ancestral curse, and the heroine with her supernatural beauty, a satanic thing without a soul, is a part of the mystery and the curse. Love seems at length to promise Undine-like a soul to this soulless creature:

He read it through—all that perfect, perfect scene. From the moment when he said,

> "I overlean,
> This length of hair and lustrous front—they turn
> Like an entire flower upward"—

his voice low, sustained, clear—till he reached the line,

> "Look at the woman here with the new soul"—

till he turned the leaf and murmured,

> "Shall to produce form out of unshaped stuff
> Be art—and, further, to evoke a soul
> From form be nothing? This new soul is mine!"—

till then he never glanced up.

But there is lack of constructive skill, lack of definiteness, lack of reality. The story sprawls at the end where it should culminate with compelling power. The last sentence is startling, but it is not connected with the *motif* and is a mere sensational addition. Everywhere there is the unusual, the overwrought, incoherent vagueness. It is not experience, it is a revel of color and of sensuousness; it is a Keats-like banquet, sweets and spicery.

The parallelism with Keats may be pressed far. She was first of all a poet, a lyrist, a dweller in Arcady rather than in a New England village. She, like so many others of her generation, had fallen under the spell of the young Tennyson, and her world is a world of cloying sweetness, of oriental sensuousness, of merely physical beauty. Poems like "Pomegranate-Flowers" and "In Titian's Garden" show her tropical temperament:

> And some girl sea-bronzed and sparkling,
> On her cheek the stain ensanguined,
> Bears aloft the bossy salver:
> As the innocent Lavinia
> Brought them in old days of revel
> Fruits and flowers amesh with sunbeams—
> No red burnish of pomegranates,
> No cleft peach in velvet vermeil,
> No bright grapes their blue bloom bursting,
> Dews between the cool globes slipping,
> Dews like drops of clouded sapphire,
> But the brighter self and spirit,
> Glowed illusive in her beauty.

The same poetic glamour she threw over all the work that now poured in swift profusion from her pen: *Sir Rohan's Ghost, Azarian,* and a score of short stories in the *Atlantic* and *Harper's* and other periodicals. It had been felt that the faults so manifest in "In a Cellar" and "The Amber Gods" would disappear as the young author gained in maturity and knowledge of her art, but they not only persisted, they increased. Like Charlotte Brontë, whom in so many ways she resembled, she knew life only as she dreamed of it in her country seclusion or read of it in romance. At length toleration ceased. In 1865 *The North American Review* condemned *Azarian* as "devoid of human nature and false to actual society," and then added the significant words: "We would earnestly exhort Miss Prescott to be *real,* to be true to something." It marks not alone the end of the first period in Miss Prescott's career; it marks the closing of an era in American fiction.

Wonder has often been expressed that one who could write "The Amber Gods" and *Sir Rohan's Ghost* should suddenly lapse into silence and refuse to work the rich vein she had opened.

The change, however, was not with the author; it was with the times. Within a year Howells was assistant editor of the *Atlantic*. The artificiality of style and the high literary tone demanded in the earlier period disappeared with the war, and in their place came simplicity and naturalness and reality. The author of *Azarian* continued to write her passionate and melodious romance, but the columns of the *Atlantic* and *Harper's* at length were closed to her tales. A volume of her work of this period still awaits a publisher.

She now turned to poetry—there was no ban upon that; the old régime died first in its prose—and poured out lyrics that are to be compared even with those of Taylor and Aldrich, lyrics full of passion and color and sensuous beauty. Among the female poets of America she must be accorded a place near the highest. Only "H. H." could have poured out a lyric like this:

> In the dew and the dark and the coolness
>   I bend to the beaker and sip,
> For the earth is the Lord's, and its fullness
>   Is held like the cup to my lip.
>
> For his are the vast opulences
>   Of color, of line, and of flight,
> And his was the joy of the senses
>   Before I was born to delight.
>
> Forever the loveliness lingers,
>   Or in flesh, or in spirit, or dream,
> For it swept from the touch of his fingers
>   While his garments trailed by in the gleam.
>
> When the dusk and the dawn in slow union
>   Bring beauty to bead at the brim,
> I take, 't is the cup of communion,
>   I drink, and I drink it with Him!

A chapter of analysis could not so completely reveal the soul of Harriet Prescott Spofford.

For a time she busied herself making books on art decoration applied to furniture, and then at last she yielded to the forces of the age and wrote stories that again commanded the magazines. With work like "A Rural Telephone," "An Old Fiddler," and "A Village Dressmaker," she entered with real distinction the field that had been preëmpted by Miss Cooke and

Miss Jewett, the depiction of New England life in its actuality. Then at the close of her literary life she wrote deeper tales, like "Ordronnaux," a story with the same underlying *motif* as "The Amber Gods"—the creation of a soul in soulless beauty—but worked out now with reality, and experience, and compelling power. But it was too late. Could she have learned her lesson when Rose Terry Cooke learned hers; could she, instead of wasting her powers upon the gorgeous *Azarian,* have sent forth in 1863 her volume *Old Madame and Other Tragedies,* she might have taken a leading place among American novelists.

III

The school of fiction that during the later period stands for the depicting of New England life and character in their actuality had as its pioneers Mrs. Stowe and Rose Terry Cooke. Both did their earlier work in the spirit and manner of the mid century; both were poets and dreamers; both until late in their lives worked with feeling rather than observation and gave to their fiction vagueness of outline and romantic unreality. *Uncle Tom's Cabin* was written by one who had never visited the South, who drew her materials largely from her feelings and her imagination, and made instead of a transcript of actual life, a book of religious emotion, a swift, unnatural succession of picturesque scene and incident, an improvisation of lyrical passion—a melodrama. It is the typical novel of the period before 1870, the period that bought enormous editions of *The Lamplighter, The Wide, Wide World,* and *St. Elmo. The Minister's Wooing,* 1859, a historical romance written in the Andover that a little later was to produce *Gates Ajar,* was also fundamentally religious and controversial: it contained the keynote of what was afterwards known as the Andover movement. It dealt with a people and an environment that the author knew as she knew her own childhood, and it had therefore, as *Uncle Tom's Cabin* has not, sympathy of comprehension and truth to local scene and character. And yet despite her knowledge and her sympathy, the shadow of the mid century lies over it from end to end. It lacked what *Elsie Venner* lacked, what the great bulk of the pre-Civil War literature lacked, organization, sharpness of line, reality. Lowell, a generation ahead of his time, saw the weakness as well as the strength of the book, and in pointing it out he criticized not alone the author but her period as well. "My advice," he wrote her with fine courage, "is to follow your own instincts—to stick to nature, and avoid what people commonly call the 'Ideal'; for that, and beauty, and pathos, and success, all lie in the simply natural. . . . There are ten thousand people who can write 'ideal' things for one who can see, and feel, and reproduce nature and character."[4] Again the voice of the new period in American literature. But Mrs. Stowe was not one to heed literary advice; her work must come by inspiration, by impulse connected with purpose, and it must work itself out without thought of laws or models. *The Pearl of Orr's Island* came by impulse, as later, in 1869, came *Oldtown Folks*. "It was more to me than a story," she wrote of it; "it is my résumé of the whole spirit and body of New England, a country that is now exerting such an influence on the civilized world that to know it truly becomes an object."[5] That these books, and the *Oldtown Fireside Stories* that followed, do furnish such a résumé is by no means true, but that they are faithful transcripts of New England life, and are pioneer books in a field that later was to be intensively cultivated, cannot be doubted.

Mrs. Stowe's influence upon later writers was greater than is warranted by her actual accomplishment. The fierce light that beat upon *Uncle Tom's Cabin* gave to all of her work extraordinary publicity and made of her a model when otherwise she would have been unknown. The real pioneer was Rose Terry Cooke, daughter of a humble family in a small Connecticut village. Educated in a seminary near her home, at sixteen she was teaching school and at eighteen she was writing for *Graham's Magazine* a novel called *The Mormon's Wife*. That she had never been in Utah and had never even seen a Mormon, mattered not at all; the tale to win its audience need be true only to its author's riotous fancy. But the author had humor as well as fancy, and her sense of humor was to save her. In her school work in rural districts she was in contact constantly with the quaint and the ludicrous, with all those strongly individualized characters that Puritanism and isolated country living had rendered abundant. They were a part of her every-day life; they appealed not only to her sense of humor, but to her sympathy.

[4] Stowe's *Life of Harriet Beecher Stowe*, 334.
[5] Fields's *Authors and Friends*, 200.

She found herself thinking of them as she sought for subjects for her fiction. Her passion and her ambition were centered upon poetry. The idealism and the loftiness that Harriet Prescott Spofford threw into her early romance, she threw into her lyrics. Fiction was a thing of less seriousness; it could be trifled with; it could even record the humor and the quaintness of the common folk amid whom she toiled. She turned to it as to a diversion and she was surprised to find that Lowell, the editor of the new and exclusive *Atlantic,* preferred it to her poetry. For the first volume of the magazine he accepted no fewer than five of her homely little sketches, and praised them for their fidelity and truth.

That the author considered this prose work an innovation and something below the high tone of real literature, cannot be doubted. In "Miss Lucinda" (*Atlantic,* 1861), as perfect a story of its kind as was ever written, she feels called upon to explain, and her explanation is a declaration of independence:

> But if I apologize for a story that is nowise tragic, nor fitted to "the fashion of these times," possibly somebody will say at its end that I should also have apologized for its subject, since it is as easy for an author to treat his readers to high themes as vulgar ones, and velvet can be thrown into a portrait as cheaply as calico; but of this apology I wash my hands. I believe nothing in place or circumstance makes romance. I have the same quick sympathy for Biddy's sorrows with Patrick that I have for the Empress of France and her august, but rather grim, lord and master. I think words are often no harder to bear than "a blue batting," and I have a reverence for poor old maids as great as for the nine Muses. Commonplace people are only commonplace from character, and no position affects that. So forgive me once more, patient reader, if I offer you no tragedy in high life, no sentimental history of fashion and wealth, but only a little story about a woman who could not be a heroine.

This is the key to her later work. She wrote simple little stories of commonplace people in a commonplace environment, and she treated them with the sympathy of one who shares, rather than as one who looks down upon a spectacle and takes sides. There is no bookish flavor about the stories: they are as artless as the narrative told by a winter hearth. In the great mass of fiction dealing with New England life and character her work excels in humor—that subdued humor which permeates every part like an atmosphere—in the picturing of the odd and the whimsical, in tenderness and sympathy, and in the perfect artlessness that is the last triumph of art.   Hers is not a realism of the severe and scientific type: it is a poetic realism like that of the earlier and more delightful Howells, a realism that sees life through a window with the afternoon light upon it.   In the whole output of the school there are few sketches more charming and more true than her "Miss Lucinda," "Freedom Wheeler's Controversy with Providence," "Old Miss Dodd," "The Deacon's Week," and "A Town and a Country Mouse."   Others, like Mrs. Slosson and Rowland E. Robinson, for instance, have caught with exquisite skill the grotesque and the humorous side of New England life, but none other has shown the whole of New England with the sympathy and the comprehension and the delicacy of Rose Terry Cooke.

IV

Of the later group, the generation born in the fifties and the early sixties, Sarah Orne Jewett is the earliest figure.   With her there was no preliminary dallying with mid-century sentiment and sensationalism; she belongs to the era of *Oldtown Folks* rather than of *Uncle Tom's Cabin*.   "It was happily in the writer's childhood," she records in her later introduction to *Deephaven*, "that Mrs. Stowe had written of those who dwelt along the wooded sea-coast and by the decaying, shipless harbors of Maine.   The first chapters of *The Pearl of Orr's Island* gave the young author of *Deephaven* to see with new eyes and to follow eagerly the old shore paths from one gray, weatherbeaten house to another, where Genius pointed her the way."   And again in a letter written in 1889: "I have been reading the beginning of *The Pearl of Orr's Island* and finding it just as clear and perfectly original and strong as it seemed to me in my thirteenth or fourteenth year, when I read it first.   I shall never forget the exquisite flavor and reality of delight it gave me.   It is classical—historical." [6]

She herself had been born by one of those same "decaying, shipless harbors of Maine," at South Berwick, a village not far from the native Portsmouth of Thomas Bailey Aldrich.   It was no ordinary town, this deserted little port.   "A stupid, common country town, some one dared to call Deephaven in a letter once,

[6] *Letters of S. O. Jewett*, 47.

and how bitterly we resented it." [7] It had seen better days. There was an atmosphere about it from a romantic past. In Miss Jewett's work it figures as Deephaven. "The place prided itself most upon having been long ago the residence of one Governor Chantrey, who was a rich ship-owner and East India merchant, and whose fame and magnificence were almost fabulous. . . . There were formerly five families who kept their coaches in Deephaven; there were balls at the Governor's and regal entertainments at other of the grand mansions; there is not a really distinguished person in the country who will not prove to have been directly or indirectly connected with Deephaven." And again, "Deephaven seemed more like one of the cozy little English seaside towns than any other. It was not in the least American."

The social régime of this early Berwick had been cavalier rather than Puritan. It had survived in a few old families like the Jewetts, a bit of the eighteenth century come down into the late nineteenth. Miss Jewett all her life seemed like her own Miss Chauncey, an exotic from an earlier day, a survival—"thoroughly at her ease, she had the manner of a lady of the olden time." Her father, a courtly man and cultivated, a graduate of Bowdoin and for a time a lecturer there, gave ever the impression that he could have filled with brilliancy a larger domain than that he had deigned to occupy. He had settled down in Berwick as physician for a wide area, much trusted and much revered, a physician who ministered to far more than the physical needs of his people. His daughter, with a daughter's loving hand, has depicted him in *A Country Doctor,* perhaps the most tender and intimate of all her studies. She owed much to him; from him had come, indeed, the greater part of all that was vital in her education. Day after day she had ridden with him along the country roads, and had called with him at the farmhouses and cottages, and had talked with him of people and flowers and birds, of olden times, of art and literature.

A story from her pen, "Mr. Bruce," signed "A. E. Eliot," had appeared in the *Atlantic* as early as 1869, but it was not until 1873 that "The Shore House," changed later to "Kate Lancaster's Plan," the first of the *Deephaven* papers, appeared in the same magazine. She had begun to write with a definite pur-

[7] *Deephaven,* 84.

pose. "When I was perhaps fifteen," she records in an autobiographical fragment, "the first city boarders began to make their appearance near Berwick, and the way they misconstrued the country people and made game of their peculiarities fired me with indignation. I determined to teach the world that country people were not the awkward, ignorant set those people seemed to think. I wanted the world to know their grand simple lives; and, so far as I had a mission, when I first began to write, I think that was it."

Mrs. Stowe and Mrs. Cooke were the depicters of the older New England, the New England at flood tide; Miss Jewett was the first to paint the ebb. With them New England was a social unit as stable as the England of Jane Austen; with her it was a society in transition, the passing of an old régime. The westward exodus had begun, with its new elements of old people left behind by their migrating children, the deserted farm, the decaying seaside town, the pathetic return of the native for a brief day, as in "A Native of Winby," and, to crown it all, the summer boarder who had come in numbers to laugh at the old and wonder at it. She would preserve all that was finest in the New England that was passing, and put it into clear light that all might see how glorious the past had been, and how beautiful and true were the pathetic fragments that still remained.

She approached her work with the serenity and the seriousness of one who goes to devotions. She was never watchful for the eccentric and the picturesque; there are no grotesque deacons and shrill old maids in her stories. She would depict only the finer and gentler side of New England life: men quiet and kindly; women sweet-tempered and serene. We may smile over her pictures of ancient mariners "sunning themselves like turtles on the wharves," her weather-beaten farmers gentle as women, and her spinsters and matrons, like Miss Debby, belonging to "a class of elderly New England women which is fast dying out," but we leave them always with the feeling that they are noblemen and ladies in disguise. Her little stretch of Maine coast with its pointed firs, its bleak farms, and its little villages redolent of the sea she has made peculiarly her own domain, just as Hardy has made Wessex his, and she has made of her native Deephaven an American counterpart of Cranford.

Many times Miss Jewett has been compared with Hawthorne,

and undoubtedly there is basis for comparison. Her style, indeed, in its simplicity and effortless strength may be likened to his, and her pictures of decaying wharves and of quaint personages in an old town by the sea have the same atmosphere and the same patrician air of distinction, but further one may not go. Of his power to trace the blighting and transforming effects of a sin and his wizard knowledge of the human heart, she had nothing. She is a writer of little books and short stories, the painter of a few subjects in a provincial little area, but within her narrow province she has no rival nearer her own times than Mrs. Gaskell.

Her kinship is with Howells rather than with Hawthorne, the Howells of the earlier manner, with his pictures of the Boston of the East India days, his half-poetic studies in background and character, his portraits etched with exquisite art, his lambent humor that plays over all like an evening glow. In her stories, too, the plot is slight, and background and characterization and atmosphere dominate; and as with him in the days before the poet had been put to death, realism is touched everywhere with romance. She paints the present ever upon the background of an old, forgotten, far-off past, with that dim light upon it that now lies over the South of the old plantation days. Over all of her work lies this gentle glamour, this softness of atmosphere, this evanescent shade of regret for something vanished forever. Hers is a transfigured New England, a New England with all its roughness and coarseness and sordidness refined away, the New England undoubtedly that her gentle eyes actually saw. Once, indeed, she wrote pure romance. Her *The Tory Lover* is her dream of New England's day of chivalry, the high tide mark from which to measure the depth of its ebb.

Her power lies in her purity of style, her humorous little touches, and her power of characterization. Work like her "A White Heron," "Miss Tempy's Watchers," and "The Dulham Ladies," has a certain lightness of touch, a pathos and a humor, a skill in delineation which wastes not a word or an effect, that places it among the most delicate and finished of American short stories. Yet brilliant as they are in technique, in characterization and background and atmosphere, they lack nevertheless the final touch of art. They are *too* literary; they are too much works of art, too much from the intellect and not enough from

the heart.   They are Sir Roger de Coverley sketches, marvelously
well done, but always from the Sir Roger standpoint.   There is
a certain "quality" in all that Miss Jewett wrote, a certain
unconscious *noblesse oblige* that kept her ever in the realm of the
gentle, the genteel, the Berwick old régime.   One feels it in her
avoidance of everything common and squalid, in her freedom
from passion and dramatic climax, in her objective attitude toward her characters.   She is always sympathetic, she is moved
at times to real pathos, but she stands apart from her picture;
she observes and describes; she never, like Rose Terry Cooke,
mingles and shares.   She cannot.   Hers is the pride that the
lady of the estate takes in her beloved peasantry; of the patrician
who steps down of an afternoon into the cottage and comes back
to tell with amusement and perhaps with tears of what she finds
there.

All her life she lived apart from that which she described.
Her winters she spent in Boston, much of the time in the home
of Mrs. James T. Fields, surrounded by memorials of the great
period of American literature.   Like Howells, she wrote ever in
the presence of the Brahmins—a task not difficult, for she herself was a Brahmin.   It was impossible for her to be common
or to be narrowly realistic.   She wrote with deliberation and she
revised and rerevised and finished her work, conscious ever of her
art—a classicist, sending forth nothing that came as a cry
from her heart, nothing that came winged with a message,
nothing that voiced a vision and a new seeing, nothing that
was not literary in the highest classical sense.   In the history of
the new period she stands midway between Mrs. Spofford and Mrs.
Freeman; a new realist whose heart was with the old school; a
romanticist, but equipped with a camera and a fountain pen.

V

Mary E. Wilkins Freeman is the typical representative of the
group born a generation after the women of the thirties, the
group that knew nothing of the emotional fifties and sixties, and
that began its work when the new literature of actuality, the
realism of Flaubert and Hardy and Howells, was in full domina-
tion.   Of hesitancy, of transition from the old to the new, her
fiction shows no trace.   From her first story she was a realist, as
enamoured of actuality and as restrained as Maupassant.   She

seems to have followed no one: realism was a thing native to her, as indeed it is native to all women. "Women are delicate and patient observers," Henry James has said in his essay on Trollope. "They hold their noses close, as it were, to the texture of life. They feel and perceive the real." But to her realism Miss Wilkins added a power usually denied her sex, the power of detachment, the epic power that excludes the subjective and hides the artist behind the picture. In all the writings of the creator of *Gates Ajar* we see but the intense and emotional soul of Elizabeth Stuart Phelps; in that of the writer of *A Humble Romance* we see only the grim lineaments of New England, a picture as remorseless and as startling as if a searchlight had been turned into the dim and cobwebbed recesses of an ancient vault. She stands not aloof like Miss Jewett; she is simply unseen. She is working in the materials of her own heart and drawing the outlines of her own home, yet she possesses the epic power to keep her creations impersonal to the point of anonymousness.

For her work, everything in her life was a preparation. She was born in Randolph not far from Boston, of an ancestry which extended back into the darkest shadows of Puritanism, to old Salem and a judge in the witchcraft trials. Her more immediate progenitors were of humble station: her father was first a builder in her native Randolph, then a store-keeper in Brattleboro, Vermont. Thus her formative years were passed in the narrow environment of New England villages. The death of her father and mother during her early girlhood must also be recorded, as should the fact that her schooling was austere and limited.

When she approached literature, therefore, it was as a daughter of the Puritans, as one who had been nurtured in repression. Love in its tropical intensity, the fierce play of the passions, color, profusion, outspoken toleration, freedom—romance in its broadest connotation—of these she knew nothing. She had lived her whole life in the warping atmosphere of inherited Puritanism, of a Puritanism that had lost its earlier vitality and had become a convention and a superstition, in a social group inbred for generations and narrowly restricted to neighborhood limits. "They were all narrow-lived country people," she writes. "Their customs had made deeper grooves in their roads; they were more fastidious and jealous of their social rights than many in higher positions." [8]

[8] *The Twelfth Guest.*

"Everything out of the broad, common track was a horror to these men, and to many of their village fellows. Strange shadows that their eyes could not pierce, lay upon such, and they were suspicious."[9] "She was a New England woman, and she discussed all topics except purely material ones shamefacedly with her sister."[10]

In the mid eighties when she began her work the primitive Puritan element had vanished from all but the more remote and sheltered nooks of New England. The toll of the war, the Western rush, and the call of the cities had left behind the old and the conservative and the helpless, the last distorted relics of a distorting old régime. To her these were the true New England: she would write the last act of the grim drama that had begun at Plymouth and Massachusetts Bay. She recorded it very largely in her first four volumes: *A Humble Romance,* twenty-four short stories as grim and austere as Puritanism itself; *A New England Nun and Other Stories; Jane Field,* a prolonged short story; and *Pembroke, a Novel.* This is the vital part of her work, the part that is to bear up and preserve her name if it is to endure.

The key to this earlier work is the word *repression.* The very style is puritanic; it is angular, unornamented, severe; it is rheumatic like the greater part of the characters it deals with; it gasps in short sentences and hobbles disconnectedly. It deals ever with repressed lives: with dwarfed and anemic old maids who have been exhorted all their lives to self-examination and to the repression of every emotion and instinct; with women unbalanced and neurotic, who subside at last into dumb endurance; with slaves of a parochial public opinion and of conventions ridiculously narrow hardened into iron laws; with lives in which the Puritan inflexibility and unquestioning obedience to duty has been inherited as stubbornness and balky setness, as in Deborah and Barnabas Thayer who in earlier ages would have figured as martyrs or pilgrims.

Her unit of measure is short. It is not hers to trace the slow development of a soul through a long period; it is hers to deal with climactic episodes, with the one moment in a repressed life when the repression gives way and the long pent-up forces sweep

[9] *Christmas Jenny.*
[10] *Amanda and Love.*

all before them, as in "The Revolt of Mother," or "A Village Singer." Her effects she accomplishes with the fewest strokes possible. Like the true New Englander that she is, she will waste not a word. In her story "Life-Everlasting," Luella—the author's miserliness with words withholds her other name—has gone to carry a pillow to the farmhouse of Oliver Weed. She wonders at the closed and deserted appearance of the premises.

Luella heard the cows low in the barn as she opened the kitchen door. "Where—did all that—blood come from?" said she.

She began to breathe in quick gasps; she stood clutching her pillow, and looking. Then she called: "Mr. Weed! Mr. Weed! Where be you? Mis' Weed! Is anything the matter? Mis' Weed!" The silence seemed to beat against her ears. She went across the kitchen to the bedroom. Here and there she held back her dress. She reached the bedroom door, and looked in.

Luella pressed back across the kitchen into the yard. She went out into the yard and turned towards the village. She still carried the life-everlasting pillow, but she carried it as if her arms and that were all stone. She met a woman whom she knew, and the woman spoke; but Luella did not notice her; she kept on. The woman stopped and looked after her.

Luella went to the house where the sheriff lived, and knocked. The sheriff himself opened the door. He was a large, pleasant man. He began saying something facetious about her being out calling early, but Luella stopped him.

"You'd—better go up to the—Weed house," said she, in a dry voice. "There's some—trouble."

That is all we are told as to what Luella saw, though it comes out later that the man and his wife had been murdered by the hired man—how we know not. There is a primitiveness about the style, its gasping shortness of sentence, its repetitions like the story told by a child, its freedom from all straining for effect, its bareness and grimness, that stamps it as a genuine human document; not art but life itself.

For external nature she cares little. Her backgrounds are meager; the human element alone interests her. There is no Mary E. Wilkins country as there is a Sarah Orne Jewett country; there are only Mary E. Wilkins people. A somber group they are—exceptions, perhaps, grim survivals, distortions, yet absolutely true to one narrow phase of New England life. Her realism as she depicts these people is as inexorable as Balzac's. "A Village Lear" would have satisfied even Maupassant. Not one jot is bated from the full horror of the picture; it is driven to its pitiless end without a moment of softening. No detail is omitted. It is *Père Goriot* reduced to a chapter. A picture like this from "Louisa" grips one by its very pitilessness:

There was nothing for supper but some bread and butter and weak tea, though the old man had his. dish of Indian-meal porridge. He could not eat much solid food. The porridge was covered with milk and molasses. He bent low over it, and ate large spoonfuls with loud noises. His daughter had tied a towel around his neck as she would have tied a pinafore on a child. She had also spread a towel over the tablecloth in front of him, and she watched him sharply lest he should spill his food.

"I wish I could have somethin' to eat that I could relish the way he does that porridge and molasses," said she [the mother]. She had scarcely tasted anything. She sipped her weak tea laboriously.

Louisa looked across at her mother's meager little figure in its neat old dress, at her poor small head bending over the teacup, showing the wide parting in the thin hair.

"Why don't you toast your bread, mother?" said she. "I'll toast it for you."

"No, I don't want it. I'd jest as soon have it this way as any. I don't want no bread, nohow. I want somethin' to relish—a herrin', or a little mite of cold meat, or somethin'. I s'pose I could eat as well as anybody if I had as much as some folks have. Mis' Mitchell was sayin' the other day that she did n't believe but what they had butcher's meat up to Mis' Nye's every day in the week. She said Jonathan he went to Wolfsborough and brought home great pieces in a market-basket every week."

She is strong only in short efforts. She has small power of construction: even *Pembroke* may be resolved into a series of short stories. The setness of Barnabas Thayer is prolonged until it ceases to be convincing: we lose sympathy; he becomes a mere Ben Jonson "humor" and not a human being. The story is strong only in its episodes—the cherry party of the tight-fisted Silas Berry, the midnight coasting of the boy Ephraim, the removal of Hannah to the poorhouse, the marriage of Rebecca— but these touch the very heart of New England. Because of their artlessness they are the perfection of art.

In her later period Miss Wilkins became sophisticated and self-conscious. The acclaim of praise that greeted her short stories tempted her to essay a larger canvas in wider fields of art. She had awakened to a realization of the bareness of her style and she sought to bring to her work ornament and the literary graces.

She experimented with verse and drama and juveniles, with long novels and romances, and even with tales of New Jersey life. In vain. Her decline began with *Madelon*, which is improbable and melodramatic, and it continued through all her later work. She wrote problem novels like *The Portion of Labor*, long and sprawling and ineffective, and stories like *By the Light of the Soul*, as impossible and as untrue to life as a young country girl's dream of city society. As a novelist and as a depicter of life outside of her narrow domain, she has small equipment. She stands for but one thing: short stories of the grim and bare New England social system; sketches austere and artless which limn the very soul of a passing old régime; photographs which are more than photographs: which are threnodies.

VI

The last phase of the school may be studied in the work of Alice Brown, representative of the influences at the end of the century. The late recognition of her fiction—she was born in 1857—which placed her a decade after Miss Wilkins who was born in 1862, compelled her to serve an apprenticeship like that of Howells, and subjected her work to the new shaping influences of the nineties. When she did gain recognition in 1895, she brought a finished art. She had mastered the newly worked-out science of the short story, she had studied the English masters—chiefest of all Stevenson, whose influence so dominated the closing century.

She was not a realist as Miss Wilkins was a realist. The New England dialect stories of *Meadow Grass* were not put forth to indicate the final field that she had chosen for her art: they were experiments just as all the others of her earlier efforts were experiments. Of her first seven books, *Fools of Nature*, with its background of spiritualism, was a serious attempt at serious fiction with a thesis worthy of a George Eliot, *Mercy Warren* and *Robert Louis Stevenson* were biographical and critical studies, *By Oak and Thorn* was a collection of travel essays, *The Road to Castelay* was a collection of poems, and *The Day of His Youth* perhaps a romance.

That she won her recognition as a writer of dialect tales rather than as a novelist, a poet, an essayist, a romancer, was due, first, to the nature of the times, and, secondly, to the fact that the tales were a section of her own life written with fullness of knowledge and sympathy. She had been born and reared in a New Hampshire town, educated in a country school and a rural "female seminary," and, like Rose Terry Cooke, she had taught school. Later she had broken from this early area of her life and had resided in Boston. The glamour of childhood grew more and more golden over the life she had left behind her; the memories of fragrant summer evenings in the green country and of the old homes she had known with all their varied inmates grew ever more tender on her pages as she wrote. It was impossible for her not to be true to this area that she knew so completely. Characters like Mrs. Blair and Miss Dyer in "Joint Owners in Spain," or Farmer Eli in "Farmer Eli's Vacation" stood living before her imagination as she told of them. She had known them in the flesh. If she were to paint the picture at all she must paint it as it was in her heart. To add to it or to subtract from it were to violate truth itself.

Her stories differ from Mrs. Cooke's and Miss Jewett's in a certain quality of atmosphere—it is difficult to explain more accurately. They have a quality of humor and of pathos, a sprightliness and freedom about them that are all their own. They never fall into carelessness like so much of the work of Mrs. Stowe and they are never poorly constructed. They are photographically true to the life they represent, and yet they possess, many of them, the beauties and the graces and the feeling of romance. They add richness to realism. In style she is the antithesis of Miss Wilkins. There is beauty in all of her prose, a half-felt tripping of feet often, a lilting rhythm as unpremeditated as a bird-song, swift turns of expression that are near to poetry. An inscription in the Tiverton churchyard halts her, and as she muses upon it she is wholly a poet:

"The purple flower of a maid"! All the blossomy sweetness, the fragrant lament of Lycidas, lies in that one line. Alas, poor love-lies-bleeding! And yet not poor according to the barren pity we accord the dead, but dowered with another youth set like a crown upon the unstained front of this. Not going with sparse blossoms ripened or decayed, but heaped with buds and dripping over in perfume. She seems so sweet in her still loveliness, the empty province of her balmy spring, that, for a moment fain are you to snatch her back into the pageant of your day. Reading that phrase, you feel the earth is poorer for her loss. And yet, not so, since the world holds other greater worlds as well. Elsewhere she may have grown to age and stature, but here she lives yet in beauteous permanence—as true a part of youth and joy and rapture as the immortal figures on the Grecian urn. While she was but a flying phantom on the frieze of time, Death fixed her there forever—a haunting spirit in perennial bliss.

Whenever she touches nature she touches it as a poet. She was of the mid nineties which saw the triumph of the nature school. Behind each of her stories lies a rich background of mountain or woodland or meadow, one that often, as in "A Sea Change," dominates in Thomas Hardy fashion the whole picture.

Only a comparatively few of Miss Brown's volumes deal with the field with which her name is chiefly associated. *Meadow Grass, Tiverton Tales,* and *The Country Road* contain the best of her dialect stories. Her heart in later years has been altogether in other work. She has written novels not provincial in their setting, and, unlike Miss Wilkins, she has succeeded in doing really distinctive work. She has the constructive power that is denied so many, especially women, who have succeeded with the short story. She has done dramatic work which has won high rewards and she has written poetry. Perhaps she is a poet first of all.

BIBLIOGRAPHY

HARRIET BEECHER STOWE. *The Mayflower,* 1843; *Uncle Tom's Cabin,* 1852; *Sunny Memories of Foreign Lands,* 1854; *Dred (Nina Gordon),* 1856; *The Minister's Wooing,* 1859; *The Pearl of Orr's Island,* 1862; *Agnes of Sorrento,* 1862; *House and Home Papers,* 1864; *Little Foxes,* 1865; *Religious Poems,* 1867; *Queer Little People,* 1867; *The Chimney Corner,* 1868; *Oldtown Folks,* 1869; *Pink and White Tyranny,* 1871; *Oldtown Fireside Stories,* 1871; *My Wife and I,* 1871; *We and Our Neighbors,* 1875; *Poganuc People,* 1878; *A Dog's Mission,* 1881; *The Life of Harriet Beecher Stowe,* Charles Edward Stowe, 1889.

ELIZABETH STUART PHELPS WARD. *Tiny,* 1866; *The Gates Ajar,* 1868; *Men, Women, and Ghosts,* 1869; *Hedged In,* 1870; *The Silent Partner,* 1870; *Poetic Studies,* 1875; *The Story of Avis,* 1877; *An Old Maid's Paradise,* 1879; *Doctor Zay,* 1882; *Beyond the Gates,* 1883; *Songs of the Silent World,* 1884; *The Madonna of the Tubs,* 1886; *The Gates Between,* 1887; *Jack the Fisherman,* 1887; *The Struggle for Immortality,* 1889; *The Master of the Magicians* [with H. D. Ward], 1890; *Come Forth* [with H. D. Ward], 1890; *Fourteen to One,* 1891; *Donald Marcy,* 1893; *A Singular Life,* 1894; *The Supply at St. Agatha's,* 1896; *Chapters from a Life,* 1896; *The Story of Jesus Christ,* 1897; *Within the Gates,* 1901; *Successors to Mary the First,* 1901; *Avery,* 1902; *Trixy,* 1904; *The Man in the Case,* 1906; *Walled In,* 1907.

HARRIET PRESCOTT SPOFFORD. *Sir Rohan's Ghost,* 1859; *The Amber Gods and Other Stories,* 1863; *Azarian,* 1864; *New England Legends,* 1871; *The Thief in the Night,* 1872; *Art Decoration Applied to Furniture,* 1881; *The Marquis of Carabas,* 1882; *Poems,* 1882; *Ballads About Authors,* 1888; *In Titian's Garden and Other Poems,* 1897; *The Children of the Valley,* 1901; *The Great Procession,* 1902; *Four Days of God,* 1905; *Old Washington,* 1906; *Old Madame and Other Tragedies,* 1910.

ROSE TERRY COOKE. *Poems by Rose Terry,* 1860; *Happy Dodd,* 1875; *Somebody's Neighbors,* 1881; *The Deacon's Week,* 1885; *Root-Bound and Other Sketches,* 1885; *No. A Story for Boys,* 1886; *The Sphynx's Children and Other People's,* 1886; *Poems by Rose Terry Cooke* (complete), 1888; *Steadfast: a Novel,* 1889; *Huckleberries Gathered from New England Hills,* 1891.

SARAH ORNE JEWETT. *Deephaven,* 1877; *Old Friends and New,* 1879; *Country By-Ways,* 1881; *The Mate of the Daylight,* 1883; *A Country Doctor,* 1884; *A Marsh Island,* 1885; *A White Heron,* 1886; *The Story of the Normans,* 1887; *The King of Folly Island,* 1888; *Betty Leicester,* 1889; *Strangers and Wayfarers,* 1890; *A Native of Winby,* 1893; *Betty Leicester's Christmas,* 1894; *The Life of Nancy,* 1895; *The Country of the Pointed Firs,* 1896; *The Queen's Twin,* 1899; *The Tory Lover,* 1901; *Letters of Sarah Orne Jewett,* Edited by Annie Fields.

MARY E. WILKINS FREEMAN. *A Humble Romance,* 1887; *A New England Nun,* 1891; *Young Lucretia,* 1892; *Jane Field,* 1892; *Giles Corey, Yeoman: a Play,* 1893; *Pembroke,* 1894; *Madelon,* 1896; *Jerome, a Poor Young Man,* 1897; *Silence,* 1898; *Evelina's Garden,* 1899; *The Love of Parson Lord,* 1900; *The Heart's Highway,* 1900; *The Portion of Labor,* 1901; *Understudies,* 1901; *Six Trees,* 1903; *The Wind in the Rose Bush,* 1903; *The Givers,* 1904; *Doc Gordon,* 1906; *By the Light of the Soul,* 1907; *Shoulders of Atlas,* 1908; *The Winning Lady,* 1909; *The Green Door,* 1910; *Butterfly House,* 1912; *Yates Pride,* 1912.

ALICE BROWN. *Fools of Nature,* 1887; *Meadow Grass,* 1895; *Mercy Otis Warren,* 1896; *By Oak and Thorn,* 1896; *The Day of His Youth,* 1896; *The Road to Castaly,* 1896; *Robert Louis Stevenson—a Study* (with Louise Imogen Guiney), 1897; *Tiverton Tales,* 1899; *King's End,* 1901; *Margaret Warrener,* 1901; *The Mannerings, High Noon, Paradise, The Country Road, The Court of Love,* 1906; *Rose MacLeod,* 1908; *The Story of Thyrza,* 1909; *County Neighbors, John Winterbourne's Family,* 1910; *The One-Footed Fairy,* 1911; *The Secret of the Clan,* 1912; *Vanishing Points, Robin Hood's Barn,* 1913; *Children of Earth,* [$10,000 prize drama], 1915.

CHAPTER XII

The novelists who began their work in the seventies found themselves in a dilemma. On one side was the new school which was becoming more and more insistent that literature in America must be a thing American, colored by American soil, and vivid and vital with the new spirit of Ibsen, Tolstoy, Hardy, Maupassant, Howells, that was thrilling everywhere like the voice of a coming era. But on the other hand there was the firmly set tradition that the new world was barren of literary material, that it lay spick and span with no romantic backgrounds save perhaps the Dutch Hudson and old Puritan Salem and colonial Boston. As late as 1872 the *North American Review* declared that the true writer of fiction "must idealize. The idealizing novelists will be the real novelists. All truth does not lie in facts." [1] And it further declared that he must look away from his own land, where there is no shadow and no antiquity, into the uncharted fields of the imagination. "One would say that the natural tendency of the American novelist would be toward romance; that the very uniformity of our social life would offer nothing tempting to the writer, unless indeed to the satirist." [1]

It was the voice of the school that had ruled the mid century, a school that was still alive and was still a dominating force of which young writers were tremendously conscious. The reading public was not prepared for the new realism: it had been nurtured on *The Token* and *The Talisman*. The new must come not as a revolution, swift and sudden; but as an evolution, slow and imperceptible. During the seventies even Howells and James were romancers; romancers, however, in process of change.

For the seventies in the history of American fiction was a period of compromise and transition. The new school would be romantic and yet at the same time it would be realistic. The

---

[1] *North American Review*, 115:373.

way opened unexpectedly. The widening of the American horizon, the sudden vogue of the Pike literature, the new exploiting
of the continent in all its wild nooks and isolated neighborhoods
—strange areas as unknown to the East as the California mines
and the canebrakes of the great river—and above all the emer-
gence of the South, brought with it another discovery: Hawthorne and the mid-century school had declared romance with
American background impossible simply because in their provincial narrowness they had supposed that America was bounded
on the south and west by the Atlantic and the Hudson. America
was discovered to be full of romantic material. It had a past
not connected at all with the Knickerbockers or even the Pilgrims. Behind whole vast areas of it lay the shadow of old
forgotten régimes, "picturesque and gloomy wrongs," with ruins
and mystery and vague tradition.

One of the earliest results, then, of the new realism, strangely
enough, was a new romanticism, new American provinces added
to the bounds of Arcady. The first gold of it, appropriately
enough, came from California, where Harte and Mrs. Jackson caught glimpses of an old Spanish civilization alive only in
the picturesque ruins of its Missions. Quickly it was found
again, rich and abundant, in New Orleans, where Spain and then
France had held dominion in a vague past; then in the plantations of the old South where Page and others caught the last
glories of that fading cavalier civilization which had been prolonged through a century of twilight by the archaic institution
of slavery; and then even in the spick-and-span new central
West with its traditions of a chivalrous old French régime.

America, indeed, was full of romantic area, full of a truly
romantic atmosphere, for it had been for centuries the battle-
field of races, the North—England, New England, Anglo-Saxons
—against the South—Spain, France, the slave-holding Cavaliers.
And romance in all lands is the record of the old crushed out
by the new, the dim tradition of a struggle between North and
South: the South with its tropic imagination, its passion, its
beauty, its imperious pride, its barbaric background; the North
with its logic, its discipline, its perseverance, its passionless force.
Romance has ever held as its theme the passing of an old Southern régime before the barbarians of the North. And romance
in America has centered always in the South. Realism might

flourish in Boston and the colder classical atmospheres, but not along the gulf and the tropic rivers. The reading public, however, and the great publishing houses were in the North. The result was compromise: the new romanticism, Southern in its atmosphere and spirit, Northern in its truth to life and conditions.

I

Harte in *Gabriel Conroy* glimpsed the new fields of romance; George Washington Cable (1844———), the earliest of the new Southern school, was the first fully to enter them. His gateway was old New Orleans, most romantic of Southern cities, unknown to Northern readers until his pen revealed it. It seemed hardly possible that the new world possessed such a Bagdad of wonder: old Spanish aristocracy, French chivalry of a forgotten *ancien régime*, creoles, Acadians from the Grand Pré dispersion, adventurers from all the picturesque ports of the earth, slavery with its barbaric atmosphere and its shuddery background of dread, and behind it all and around it all like a mighty moat shutting it close in upon itself and rendering all else in the world a mere hearsay and dream, the swamps and lagoons of the great river.

Cable was a native of the old city. During a happy boyhood he played and rambled over the whole of it and learned to know it as only a boy can know the surroundings of his home. His boyhood ended when he was fourteen with the death of his father and the responsibility that devolved upon him to help support his mother and her little family left with scanty means. There was to be no more schooling. He marked boxes in the custom house until the war broke out, and then at seventeen he enlisted in the Confederate army and served to the end. Returning to New Orleans, he found employment in a newpaper office, where he proved a failure; he studied surveying until he was forced by malarial fever caught in the swamps to abandon it; then, after a slow recovery, he entered the employ of a firm of cotton factors and for years served them as an accountant. It was an unpromising beginning. At thirty-five he was still recording transfers of cotton, and weights and prices and commissions.

But his heart, like Charles Lamb's, was in volumes far different from those upon his office desk. He had always been a studious youth. He had read much: Dickens, Thackeray, Poe, Irving, Scott; and, like a true native of the old city to whom French was a mother tongue, Hugo, Mérimée, About. He loved also to pore over antiquarian records: *Relations* of the priest explorers, and old French documents and writings. His first impulse to write came to him as he sat amid these dusty records. "It would give me pleasure," he once wrote in a letter, "to tell you how I came to drop into the writing of romances, but I cannot; I just dropt. Money, fame, didactic or controversial impulse I scarcely felt a throb of. I just wanted to do it because it seemed a pity for the stuff to go so to waste."

Cable's first story, " 'Sieur George," appeared in *Scribner's Monthly* in October, 1873. Edward King, touring the Southern States in 1872 for his series of papers entitled *The Great South*, had found the young accountant pottering away at his local history and his studies of local conditions and had secured some of his work for Dr. Holland. During the next three years five other articles were published in the magazine and one, "Posson Jone," in *Appleton's*, but they caused no sensation. It was not until 1879, when the seven stories were issued in book form as *Old Creole Days*, that recognition came. The long delay was good for Cable: it compelled him, in Hawthorne fashion, to brood over his early work in his rare intervals of leisure, to contemplate each piece a long time, and to finish it and enrich it. He put forth no immaturities; he began to publish at the point where his art was perfect.

The reception accorded to *Old Creole Days* was like that accorded to Harte's *Luck of Roaring Camp*. It took its place at once as a classic, and the verdict has never been questioned. There is about the book, and the two books which quickly followed it, an exotic quality, an *aura* of strangeness, that is like nothing else in our literature. They seem not American at all; surely such a background and such an atmosphere as that never could have existed "within the bounds of our stalwart republic." They are romance, one feels; pure creations of fancy, prolongations of the Longfellowism of the mid century—and yet, as one reads on and on, the conviction grows that they are not romance; they are really true. Surely "Posson Jone" and "Madame Delphine" are not creations of fancy. The elided and softly lisping

dialect, broken-down French rather than debased English, is not
an invention of the author's: it carries conviction the more one
studies it; it is not brought in to show: it adds at every point to
the reality of the work. And the carefully worked-in backgrounds—let Lafcadio Hearn speak, who settled in the city a few
months after "Jean-ah Poquelin" came out in *Scribner's
Monthly:*

The strict perfection of his Creole architecture is readily recognized
by all who have resided in New Orleans. Each one of those charming
pictures of places—veritable pastels—was painted after some carefully
selected model of French or Franco-Spanish origin—typifying fashions
of building which prevailed in the colonial days. . . . The author of
Madame Delphine must have made many a pilgrimage into the quaint
district, to study the wrinkled faces of the houses, or perhaps to read
the queer names upon the signs—as Balzac loved to do in old-fashioned
Paris.[2]

It is realism, and yet how far removed from Zola and Flaubert—Flaubert with his "sentiment is the devil"! It is realism
tempered with romance; it is the new romance of the transition.
There is seemingly no art about it, no striving for effect, and
there is no exhibition of quaint and unusual things just because
they *are* quaint and unusual. Rather are we transported into
a charmed atmosphere, "the tepid, orange-scented air of the
South," with the soft Creole *patois* about us and romance become
real. The very style is Creole—Creole as Cable knew the Creoles of the quadroon type. There is a childish simplicity about
it, and there is a lightness, an epigrammatic finesse, an elision of
all that can be suggested, that is Gallic and not Saxon at all.

One can feel this exotic quality most fully in the portraits of
women: 'Tite Poulette, Madame Delphine, Aurora Nancanou,
Clotilde, and the others, portraits etched in with infinitesimal
lightness of touch, suggested rather than described, felt rather
than seen. These are not Northern women, these daintily feminine survivals of a decadent nobility, these shrinking, coquettish,
clinging, distant, tearful, proud, explosive, half barbarous, altogether bewitching creatures. A suggestion here, a glimpse there,
an exclamation, a flash of the eyes, and they are alive and real
as few feminine creations in the fiction of any period. One may
forget the story, but one may not forget Madame Delphine. If

2 "Scenes of Cable's Romances," *Century,* 5:40.

one would understand the secret of Cable's art, that Gallic
lightness of touch, that subtle elision, that perfect balance between the suggested and the expressed, let him read the last chapter of *The Grandissimes.* It is a Cable epitome.

"Posson Jone," "Jean-ah Poquelin," and *Madame Delphine,*
which, despite its length and its separate publication, is a short
story belonging to the *Old Creole Days* group, are among the
most perfect of American short stories and mark the highest
reach of Cable's art.

The Grandissimes, his first long romance, appeared in 1880.
Never was work of art painted on broader canvas or with elements more varied and picturesque. Though centering in a
little nook among the bayous, it contains all Louisiana. Everywhere perspectives down a long past: glimpses of the explorers,
family histories, old forgotten wrongs, vendettas, survivals from
a feudal past, wild traditions, superstitions. Grandissime and
Fusilier, young men of the D'Iberville exploring party, get lost
in the swamps. "When they had lain down to die and had
only succeeded in falling to sleep, the Diana of the Tchoupi-
toulas, ranging the magnolia groves with bow and quiver, came
upon them in all the poetry of their hope-forsaken strength and
beauty, and fell sick of love." The love of this Indian queen
begins the romance. Both eager to possess her, they can settle the
matter only with dice. Fusilier wins and becomes the founder
of a proud line, semibarbarous in its haughtiness and beauty,
the Capulets to De Grapion's Montagues. The culmination
comes a century later when the old feudal régime in Louisiana
was closed by Napoleon and the remnants of the warring families were united according to the approved Montague-Capulet
formula.

But the theme of the book is wider than this quarrel of families, wider than the conflict of two irreconcilable civilizations
and the passing of the outworn. In a vague way it centers in
the episode of Bras Coupé, the African king who refused to be
a slave and held firm until his haughty soul was crushed out with
inconceivable brutality. The cumulative and soul-withering
power of an ancient wrong, the curse of a dying man which works
its awful way until the pure love of innocent lovers removes it—
it is *The House of the Seven Gables* transferred to the barbarous swamps of the Atchafalaya.

The strangeness of the book grows upon one as one reads. It is a book of lurid pictures—the torture and death of Bras Coupé, the murder of the *négresse* Clemence, which in sheer horror and brutal, unsparing realism surpasses anything in *Uncle Tom's Cabin*, anything indeed in the Russian realists. It is a book too with a monotone of fear: the nameless dread that comes of holding down a race by force, or as Joel C. Harris has phrased it, "that vague and mysterious danger that seemed to be forever lurking on the outskirts of slavery, ready to sound a shrill and ghostly signal in the impenetrable swamps and steal forth under the midnight stars to murder and rapine and pillage"; the superstitious thrill when at dead of night throbs up from a neighboring slave yard "the monotonous chant and machine-like time-beat of the African dance"; the horror of finding morning after morning on one's pillow voodoo warnings and ghastly death charms placed seemingly by supernatural hands. No one has ever surpassed Cable in making felt this uncanny side of the negro. His characterization of the voodoo quadroon woman Palmyre with her high Latin, Jaloff-African ancestry, her "barbaric and magnetic beauty that startled the beholder like the unexpected drawing out of a jeweled sword," her physical perfection—lithe of body as a tigress and as cruel, witching and alluring, yet a thing of horror, "a creature that one would want to find chained"—it fingers at one's heart and makes one fear.

And with all this strangeness, this flash after flash of vivid characterization, a style to match. "Victor Hugo," one exclaims often as one reads. Let us quote, say from chapter five. The stars are Cable's:

There Georges De Grapion settled, with the laudable determination to make a fresh start against the mortifyingly numerous Grandissimes.

"My father's policy was every way bad," he said to his spouse; "it is useless, and probably wrong, this trying to thin them out by duels; we will try another plan. Thank you," he added, as she handed his coat back to him, with the shoulder-straps cut off. In pursuance of the new plan, Madame De Grapion—the precious little heroine!—before the myrtles offered another crop of berries, bore him a boy not much smaller (saith tradition) than herself.

Only one thing qualified the father's elation. On that very day Numa Grandissime (Brahmin-Mandarin de Grandissime), a mere child, received from Governor De Vaudreuil a cadetship.

"Never mind, Messieurs Grandissime, go on with your tricks; we shall see! Ha! we shall see!"

"We shall see what?" asked a remote relative of that family. "Will Monsieur be so good as to explain himself?"

* * * * * * * * * *

Bang! Bang!

Alas, Madame De Grapion!

It may be recorded that no affair of honor in Louisiana ever left a braver little widow.

It is French, too, in its sudden turns, its fragmentary paragraphs, its sly humor, its swift summings-up with an epigram:

"Now, sir," thought he to himself, "we'll return to our senses."
"Now I'll put on my feathers again," says the plucked bird.

But as one reads on one realizes more and more that this style comes from no mere imitation of a master: it is Creole; it is the style that is the counterpart of the Creole temperament. It is verisimilitude; it is interpretation.

Thus far the strength of the book; there are weaknesses as great. Cable failed, as Harte failed, as most of the masters of the short story have failed, in constructive power. The magnificent thesis of the romance is not worked out; it is barely suggested rather than made to dominate the piece. Moreover, the interest does not accumulate and culminate at the end. It is a rich mass of materials rather than a finished romance. The emphasis is laid upon characters, episodes, conditions, atmosphere, to the neglect of construction. From it Cable might have woven a series of perfect short stories: some parts indeed, like the tale of Bras Coupé, *are* complete short stories as they stand. The book is a gallery rather than a single work of art.

Dr. Sevier, 1885, marks the beginning of Cable's later style, the beginning of the decline in his art. The year before he had taken up his permanent residence in Massachusetts and now as a literary celebrity, with Boston not far, he became self-conscious and timid. His art had matured in isolation; there had been an elemental quality about it that had come from his very narrowness and lack of formal education. In the classic New England atmosphere the Gallic element, the naïve simplicity, the elfin charm that had made his early writings like no others, faded out of his art. It was as if Burns after the Kilmarnock edition had studied poetry at Oxford and then had settled in literary London. *Doctor Sevier* is not a romance at all; it is a realistic

novel of the Howells type, a study of the Civil War period as
it had passed under Cable's own eyes, with no plot and no culminating love interest. It is a running chronicle of ten years in
the lives of John and Mary Richling, tedious at times, impeded
with problem discussion and philosophizing. Its strength lies
in its characterization: the Italian Ristofalo and his Irish wife are
set off to the life; but why should the creator of Madame Delphine and Posson Jone and Palmyre turn to Irish and Italian
characterization? The story, too, has the same defects as *The
Grandissimes:* it lacks proportion and balance. With a large
canvas Cable becomes always awkward and ineffective. With
Bonaventure, graphic as parts of it unquestionably are, one posi-
tively loses patience. Its plan is chaotic. At the end, where
should come the climax of the plot, are inserted three long chapters telling with minute and terrifying realism the incidents of
a flood in the canebrakes. It is magnificent, yet it is "lumber."
It is introduced apparently to furnish background for the death
of the "Cajun," but the "Cajun" is only an incidental figure
in the book. To deserve such "limelight" he should have been
the central character who had been hunted with increasing interest up to the end and his crime and his punishment should
have been the central theme.

With *Madame Delphine* (1881) had closed the first and the
great period in Cable's literary career. The second period was
a period of miscellany: journalized articles on the history and
the characteristics of the Creoles, on New Orleans and its life,
on Louisiana, its history and traditions, on phases of social reform. Necessary as this work may have been, one feels inclined
to deplore it. When one has discovered new provinces in the
realm of gold one does not well, it would seem, to lay aside his
magic flute and prepare guide books to the region.

The New England atmosphere brought to life a native area in
Cable. His mother had been of New England ancestry. Moral
wrestlings, questions of reform, problems of conscience, were a
part of his birthright. One feels it even in his earliest work:
he had seen, we feel, the problem of *The Grandissimes* before he
had found the story. After his removal to Northampton, Massachusetts, it may be said that reform work became his real profession. Not that we criticize his choice, for life ever is greater
than mere art; we record it simply because it explains. He

formed home culture clubs for the education and the esthetic
culture of wage-earners, and conducted a magazine in the interest of the work; he interested himself actively in the cause of
the negro; so actively, indeed, that after his *Silent South* and
The Negro Question and the problem novel *John March, Southerner*, the South practically disowned him.

His third period begins, perhaps, with his novel *Strong Hearts*
in 1899. The pen that so long had been dipped in controversy
and journalism and philanthropic propaganda again essayed
fiction, but it was too late. The old witchery was gone. His
later novels, all his fiction indeed after *Madame Delphine*, with
the exception perhaps of parts of *Bonaventure*, read as if written by a disciple of the earlier Cable. The verve, the sly humor,
the Gallic finesse, the Creole strangeness and charm, have disappeared. There is a tightening in the throat as one reads the
last page of *Madame Delphine*, there is a flutter of the heart as
one reads the love story of Honoré and Aurora, but nothing
grips one as he reads *The Cavalier*. A pretty little story, undoubtedly, but is it possible that the author of it once wrote
"Posson Jone" and "Jean-ah Poquelin"? And *Gideon's
Band*, a romance with an attempt to win back the old witchery
of style—it was all in vain. Why say more?

Cable as a short story writer, a maker of miniatures with marvelous skill of touch, was most successful perhaps with dainty
femininities of the old régime. Once, twice, thrice the light of
romance glowed upon his page. Then he became a reformer,
a journalist, a man with a problem. But he who gave to American literature *Madame Delphine* and *Old Creole Days* need not
fear the verdict of coming days. Already have these works become classics.

II

The old Spanish régime in America furnished the theme of
Lewis Wallace's (1827–1905) first romance, *The Fair God*, published the year " 'Sieur George" appeared in *Scribner's*. He
had returned from the Mexican War interested in Aztec an-
tiquities. After the Civil War, in which he took a prominent
part, he began in the intervals of his law practice to write a military romance centering about Cortez and the conquest, and in
1873, through the efforts of Whitelaw Reid, succeeded in having

it published in Boston. It was not, however, until 1884, after the enormous popularity of *Ben Hur*, that it was discovered by the reading public. It is really better in workmanship and proportions than its more highly colored and vastly more exploited companion; it moves strongly, its battle scenes have a resonance and excitement about them that make them comparable even with Scott's, but its tendency is to sentiment and melodrama: it is a blending of Prescott and Bulwer-Lytton.

A far more distinctive study of old Spanish days is to be found in Helen Hunt Jackson's *Ramona*, undoubtedly the strongest romance of the period. Mrs. Jackson was a daughter of Professor Nathan W. Fiske of Amherst, Massachusetts, and until the last decade of her life was a resident of her native New England. Not until she was thirty-five and had been bereft of husband and children did she attempt literature. Her first form of expression was poetry, the short, sharp cry of desolation, narrowly personal and feminine. Then she wrote travel sketches and juveniles and moral essays, and then an outpouring of fiction intense and sentimental. During the seventies and the early eighties her work was in all the magazines. So versatile and abundant was she that at one time Dr. Holland seriously contemplated an issue of *Scribner's* made up wholly of her contributions.

To almost nothing of her work, save that at the very last, did she sign her own name. She had an aversion to publicity that became really a mannerism. Her early work she signed variously or not at all, then for a time she settled upon the initials "H. H." It is no secret now that she wrote the much-speculated-upon novels *Mercy Philbrick's Choice* and *Hetty's Strange History* in the No-Name Series, and that the *Saxe Holm Stories*, which furnished the literary mystery of the seventies, were from her pen. They are love stories of the *Lamplighter* school of fiction, sentimental, over-intense, moralizing. General and colorless as most of them are, they here and there display a rare power of characterization and a sharply drawn study of background and conditions. Parts of "Farmer Bassett's Romance," with its analysis of the "pagan element" in New England character, are worthy of Mary E. Wilkins. The stories, however, belong with the old rather than the new, and have been forgotten.

It is impossible to understand "H. H." without taking into account her New Englandism. She was a daughter of the Brahmins, in many ways a counterpart of Elizabeth Stuart Phelps—intensely conscientious, emotional, eager in the reform of abuses, brilliant, impetuous. While visiting California in the mid seventies she came in contact with the Indian problem and with characteristic impulsiveness set out to arouse the nation. After six months of intense work in the Lenox library of New York she published her *Century of Dishonor*, a bitter arraignment of the national Indian policy, and at her own expense sent a copy to every member of Congress. As a result she was appointed one of two commissioners to examine and report upon "the condition and need of the Mission Indians of California." Her report was thorough and businesslike, but it accomplished little.

Then she conceived the purpose of enlarging her area of appeal by the publication of a story—on the title page it stands *Ramona. A Story.* The problem preceded plot and materials and background. "You have never fully realized," she wrote only a few weeks before her death, "how for the last four years my whole heart has been full of the Indian cause—how I have felt, as the Quakers say, 'a concern' to work for it. My *Century of Dishonor* and *Ramona* are the only things I have done of which I am glad now." [3] And earlier than that she had written: "I have for three or four years longed to write a story that should 'tell' on the Indian question. But I knew I could not do it; I knew I had no background—no local color." [4]

Ramona was conceived of, therefore, as a tract, as a piece of propaganda, like Elizabeth Stuart Phelps's *Loveliness*. It was written with passion, flaming hot from a woman's heart—not many have been the romances written in heat. In this one respect it may be likened to Mrs. Stowe's great work, but to call it, as so often it has been called, "the *Uncle Tom's Cabin* of the Indian," is to speak with inaptness. The book is a romance, and only a romance; its whole appeal is the appeal of romance. She had found at last her background, but it was a background that dominated and destroyed her problem. Unconsciously she surrendered herself to the charm of it until to-day the book is no

[3] *The Nation*, August 20, 1885.
[4] *The Atlantic Monthly*, 86:713.

more a problem novel than is the *House of the Seven Gables,* which also makes use of the excesses and crimes of a system.

No background could be more fitted for romance: southern California with its "delicious, languid, semi-tropic summer"; the old Spanish régime, "half barbaric, half elegant, wholly generous and free handed," "when the laws of the Indies were still the law of the land, and its old name, 'New Spain,' was an ever-present link and stimulus";[5] and over it all like a soft, old-world atmosphere the Romish church with its mystery and its medieval splendor. "It was a picturesque life, with more of sentiment and gaiety in it, more also that was truly dramatic, more romance, than will ever be seen again on those sunny shores. The aroma of it all lingers there still."[5]

It had been the plan of the author first to elicit strongly the reader's sympathy for Ramona and the Indian Alessandro, then to harrow him with the persecutions wreaked upon them because they were Indians. But the purpose fails from the start. Ramona's Indian blood is not convincing to the reader. Until the story is well under way no one of the characters except the Señora and the priest, not even Ramona herself, suspects that she is not a daughter of the old Spanish house of Ortegna. There was small trace of the Indian about her: her beauty was by no means Indian—steel blue eyes and "just enough olive tint in her complexion to underlie and enrich her skin without making it swarthy." She had been reared as a member of the patriarchal household of the Morenos, and in education and habit of life was as much Spanish as her foster brother Felipe. And Alessandro—even the author explains that Ramona "looked at him with no thought of his being an Indian—a thought there had surely been no need of her having, since his skin was not a shade darker than Felipe's." He is an Indian, we must admit, and yet an Indian who looks like a Spaniard, an Indian who has been educated carefully in the Mission like a priest, an Indian who can sing Latin hymns with marvelous sweetness and play the violin like a master, an Indian with all the characteristics of a courtly señor, more nobly Spanish in soul than even Felipe himself, the heir of the great Moreno estate—the imagination refuses to accept either of the two characters as Indians. *Uncle*

[5] *Ramona,* Chap. II.

Tom's Cabin was worked out with the blackest of negroes; its central figure was a typical slave, who died at the end a victim of the system, but as one reads *Ramona* one thinks of Indians only as incidental figures in the background.

It is a romance of the days of the passing of the haughty old Spanish régime. A maiden of inferior birth, or, in terms of the ordinary continental romance, a maiden whose mother was of the peasant class, is brought up side by side and on a perfect equality with the heir of the noble house. He falls in love with her, but he tells of his love neither to her nor to his proud Castilian mother, who alone in the family knows the secret of the girl's birth. Then the maiden clandestinely marries, out of her caste as all but the Señora supposes, a peasant, as her mother had been a peasant, and is driven out of the home with harshness. A tenderly reared maiden, married to poverty, forced to live for a period in squalor, bereaved at last of her husband, rescued by her old lover when she is at the lowest point of her misery, and taken back to the old home where the implacable mother has died, and there wooed until she surrenders her new future to the high-born foster brother, who, even though he has learned of her peasant strain, has never ceased to love her—that is the romance. The Indians, even Alessandro, are felt to be only incidental parts of the story. The center of the romance is the slow, faithful, thwarted, but finally triumphing, love of Felipe. The thing that really grips is not the incidental wrongs and sufferings of the Indians, but the relentlessly drawn picture of the old Señora and the last chapter where the two lovers, united at last, have left behind them the old land, no longer theirs—its deserted and melancholy Missions, its valleys and long pastures which ring now with the shouts of a conquering race, and turn their faces southward into a new world and a new and more joyous life. Then it was that Ramona blossomed into her full beauty. "A loyal and loving heart indeed it was —loyal, loving, serene. Few husbands so blest as the Señor Filipe Moreno. Sons and daughters came to bear his name. The daughters were all beautiful; but the most beautiful of them all, and, it was said, the most beloved by both father and mother, was the eldest one: the one who bore the mother's name, and was only step-daughter to the Señor—Ramona, daughter of Alessandro the Indian." And so the romance ends, as romance should end, with all trouble and uncertainty a mere cloud in the far past.

Ramona is a bombshell that all unknowingly to its creator turned out to be not a bombshell at all, but an exquisite work of art. The intensity and the passion, which came from the viewing of abuses and the desire to work reform, wove themselves into the very substance of it. It is a blending of realism and romanticism and ethic earnestness into a rounded romance. More and more is it evident that aside from this and perhaps two or three sonnets, nothing else that its author wrote is of permanent value. *Ramona,* however, is alone enough to give her a place in American literature, a place indeed with the two or three best writers of American romance.

III

The French occupation of the northern area of the continent has also proved a rich literary field. It seems, as Howells has observed, that the French have touched America "with romance wherever they have touched it at all as soldiers, priests, exiles, or mere adventurers." The bare history of their adventures is, as Parkman has recorded it, romance. Cooper caught a glimpse of the richness of the field, and a grand-niece of his, Constance Fenimore Woolson, made a new discovery of it during the "local color" period that followed the advent of Bret Harte. Her collection of stories, *Castle Nowhere,* 1875, pictured with graphic realism the life of the rude settlements along the upper lakes, but once or twice she dipped her pen into pure romance and became a pioneer. Her sketch, "The Old Agency," which deals with the ancient building at Mackinac with its memories of the Jesuits, and her strong story "St. Clair Flats" reveal what she might have done had she not turned her attention to other regions.

The field that she abandoned was taken later by Mary Hartwell Catherwood, a native of Ohio, the first woman novelist of the period to be born west of the Alleghenies. She was, moreover, the first woman of any prominence in American literary ranks to acquire a college education, graduating not in the East, as one might suppose, but from a new college in the new West. The fact is significant. After a brief period of teaching in Illinois, she became a newspaper writer and a general literary worker, and she published her first book, *A Woman in Armor,* as early as 1875. Juveniles, marketable stories, sketches, critiques, flowed from her pen for nearly twenty years, and yet in 1888 she had settled upon no fixed style or field of work and she was completely unknown to the reading public. She seems to have been trying the literary currents of the time. Her first experiment, not to mention her juveniles, was her *Craque-O'- Doom*, 1881, an E. P. Roe-like novel of the *He Fell in Love with His Wife* type, but it made no impression. "Don't you know," she makes one of her characters say in words that are an explanation, "that the key of the times is not sentiment but practical common sense? Just after the war when the country was wrought to a high pitch of nerves, current literature overflowed with self-sacrifice. According to that showing—and current literature ought to be a good reflection of the times—everybody was running around trying to outdo his neighbor in the broken heart and self-renunciation business." Next she assayed to enter the "practical sense" school, and her "Serena," *Atlantic*, 1882, with its unsparingly realistic picture of a death and funeral in an Ohio farmhouse, shows that she might have made herself the Miss Jewett or the Miss Wilkins of her native region. But minute studies of contemporary life failed to satisfy the demands within her. She awoke at last to her true vocation over a volume of Parkman, let us suppose over the sixth and the sixteenth chapters of *The Old Régime in Canada*. From the glowing pages of this master of narrative she caught a full breath of romance and for the first time she realized her powers.

The Romance of Dollard, which appeared in the *Century* in 1888, and the other romances that swiftly followed, are no more like the earlier work of the author than if they had been written by another hand. It was as if a new and brilliant writer had suddenly appeared. The suddenness, however, was only a seeming suddenness: the romances were in reality the culmination of a long and careful period of apprenticeship. Her style, to be sure, had been influenced by Parkman: one cannot read a page without feeling that. There is the same incisive, nervous manner; the same impetuous rush and vigor as if the wild Northern winds were filling the paragraphs; the same short and breathless sentences in descriptions of action, packed with excitement and dramatic force. Yet there is vastly more than Parkman in her work. There is a wealth of poetry and spiritual force in it a healthy sentiment, a skilful selecting and blending of romantic elements, and a Hardy-like power to catch the spirit of a locality so as to make it almost a personality in the tragedy. This background of wilderness, this monotone of the savage North, is never absent. At the beginning of every story and every chapter is struck, as it were, the dominating key. Here is the opening paragraph of ''The Windigo'':

The cry of those rapids in Ste. Marie's River called the Sault could be heard at all hours through the settlement on the rising shore and into the forest beyond. Three quarters of a mile of frothing billows, like some colossal instrument, never ceased playing music down an inclined channel until the trance of winter locked it up. At August dusk, when all that shaggy world was sinking to darkness, the gushing monotone became very distinct.

These rapids with their mournful cry become a character in the story; they dominate every page until at the end they rescue the hero, bearing in his arms the frightful ''windigo,'' in a page of action that stirs the blood. The Canadian wilds of the *coureurs de bois,* the roar of swollen rivers, the sudden storms that lash the forests, the terror and the mystery of night in the savage woods, and evermore the river, the black St. Lawrence— one feels them like a presence. Like Cable, too, she can make her reader share the superstitious thrill of the region. Her *windigos* and *loup-garous* lay hold on one like a hand out of the dark.

Amid this wild landscape a wild social order—savage Indians, explorers, *voyageurs,* flaming Jesuits, *habitants, grands seigneurs,* soldiers of fortune—Frontenac, Tonty, Dollard, La Salle, Bigot, Montcalm, and perhaps the lost dauphin, son of Louis XVI and Marie Antoinette—and in the heart of it all and the moving force of it all, beautiful women, exiles from France, exquisite maidens educated in convents, charmingly innocent, lithe Indian girls, Indian queens, robust daughters of *habitants.* Swords flash in duel and battle, love rules utterly even such stormy souls as La Salle's, plots with roots that extend even across the ocean into France are worked out in secret fastness—with such material and such background romantic combinations are endless.

The strength of Mrs. Catherwood's work lies in its tensity and excitement, its vigor of narrative, its picturesque setting, its power of characterization. From this very element of strength comes a weakness. Romance must tread ever near the verge of the impossible, and at times she pushes her situations too far and falls over into the realm of melodrama. In *The White Islander*, for instance, the Indians have the hero burning at the stake when suddenly Marie, the French "white islander" who loves him, leaps into the circle of flames, declaring that she will die with him. Then realizing there is no hope of saving the two, the Jesuit father unites them in marriage, side by side at the stake, while the flames are crackling, but the moment he pronounces them man and wife the yells of the rescuing party resound from the near forest and they are saved.

There is another weakness, one that lies far deeper, one indeed that applies to the whole school of historical novelists that so flourished in the nineties. The author had a passion for "documenting" her romances. She studied her sources as carefully as if she were to write a history; she used all the known facts that could be found; then she supplemented these known facts copiously from her imagination. For her *Romance of Dollard* she got Parkman to write an introduction commending its historical accuracy; she strewed the chapters with corroborating footnotes; and she tried in all ways to give the impression that it was a genuine piece of history. But there is no evidence that Dollard ever married, and there is not a scrap even of tradition that his bride died with him at the battle of the Long Saut. To make an historical personage like Dollard or La Salle or Tonty the leading, speaking character in a romance is to falsify the facts. Historical romance is not history; it is pure fiction, true only to the spirit of the age and the place represented and to the fundamentals of human character and the ways of the human soul. It should be worked out always with non-historical characters.

Of Mrs. Catherwood's romances the best is *The Lady of Fort St. John*, made so perhaps on account of the unique character Rossignol. Her strongest work, however, lies in her shorter stories. It was a peculiarity of the whole period that nearly all of its writers of fiction should have been restricted in their powers of creation to the small effort rather than to the large. It was the age of cameos rather than canvases. Her volume, *The Chase of St. Castin and Other Stories of the French in the New World*, and her *Mackinac and Lake Stories*, which deal with

the mixed populations dwelling on the islands of the Great
Lakes, show her at her highest level. Her versatility, however,
was remarkable. Her *Spirit of an Illinois Town,* a realistic
story of a typical boom town, has in it the very soul of the new
West, and her *The Days of Jeanne d'Arc,* written after much
observation of the Vosges and Lorraine peasants in France and
a year of work in the best libraries, is as brilliant a piece of historical work as was produced during the period.

Whatever her failings as a romancer she must be reckoned
with always as perhaps the earliest American pioneer of that
later school of historical fiction writers that so flourished in the
nineties. After her stirring tales had appeared, *Alice of Old
Vincennes,* and *Monsieur Beaucaire,* and *The Seats of the
Mighty,* and all the others, were foregone conclusions.

IV

The latest field in America for romance was that created by
the Civil War. The patriarchal life of the great Southern
plantations had in it a peculiar picturesqueness, especially when
viewed through the fading smoke of the conflict that destroyed it.
An old aristocracy had been overthrown by Northern invaders—
field enough for romance. It had been a peculiar aristocracy—a
"democratic aristocracy," as it was fond of explaining itself,
"not of blood but of influence and of influence exerted among
equals,"[6] but none the less it was an aristocracy in the heart of
democratic America, Roman in its patrician pride, its jealously
guarded principle of caste, its lavish wealth, and its slavery
centered, social régime. Like all aristocracies it was small in
numbers. "Only about 10,781 families held as many as fifty
or more slaves in 1860, and these may, without great error, be
taken as representing the number of the larger productive estates
of the South."[7] But of these estates very many were only commercial establishments with little social significance. The real
aristocracy was to be found in a few old families, notably in Virginia, in numbers not exceeding the New England aristocracy of
the Brahmins, which had been set apart by a principle so
radically different. Both were narrowly provincial rather than
national, both were centered within themselves, both were intol-

6 Woodrow Wilson, *Division and Reunion,* 106.
7 F. E. Chadwick, *Causes of the Civil War,* 32.

erant and self-satisfied, and both alike disappeared in the flames of the war to make way for the new national spirit which was to rule the new age.

To feel the atmosphere of this Southern old régime, this exclusive aristocracy, far older than the republic, one must read Thomas Nelson Page's *The Old South*, or his earliest published sketch, "Old Yorktown," *Scribner's Monthly*, 1881, a sketch that is in reality the preface to his romances. It may be profitable, perhaps, to quote a few paragraphs. After his description of the old custom house of York, the first erected in America, he writes:

> There the young bucks in velvet and ruffles gathered to talk over the news or plan new plots of surprising a governor or a lady-love. It was there the haughty young aristocrats, as they took snuff or fondled their hounds, probably laughed over the story of how that young fellow, Washington, who, because he had acquired some little reputation fighting Indians, had thought himself good enough for anybody, had courted Mary Cary, and very properly had been asked out of the house of the old Colonel, on the ground that his daughter had been accustomed to ride in her own coach. . . . It would be difficult to find a fitter illustration of the old colonial Virginia life than that which this little town affords. It was a typical Old Dominion borough, and was one of the eight boroughs into which Virginia was originally divided. One or two families owned the place, ruling with a sway despotic in fact, though in the main temperate and just, for the lower orders were too dependent and inert to dream of thwarting the "gentlefolk," and the southerner uncrossed was ever the most amiable of men.

Among these ruling families were the Nelsons and the Pages:

> The founder of the Page family in Virginia was "Colonel John Page," who, thinking that a principality in Utopia might prove better than an acre in Middlesex, where he resided, came over in 1656. He had an eye for "bottom land," and left his son Matthew an immense landed estate, which he dutifully increased by marrying Mary Mann, the rich heiress of Timber Neck. Their son, Mann, was a lad thirteen years old when his father died. After being sent to Eton, he came back and took his place at the "Council Board," as his fathers did before him and as his descendants did after him.

It reminds one of Hawthorne's account of his own family in the introduction to *The Scarlet Letter*.

Before the war the South had had its romancers. Kennedy and Simms and others had tried early to do for it what Cooper had done for the more northerly area. Then in the fifties John

Esten Cooke (1830–1886), the best novelist the South produced during the earlier period, put forth a series of Virginia romances, the strongest of which undoubtedly was *The Virginia Comedians,* 1854, republished in 1883. The strength of the book, as indeed of all of Cooke's romances, lay in its vivacity, its enthusiasm, its stirring pictures of the more picturesque elements of the old Southern life: barbecues, horse races, contests between fiddlers, the doings of negroes, and the like. Its weakness, in addition to hasty workmanship and lack of cumulative power, was the common weakness of all the mid-century fiction. It had a *St. Elmo* atmosphere. Like all the rest of his fiction, it is tainted with profuse sentimentality, with sensationalism, with a straining for the unexpected and the picturesque. Panels in the wall slide apart mysteriously, accidents happen in the nick of time, villains in the form of French dancing masters are foiled at last by the hero. One is in old Williamsburg, to be sure, "the Southern Boston" in its golden prime, and is impressed with its courtly manners, its beautiful women, its chivalrous heroes, its frequent duels; yet one is never quite sure whether it is the real South or whether it is not after all the story-world of an old-fashioned romancer who perhaps has never visited the South at all save in imagination. It is romanticism overdone; it is everything too much. Even its sprightliness and its occasional touches of realism cannot rescue it from oblivion.

A dwelling upon the merely quaint and unusual in the local environment to arouse laughter and interest was perhaps the leading source of failure in Southern fiction even to the time of the later seventies. From the days of Longstreet's *Georgia Scenes,* pictures there had been of the "cracker," the mountaineer, the Pike, the conventional negro of the Jim Crow and the Zip Coon or the Uncle Tom type, the colonel of the fire-eating, whisky-drinking variety, but there had been no painstaking picture of real Southern life drawn with loving hand, not for mirth and wonder, not for the pointing of a moral, but for sympathy and comprehension. Horace E. Scudder as late as 1880 noted that "the South is still a foreign land to the North, and travelers are likely to bring back from it only what does not grow in the North."[8] It was true also of travelers in its books as well, for

8 *Atlantic Monthly,* 46:828.

the most of its books had been written for Northern publication. The first writer really to picture the South from the heart outward, to show it not as a picturesque spectacle but as a quivering section of human life, was Thomas Nelson Page (1853————), whose first distinctive story, "Marse Chan," appeared as late as 1884.

At the opening of the Civil War Page was eight years old. During the years of conflict his home, one of the great plantations of Virginia, was a center of Confederate activities, and time and again the region about it was overrun by the invading armies. It was a marvelous training for the future novelist. He had been born at precisely the right moment. He had been a part of the old régime during the early impressionable years that are golden in a life, the years that color and direct the imagination in all its future workings, and he was young enough when the era closed to adapt himself to the new order. At the close of the war he studied the classics with his father, a scholar of the old Southern type, took the course in the Virginia university presided over by Robert E. Lee, studied law at the University of Virginia, and then from 1875 to 1893 practised law in Richmond. These are the essentials of his biography.

It was while he was establishing himself in his profession at the old capital of the Confederacy that he did his first literary work. *Scribner's Monthly* had heard from the ruined South the first murmurings of a new literature and was giving it every encouragement. It had published King's series of articles on *The Great South,* it had discovered Cable in 1873, it had encouraged Lanier, and in January, 1876, it had begun to issue a series of negro dialect poems by Irwin Russell, a native of Port Gibson, Mississippi, poems that undoubtedly had been suggested by the Pike balladry, and yet were so fresh and original in material and manner that they in turn became a strong influence on their times. That the poems launched Page in his literary career he has freely admitted.

Personally I owe much to him. It was the light of his genius shining through his dialect poems—first of dialect poems then and still first—that led my feet in the direction I have since tried to follow. Had he but lived, we should have had proof of what might be done with true negro dialect; the complement of "Uncle Remus." [9]

[9] *The Southern Poets.* Weber, xxv.

In April, 1877, came his first contribution to *Scribner's*, "Uncle Gabe's White Folks," a dialect poem of the Russell order, yet one that strikes the keynote of all its author's later work:

> Fine ole place? Yes, sah, 't is so;
>   An' mighty fine people my white folks war—
> But you ought ter 'a' seen it years ago,
>   When de Marster an' de Mistis lived up dyah;
> When de niggers 'd stan' all roun' de do',
> Like grains o' corn on de cornhouse flo'.

Together with Armistead C. Gordon of Staunton, Virginia, he wrote other ballads and poetical studies which were issued as a joint volume a decade later with the title *Befo' de War, Echoes in Negro Dialect*. But in the meantime he had been experimenting with prose dialect, and late in the seventies he submitted to the magazine a long story told wholly in the negro vernacular. It was a bold venture: even *Scribner's* hesitated. They might print humorous dialect poems and Macon's "Aphorisms from the Quarters" in their "Bric-à-Brac" department, but a serious story all of it in a dialect that changed many words almost beyond recognition—they held it for over four years. When it did appear, however, as "Marse Chan" in 1884, it seemed that their fears had been groundless. It was everywhere hailed as a masterpiece. "Unc' Edinburg's Drowndin'," "Meh Lady," and others quickly followed, and in 1887 the series was issued as a collection with the title *In Ole Virginia*, a book that is to Page what *The Luck of Roaring Camp* is to Harte and *Old Creole Days* is to Cable.

The method of Page in these early stories was original. The phrase "befo' de war" explains it. He would reproduce the atmosphere of the old South, or what is more nearly the truth, the atmosphere of aristocratic old Virginia plantation life. "No doubt the phrase 'Before the war' is at times somewhat abused. It is just possible that there is a certain Caleb Balderstonism in the speech at times. But for those who knew the old county as it was then, and contrast it with what it has become since, no wonder it seems that even the moonlight was richer and mellower 'before the war' than it is now. For one thing, the moonlight as well as the sunlight shines brighter in our youth than in maturer age.'' [10] But Page expressed the phrase in negro dialect— ''befo' de war.'' The story of the vanished era, the gallantry and spirit of its men, the beauty of its women, the nameless glow that hovers over remembered youthful days, he would show through the medium of the negro. It is exquisite art done with seemingly impossible materials. An old slave tells the story in his own picturesque way and wholly from his own viewpoint, yet so simply, so inevitably, that one forgets the art and surrenders oneself as one surrenders to actual life with its humor and its pathos and its tragedy. It is romance—an idealized world, and an idealized negro. Surely no freed slave ever told a consecutive tale like that, perfect in its proportions and faultless in its lights and shadows, yet such a criticism never for a moment occurs to the reader. The illusion is complete. The old South lives again and we are in it both in sympathy and comprehension.

In the decade that followed this first book Page gave himself to the writing of short stories and studies of Southern life, but only once or twice did he catch again the magic atmosphere of the earlier tales. *Two Little Confederates* is exquisite work, but *Elsket,* which followed, was full of inferior elements. Its negro stories, ''George Washington's Last Duel'' and ''P'laski's Tunament,'' are only good vaudeville—they show but the surface of negro life; ''Run to Seed'' is pitched almost with shrillness, and ''Elsket'' and ''A Soldier of the Empire,'' the one dealing with the last of her race, the other with the last of his order, are European sketches a trifle theatrical in spite of their touches of pathos.

Red Rock (1898) marks the beginning of Page's second period, the period of long romances. Once before with *On Newfound River* he had tried the border canvas and he had failed save in certain of his characterizations and detached episodes. Now with *Red Rock* he set out to write what should stand among his works as *The Grandissimes* stands among Cable's. Its sub-title, *A Chronicle of Reconstruction,* explains at once its strength and its weakness. Its author approached it as Mrs. Jackson had approached *Ramona,* with a purpose, and, unlike Mrs. Jackson, he accomplished his purpose. The wrongs of the South during the period are made vivid, but at the expense of the novel.

[10] Preface to *Red Rock.*

The opening pages are perfect. Chapter two with its merrymaking at the great plantation, and all its glimpses of traits and scenes peculiarly Southern, leads the reader to feel that he has in his hands at last the great romance of Southern life. There is the background of an ancient wrong. The red stain on the great rock is supposed to be the blood of the first mistress of the plantation murdered there by an Indian; and the haunting picture over the fireplace of the first master who had killed the Indian with his bare hands, then had glared from his portrait until he had become the dominating center of the plantation, is felt to be the dominating center also of the romance as the Bras Coupé episode is the motif of *The Grandissimes.* But one is soon disappointed. The problem dominates the romance; the book is primarily a treatise, a bit of special pleading. It is undoubtedly all true, but one set out to read a romance of the old South. True as its facts may be, from the art side it is full of weaknesses. Leech, the carpet-bagger, and Still, the rascally overseer, are villains of the melodramatic type; they are a dead black in character from first to last. The turning points of the action are accidents, the atmosphere is too often that of *St. Elmo.* When the master is killed in battle the picture of the Indian killer falls to the hearth, and again when Leech is beating to death the wounded heir to the estate it falls upon the assassin as if in vengeance and nearly crushes him. The plot is chaotic. We are led to believe that Blair Cary, the doctor's daughter, who in the opening chapters is as charming as even Polly herself in *In Ole Virginia,* is to be the central figure, but Blair is abandoned for no real reason and Miss Welsh, a Northern girl, finishes the tale. Jacquelin, too, who dominates the earlier pages, peters out, and it is not clear why Middleton, the Northern soldier, is brought in near the close of the book, perhaps to marry Blair, who by every right of romance belongs to Jacquelin. It is enough to say that the story is weak just as *Gabriel Conroy* is weak, just as *The Grandissimes* and *Pembroke* are weak. The materials are better than the construction.

The fame of Page then must stand or fall, as Harte's must, or Cable's or Miss Wilkins's, on the strength of his first book. His essays on the Old South and other volumes are charming and valuable studies, his novels are documents in the history of a stirring era, but his *In Ole Virginia* is a work of art, one of the real classics of American literature.

Several others have used Virginia as a background for romance, notably Mary Virginia Terhune, (1831———), who wrote under the pseudonym "Marion Harland" something like twenty novels, the most of them in the manner in vogue before 1870, and F. Hopkinson Smith (1838–1915), whose *Colonel Carter of Cartersville* (1891) is one of the most sympathetic studies of Southern life ever written. Its sly humor, its negro dialect, its power of characterization, its tender sentiment, its lovable, whimsical central figure, and its glimpses of an old South that has forever disappeared, make it one of the few books of the period concerning which one may even now prophesy with confidence.

BIBLIOGRAPHY

GEORGE W. CABLE. *Old Creole Days*, 1879; *The Grandissimes*, 1880; *Madame Delphine*, 1881; *The Creoles of Louisiana*, 1884; *Dr. Sevier*, 1885; *The Silent South*, 1885; *Bonaventure*, 1888; *Strange True Stories of Louisiana*, 1889; *The Negro Question*, 1890; *The Busy Man's Bible*, 1891; *John March, Southerner*, 1894; *Strong Hearts*, 1899; *The Cavalier*, 1901; *Byelow Hill*, 1902; *Kincaid's Battery*, 1908; *Gideon's Band*, 1914; *The Amateur Garden*, 1914.

HELEN HUNT JACKSON. *Verses*, 1870, 1874; *Bits of Travel*, 1872; *Saxe Holm Stories*, 1873; *Bits of Talk About Home Matters*, 1873; *Bits of Talk for Young People*, 1876; *Mercy Philbrick's Choice* (No Name Series), 1876; *Hetty's Strange History* (No Name Series), 1877; *Bits of Travel at Home*, 1878; *Nelly's Silver Mine*, 1878; *Saxe Holm Stories* (Second Series), 1878; *The Story of Boon* (a Poem), 1879; *A Century of Dishonor*, 1881; *Mammy Tittleback and Her Family*, 1881; *The Training of Children*, 1882; *The Hunter Cats of Connorloa*, 1884; *Ramona* [First Published in the *Christian Union*], 1884; *Zeph*, 1886; *Glimpses of Three Coasts*, 1886; *Sonnets and Lyrics*, 1886; *Between Whiles*, 1887.

MARY HARTWELL CATHERWOOD. *A Woman in Armor*, 1875; *Craque-O'-Doom*, 1881; *Rocky Fork*, 1882; *Old Caravan Days*, 1884; *The Secrets of Roseladies*, 1888; *The Romance of Dollard*, 1889; *The Story of Tonty*, 1890; *The Lady of Fort St. John*, 1891; *Old Kaskaskia, The White Islander*, 1893; *The Chase of St. Castin*, 1894; *The Spirit of an Illinois Town, Little Renault, The Days of Jeanne d'Arc*, 1897; *Heroes of the Middle West*, 1898; *Spanish Peggy*, 1899; *The Queen of the Swamp*, 1899; *Lazarre*, 1901.

JOHN ESTEN COOKE. *Leather Stocking and Silk; or, Hunter John Myers and His Times*, 1854; *The Virginia Comedians; or Old Days in the Old Dominion*, 1854; *The Youth of Jefferson*, 1854; *Ellie; or, The Human Comedy*, 1855; *The Last of the Foresters*, 1856; *Henry St. John, Gentleman: a Tale of 1874–75*, 1859; *A Life of Stonewall Jackson*, 1863;

Stonewall Jackson: a Military Biography, 1866; *Surrey of Eagle's Nest*, 1866; *The Wearing of the Gray*, 1867; *Mohun; or the Last Days of Lee and His Paladins*, 1868; *Fairfax, the Maker of Greenway Court*, 1868; *Hilt to Hilt*, 1869; *Out of the Foam*, 1869; *Hammer and Rapier*, 1870; *The Heir to Gaymount*, 1870; *A Life of General R. E. Lee*, 1871; *Dr. Vandyke*, 1872; *Her Majesty the Queen*, 1873; *Pretty Mrs. Gaston, and Other Stories*, 1874; *Justin Hartley*, 1874; *Canolles: the Fortunes of a Partisan of '81*, 1877; *Professor Presseusee, Materialist and Inventor*, 1878; *Mr. Grantley's Idea*, 1879; *Stories of the Old Dominion*, 1879; *The Virginia Bohemians*, 1880; *Virginia*, 1885; *The Maurice Mystery*, 1885; *My Lady Pokahontas*, 1885.

THOMAS NELSON PAGE. *In Ole Virginia*, 1887; *Two Little Confederates, Befo' de War*, 1888; *Elsket and Other Stories, On Newfound River, The Old South, Among the Camps*, 1891; *Pastime Stories, The Burial of the Guns*, 1894; *Social Life in Old Virginia Before the War, The Old Gentleman of the Black Stock*, 1896; *Two Prisoners*, 1897; *Red Rock, a Chronicle of Reconstruction*, 1898; *Santa Claus's Partner*, 1899; *A Captured Santa Claus*, 1902; *Gordon Keith*, 1903; *The Negro: the Southerner's Problem*, 1904; *Bred in the Bone*, 1905; *The Coast of Bohemia* [poems], 1906; *Novels, Stories, Sketches, and Poems*. Plantation Edition. 12 volumes, 1906; *Under the Crust*, 1907; *The Old Dominion—Her Making and Her Manners, Robert E. Lee, the Southerner, Tommy Trot's Visit to Santa Claus*, 1908; *John Marvel, Assistant*, 1909; *Robert E. Lee, Man and Soldier*, 1912; *The Land of the Spirit*, 1913.

CHAPTER XIII

LATER POETS OF THE SOUTH

The year 1866 saw the low-water mark, perhaps, not only of the American novel, but of American literature generally. On May 12 of this year *The Round Table* of New York, in an editorial entitled "Plain Talk with American Writers," declared that "The literary field was never so barren, never so utterly without hope of life. . . . The era of genius and vigor that seemed ready to burst on us only a few months ago has not been fulfilled. There is a lack of boldness and power. Men do not seem to strike out in new paths as bravely as of old." Then it issued a challenge to the new generation of literary men: "We have very little strong, original writing. Who will awaken us from this sleep? Who will first show us the first signs of a genuine literary reviving? . . . If ever there was a time when a magnificent field opened for young aspirants for literary renown, that time is the present. Every door is wide open."

We know now that the reviving was close at hand. Within five years the flood-gates were opened, and Clemens, Harte, Hay, Burroughs, Howells, Miller, and all the group were publishing their first work. Among others a young Georgia school-teacher felt the thrill as he read the *Round Table* call, and he made haste to send to the paper a budget of poems—"Barnacles," "Laughter in the Senate," and some others, to be, if possible, the first fruits of this new period. A year later, in 1867, he went himself to New York to bring out a novel, *Tiger Lilies,* a book sent forth with eagerness and infinite hope, for was not every door wide open? It is a book to linger over: crude as it is, it was the first real voice from the new South.

I

The little group of Southern poets that had gathered itself about Paul Hamilton Hayne (1831–1886), the chief of whom

were Margaret Junkin Preston (1820–1897), Francis Orrery
Ticknor (1822–1874), and Henry Timrod (1829–1867)—poets
who were contemporary with Bayard Taylor and his group—belongs rather with the period before the war than with the new
national period that followed it. They were poets of beauty like
Stoddard, singing the music of Keats and Tennyson and the old
Cavalier poets—dreamers, makers of dainty conceits and pretty
similes, full of grace and often of real melody, but with little
originality either of manner or message. The war came into their
lives sharply and suddenly, a cataclysm that shook all their plans
into ruins about them. It swept away their property, their
homes, their libraries, even their health. For a time during the
conflict they turned their poetry into martial channels: invec-
tives on the invading "Huns," rallying songs, battle lyrics,
patriotic calls. When the war was over they found themselves
powerless to adjust themselves. Hayne before the war was a
graceful sonneteer, a worshiper of classic beauty, a writer of
odes, not to the nightingale but to the mocking bird:

> A golden pallor of voluptuous light
> Filled the warm southern night:
> The moon, clear orbed, above the sylvan scene
> Moved like a stately queen,
> So rife with conscious beauty all the while,
> What could she do but smile
> At her own perfect loveliness below,
> Glassed in the tranquil flow
> Of crystal fountains and unruffled streams?

Even his war poems are gentle and softly poetic. After the war
he lapsed into lyrics of retrospect and contemplation with a
minor note always of gentle resignation. He lived to write
elegies on Timrod and Lanier and to make himself the threnodist
of the old South:

> Forgotten! Tho' a thousand years should pass,
> Methinks our air will throb with memory's thrills,
> A common grief weigh down the faltering grass,
> A pathos shroud the hills;
> Waves roll lamenting; autumn sunsets yearn
> For the old time's return.

A more sensitively imaginative poet was Timrod, yet even he
was not strong enough to lead his time and become more than

a minor singer. He was of the old South and would have been wholly out of place in the new even had he lived. More fire and Hebraic rage there were in him than in Hayne, indeed than in any other American poet save Whittier. Once or twice when his life was shaken to the center by the brutalities of war he burst into cries that still quiver with passion:

> Oh! standing on this desecrated mold,
> Methinks that I behold,
> Lifting her bloody daisies up to God,
> Spring kneeling on the sod,
> And calling with the voice of all her rills,
> Upon the ancient hills
> To fall and crush the tyrants and the slaves
> That turn her meads to graves.

And again at the climax of "The Cotton Boll":

> Oh, help us, Lord! to roll the crimson flood
> Back on its course, and, while our banners wing
> Northward, strike with us! till the Goth shall cling
> To his own blasted altar-stones, and crave
> Mercy; and we shall grant it, and dictate
> The lenient future of his fate
> There, where some rotting ships and crumbling quays
> Shall one day mark the port which ruled the Western
>   seas.

And what other poet save Whittier could after victory burst into Hebraic ecstasy of joy like this?

> Our foes are fallen! Flash, ye wires!
>   The mighty tidings far and nigh!
>   Ye cities! write them on the sky
> In purple and in emerald fires!
>
> They came with many a haughty boast;
>   Their threats were heard on every breeze;
>   They darkened half the neighboring seas;
> And swooped like vultures on the coast.
>
> False recreants in all knightly strife,
>   Their way was wet with woman's tears;
>   Behind them flamed the toil of years,
> And bloodshed stained the sheaves of life.
>
> They fought as tyrants fight, or slaves;
>   God gave the dastards to our hands;
>   Their bones are bleaching on the sands,
> Or moldering slow in shallow graves.

But it was like pouring molten bullet lead from Satsuma vase. The fragile, beautiful life that should have known nothing harsher than the music of poets and the laughter of children and lovers, broke under the strain of war and poverty and neglect, and his life went out miserably at thirty-eight.

II

Sidney Lanier's life was as brief as Timrod's and as full of harshness and poverty, but the end of the war found him young enough to have resiliency and the ability to adapt himself to the new régime of which willy-nilly he found himself a part. He was thirteen years younger than Timrod and twelve years younger than Hayne. His temperament was different: he was broader in his sympathies—no man ever threw himself more completely into the cause of the Confederacy, yet a decade after the war we find him with a nation-wide vision of the new era; he was more democratic of soul than Hayne or Timrod—he could worship beauty as passionately as they and he could also write ballads of the Pike County order; he suffered just as acutely from the war as did Timrod, yet one may search long through his poems or his letters for a single despondent note. He was buoyant and impetuous: his winning of literary recognition in the face of physical disabilities seemingly insuperable places him beside Parkman.

In point of time Lanier was the first of what may be called the Georgia school of writers. It is notable that the State most harshly dealt with by the war was the first to arise from its ruins, the first to receive the vision of a new South, and the first to catch the new national spirit. Macon, Lanier's birthplace, had about it all the best elements of the Old South. It was the seat of an influential college for women, it possessed a cultured society, and it had an art atmosphere—music, poetry, literary conversation—unusual in that period outside of New England and some of the larger cities. Lanier's home was in every way ideal: his father, a lawyer of the old Southern type, was "a man of considerable literary acquirements and exquisite taste," and, moreover, like most Southerners of his class, he had a library stocked with the older classics, a treasure-house of which his son, bookish from his earliest childhood, made the fullest use. "Sir Walter Scott, the romances of Froissart, the adventures of Gil Blas," all the older poets—he read them until he seemed to his boyish companions as one who lived apart in a different world from theirs.

His formal schooling was meager, yet at fifteen he was able to enter the sophomore class of Oglethorpe University, a small denominational college at Midway, Georgia, and in 1860 he was ready for graduation with the highest honors of his class. Compared with the larger Northern institutions, the college was pitifully primitive; Lanier in later years could even call it "farcical," nevertheless it is doubtful if any university could have done more for the young poet. It brought him in contact with a man, James Woodrow of the department of science, a man who was to become later the president of the University of South Carolina and the author of the famous book, *An Examination of Certain Recent Assaults on Physical Science* (1873).

"Such a man," says his biographer, "coming into the life of Lanier at a formative period, influenced him profoundly. He set his mind going in the direction which he afterwards followed with great zest, the value of science in modern life and its relation to poetry and religion. He also revealed to him the meaning of genuine scholarship." [1]

This influence it may have been which made Lanier in later years so tolerant and so broad of view. The attraction between pupil and teacher seems to have been mutual. Through Woodrow it was that Lanier received his appointment as tutor in the college, a position which he held during the year that followed.

It was a year of close study and of wide reading. Throughout his undergraduate period he had read enormously: often in unusual books: Burton's *Anatomy of Melancholy*, Jeremy Taylor, Keats's *Endymion*, Chatterton, Christopher North, Tennyson, whose *Maud* he learned by heart, Carlyle, and a long list of others. "Without a doubt it was Carlyle who first enkindled in Lanier a love of German literature and a desire to know more of that language." He studied with eagerness. His dream now was to enter a German university and do scholarly work as Basil Gildersleeve had just done, and Thomas R. Price, two other young men of the new South, but suddenly as he dreamed all his life plans fell in ruins about him. The crash of war resounded in his ears. All in a moment he found himself in an atmosphere of fierce excitement. The college became an armed camp; Macon became

[1] *Sidney Lanier*, Mims, 29.

a military center. Before he had fairly realized it the young tutor, just turned twenty, had enlisted in the first company to leave the State, and was marching away to the front.

His career as a soldier need not detain us. It was varied and it was four years long and it ended dramatically on the stormy night of November 2, 1864, when the Federal cruiser *Santiago-de-Cuba* picked up the blockade runner *Lucy* off Wilmington, North Carolina, and sent her crew, among them signal officer Lanier, to Point Lookout prison. A fellow prisoner and a close friend during the hard days that followed was another Southern poet, John Bannister Tabb (1845–1909), whose brief lyrics as we know them to-day possess beauty and finish and often distinction.

Lanier was released in March, 1865, and after incredible hardships succeeded in reaching his home in Macon more dead than alive to find his mother dying of consumption. The poet's tendency to the disease was congenital; the prison hardships and exposure had broken down his physical vigor; and two years later while teaching a small country school in Prattville, Alabama, as he was forced to do by the poverty of the South and his own lack of money or profession, hemorrhages from the lungs began, and the rest of his life, like Stevenson's under the same conditions, was a fight with tuberculosis, a perpetual changing from place to place that he might find some climate that would afford relief. With unparalleled heroism he fought off the disease for fifteen years, and under physical weakness that would have sent the average man to his bed and his grave he made himself recognized as the leading poetic voice of the new South, and one of the few poetic voices of his era.

His life divides itself into three periods: the first one his time of dreaming, as he himself styled it—his boyhood, ending with the call to arms in 1861; the second his period of storm and stress, his period of struggle and uncertainty and final adjustment, ending in 1873 with his determination to devote his life to music and poetry; and finally the seven or eight years in which eagerly and unremittingly, with failing health and long periods of total incapacity, he wrote all those books and poems for which he is now known.

III

Lanier's work more than that of any other writer of his time illustrates the difference between the mid-century literature and

that of the later national period. He is distinctively a transition
figure: he heard both voices and he obeyed both. Until after the
war he was what Hayne and Timrod had been, and Taylor and
Stoddard—a disciple of Keats, a poet of merely sensuous beauty.
But for the war he would have been a Longfellow bringing from
Germany *Hyperions* and *Voices of the Night*. The four vital
years in the camps, on the blockade runner, in the military prison,
with their close contact with life in its elemental conditions, was
a university course far different from any that he had dreamed
of in his college days. It was this that differentiates him from
Hayne and Timrod and that brings him into our period.

Tiger Lilies, his first published book (1867), is a document not
only in the life of Lanier but also in the transition period of the
sixties. It is a crude first novel full of a strange mixture of weakness and strength. It has been likened to Longfellow's *Hyperion*,
but the likeness extends no further than this: *Tiger Lilies* is the
novel transitional to the seventies as *Hyperion* was transitional
to the romantic thirties and forties. In parts it belongs completely
to the older period. It opens with this outburst, not by Paul
Fleming, but by Paul Rübetsahl:

"Himmel! Cospetto! Cielo! May our nests be built on the strongest and leafiest bough of the great tree Ygdrasil! May they be lined
with love, soft and warm, and may the storms be kind to them: Amen
and Amen!" said Paul Rübetsahl.

The first part is florid in the extreme and artificial, full of literary affectations and conceits:

On the last day of September, 1860, huntsman Dawn leapt out of
the East, quickly ran to earth that old fox, Night, and sat down on the
top of Smoky Mountain to draw breath, etc.

Its discussions of poetry, of music, of the meaning of art and of
life generally are all in the dream-world of German romance, and
its chaotic plot and its impossible characters and happenings are
in full keeping. But with part two the book comes suddenly to
life. The hero enters the war and all at once there is realism,
passages like this as graphic even as Whitman:

The wounded increase. Here is a musket in the road: there is the
languid hand that dropped it, pressing its fingers over a blue edged
wound in the breast. Weary pressure, and vain—the blood flows
steadily.

More muskets, cartridge-boxes, belts, greasy haversacks, strew the ground.
. Here come the stretcher-bearers. They leave a dripping line of blood. "Walk easy as you kin, boys," comes from the blanket which the men are carrying by the corners. Easy walking is desirable when each step of your four carriers spurts out the blood afresh or grates the rough edges of a shot bone in your leg.
The sound of a thousand voices, eager, hoarse, fierce, all speaking together yet differently, comes through the leaves of the undergrowth. A strange multitudinous noise accompanies it—a noise like the tremendous sibilation of a mile-long wave just before it breaks. It is the shuffling of two thousand feet as they march over dead leaves.

The novel is laid in the Tennessee Mountains in the same region that was to figure a decade later in the stories of Charles Egbert Craddock. The Great Smoky Mountains and Chilhowee Mountain—familiar names now—form the background, but the author puts no individuality into the landscape. It might be Germany. His mountaineers, however, are alive and they are sharply characterized. Gorm Smallin and his brother Cain are among the earliest figures in that vast gallery of realistically portrayed local types that soon was to figure so prominently in American literature. The chapter that records the desertion of Gorm and his arraignment by his brother Cain is worthy of standing with the best work of Charles Egbert Craddock or Octave Thanet. The prison scenes, drawn from the author's own first-hand experience, are documents in the history of the war. On every line is the stamp of reality. Here is a bivouac scene:

Cain Smallin sat, stiff backed upon the ground, sternly regarding his packed circle of biscuits in the skillet.
"How do they come on, Cain? Most done?" . . .
"Bully! Brownin' a little some of 'em. 'Bout ten minutes yit."

At that moment a shell that has buried itself in the ground explodes in the midst of the group, literally burying the party and scattering havoc. Cain Smallin, unhurt, digs himself from the ruins and scrapes the dirt from his face.

"Boys," said he, in a broken voice of indignant but mournful inquiry, "have any of ye seed the skillet?"

In the words of its preface, the book was a cry, "a faint cry, sent from a region where there are few artists, to happier lands

who own many; calling on these last for more sunshine and less
night in their art. . . . There are those even here in the South
who still love beautiful things with sincere passion.''

But necessity was upon the young dreamer. He was without
a profession, and he had married a wife. There was no refuge
but his father's profession, which always had been the last as well
as the first resort of young Southerners. His father's law firm
was glad to employ him, though it could offer but meager compensation. No more novels, no more dreams of the scholar's life,
of Heidelberg, and poetry. Until 1873 he was busy, like Cable
during the same period, with his conveyances and his bills of sale.
The ambitious plan of a long poem of medieval France, ''The
Jacquerie,'' he kept in his desk, a beautiful dream that often
he returned to. He wrote exquisite little songs for it:

> May the maiden,
> Violet-laden
> Out of the violet sea,
> Comes and hovers
> Over lovers,
> Over thee, Marie, and me,
> Over me and thee.

His poetic experiments of this period one may find at the back
of the definitive edition of his work. With Timrod and Hayne he
was still dreamy and imaginative, more prone to look at the beautiful than at the harsher realities of humanity, yet even as he
was dreaming over his ''Jacquerie'' he was not oblivious to the
problems of his own time. He wrote dialect poems: ''Jones's
Private Argument,'' ''Thar's More in the Man than Thar Is in
the Land,'' ''Nine from Eight,'' and the like, and published them
in Southern papers. They deal with the Georgia ''Crackers'' and
with the social and financial conditions of the times, and they were
written in 1868, two years before the Pike County balladry. In
1875 with his brother Clifford he published in *Scribner's Monthly*
''The Power of Prayer; or, the First Steamboat up the Alabama,''
a negro dialect poem adapted undoubtedly from a similar episode
recounted in Mark Twain's *The Gilded Age*, yet original in tone
and realistically true. Had it been unsigned we should attribute
it without hesitation to Irwin Russell, who by many is believed to
have been the first to discover the literary possibilities of the

negro, at least in the field of poetic balladry. How like Russell is a stanza like this:

> It 'pear to me dis mornin' I kin smell de fust o' June.
> I 'clar', I b'lieve dat mockin'-bird could play de fiddle soon!
> Dem yonder town-bells sounds like dey was ringin' in de moon.

But Russell's first poem, "Uncle Cap Interviewed," appeared in *Scribner's* almost a year later. The Lanier brothers contributed to the magazine at least one more dialect poem, "Uncle Jim's Baptist Revival Hymn," a product as realistically true to the negro as anything written later by Harris or Page:

> Sin's rooster's crowed, Ole Mahster's riz,
> De sleepin'-time is pas';
> Wake up dem lazy Baptissis,
> *Chorus.*   *Dey's mightily in de grass, grass,*
>   *Dey's mightily in de grass.*
>
> De Meth'dis team's done hitched; O fool,
> De day's a-breakin' fas';
> Gear up dat lean old Baptis' mule,
> *Dey's mightily in de grass, grass,*
> *Dey's mightily in de grass.* Etc.

Lanier was a pioneer in a rich field.

IV

The turning point came in 1873. The poet's physical condition had become so alarming that he had been sent to spend the winter at San Antonio, Texas. He found what least he was looking for. The German Maennerchor of the city, an unusual circle of musicians, discovered him and asked him to play to them the flute, an instrument that had been his companion since boyhood. "To my utter astonishment," he wrote his wife, "I was master of the instrument. Is not this most strange? Thou knowest I had never learned it; and thou rememberest what a poor muddle I made at Marietta in playing difficult passages; and I certainly have not practised; and yet there I commanded and the blessed notes obeyed me, and when I had finished, amid a storm of applause, Herr Thielepape arose and ran to me and grasped my hand, and declared that he hat never heert de flude accompany itself pefore." [2]

[2] Mims's *Sidney Lanier*, 122.

Judging from contemporary testimony, we are compelled to rate Lanier as a musical genius. Though he never had had formal training in the art, from his childhood music had been with him a consuming passion. He had taken his flute to the war, he had smuggled it into the prison, and he had moved all his life amid a chorus of exclamations over the magic beauty of his improvisations. The masters were praising him now: he would be a master himself. He would toil no longer at the task he despised; he would live now for art. In November, 1873, he wrote to his father:

How can I settle myself down to be a third-rate struggling lawyer for the balance of my little life, as long as there is a certainty almost absolute that I can do something so much better? Several persons, from whose judgment in such matters there can be no appeal, have told me, for instance, that I am the greatest flute-player in the world; and several others, of equally authoritative judgment, have given me an almost equal encouragement to work with my pen. My dear father, think how, for twenty years, through poverty, through pain, through weariness, through sickness, through the uncongenial atmosphere of a farcical college and of a bare army and then of an exacting business life, through all the discouragement of being wholly unacquainted with literary people and literary ways—I say, think how, in spite of all these depressing circumstances, and of a thousand more which I could enumerate, these two figures of music and poetry have steadily kept in my heart so that I could not banish them. Does it not seem to you as to me, that I begin to have the right to enroll myself among the devotees of these two sublime arts, after having followed them so long and so humbly, and through so much bitterness? [3]

He gave himself first to music. So perfect was his mastery of his instrument that he secured without difficulty the position of first flute in Hamerik's Peabody Orchestra of Baltimore, and he played at times even with Thomas's Orchestra of New York. It was the opinion of Hamerik, himself a rare artist, that Lanier was a musician of highest distinction:

His human nature was like an enchanted instrument, a magic flute, or the lyre of Apollo, needing but a breath or a touch to send its beauty out into the world. . . . In his hands the flute no longer remained a mere material instrument, but was transformed into a voice that set heavenly harmonies into vibration. Its tones developed colors, warmth, and a low sweetness of unspeakable poetry—His playing appealed alike to the musically learned and to the unlearned—for he would magnetize the listener; but the artist felt in his performance the supe-

[3] Quoted by William Hayes Ward, 1884, edition of the *Poems.*

riority of the momentary inspiration to all the rules and shifts of mere technical scholarship. His art was not only the art of art, but an art above art. I will never forget the impression he made on me when he played the flute concerta of Emil Hartman at a Peabody symphony concert, in 1878—his tall, handsome, manly presence, his flute breathing noble sorrows, noble joys, the orchestra softly responding. The audience was spellbound. Such distinction, such refinement! He stood the master, the genius.[4]

His first recognition as a poet came in 1875 with the publication of "Corn" in *Lippincott's Magazine*. The poem caught the attention of Taylor and brought to the poet the commission to furnish the words for the Cantata to be sung at the Centennial Exposition. After that commission Lanier was a national figure.

During the scant six years that followed, the years of his literary life in which he wrote all that is distinctive in his poetry, he lived in a whirlwind of activity, of study in the large libraries to which he now had access, of music, of literary hack-work, or he lay totally incapacitated by sickness that threatened always the speedy termination of all. Poetry he could write only in moments stolen from more imperative things. He compiled a guide book to Florida, he prepared courses of lectures on Shakespeare for clubs of women, he delivered two scholarly courses of lectures at Johns Hopkins University, and he published four juveniles that adapted for boys the old romances of chivalry. He wrote lyrics and songs, but his future as a poet must rest on five poems: "Corn," the first significant poem from the new South; "The Symphony," a latter-day ode to St. Cecilia; "The Psalm of the West," which he intended should do for the centennial year what Taylor had failed so lamentably to do in his Fourth of July ode; "The Marshes of Glynn," a symphony without musical score; and, finally on his death bed, held in life only by his imperious will, "Sunrise," his most joyous and most inspired improvisation of all.

V

For Lanier was essentially an improvisatore. He left behind him no really finished work: he is a poet of magnificent fragments. He was too excited, too impetuous, to finish anything. Poetry was a thing of rhapsodic outbursts, of tiptoe glimpses: his eager jottings for poems made on the backs of envelopes, scraps of

[4] Quoted by William Hayes Ward, 1884, edition of the *Poems*.

paper, anything that was at hand, fill a volume. He may be likened to a child in a meadow of daisies: he filled his hands, his arms, full of the marvelous things, then threw them aside to gather more and ever more. There was no time to arrange them, no time even to look at them twice. Ideas came in flocks; he lived in a tumult of emotion. His letters quiver with excitement as do those of no other American poet. "All day my soul hath been cutting swiftly into the great space of the subtle, unspeakable deep, driven by wind after wind of heavenly melody." "I cannot tell you with what eagerness I devoured *Felix Holt.*" "My heart was all a-cry." "The fury of creation is on me to-day." "Lying in the music-waters, I floated and flowed, my soul utterly bent and prostrate." "The very inner spirit and essence of all wind-songs, bird-songs, passion-songs, folk-songs, country-songs, sex-songs, soul-songs, and body-songs hath blown me in quick gusts like the breath of passion and sailed me into a sea of vast dreams." One may quote interminably.

Hamerik's characterization of his flute-playing may be taken as the key to all his work: "The artist felt in his performance the superiority of the *momentary inspiration* to all the rules and shifts of mere technical scholarship." It explains the unevenness of his work and its lack of finish. He had no patience to return to a poem and labor upon it. Other and more rapturous melodies were calling to him. It explains his lack of constructive power: inspiration is a thing of rapturous glimpses, not of long, patient coördinating effort. His poems are chaotic in structure even to the point often of obscurity. "Corn," for example, was intended to be a poem with a message, and that message doubtless the superiority of corn over cotton as a crop for the new South. But half the poem has only the vaguest connection with the subject. One-third of it outlines the duties and privileges of the poet soul. The message is not brought home: one has to labor to find it. There is a succession of beautiful images expressed often with rare melody and distinction, but inconsecutive even to vagueness.

His prose has the same characteristics. The lectures on the English novel seem like the first draft of work rather than like a finished product. He changes his plan as he proceeds. It was to be a study of the novel as a literary form, but as he progresses he changes it into a study of the development of personality in literature, and finally ends it by devoting half his total space to a rhapsody upon George Eliot. *The Science of English Verse* has the same faults. He rides a pet theory through chapters and dismisses really basic principles with a paragraph. It is a book of magnificent, even at times of inspired sections, but as a complete treatise it has no great value. The same may be said of all his prose work : he had flashes of inspiration but no consecutive message. The cause for it was partly pathological, partly temperamental. He was first of all a musician, a genius, an improvisatore.

That his conception of the poet's office was a broader and saner and more modern one than that of most of his contemporaries was undoubtedly true. In ''Corn'' he addresses thus the stalk that stands high above its fellows :

> Still shalt thou type the poet-soul sublime
> That leads the vanward of his timid time
> And sings up cowards with commanding rime—
> Soul calm, like thee, yet fain, like thee, to grow
> By double increment, above, below;
> Soul homely, as thou art, yet rich in grace like thee,
> Teaching the yeomen selfless chivalry

The poet then is not to be a mere dreamer of beauty, a dweller in the clouds apart from the men of his time. He is to stand squarely on the earth :

> Thou lift'st more stature than a mortal man's,
> Yet ever piercest downward in the mold
> And keepest hold
> Upon the reverend and steadfast earth
> That gave thee birth.

But despite his conception of the poet's office, Lanier himself is not often a leader and a prophet. He had ceased to be Georgia-minded and he had felt the national thrill that was making a new America, but it was not his to be the strong voice of the new era. ''The Psalm of the West,'' which casts into poetic form certain vital episodes of American history, has no message. One searches it in vain for any interpretation of the soul of the great republic, or any forecasting of the future years, or any passages expressing what America is to stand for among the nations. It is a fragment, the introduction to what should have been the poem.

In ''The Symphony'' more than elsewhere, perhaps, he is the

poet of his period. The poem is a cry against the materialism
that Lanier felt was crushing the higher things out of American
life:

> "O Trade! O, Trade! Would thou wert dead!
> The Time needs heart—'t is tired of head:
> We 're all for love," the violins said.

Each instrument in the orchestra joins in the argument. "A
velvet flute note" followed the passion of the violins, the reeds
whispered, "the bold straightforward horn" spoke out,

> And then the hautboy played and smiled
> And sang like any large-eyed child.

The solution of the problem was the same that Shelley had
brought. Love alone could master the evils of the time:

> Life! Life! thou sea-fugue, writ from east to west,
> Love, love alone can pore
> On thy dissolving score
> Of harsh half-phrasings,
> Blotted ere writ,
> And double erasings
> Of chords most fit.

And love was to come through music:

> Music is love in search of a word.

The poem is indeed a symphony. One feels that the poet is com-
posing rather than writing, that he is thinking in terms of or-
chestration, balancing parts and instruments, and working out
tone values. The same is true of "The Marshes of Glynn" and
"Sunrise": they are symphonies.

One must appreciate fully this musical basis of Lanier's art if
one is to understand him. He thought in musical forms. The
best illustration, perhaps, may be found in his Centennial Cantata. To the average man the poem meant little. One must read
it and reread it and study it if one is to get any consecutive
thought from it. But read after Lanier's explanation, it becomes not only clear but illuminating:

The principal matter over which the United States can legitimately
exult is *its present existence as a Republic,* in spite of so much oppo-
sition from Nature and from man. I therefore made the refrain of
the song—about which all its train of thought moves—concern itself
wholly with the *Fact of existence:* the waves cry *"It shall not be"; * the

powers of nature cry "It shall not *be"; * the wars, etc., utter the same cry. This Refrain is the key to the whole poem.

A knowledge of the inability of music to represent any shades of meaning save those which are very intense, and very highly and sharply contrasted, led me to divide the poem into the eight paragraphs or movements which it presents, and make these vividly opposed to each other in sentiment. Thus the first movement is reflection, measured and sober: this suddenly changes into the *agitato* of the second: this agitato, culminating in the unison shout *"No! It shall not be,"* yields in the third movement to the *pianissimo* and meager effect of the skeleton voices from Jamestown, etc.: this *pianissimo* in the fourth movement is turned into a climax of the wars of armies and of faiths, again ending in the shout, "No!" etc.: the fifth movement opposes this with a *whispered* chorus—Huguenots whispering *Yea,* etc.: the sixth opposes again with loud exultation, "Now praise," etc.: the seventh opposes this with the single voice singing the Angels' song; and the last concludes the series of contrasts with a broad full chorus of measured and firm sentiment.

The metrical forms were selected purely with reference to their descriptive nature: the four trochaic feet of the opening strophe measure off reflection, the next (Mayflower) strophe swings and yaws like a ship, the next I made outre and bizarre and bony simply by the device of interposing the line of two and a half trochees amongst the four trochee lines: the swift action of the Huguenot strophe of course required dactyls: and having thus kept the first part of the poem (which describes the time *before* we were a real nation) in meters which are as it were exotic to our tongue, I now fall into the iambic meter—which is the genius of English words—as soon as the Nation becomes secure and firm.

My business as member of the orchestra for three years having caused me to sit immediately in front of the bassoons, I had often been struck with the possibility of producing the ghostly effects of that part of the bassoon register so well known to students of Berlioz and Meyerbeer—by the use of the syllable *ee* sung by a chorus. With this view I filled the ghostly Jamestown stanza with *ee*'s and would have put in more if I could have found them appropriate to the sense.[5]

No one can read this without thinking of Poe's "Philosophy of Composition." It explains much of Lanier's work.

VI

Had Lanier lived a decade longer, had he had time and strength to devote himself completely to his poetry, had his impetuous soul had time to gain patience and poise, and divest itself of florid extravagance and vague dithyramb, he might have gained a much higher place as a poet. He was gaining in power: his last poem

---

[5] *Letters of Sidney Lanier,* 162.

is his greatest. He was laying plans that would, we feel sure,
have worked themselves out to high poetic achievement. For at
least four books of poetry he had already selected titles: *Hymns
of the Mountains, Hymns of the Marshes, Songs of Aldheim,* and
Poems on Agriculture. What they were to be we can judge only
from "The Marshes of Glynn" and "Sunrise."

In these two poems we have work that is timeless and essentially
placeless. There is a breadth and sweep about it that one finds
only in the greater poets:

> And invisible wings, fast fleeting, fast fleeting,
>   Are beating
> The dark overhead as my heart beats—and steady and free
> Is the ebb-tide flowing from marsh to sea.

Oh, what is abroad in the marsh and the terminal sea?
Somehow my soul seems suddenly free
From the weighing of fate and the sad discussions of sin,
By the length and the breadth and the sweep of the marshes of Glynn.

As the marsh-hen secretly builds on the watery sod,
Behold I will build me a nest on the greatness of God:
I will fly in the greatness of God as the marsh-hen flies
In the freedom that fills all the space 'twixt the marsh and the skies:
By so many roots as the marsh-grass sends in the sod
I will heartily lay me a-hold on the greatness of God:
Oh, like the greatness of God is the greatness within
The range of the marshes, the liberal marshes of Glynn.

The jottings that he made in his notebooks and the fragments of
poems that he noted down as the inspiration came to him remind
us often of Whitman. They have sweep and range:

    I fled in tears from the men's ungodly quarrel about God: I fled
in tears to the woods, and laid me down on the earth; then somewhat
like the beating of many hearts came up to me out of the ground, and
I looked and my cheek lay close by a violet; then my heart took courage
and I said:

> "I know that thou art the word of God, dear violet.
> And, oh, the ladder is not long that to my heaven leads!
> Measure the space a violet stands above the ground,
>   'T is no farther climbing that my soul and angels have to do
>   than that!"

> > I went to the church to find my Lord.
> > They said He is here. He lives here.
> > But I could not see him
> > For the creed-tables and bonnet flowers.

Lanier is essentially a poet of unfulfilled promise. He seems always about to do greater things than in reality he ever does. His lyrics like "Evening Song," and "The Trees and the Master" and "The Song of the Chattahoochee," have strains in them almost Shelley-like, but there is always the fatal defect somewhere. Nothing is perfect. It seems strange sometimes that one who could at moments go so far could not go the whole way and remain long. He must hold his place among the American poets by virtue of a few fragments. A few times was he rapt into the pure ether of poetry, but he was allowed to catch only fleeting glimpses.

VII

The period may be said to have produced in the South two inspired poets, Lanier and Irwin Russell, and in many ways the two were alike. Both were frail of body and sensitive of temperament, both were passionately given to music and found their poetic field by means of it, both were educated men, eager students of the older literatures, both discovered the negro as poetic material, and both died when their work was just beginning, Russell, like Keats, at the boyish age of twenty-six. But Russell added what Lanier had no trace of, a waywardness of character and a genius for goodfellowship that wrecked him even earlier than it did Burns.

The life of Russell is associated with four cities: Port Gibson, Mississippi, where he was born in 1853; St. Louis, where he spent the earlier years of his life and where later he completed the course at the Jesuit University; Port Gibson again, where he studied law and was admitted to the bar; New York City, of which he was a resident from January until July, 1879; and New Orleans, where he died in December of the same year. His life was fitful and restless. He did little with his profession, turning from it to learn the printer's trade, and then after a few listless months, drifting into other things. He had dreams of California and wandered on foot in its direction as far as Texas; he attempted to run away to sea, and he spent much time on the river boats making jovial friends of the captains and the pilots. His banjo assured him of a welcome wherever he might go.

The writing of poetry was never to him a serious occupation. He composed with abandon when the mood was on him, he seldom

revised, and he cared little for the finished product save as it
might please his friends. One finds many evidences in his work
that he learned his art from Burns, whom he considered the greatest poet the world had ever produced. He had saturated himself
too with the English balladists and the genuine old poets of the
early periods. The poetry of his own time angered him. In ''The
Hysteriad'' (*Scribner's*, 16:759) he satirizes with bitterness the
contemporary product. ''A poem of the period,'' he said, ''or a
periodical poem, is a thing that is altogether emotional, and is
not intended to convey any idea in particular.'' To him poetry
meant something not esoteric and idealized, but something that lay
very close to the life of every day, something redolent of humanity, like Burns's songs. He maintained that his own inspiration had come not at all from other poets, but from actual contact
with the material that he made use of. His own words concerning
the composition of his first poem have a peculiar value. They are
a part of the history of the period:

You know I am something of a banjoist. Well, one evening I was
sitting in our back yard in old Mississippi "twanging" on the banjo,
when I heard the missis—our colored domestic, an old darkey of the
Aunt Dinah pattern—singing one of the outlandish camp-meeting
hymns of which the race is so fond. She was an extremely " 'ligious"
character and, although seized with the impulse to do so, I hesitated
to take up the tune and finish it. I did so, however, in the dialect I
have adopted, and which I then thought and still think is in strict con-
formity to their use of it, I proceeded, as one inspired, to compose
verse after verse of the most absurd, extravagant, and, to her, irreverent
rime ever before invented, all the while accompanying it on the banjo
and imitating the fashion of the plantation negro. . . . I was then
about sixteen and as I had soon after a like inclination to versify, was
myself pleased with the performance, and it was accepted by a publisher, I have continued to work the vein indefinitely.[6]

To what extent the poet was indebted to the Pike balladry that
had preceded his first work, at least so far as wide publication in
Northern magazines was concerned, is not easily determined. It
seems extremely probable that he had seen it. Lanier, as has
been shown, had published negro dialect poetry in *Scribner's*
nearly a year before Russell, but whoever was pioneer, the author
of ''Christmas-night in the Quarters'' was the one who first
caught the attention of the reading public and exerted the great-

[6] *The Critic*, November 3, 1888.

est influence upon the period. He undoubtedly was the leading pioneer. Page and Gordon dedicated their *Befo' de War* "To Irwin Russell, who awoke the first echo," and Joel Chandler Harris, manifestly an authority, declared that "Irwin Russell was among the first—if not the very first—of Southern writers to appreciate the literary possibilities of the negro character, and of the unique relations existing between the two races before the war, and was among the first to develop them." [7]

In the last year of his life Russell, encouraged by the reception of his magazine poems, went to New York to make literature his profession. Bunner, the editor of *Puck,* and Gilder and Robert Underwood Johnson of the *Century* staff, and others, recognized his ability, and gave him every encouragement possible. One of the most prominent of the poets of the older school, it may be remarked, also became interested in him and urged him to drop the ephemeral type of verse to which he had addicted himself and devote his talents to really serious work. For a brief period he obeyed, with what success one may judge from the poems at the end of his volume.

Success came too late. His friends were powerless to control his wayward genius. His frail constitution gave way. From a bed of fever he arose still half delirious, staggered to the docks, engaged to work his way on a New Orleans boat as a coal-heaver, and in New Orleans secured a position on the *Times.* But the end was near. To a member of the *Times* staff he opened his heart in words that might have come from Poe:

It has been the romance of a weak young man threaded in with the pure love of a mother, a beautiful girl who hoped to be my wife, and friends who believed in my future. I have watched them lose heart, lose faith, and again and again I have been so stung and startled that I have resolved to save myself in spite of myself. . . . I never shall.[8]

He died a few weeks later.

VIII

The value of Russell's work depends not so much upon the poetic quality of it as upon the faithfulness and the skill with which he has portrayed the negro. Within this narrow field he has had no superior. Harris has summed it up thus:

[7] Introduction to Russell's Poems.
[8] *Library of Southern Literature,* 4663.

The most wonderful thing about the dialect poetry of Irwin Russell is his accurate conception of the negro character. The dialect is not always the best—it is often carelessly written—but the negro is there, the old-fashioned, unadulterated negro, who is still dear to the Southern heart. There is no straining after effect—indeed the poems produce their result by indirection; but I do not know where could be found to-day a happier or a more perfect representation of negro character.[9]

Russell is less romantic in his picture of the negro than are Page and Harris. Once in a while he throws the mellow light over the old days, as in "Mahsr John," where he represents the freed slave dwelling in imagination upon the glories that he has once known, but he holds the strain not long:

> I only has to shet my eyes, an' den it seems to me
> I sees him right afore me now, jes' like he use' to be,
> A-settin' on de gal'ry, lookin' awful big an' wise,
> Wid little niggers fannin' him to keep away de flies.

> He alluz wore de berry bes' ob planters' linen suits,
> An' kep' a nigger busy jes' a-blackin' ob his boots;
> De buckles on his galluses wuz made of solid gol',
> An' diamon's!—dey wuz in his shut as thick as it would hol'.

Page would have stopped after the old negro had ended his glorification of the old days, but Russell hastens to bring the picture to present-day conditions:

> Well, times is changed. De war it come an' sot de niggers free,
> An' now ol' Mahsr John ain't hardly wuf as much as me;
> He had to pay his debts, an' so his lan' is mos'ly gone—
> An' I declar' I 's sorry fur my pore ol' Mahsr John.

It was essentially the later negro, the negro of the poet's own day, that is represented in the poems. He has become a farmer for himself now and tries sly tricks when he takes his cotton to market. Detected, he is voluble in his explanations:

> Rocks in dat ar cotton! How de debbil kin dat be?
> I packed dat bale mys'f—hol' on a minute, le'—me—see—
> My stars! I mus' be crazy! Mahsr Johnny, dis is fine!
> I 's gone an' hauled my brudder's cotton in, stead ob mine!

He sends his boy to work as waiter on the river boats and as he is departing overwhelms him with advice:

Dem niggers what runs on de ribber is mos'ly a mighty sharp set;
Dey 'd fin' out some way fur to beat you, ef you bet 'em de water
        wuz wet;

[9] Introduction to Russell's Poems.

You's got to watch out for dem fellers; dey'd cheat off de horns ob
a cow.
I knows 'em; I follered de ribber 'fore ebber I follered a plow.

He is inordinately fond of preaching, as witness "Half-way
Doin's" and "A Sermon for the Sisters." He delights to interpret the Scriptures, and his exegesis is often full of local color:

"Dar's gwine to be a' oberflow," said Noah, lookin' solemn—
Fur Noah tuk the *Herald,* an' he read de ribber column—
An' so he sot his hands to wuk a-cl'arin' timber-patches,
An' 'lowed he's gwine to build a boat to beat the steamah *Natchez.*

All the characteristics of the negro are touched upon with the
certainty of perfect knowledge: his superstitions, his ignorance
of the world, his awe of legal terms, his humor, his simple trust
in his religion, his childlike attitude toward nature, his habit of
addressing sententious language to his beasts of burden as if they
understood all he said, his conceit, and his firm belief in immortality.

Russell was one of the pioneers of the new era which had as its
most marked characteristic the use of American themes and backgrounds and absolute truth to American life. No section of the
social era was too lowly or unknown for him to take as material
for his art. He could even plan to write a negro novel with all
of its characters negroes and write the first chapters. Little,
however, that he planned ever came to completion. The thin
volume of poems published after his death was but a fragment of
what he might have written under happier conditions. As it is,
he must, like Lanier, be treated as one of those brief excited lives
that are found ever at the opening of new romantic eras—Novalis,
Chatterton, Burns, Keats—poets who left behind only fragments
of what might have been, but who influenced enormously the
writers that were to be.

BIBLIOGRAPHY

PAUL HAMILTON HAYNE. (1830–1886.) *Poems,* Boston, 1855; *Sonnets
and Other Poems,* 1857; *Avolio: A Legend of the Island of Cos,* 1860;
Legends and Lyrics, Philadelphia, 1872; *The Mountain of the Lovers,
with Poems of Nature and Tradition,* 1875; *Life of Robert Young Hayne,*
1878; *Life of Hugh Swinton Legare,* 1878; Complete edition of the Poems
with a sketch by Margaret J. Preston, 1882.
HENRY TIMROD. (1829–1867.) *Poems,* Boston, 1860; Complete edition

of the Poems with biographical introduction of 60 pages by Paul Hamilton Hayne, 1872; Poems of Henry Timrod, 1901.

SIDNEY LANIER. (1842–1881.) *Tiger Lilies: a Novel*, 1867; *Florida: Its Scenery, Climate, and History*, 1876; *Poems*, 1877; *The Boy's Froissart. Being Sir John Froissart's Chronicles of Adventure, Battle, and Custom in England, France, Spain, etc. Edited for Boys*, 1878; *The Science of English Verse*, 1880; *The Boy's King Arthur. Being Sir Thomas Malory's History of King Arthur and His Knights of the Round Table. Edited for Boys*, 1880; *The Boy's Mabinogion. Being the Earliest Welsh Tales of King Arthur in the Famous Red Book of Hergest. Edited for Boys*, 1881; *The Boy's Percy. Being Old Ballads of War, Adventure, and Love, from Bishop, Thomas Percy's Reliques of Ancient English Poetry. Edited for Boys*, 1882; *The English Novel and the Principles of Its Development*, 1883; *Poems of Sidney Lanier, Edited by His Wife*, with a Memorial by William Hayes Ward, 1884; Select Poems of Sidney Lanier, edited with an Introduction, Notes, and Bibliography, by Morgan Callaway, 1895; *Music and Poetry: Essays*, 1898; *Retrospects and Prospects: Descriptive and Historical Essays*, 1899; *Letters of Sidney Lanier*. Selections from His Correspondence 1866–1881, 1899; *Shakespeare and His Forerunners*, 1902; *Sidney Lanier*, by Edwin Mims, 1905. *Some Reminiscences and Early Letters of Sidney Lanier*, G. H. Clarke, 1907; *Poem Outlines*, 1908; *Synthesis and Analysis of the Poetry of Sidney Lanier*, C. C. Carroll, 1910.

IRWIN RUSSELL. *Poems by Irwin Russell*. With an introduction by Joel Chandler Harris. New York. 1888.

CHAPTER XIV

Just as the West of Mark Twain, Harte, Miller, Eggleston, and others had been central in the literature, especially in the fiction, of the seventies, so the South became central in the eighties. Southern writers like Cable, Lanier, and Russell began their distinctive work not long after the opening of the Bret Harte period, yet it was not until after *Old Creole Days,* 1879, the death of Russell in the same year and of Lanier in 1881, and the publication of Miss Woolson's *Rodman the Keeper* and the first Uncle Remus book in 1880, Johnston's *Dukesborough Tales,* 1883, and Craddock's *In the Tennessee Mountains,* 1884, that what we may call the era of Southern themes and Southern writers may be said fully to have taken possession of American literature. By 1888 Albion W. Tourgee could write in the *Forum,* ''It cannot be denied that American fiction of to-day, whatever may be its origin, is predominatingly Southern in type and character. . . . A foreigner studying our current literature, without knowledge of our history, and judging our civilization by our fiction, would undoubtedly conclude that the South was the seat of intellectual empire in America and the African the chief romantic element of our population.''

The real cause of this outburst has not often been touched upon. The sudden vogue of Southern themes and Southern writers came not, as some have explained, from the fact that a distinctive Southern literature had arisen, or that a peculiar school had sprung up in one section of the country, just as, for instance, we may speak of the New England school earlier in the century. Nor is it explained by the theory that the close of the war brought a new feeling of individuality to the South, a consciousness of its own self which was to find expression in a group of writers, as England after the wars with Spain found expression in the Elizabethans. It was not a merely local manifestation. The term ''Southern Literature,'' as now found in the titles of an increasing number of books and studies, is misleading. If the South, or any other section, is to produce a distinct literature of its own, that section must possess not alone themes and writers, but publishers as well, and widely circulated magazines of the type of the *Atlantic* and the *Century* and *Harper's*. It must have also critics and adequate critical standards, and, most important of all, it must have a clientele, readers enough to dispose of its own literary product. The South has had practically none of these save the literary themes and the writers. The turn of the tide from Western material and Western workers to material and workers from the South was a national phenomenon. It was in reality more a thing of the North than it was of the South. Without Northern publishers and magazines and criticism and readers there would have been no Southern literature.

To illustrate with a concrete example: Richard Malcolm Johnston published at Augusta, Georgia, in 1864, *Georgia Sketches by an Old Man*. In 1871 he added more tales to the collection, published them in the *Southern Magazine* of Baltimore, issued them in book form in the same city, with the title *Dukesborough Tales*, and a little later put forth a second and enlarged edition. Yet Edward Eggleston could say when Johnston as late as 1879 published his first story in a Northern magazine, "Mr. Neelus Peeler's Conditions," in *Scribner's Monthly*, that the reading public everywhere hailed his advent as that of a new and promising young man who had sent in his first story. It was not until the Harpers in 1883 issued a Northern edition of the much-published *Dukesborough Tales* that Johnston ceased to be a producer of merely Southern literature.

The cause of the Southern tone which American literature took on during the eighties lies in the single fact that the South had the literary material. The California gold, rich as it was when first discovered by the East, was quickly exhausted. There were no deep mines; it was surface gold, pockets and startling nuggets. Suddenly it was discovered that the South was a field infinitely richer, and the tide turned. Nowhere else were to be found such a variety of picturesque types of humanity: negroes, crackers, creoles, mountaineers, moonshiners, and all those incongruous elements that had resulted from the great social upheaval of 1861–1865. Behind it in an increasingly romantic perspective lay the old régime destroyed by the war; nearer was the war itself, most heroic of struggles; and still nearer was the tragedy of reconstruction with its carpet-bagger, its freed slaves, and its Klu-Klux terror. Never before in America, even in California, had there been such richness of literary material. That a group of Southern-born writers should have arisen to deal with it was inevitable. Who else *could* have dealt with it, especially in the new era that demanded reality and absolute genuineness? No Northerner could have revealed, for instance, the heart of the old plantation negro. Miss Woolson's stories of the South, brilliant as they are, are in a different world from those of Joel Chandler Harris.

The writers themselves made no claim that they were producing a Southern literature. They had, all of them, been touched by the new after-the-war spirit, and their outlook was nation wide. Cable in an address at Oxford, Mississippi, in June, 1882, pleaded for home subjects as a basis for literature, but for home subjects treated in a spirit of the broadest nationality: "Only let them be written," he urged, "to and for the whole nation and you shall put your own State not the less but the more in your debt." [1] He declared himself to be not at all in favor of the popular new phrase "the new South"; he would change it, he said, to "the *no* South." Lanier, as we have seen, was American in the broadest sense, and Joel Chandler Harris could say: "What does it matter whether I am a Northerner or Southerner if I am true to truth and true to that larger truth, my own true self? My idea is that truth is more important than sectionalism and that literature that can be labeled Northern, Southern, Western, Eastern, is not worth labeling." [2]

It was the voice of the new spirit of the new age.

I

That the enormous vogue of the Bret Harte and the *Pike County Ballads* literature of the early seventies could have passed unnoticed even in the remotest sections of America seems improbable, but to attempt to trace the influence it exerted on the group of Southern writers that sprang up shortly after it had made its appearance is useless and worse than useless Not for a

---

1 Boston *Literary World*, June 28, 1882.
2 Mims's *Sidney Lanier*, 284.

moment must it be forgotten that this earlier Western outburst was not a local evolution that succeeded in attracting the attention of the nation; it was rather the first result of a condition which was general and nation wide. It was the new after-the-war demand for life and reality and democracy, and it broke out first in the West because the West at that moment had material which was peculiarly fitted to make an appeal. Had the West at that crisis had no writers ready to exploit this material, the outburst undoubtedly would have come from the South. Cable and Lanier and Johnston and Russell would have written very much as they did write had Bret Harte and Mark Twain and Edward Eggleston never lived.

There were influences and conditions in the South that were peculiarly favorable to the production of the type of literature demanded by the time. Georgia in particular offered congenial soil. The middle region of the State was the most democratic part of the South. It had been settled by a sturdy race which separation from the more aristocratic areas had rendered peculiarly individual. At one extreme was the mountain cracker, a type which had been made peculiar only by isolation, at the other were such remarkable men as Alexander H. Stephens, Atticus G. Haygood, Benjamin H. Hill, John B. Gordon, and Henry W. Grady. The social system was peculiar. Relations between master and slave were far different from those found on the larger plantations where overseers were employed. The negroes were known personally; they were a part of the family. Relations like those described so delightfully by Joel Chandler Harris were common. "There was no selling," as Johnston expressed it; "black and white children grew up together. Servants descended from father to son." The result of this democracy was a natural tendency toward the new realistic type of localized literature. While the rest of the South had been romantic and little inclined to use its own backgrounds and its own local types of character, Georgia had been producing since the mid years of the century studies of its own peculiar types and institutions.

As early as 1835 had appeared *Georgia Scenes, Characters, Incidents, etc., in the First Half Century of the Republic. By a Native Georgian,* from the pen of Augustus B. Longstreet, graduate of Yale, lawyer, preacher, college president. It was republished in New York in 1840 and from that day it has never been out of print. A realistic, brutal series of sketches it is, full of ear-chewing fights, cruel gougings, horse-racings, horse-swaps, coarse practical jokes, and all the barbarous diversions of a primitive people in a primitive time. Its author apologizes in his preface for the ephemeral character of the book: the stories and sketches, he explains, are "nothing more than fanciful combinations of real incidents and characters." Yet few books of its decade have had more vitality. The author worked first hand in the materials of the life that he himself had seen about him. It is true at every point. Its author, a generation ahead of his times, summed up in one phrase the new realism that was to come: "real people and real incidents in fanciful combinations."

Associated with Longstreet in this earlier realistic period of Georgia were Oliver Hillhouse Prince (1787–1837), who contributed to *Georgia Scenes* "The Militia Drill," a sketch read perhaps by Thomas Hardy before he wrote his *Trumpet-Major,* and William Tappan Thompson (1812–1882), whose *Major Jones's Chronicles* appeared in book form in Philadelphia in 1840.

There was another element in Georgia during the earlier period which had strong influence upon the later group of writers, and allowed it to produce not only Richard Malcolm Johnston and Joel Chandler Harris and "Bill Arp," but poets like Ticknor and Lanier as well. In the cities and larger towns of the State there was an atmosphere of culture unique in the South. Harry Stillwell Edwards would account for it by calling attention to an element usually overlooked:

In the late thirties—1839 to be exact—Wesleyan Female College came into being at Macon—the first chartered college for women in the world, and soon began to turn out large classes of highly educated and accomplished graduates. The majority of these came from Georgia, but the whole South has always been represented in Wesleyan. Without going into this subject, I wish to state as my personal opinion that Georgia's literary development, which is undoubtedly more extensive than that of other Southern States, is due to the intellectual and spiritual soil or environment produced by this College in the fifty years of its existence previous to 1890. You will understand how this can be true though the mothers of the State's best known writers may not have been graduates. In my youth, every girl associate I had was of this college. Its atmosphere was everywhere apparent. To-day its graduates lead all over the State.[3]

One may trace these elements—the Longstreet realism at the one extreme and the Macon College influence at the other—in all the later Georgia writers. We have found how Lanier in his earlier work alternated between broad cracker sketches and dialect ballads and the more elegant forms of prose and poetry. Even a poem as rhapsodic as his "Corn" contains within it a realistic picture of the thriftless Georgia planter. It was from the blending of these two streams of influence that there came some of the strongest literature of the new period.

II

The link between Longstreet and the younger Georgia writers is to be found in Richard Malcolm Johnston. Chronologically— he was born in 1822—he belongs to the earlier group, the generation of Lowell and Story, Boker and Read and Edward Everett Hale, and he seems to have been touched not at all by the literary influences that had so strongly exerted themselves upon the writers of the seventies. He was reared on a central Georgia plantation with all the surroundings of the old régime; he had been educated in the type of rural school so graphically described in his earlier sketches and then later at Mercer College, from which he was graduated in 1841; he gave the vigorous years of his life to the law and then to teaching; and after he was sixty years of age began seriously to devote himself to the profession of literature.

As early as 1857 he had begun writing sketches of provincial life after the Longstreet pattern. His first piece, "The Goose Pond School" was followed at long intervals by others in the same vein, written, the greater part of them, after his removal to Baltimore partly to assist his friend Turnbull, the editor of the *Southern Magazine,* who had asked for his help, and partly "to subdue as far as possible the feeling of homesickness for my native region. It never occurred to me that they were of any sort of value. Yet when a collection of them, nine in all, was printed by Mr. Turnbull, who about that time ended publication of his magazine, and when a copy of this collection fell into the

[3] Letter to the Author, December, 1914.

hands of Henry M. Alden, of *Harper's Magazine,* whose acquaint-ance I had lately made, he expressed much surprise that I had not received any pecuniary compensation, and added that he would have readily accepted them if they had been offered to him. Several things he said about them that surprised and gratified me much. I then set into the pursuit of that kind of work."[4]

Johnston owed his introduction to Northern readers almost wholly to Lanier, who also was an exile in Baltimore. His in-fluence it was that induced Gilder to accept for *Scribner's Monthly* the first of the *Dukesborough Tales* to be published in the North. He did far more than this: he gave him constructive criticism; he pointed out to him weaknesses which might be tolerated in a pioneer like Longstreet, but not in the work of a later artist. Certain phases of his sketches he found exceedingly strong: ''The story strikes me as exquisitely funny, and your reproduction of the modes of thought and of speech among the rural Georgians is really wonderful.''[5] There were, however, frequent ''verbal lapses'' which were almost fatal, ''the action of the story does not move fast enough,'' and the catastrophe is clumsily handled. ''I will try to see you in a day or two and do this'' [read the manuscript aloud to him with running criticisms]. It was an opportunity that few authors ever get; and Johnston was wise enough to make the fullest use of it. Through Lanier it was that Alden became acquainted with his work and that the enlarged *Dukesborough Tales* was taken over by the Harpers, and it was only after the Northern issue of this book in 1883 that its author took a place among the writers of the period. During the following fifteen years he wrote vo-luminously.

Lanier's criticism touches with skill the strength and the weak-ness of Johnston as a writer of fiction. Like Longstreet, he was preëminently a maker of sketches. In his novels like *Old Mark Langston* and *Widow Guthrie* he failed dismally. Local color there is and humor and characterization, but in all that pertains to plot management the novels are feeble. The center and soul of his art was the Georgia environment. ''As long as the people in my stories have no fixed surroundings, they are nowhere to

---

4 *Autobiography,* 72.
5 Mims's *Sidney Lanier,* 297.

me; I cannot get along with them at all." There is little of story, little of action, little consideration of the deeper passions and motives of life: there is rather an artless presentation of the archaic provincial types and surroundings that he had known in his boyhood. Even within this restricted area his range was narrow. He seemed to be attracted, as was Longstreet, by the eccentric and the exceptional. As he looked back into his earlier years it was only the highly individualized characters and surroundings that stood out in his memory, and he peopled his stories largely with these. Like Lincoln he had traveled a primitive legal circuit in primitive days and he had had unique experiences highly laughable. His range of characters also is small. There is little of the negro in his work: he deals almost wholly with the class of middle Georgia common people that are but one step removed from the mountain cracker of Harris and Harbin.

Johnston was to the Southern movement what Eggleston was to the Western. The two have many points of resemblance. Both were humorists, both worked in the crude materials of early American life, and both seem to have evolved their methods and their literary ideals very largely from themselves. Neither was an artist. They will live largely because of their fidelity to a vanished area of American life.

III

Joel Chandler Harris also continued the tradition of Long-street and worked in the materials of Georgia life with little suggestion from without. There are few instances of a more spontaneous lapsing into literary expression. He had been reared in an environment as unliterary as Mark Twain's. Longstreet and Johnston, Russell and Lanier, were all college men, but Harris's school education ended when he was twelve, and the episode that ended it, a most unusual one, he has described thus:

One day while Joe Maxwell was sitting in the post-office looking over the Milledgeville papers, his eye fell on an advertisement that interested him greatly. It seemed to bring the whole world nearer to him. The advertisement set forth the fact that on next Tuesday the first number of the *Countryman,* a weekly paper, would be published. It would be modeled after Mr. Addison's little paper, the *Spectator,* Mr. Gold-smith's little paper, the *Bee,* and Mr. Johnson's little paper, the *Ram-*

bler. It would be edited by J. A. Turner, and it would be issued on the plantation of the editor, nine miles from Hillsborough. Joe read this advertisement over a dozen times, and it was with a great deal of impatience that he waited for the next Tuesday to come.

But the day did come, and with it came the first issue of the *Countryman.* Joe read it from beginning to end, advertisements and all, and he thought it the most entertaining little paper he had ever seen. Among the interesting things was an announcement by the editor that he wanted a boy to learn the printing business. Joe borrowed pen and ink and some paper from the friendly postmaster, and wrote a letter to the editor, saying that he would be glad to learn the printing business. The letter was no doubt an awkward one, but it served its purpose, for when the editor of the *Countryman* came to Hillsborough he hunted Joe up, and told him to get ready to go to the plantation. . . .

[The office] was a very small affair; the type was old and worn, and the hand-press—a Washington No. 2—had seen considerable service. . . . He quickly mastered the boxes of the printer's case, and before many days was able to set type swiftly enough to be of considerable help to Mr. Snelson, who was foreman, compositor, and pressman. The one queer feature about the *Countryman* was the fact that it was the only plantation newspaper that has ever been published, the nearest post-office being nine miles away. It might be supposed that such a newspaper would be a failure; but the *Countryman* was a success from the start, and at one time it reached a circulation of nearly two thousand copies. The editor was a very original writer.

On the Plantation: a Story of a Georgia Boy's Adventures during the War is the record, slightly disguised—Joe Maxwell is Joe Harris, and Hillsborough is Eatonton—of the four years in the boy's life that made of him the Joel Chandler Harris that we know to-day. It was his college course, and it was a marvelously complete one. He became a part of the great plantation; he shared its rude festivities; he came closely in contact with the old-time type of plantation negro; and, more important still, he discovered his employer's great library and was directed in his reading by Mrs. Turner, who took pains with the diffident young lad. In time he became himself a contributor to the paper, secretly at first, then openly with the editor's approval. The end of the war and with it the end of the old plantation régime, ended also the *Countryman* and sent Harris into wider fields.

For a time he worked at Macon, home of Lanier, then at New Orleans, where Cable in the intervals of office work was dreaming over the old French and Spanish records, then for a time he was editor of the Forsyth, Georgia, *Advertiser.* The force and originality of his editorials attracted at length the attention of W. T. Thompson, author of the Georgia classic, *Major Jones's Courtship*, and in 1871 he secured him for his own paper, the *Savannah News*. Five years later, Harris went over to the *Atlanta Constitution* and during the twenty-five years that followed his life was a vital part of that journal's history.

One must approach the literary work of Harris always with full realization that he was first of all a journalist. During the greater part of his life he gave the best of every day unreservedly to the making of his paper. Literary fame came to him almost by accident. To fill the inexorable columns of his paper he threw in what came easiest for him to write and he thought no more about it. Then one day he looked up from his desk to find himself hailed as a rising man of letters. It amazed him; he never half believed it; he never got accustomed to it. Years later in the full noon of his success he could say: "People insist on considering me a literary man when I am a journalist and nothing else. I have no literary training and know nothing at all of what is termed literary art. I have had no opportunity to nourish any serious literary ambition, and the probability is that if such an opportunity had presented itself I would have refused to take advantage of it." Never once did he seek for publication; never once did he send a manuscript to any publisher or magazine that had not earnestly begged for it; never once did he write a line with merely literary intent.

His first recognition by the literary world came through a bit of mere journalism. The story is told best in the words of Harry Stillwell Edwards:

About 1880, Sam Small of Atlanta, Georgia, on the local staff of the *Constitution*, began writing negro sketches, using "Old Si" or "Uncle Si" as his vehicle, and soon made the character famous. Small, however, was very dissipated, and frequently the Sunday morning Old Si contribution failed to appear. Joel Chandler Harris, the paragrapher for the *Constitution* as he had been for the *Sanannah News*, was called on to supply something in place of the missing Si sketches and began with "Uncle Remus." His first contributions were not folk lore, but local. He soon drifted into the folk lore, however, and recognizing the beauty and perfection of his work, people generally who remembered the stories of their childhood, wrote out for him the main points and sent them. I, myself, contributed probably a dozen of the adventures of Brer Rabbit as I had heard them. This service he afterwards acknowledged in a graceful card of thanks. Uncle Remus became, soon, the mouthpiece of the generation, so far as animal legends are concerned.

The stories at once attracted attention in the North. The *New York Evening Post* and the *Springfield Republican* in particular made much of them. As a direct result, *Uncle Remus: His Songs and Sayings; The Folk-lore of the old Plantation,* appeared in 1880 and its author quickly found himself a national and indeed an international personage.

The really vital work of Harris lies in two fields: sketches of the old-time negro and sketches of the mountain cracker of the later period. It is upon the first that his permanence as a writer must depend. He worked in negro folk lore, in that vast field of animal stories which seems to be a part of the childhood of races, but it is not his folk lore, valuable as it may be, that gives him distinction. Ethnological and philological societies have done the work more scientifically. Many of the animal legends in common use among the slaves of the South were already in print before he began to write.[6] What he did was to paint a picture, minutely accurate, of the negro whom he had known intimately on the plantation of Mr. Turner at the transition moment when the old was passing into the new. With a thousand almost imperceptible touches he has made a picture that is complete and that is alive. The childish ignorance of the race and yet its subtle cunning, its quaint humor, its pathos, its philosophy, its conceit, its mendacity and yet its depth of character, its quickness at repartee—nothing has been omitted. The story teller is more valuable than his story: he is recording unconsciously to himself his own soul and the soul of his race. Brer Rabbit after all is but a negro in thinnest disguise, one does not have to see Frost's marvelous drawings to realize that. The rabbit's helplessness typifies the helplessness of the negro, and yet Brer Rabbit always wins. Suavity and duplicity and shifty tricks are the only defense the weak may have. His ruses are the ruses of a childlike mind. Clumsy in the extreme and founded on what seems like the absolute stupidity of Brer Fox and Brer Wolf and the others who are beguiled, these ruses always succeed. The helpless little creature is surrounded on all sides by brutality and superior force; they seemingly over-

---

6 See *Riverside Magazine,* November, 1868, and March, 1869; also *Independent,* September 2, 1875.

come him, but in the end they are defeated and always by force of superior cunning and skilful mendacity at the supreme moment. It is the very essence of the child story—the giant killed by Jack, the wolf powerless to overcome Little Red Riding Hood, and all the others—for the negro himself was but a child.

Page uses the negro as an accessory. The pathos of the black race adds pathos to the story of the destroyed white régime. Harris rose superior to Page in that he made the negro not the background for a white aristocracy, but a living creature valuable for himself alone; and he rose superior to Russell inasmuch as he embodied the result of his studies not in a type but in a single negro personality to which he gave the breath of life. Harris's negro is the type plus the personal equation of an individual—Uncle Remus, one of the few original characters which America has added to the world's gallery.

It is worthy of note too that he interpreted with the same patience and thoroughness the music and the poetry of the negro. Russell was a lyrist with the gift of intuition and improvisation; Harris was a deliberate recorder. The songs he wrote are not literary adaptations, nor are they framed after the conventional minstrel pattern. They are reproductions. In his first introduction to *Uncle Remus, His Songs and His Sayings* he wrote:

As to the songs, the reader is warned that it will be found difficult to make them conform to the ordinary rules of versification, nor is it intended that they should so conform. They are written, and are intended to be read, solely in reference to the regular invariable recurrence of the cæsura, as, for instance, the first stanza of the Revival Hymn:

Oh, whar | shill we go | w'en de great | day comes |
Wid de blow | in' er de trumpits | en de bang | in' er de drums |
Hoy man | y po' sin | ers 'll be kotch'd | out late |
En fine | no latch | ter de gold | en gate |

In other words, the songs depend for their melody and rhythm upon the musical quality of *time,* and not upon long or short, accented or unaccented, syllables. I am persuaded that this fact led Mr. Sidney Lanier, who is thoroughly familiar with the metrical peculiarities of negro songs, into the exhaustive investigation which has resulted in the publication of his scholarly treatise on The Science of English Verse.

Nowhere else does one come so completely into the feeling of negro music as in Harris. In "The Night Before Christmas," in *Nights with Uncle Remus,* a latter-day "Sir Roger de Coverley Paper," we feel the tone of it:

His voice was strong and powerful, and sweet, and its range was as astonishing as its volume. More than this, the melody to which he tuned it, and which was caught up by a hundred voices almost as sweet and as powerful as his own, was charged with a mysterious and pathetic tenderness. The fine company of men and women at the big house— men and women who had made the tour of all the capitals of Europe— listened with swelling hearts and with tears in their eyes as the song rose and fell upon the air—at one moment a tempest of melody, at another a heart-breaking strain breathed softly and sweetly to the gentle winds. The song that the little boy and the fine company heard was something like this—ridiculous enough when put in cold type, but powerful and thrilling when joined to the melody with which the negroes had invested it:

> De big Owl holler en cry fer his mate,
> My honey, my love!
> Oh, don't stay long! oh, don't stay late!
> My honey, my love!
> Hit ain't so mighty fur ter de good-by gate,
> My honey, my love!
> Whar we all got ter go w'en we sing out de night,
> My honey, my love!
> My honey, my love, my heart's delight—
> My honey, my love!

IV

With the success of the first Uncle Remus book there came the greatest flood of dialect literature that America has ever known. The years 1883 and 1884 mark the high tide of this peculiar out- break, and to Georgia more than to any other locality may be traced the primal cause. In 1883 came what may be called the resurgence of the cracker, that Southeastern variety of the Pike which now came to the North as a new discovery. The leading characteristics of the type were thus set forth by Harris in his story of "Mingo":

Slow in manner and speech, shiftless in appearance, hospitable but suspicious toward strangers, unprogressive, toughly enduring the poor, hard conditions of their lives, and oppressed with the melancholy silences of the vast, shaggy mountain solitudes among which they dwell. The women are lank, sallow, dirty. They rub snuff, smoke pipes— even the young girls—and are great at the frying pan; full of a com- plaining patience and a sullen fidelity.

Again America became excited over a new Pike County type. Johnston's *Dukesborough Tales* were issued for the first time in the North; Harris's "At Teague Poteet's, a Sketch of the Hog Mountain Range," appeared in the June *Century*, and Charles Egbert Craddock's story of the same mountains, "The Harnt that Walks Chilhowee," came out the same month in the *Atlantic*. That was in 1883. The next year appeared Harris's *Mingo*, and Craddock's *In the Tennessee Mountains*. Then the flood gates of dialect were loosened. The *Century* published Page's story "Mars Chan," which it had been holding for four years, a story told entirely in the negro dialect. The new and mysterious Craddock, who was found now to be Miss Mary N. Murfree, created a wide-spread sensation. In 1883 appeared James Whitcomb Riley's first book *The Old Swimmin'-Hole and 'Leven More Poems* and Mary Hallock Foote's *The Led-Horse Claim;* in 1887 came Octave Thanet's *Knitters in the Sun*, dialect tales of the Arkansas canebrakes, and shortly afterwards Hamlin Garland's studies of farm life in the middle West. The eighties stand for the complete triumph of dialect and of local color.

Henry James, viewing the phenomenon from his English standpoint, offered an explanation that is worthy of note: "Nothing is more striking," he wrote, "than the invasive part played by the element of dialect in the subject-matter of the American fictions of the day. Nothing like it, probably—nothing like any such predominance—exists in English, in French, in German work of the same order. It is a part, in its way, to all appearance, of the great general wave of curiosity on the subject of the soul aboundingly *not* civilized that has lately begun to well over the Anglo-Saxon globe and that has borne Mr. Rudyard Kipling, say, so supremely high on its crest."

Harris's work with the Georgia cracker, though small in quantity, is of permanent value. Unlike Craddock, he was upon his native ground and he worked with sympathy. He had not the artistic distinction and the ideality of Page, but he was able to bring his reader nearer to the material in which he worked. Page was romantic and his standpoint was essentially aristocratic; Harris was realistic and democratic. He worked close always to the fundamentals of human life and his creations have always the seeming spontaneousness of nature itself.

As a writer Harris must be summed up as being essentially fragmentary. His literary output was the work of a man who could write only in the odd moments stolen from an exacting profession. It is work done by snatches. He left no long masterpiece; his novels like *Gabriel Tolliver* and the rest are full of delightful fragments, but they are rambling and incoherent. Of *Plantation Pageants* its author himself could say, "Glancing back over its pages, it seems to be but a patchwork of memories and fancies, a confused dream of old times." With his Brer Rabbit sketches, however, this criticism does not hold. By their very nature they are fragmentary; there was no call for continued effort or for constructive power; the only demand was for a consistent personality that should emerge from the final collection and dominate it, and this demand he met to the full.

No summary of Harris's work can be better than his own comment once uttered upon *Huckleberry Finn:* "It is history, it is romance, it is life. Here we behold a human character stripped of all tiresome details; we see people growing and living; we laugh at their humor, share their griefs, and, in the midst of it all, behold we are taught the lesson of honesty, justice, and mercy." To no one could this verdict apply more conspicuously than to the creator of Uncle Remus and of Teague Poteet.

V

To the Georgia group belongs in reality Mary Noailles Murfree, better known as Charles Egbert Craddock. Tennessee, her native State—she was born at Murfreesboro in 1850—was of Georgia settlement. On one side of the border as on the other one found a certain wild independence and originality and crude democracy, the same that voiced itself in Longstreet and Thompson, and later in Johnston and Harris. Moreover, the mountains of the Craddock tales lie along the Georgia border and their inhabitants are the same people who figured in Longstreet's "Gander Pulling" and furnished Gorm Smallin and Teague Poteet for Lanier and Harris.

During the seventeen years of her later childhood and youth, or from 1856 to 1873, Miss Murfree lived at Nashville, Tennessee, where her father had an extensive legal practice, and then until

1882 she made her home at St. Louis, Missouri. She was, therefore, unlike Johnston and Harris, metropolitan in training and
in point of view.   Lameness and a certain frailness of physique
caused by a fever debarred her from the activities of childhood
and drove her in upon herself for entertainment.   She was precocious and she read enormously, pursuing her studies even into
the French and the Italian.   Later she attended the academy at
Nashville and then a seminary at Philadelphia, and, on her return home, even began the study of law in her father's library.

For such a woman, especially in the seventies, literature as a
profession was inevitable.   She began to write early and some of
her apprentice papers, signed even then with the pen name
Charles E. Craddock, found publication, notably a few sketches
and tales in the weekly *Appleton's Journal.*   It was conventional
work and it promised little.   Between a sketch like "Taking the
Blue Ribbon at the Fair" and "The Dancin' Party at Harrison's
Cove," which appeared in the May issue of the *Atlantic,* 1878,
there is a gulf that even yet has not been fully explained.   Undoubtedly the early models that influenced her were George
Eliot, Thomas Hardy, and Bret Harte, but she has preserved little of her transition work.   She came unheralded with her art
fully matured.   Whoever may have been her early masters, she
was from the first autochthonic in style and material and in the
atmosphere that she threw over all that she wrote.   There was a
newness to her work, a tang of the wild and elemental in the
dialect, a convincing quality to the backgrounds painted in
sentences like "An early moon was riding, clear and full, over
this wild spur of the Alleghanies," that excited wide comment.
It was not until 1884, however, that the new author may be
said definitely to have arrived, for it was not until then that her
stories were given the dignity of book form.

With the publication of *In the Tennessee Mountains* came one
of the most dramatic happenings that ever gave wings to a new
book.   Charles Egbert Craddock visited the *Atlantic* office and,
to the amazement of Aldrich and Howells and Dr. Holmes, he
was a woman.   The sensation, coming as it did from the center
of the old New England tradition, gave the book at once an international fame and made Charles Egbert Craddock a name as
widely known as Dr. Holmes.   She followed her early success
with a long series of Tennessee mountain novels.   Six of them—

The Prophet of the Great Smoky Mountains, In the Clouds, The Despot of Broomsedge Cove, His Vanished Star, The Mystery of Witchface Mountain, and *The Juggler*—first appeared serially in the *Atlantic,* and, for a time at least, it seemed as if her work had taken its place among the American classics.

VI

Criticism of the Craddock novels must begin always with the statement that their author was not a native of the region with which she dealt.   She had been born into an old Southern family with wealth and traditions, and she had been reared in a city amid culture and a Southern social régime.   The Tennessee mountains she knew only as a summer visitor may know them.   For fifteen summers she went to the littie mountain town of Beersheba, prototype undoubtedly of the ''New Helvetia Springs'' of her novels, and from there made excursions into the wilder regions. She saw the mountains with the eyes of the city vacationist: she was impressed with their wildness, their summer moods with light and shadow, their loneliness and their remote spurs and coves and ragged gaps.   She saw them with the picture sense of the artist and she described them with a wealth of coloring that reminds one of Ruskin.   In every chapter, often many times repeated, gorgeous paintings like these:

A subtle amethystine mist had gradually overlaid the slopes of the T' other Mounting, mellowing the brilliant tints of the variegated foliage to a delicious hazy sheen of mosaics; but about the base the air seemed dun-colored, though transparent; seen through it, even the red of the crowded trees was but a somber sort of magnificence, and the great masses of gray rocks, jutting out among them here and there, wore a darkly frowning aspect.   Along the summit there was a blaze of scarlet and gold in the full glory of the sunshine; the topmost cliffs caught its rays, and gave them back in unexpected gleams of green or grayish-yellow, as of mosses, or vines, or huckleberry bushes, nourished in the heart of the deep fissures.

Mink, trotting along the red clay road, came suddenly upon the banks of the Scolacutta River, riotous with the late floods, fringed with the papaw and the ivy bush.   Beyond its steely glint he could see the sun-flooded summit of Chilhowee, a bronze green, above the intermediate ranges: behind him was the Great Smoky, all unfamiliar viewed from an unaccustomed standpoint, massive, solemn, of dusky hue; white and amber clouds were slowly settling on the bald.   There had been a shower among the mountains, and a great rainbow, showing now only green and rose and yellow, threw a splendid slant of translucent color on the purple slope. In such an environment the little rickety wooden mill—with its dilapidated leaking race, with its motionless wheel moss-grown, with its tottering supports throbbing in the rush of the water which rose around them, with a loitering dozen or more mountaineers about the door—might seem a feeble expression of humanity. To Mink the scene was the acme of excitement and interest.

A picture of summer it is for the most part painted lavishly with adjectives, and presented with impressionistic rather than realistic effect. Every detail is intensified. The mountains of eastern Tennessee are only moderate ridges, yet in the Craddock tales they take on the proportions of the Canadian Rockies or the Alps. The peak that dominates *In the Clouds* seems to soar like a Mont Blanc:

In the semblance of the cumulus-cloud from which it takes its name, charged with the portent of the storm, the massive peak of Thunderhead towers preëminent among the summits of the Great Smoky Mountains, unique, impressive, most subtly significant. What strange attraction of the earth laid hold on this vagrant cloud-form? What unexplained permanence of destiny solidified it and fixed it forever in the foundations of the range? Kindred thunderheads of the air lift above the horizon, lure, loiter, lean on its shoulder with similitudes and contrasts. Then with all the buoyant liberties of cloudage they rise—rise! . . . Sometimes it was purple against the azure heavens; or gray and sharp of outline on faint green spaces of the sky; or misty, immaterial, beset with clouds, as if the clans had gathered to claim the changeling.

Always the scenery dominates the book. It is significant that all of her early titles have in them the name of a locality,—the setting is the chief thing: Lost Creek, Big Injun Mounting, Harrison's Cove, Chilhowee, the Great Smoky Mountains, Broomsedge Cove, Keedon Bluffs. In stories like *The Mystery of Witch-Face Mountain* the background becomes supreme: the human element seems to have been added afterwards by a sort of necessity; the central character is the great witch-face on the mountain.

It reminds one of Hardy, and then one remembers that when "The Dancin' Party at Harrison's Cove" appeared in the *Atlantic*, *The Return of the Native* had for three months been running as a serial in *Harper's Monthly*, and that, somewhat later, *In the "Stranger-People's" Country* and *Wessex Folk* ran for months parallel in the same magazine. It is impossible not to think of Hardy as one reads *Where the Battle Was Fought,* 1884. The battle-field dominates the book as completely as does Egdon Heath *The Return of the Native,* and it dominates it in the same symbolic way:

> By wintry daylight the battle-field is still more ghastly. Gray with the pallid crab-grass which so eagerly usurps the place of the last summer's crops, it stretches out on every side to meet the bending sky. The armies that successively encamped upon it did not leave a tree for miles, but here and there thickets have sprung up since the war, and bare and black they intensify the gloom of the landscape. The turf in these segregated spots is never turned. Beneath the branches are rows of empty, yawning graves, where the bodies of soldiers were temporarily buried. Here, most often, their spirits walk, and no hire can induce the hardiest plowman to break the ground. Thus the owner of the land is fain to concede these acres to his ghostly tenants, who pay no rent. A great brick house, dismantled and desolate, rises starkly above the dismantled desolation of the plain.

The title of the book—*Where the Battle Was Fought*—makes the battle-field central in the tragedy, and so it is with the short stories " 'Way Down in Lonesome Cove" and "Drifting Down Lost Creek." Nature is always cognizant of the human tragedy enacted before it and always makes itself felt. In *The Juggler,* Tubal Cain Sims believes that murder has been done:

> "He sighed an' groaned like suthin' in agony. An' then he says, so painful, 'But the one who lives—oh, what can I do—the one who lives!'" He paused abruptly to mark the petrified astonishment on the group of faces growing white in the closing dusk.
> An owl began to hoot in the bosky recesses far up the slope. At the sound, carrying far in the twilight stillness, a hound bayed from the door of the little cabin in the Cove, by the river. A light, stellular in the gloom that hung about the lower levels, suddenly sprung up in the window. A tremulous elongated reflection shimmered in the shallows.

But such effects in her work are fitful: one feels them strongly at times, then forgets them in the long stretches of dialect conversation and description seemingly introduced for its own sake. Of the art that could make of Egdon Heath a constantly felt, implacable, malignant presence that harried and compelled its dwellers until the reader at last must shake himself awake as from a nightmare, of this she knew little. She worked by means of brilliant sketches; she relied upon her picturing power to carry the story, and as a result the effect is scattered.

In her characterization she had all the defects of Scott: she worked largely with externals. She had an eye for groups posed artistically against a picturesque background as in that marvelous opening picture in " 'Way Down on Lonesome Cove.'' She expended the greatest of care on costume, features, habits of carriage and posture, tricks of expression, individual oddities, but she seldom went deeper. We see her characters distinctly; not often do we feel them. In her major personages, like the Prophet, the Despot, the Juggler, we have little sympathetic interest, and it is impossible to believe that they were much more than picturesque specimens even to the author herself. To get upon the heart of the reader a character must first have been upon the heart of his creator. Here and there undoubtedly she did feel the thrill of comprehension as she created, a few times so keenly indeed that she could forget her art, her note book, and her audience. The one thing that seems to have touched her heart as she journeyed through the summer valleys and into the remote coves seems to have been the pitiful loneliness and heart-hunger of the women. Could she have done for all of her characters what she did for Celia Shaw and Madeline and Dorinda and a few other feminine souls, the final verdict upon her work might have been far different from what it must be now.

Her stories necessarily are woven from scanty materials. In the tale of a scattered and primitive mountain community there can be little complication of plot. The movement of the story must be slow, as slow indeed as the round of life in the coves and the lonesome valleys. But in her long-drawn narratives often there is no movement at all. She elaborates details with tediousness and records interminable conversations, and breaks the thread to insert whole chapters of description, as in Chapter VI of *The Juggler,* which records the doings at a mountain revival meeting seemingly for the mere sake of the local color. Nearly all of her longer novels lack in constructive power. Like Harte, whom in so many ways she resembled, she could deal strongly with picturesque moments and people, but she lacked the ability to trace the growth of character or the slow transforming power of a passion or an ideal or a sin.

Her style was peculiarly her own; in this she was strong. It is worthy of note that in an age rendered styleless by the newspaper and the public school she was able to be individual to the extent that one may identify any page of her writings by the style alone. It is not always admirable: there is a Southern floridness about it, a fondness for stately epithet that one does not find in Harris or in others of the Georgia group. She can write that the search light made "a rayonnant halo in the dim glooms of the riparian midnight," and she can follow the jocose observation of a woman washing dishes with this tremendous sentence: " 'What fur?' demanded the lord of the house, whose sense of humor was too blunted by his speculations, and a haunting anxiety, and a troublous eagerness to discuss the question of his discovery, to perceive aught of the ludicrous in the lightsome metaphor with which his weighty spouse had characterized her dissatisfaction with the ordering of events." It may be interesting to know that the woman vouchsafed no reply. Rather, "she wheezed one more line of her matutinal hymn in a dolorous cadence and with breathy interstices between the spondees."

She is at her best when describing some lonely valley among the ridges, or the moonlight as it plays fitfully over some scene of mountain lawlessness, or some remote cabin "deep among the wooded spurs." In such work she creates an atmosphere all her own. Few other writers have so made landscape felt. One may choose illustrations almost at random:

On a certain steep and savage slope of the Great Smoky Mountains, the primeval wilderness for many miles is unbroken save for one meager clearing.

Deep among the wooded spurs Lonesome Cove nestles, sequestered from the world. Naught emigrates from thence except an importunate stream that forces its way through a rocky gap, and so to freedom beyond. No stranger intrudes; only the moon looks in once in a while. The roaring wind may explore its solitudes; and it is but the vertical sun that strikes to the heart of the little basin, because of the massive mountains that wall it round and serve to isolate it.

The night wind rose. The stars all seemed to have burst from their moorings and were wildly adrift in the sky. There was a broken tumult of billowy clouds, and the moon tossed hopelessly among them, a lunar wreck, sometimes on her beam ends, sometimes half submerged, once more gallantly struggling to the surface, and again sunk. The bare boughs of the trees beat together in a dirgelike monotone.

Nowhere is she commonplace; nowhere does she come down from the stately plane that she reaches always with her opening paragraph. Even her dialect is individual. Doubtless other writers have handled the mountain speech more correctly, doubtless there is as much of Charles Egbert Craddock in the curious forms and perversions as there is of the Tennessee mountaineers, yet no one has ever used dialect more convincingly than she or more effectively. She has made it a part of her style.

The story of Charles Egbert Craddock is a story of gradual decline. *In the Tennessee Mountains* was received with a universality of approval comparable only with that accorded to *The Luck of Roaring Camp*. In her second venture, *Where the Battle Was Fought*, she attempted to break from the narrow limits of her first success and to write a Hardy-like novel of the section of Southern life in which she herself belonged, but it failed. From all sides came the demand that she return again to her own peculiar domain. And she returned with *The Prophet of the Great Smoky Mountains*. It was praised, but with the praise came a note of dissatisfaction, a note that became more and more dominant with every novel that followed. Her first short stories had appealed because of their freshness and the strangeness of their setting. Moreover, since they were the first work of a young writer they were a promise of better things to come. But the promise was not fulfilled. After *The Juggler*, her last attempt on a large scale to create a great Tennessee-mountains novel, she took the advice of many of her critics and left the narrow field that she had cultivated so carefully. She wrote historical romances and novels of contemporary life, but the freshness of her early work was gone. After 1897 she produced nothing that had not been done better by other writers.

Her failure came not, as many have believed, from the poverty of her materials and the narrowness of her field. Thomas Hardy deliberately had chosen for his novels a region and a people just as primitive. A great novel should concern itself with the common fundamentals of humanity, and these fundamentals, he believed, may be studied with more of accuracy in the isolated places where the conventions of polite society have not prevented natural expression. Or, to quote Hardy's own words:

Social environment operates upon character in a way that is oftener than not prejudicial to vigorous portraiture by making the exteriors of men their screen rather than their index, as with untutored mankind. Contrasts are disguised by the crust of conventionality, picturesqueness obliterated, and a subjective system of description necessitated for the differentiation of character. In the one case the author's word has to be taken as to the nerves and muscles of his figures; in the other they can be seen as in an écorché.[7]

The failure of Charles Egbert Craddock came rather from her inability to work with large masses of material and coördinate it and shape it into a culminating force. She was picturesque rather than penetrating, melodramatic rather than simple, a showman rather than a discerning interpreter of the inner meanings of life. She could make vivid sketches of a moment or of a group or a landscape, but she could not build up touch by touch a consistent and compelling human character. Her genius was fitted to express itself in the short story and the sketch, and she devoted the golden years of her productive life to the making of elaborate novels. A little story like " 'Way Down on Lonesome Cove" is worth the whole of the *The Juggler* or *In the Clouds*. The short stories with which she won her first fame must stand as her highest achievement.

VII

Later members of the Georgia group, Sarah Barnwell Elliott, Harry Stillwell Edwards, and William Nathaniel Harben, have continued the tradition of Longstreet and have dealt more or less realistically with the humbler life of their region. Miss Elliott with her *The Durket Sperrit* entered the domain of Charles Egbert Craddock and gave a new version of the mountain dialect. A comparison of this novel with *The Juggler*, which appeared the same year, is illuminating. The two writers seem to be complements of each other, the one strong where the other is weak. The story lacks the atmosphere, the poetic dignity, the sense of mystery and of mountain majesty so notable in the elder novelist, but it surpasses her in characterization and in sympathy. The people are tremendously alive. The tyrannical old woman about whom the tale centers, with her narrow ideals and her haughty "Durket sperrit," dominates every page

[7] *The Forum*, 1888.

as Egdon Heath dominates *The Return of the Native*. She is felt during every moment of the story and so is the pathetic little mountain waif in the earlier chapters of *Jerry*. Miss Elliott's distinctive work is limited to these two books. Had she had the courage to work out with clearness the central tragedy of *The Durket Sperrit*, the deliberate disgracing of Hannah by her discarded lover, the book might take its place among the few great novels of the period.

Edwards inclined more toward the old Georgia type of human-nature sketch. His best work is to be found in his short studies in black and white after the Johnston pattern. Indeed, his first story, "Elder Brown's Backslide," *Harper's Monthly*, 1885, without his name would have been regarded as a Dukesborough Tale. He has written two novels, one of which, *Sons and Fathers*, was awarded the $10,000 prize offered by the *Chicago Record* for a mystery story, but he is not a novelist. He is humorous and picturesque and often he is for a moment the master of pathos, but he has added nothing new and nothing commandingly distinctive.

VIII

Constance Fenimore Woolson's *Rodman the Keeper*, 1880, undoubtedly was a strong force in the new Southern revival. During the eighties Miss Woolson was regarded as the most promising of the younger writers. She was a grand niece of Cooper, a fact made much of, and she had written short stories of unusual brilliance, her collection, *Castle Nowhere*, indeed, ranking as a pioneer book in a new field. Again was she destined to be a pioneer. In 1873 the frail health of her mother sent her into the South and for six years she made her home in Florida, spending her summers in the mountains of North Carolina, Virginia, South Carolina, and Georgia. During the rest of her life her stories were studies of Southern life and Southern conditions. Only *Anne* of her novels and two late collections of Italian tales may be noted as exceptions.

It was in *Rodman the Keeper*, a collection of her magazine stories of the late seventies, that the North found its first adequate picture of the territory over which had been fought the Civil War. The Tourgee novels, which had created a real sensation, were political documents, but here were studies carefully wrought by one who did not take sides. It showed the desolation wrought by the armies during the four years, the pathos of broken homes and ruined plantations, the rankling bitterness, especially in the hearts of women, the helpless pride of the survivors, and the curious differences between the Northern and the Southern temperaments. It was careful work. Contemporary opinion seemed to be voiced by the Boston *Literary World:* The stories "more thoroughly represent the South than anything of the kind that has been written since the war."

Necessarily the standpoint was that of an observer from without. There was no dialect in the tales, there were no revealings of the heart of Southern life as in Harris and Page and the others who had arisen from the material they used, but there was beauty and pathos and a careful realism that carried conviction. A sketch like "Felipe," for example, is a prose idyl, "Up the Blue Ridge" is the Craddock region seen with Northern eyes, and the story that gives the title to the book catches the spirit of the defeated South as few writers not Southern born have ever done.

For a time Miss Woolson held a commanding place among the novelists of the period. After her untimely death in 1894 Stedman wrote that she "was one of the leading women in the American literature of the century," and again, "No woman of rarer personal qualities, or with more decided gifts as a novelist, figured in her own generation of American writers." But time has not sustained this contemporary verdict. Her ambitious novel *Anne,* over which she toiled for three years, brilliant as it may be in parts, has not held its place. And her short stories, rare though they may have been in the day of their newness, are not to be compared with the perfect art of such later writers as Miss King and Mrs. Chopin. She must take her place as one of the pioneers of the period who discovered a field and prepared an audience for writers who were to follow.

IX

The appearance of Page's *In Ole Virginia,* 1887, marks the culmination of the period of Southern themes. The sensation caused by *The Quick or the Dead?* by Amélie Rives (later Princess Troubetzkoy) in 1888 need only be referred to. It had little significance either local or otherwise. The younger writers, born for the most part at a later date, like John Fox, Jr., Mary Johnston, and Ellen Glasgow, belong to another period.

BIBLIOGRAPHY

RICHARD MALCOLM JOHNSTON. (1822–1898.) *The English Classics,* 1860; *Georgia Sketches, by an Old Man,* 1864; *Dukesborough Tales,* 1871, 1874, 1883, 1892; *English Literature* (with William Hand Browne), 1872; *Life of Alexander H. Stephens* (with William Hand Browne), 1878; *Old Mark Langston, a Tale of Duke's Creek,* 1883; *Mr. Absalom Billingslea and Other Georgia Folk,* 1888; *Ogeechee Cross Firings,* 1889; *The Primes and Their Neighbors,* 1891; *Studies Literary and Scientific,* 1891; *Mr. Billy Downs and His Likes,* 1892; *Mr. Fortner's Marital Claims and Other Stories,* 1892; *Two Gray Tourists,* 1893; *Widow Guthrie,* 1893; *Little Ike Templin and Other Stories,* 1894; *Old Times in Middle Georgia,* 1897; *Pearce Amerson's Will,* 1898.

JOEL CHANDLER HARRIS. (1848–1908.) *Uncle Remus, His Songs and His Sayings,* 1880; *Nights with Uncle Remus, Myths and Legends of the Old Plantation,* 1883; *Mingo and Other Sketches in Black and White,* 1884; *Story of Aaron,* 1885; *Free Joe and Other Georgian Sketches,* 1887; *Daddy Jake the Runaway, and Short Stories Told After Dark,* 1889; *Balaam and His Master, and Other Sketches and Stories,* 1891; *On the Plantation, a Story of a Georgia Boy's Adventures During the War,* 1892; *Uncle Remus and His Friends,* 1892; *Little Mr. Thimblefinger and His Queer Country,* 1894; *Mr. Rabbit at Home,* 1895; *Sister Jane, Her Friends and Acquaintances,* 1896; *Georgia from the Invasion of De Soto to Recent Times,* 1896; *Stories of Georgia,* 1896; *Aaron in the Wildwoods,* 1897; *Tales of the Home Folks in Peace and War,* 1898; *Chronicles of Aunt Minerva Ann,* 1899; *Plantation Pageants,* 1899; *On the Wing of Occasions,* 1900; *Gabriel Tolliver, a Story of Reconstruction,* 1902; *Making of a Statesman, and Other Stories,* 1902; *Wally Wanderoon,* 1903; *Little Union Scout,* 1904; *Tar Baby and Other Rimes of Uncle Remus,* 1904; *Told by Uncle Remus; New Stories of the Old Plantation,* 1905.

CONSTANCE FENIMORE WOOLSON. (1840–1894.) *The Old Stone House,* 1873; *Castle Nowhere,* 1875; *Lake-Country Sketches,* 1875; *Rodman the Keeper,* 1880; *Anne,* 1882; *East Angels,* 1886; *Jupiter Lights,* 1889; *Horace Chase, a Novel,* 1894; *The Front Yard and Other Italian Stories,* 1895; *Dorothy, and Other Italian Stories,* 1896; *Mentone, Cairo, and Corfu,* 1896.

CHARLES EGBERT CRADDOCK. (1850——.) *In the Tennessee Mountains,* 1884; *Where the Battle Was Fought,* 1885; *Down the Ravine,* 1885; *The Prophet of the Great Smoky Mountains,* 1885; *In the Clouds,* 1886; *The Story of Keedon Bluffs,* 1887; *The Despot of Broomsedge Cove,* 1888; *In the "Stranger People's" Country,* 1891; *His Vanished Star,* 1894; *The Phantoms of the Footbridge,* 1895; *The Mystery of Witchface Mountain,* 1895; *The Juggler,* 1897; *The Young Mountaineers,* 1897; *The Story of

Old Fort Louden, 1899; *The Bushwhackers and Other Stories,* 1899; *The Champion,* 1902; *A Specter of Power,* 1903; *Storm Center,* 1905; *The Frontiersman,* 1905; *The Amulet,* 1906; *The Windfall,* 1907; *The Fair Mississippian,* 1908; *Ordeal—A Mountain Story of Tennessee,* 1912; *Raid of the Guerrilla,* 1912; *The Story of Duciehurst,* 1914.

SARAH BARNWELL ELLIOTT. *The Felmeres,* 1880; *A Simple Heart,* 1886; *Jerry,* 1890; *John Paget,* 1893; *The Durket Sperret,* 1897; *An Incident and Other Happenings,* 1899; *Sam Houston,* 1900; *The Making of Jane,* 1901; *His Majesty's Service and Other Plays.*

HARRY STILLWELL EDWARDS. (1855———.) *Two Runaways and Other Stories,* 1889; *Sons and Fathers,* 1896; *The Marbeau Cousins,* 1898; *His Defense, and Other Stories,* 1898.

CHAPTER XV

THE LATER POETS

Although prose forms, especially the novel and the short story, dominated the period, yet the amount of poetry published from 1860 to 1899 surpasses, in mere bulk at least, all that had been produced in America before that date. In quality also it is notable. Stedman's *An American Anthology* has 773 pages of selections, and of this space 462 pages, or almost two-thirds, are given to the poets who made their first appearance during these forty years. Very many whom he mentions were only incidentally poets. A surprising number of those who are known to-day only as novelists or short story writers began their career with a volume and in some cases with several volumes of verse. Few indeed have been the writers who have not contributed poetical material. Among the poets are to be numbered writers as inseparably connected with prose as Thoreau, Burroughs, Howells, Mrs. Stuart Phelps Ward, S. Weir Mitchell, Miss Woolson, Lew Wallace, Mrs. Wilkins Freeman, Harris, Page, Mrs. Cooke, Ambrose Bierce, Alice Brown, Hamlin Garland, and A. S. Hardy.

Those who may be counted as the distinctive poets of the era, the third generation of poets in America, make not a long list if only those be taken who have done new and distinctive work. Not many names need be added to the following twenty-five whose first significant collections were published during the twenty years following 1870:

1870. Bret Harte. *Plain Language from Truthful James.*
1871. John Hay. *Pike County Ballads.*
1871. Joaquin Miller. *Songs of the Sierras.*
1871. Will Carleton. *Poems.*
1872. Celia Thaxter. *Poems.*
1873. John Boyle O'Reilly. *Songs of the Southern Seas.*
1875. Richard Watson Gilder. *The New Day.*
1877. Sidney Lanier. *Poems.*

1881. Ina Coolbrith. *A Perfect Day and Other Poems.*
1882. John Bannister Tabb. *Poems.*
1883. James Whitcomb Riley. *The Old Swimmin'-Hole.*
1883. George Edward Woodberry. *The North Shore Watch.*
1884. Edith M. Thomas. *A New Year's Masque.*
1884. Henry Cuyler Bunner. *Airs from Arcady.*
1884. Louise Imogen Guiney. *Songs at the Start.*
1886. Clinton Scollard. *With Reed and Lyre.*
1887. Eugene Field. *Culture's Garland.*
1887. Madison Cawein. *Blooms of the Berry.*
1887. Robert Burns Wilson. *Life and Love.*
1888. Irwin Russell. *Dialect Poems.*
1889. Richard Hovey. *The Laurel: an Ode.*

John James Piatt, Emma Lazarus, Emily Dickinson, and E. R, Sill, whose first volumes fall outside of the twenty-years period, complete the number.

I

For the greater part these later poets were children of the new era who with Whitman voiced their own hearts and looked at the life close about them with their own eyes. The more individual of them, the leading innovators who most impressed themselves upon their times—Whitman, Hay and Harte, Miller, Lanier and Russell—we have already considered. They rose above conventions and rules and looked only at life; they stood for the new Americanism of the period, and they had the courage that dared in a critical and fastidious age to break away into what seemed like crude and unpoetic regions. Not many of them could go to the extremes of Whitman, or even of Harte and Hay. Some would voice the new message of the times in the old key and the old forms; others would adopt the new fashions but change not at all the old themes and the old sentiments.

Of the latter class Will Carleton perhaps is the typical representative. By birth and training he belonged to the Western group of innovators represented by Mark Twain and Eggleston and Miller. He had been born in a log cabin in Michigan and he had spent all of his boyhood on a small, secluded farm. He had broken from his environment at twenty, had gained a college degree, and following the lead of his inclination had become a journalist, first in Detroit, then in Chicago, Boston, and New York. From journalism, especially in the seventies, it was but a step to literature. He would be a poet, and led by the spirit of his period he turned for material to the homely life of his boyhood. He would make no realistic picture—no man was ever less fitted than he to reproduce the external features of a scene or a region—he would touch the sentiments and the emotions. "Betsey and I Are Out," published in the *Toledo Blade* in 1871, was the beginning. Then in 1873 came *Farm Ballads*, with such popular favorites as "Over the Hills to the Poor-House" and "Gone with a Handsomer Man," a thin book that sold forty thousand copies in eighteen months. No poet since Longfellow had so appealed to the common people. At his death in 1912 there had been sold of his various collections more than six hundred thousand copies.

His poetry as we read it to-day has in it little of distinction; it is crude, for the most part, and conventional. It made its appeal largely because of its kindly sympathy, its homeliness, and its lavish sentiment. The poet played upon the chords of memory and home and childhood, the message of the earlier Longfellow cast into a heavily stressed and swinging melody that found a prepared audience. With E. P. Roe, his counterpart in prose, Will Carleton is largely responsible for prolonging the age of sentiment.

A singer of a different type was John James Piatt, born in Indiana in 1835 and joint author with W. D. Howells of *Poems of Two Friends,* 1859. He was a classicist who caught the new vision and sought to compromise. Everywhere in his work a blending of the new and the old: the Western spirit that would voice the new notes of the Wabash rather than echo the old music of the Thames, that syren melody that had been the undoing of Taylor and Stoddard. In an early review of Stedman, Piatt had found, as he characteristically termed it, "a too frequent betrayal of Tennyson's floating musk in his singing-garments," and he had noted as his chief strength that "his representative subjects are American." [1] In making the criticism he touched upon his own weakness and his own strength. In all his volumes conventional work like "Rose and Root," "The Sunshine of Shadows," and "The Unheard" alternates with more original

[1] *Atlantic Monthly,* 41:313.

poems, native in theme and to a degree native in spirit, like "The Mower in Ohio," "The Pioneer's Chimney," "Fires in Illinois," and "Riding to Vote." There is no dialect, no straining for realistic effect, no sentimentality. In all that makes for art the poems have little for criticism: they are classical and finished and beautiful. But they lack life. There is nothing about them that grips the reader's heart, nothing that fixes itself in the memory, no single line that has distinction of phrase. Even in the Western poems like "The Mower in Ohio" there is no sharpness, no atmosphere, no feeling of reality. It is art rather than life; it is a conscious effort to make a poem. The case is typical. With the criticism one may sweep away once for all great areas of the poetry of the time.

Far stronger are the vigorous lyrics of Maurice Thompson, whose work is to be found in so many literary fields of the period. His poetry, small in quantity, has a spirit of its own that is distinctive. It is tonic with the out-of-doors and it is masculine. One stanza from the poem "At Lincoln's Grave," delivered before the Phi Beta Kappa at Harvard in 1893, voices the new Western soul:

> His humor, born of virile opulence,
> Stung like a pungent sap or wild-fruit zest,
> And satisfied a universal sense
> Of manliness, the strongest and the best;
> A soft Kentucky strain was in his voice, ·
> And the Ohio's deeper boom was there,
> With some wild accents of old Wabash days,
>   And winds of Illinois;
> And when he spoke he took us unaware,
> With his high courage and unselfish ways.

II

The successor of Carleton is James Whitcomb Riley of Indiana, the leading producer during the later period of platform and newspaper balladry. The early life of Riley was urban rather than rural. His father was a lawyer at Greenfield, a typical Western county seat, and after sending the boy to the village school he sought to turn him to his own profession. But there was a stratum of the wayward and the unconventional in Riley even from the first. The professions and the ordinary oc-

cupations open to youth did not appeal to the imaginative lad.
He learned the trade of sign-painting and then for a year
traveled with a patent medicine "doctor" as advertising agent.
Following this picturesque experience came three or four years
as a traveling entertainer with a congenial troupe, then desultory
newspaper work, and finally, from 1877 to 1885, a steady position on the Indianapolis *Journal*. His recognition as a poet came
in the mid eighties, and following it came a long period on the
lecture circuit, reading his own productions, at one time working
in conjunction with Eugene Field and Edgar W. Nye,—"Bill
Nye."

His earliest work seems to have been declamatory and journalistic in origin. "I was always trying to write of the kind of
people I knew and especially to write verse that I could read just
as if it were being spoken for the first time." And again, "I
always took naturally to anything theatrical." [2] For years the
newspaper was his only medium. He contributed to most of the
Indiana journals with pseudonyms ranging all the way from
"Edyrn" to "Jay Whitt" and "Benjamin F. Johnson of
Boone," and it was while writing under the last of these for
the Indianapolis *Journal* that he first became known beyond the
confines of Indiana. The device of printing poems that osten-
sibly were contributed by a crude farmer from a back country
was not particularly original. Lowell had used it and Artemus
Ward. Moreover, the fiction of accompanying these poems with
editorial comment and specimen letters from the author was as
old at least as *The Biglow Papers*, but there was a Western, Pike
County freshness about the Benjamin F. Johnson material. The
first poem in the series, for instance, was accompanied by material
like this:

Mr. Johnson thoughtfully informs us that he is "no edjucated man,"
but that he has, "from childhood up tel old enugh to vote, allus wrote
more or less poetry, as many of an albun in the neghborhood can
testify." Again, he says that he writes "from the hart out"; and there
is a touch of genuine pathos in the frank avowal, "Thare is times when
I write the tears rolls down my cheeks."

The poems that followed,—"Thoughts fer the Discuraged
Farmer," "When the Frost is on the Punkin," "Wortermelon
Time," and the others—were written primarily as humorous

[2] *McClure's Magazine*, 2:222.

exercises just as Browne had written his first Artemus Ward contributions. There is a histrionic element about them that must
not be overlooked. The author is playing a part. Riley, we
know, had, at least in his youth, very little sympathy with farm
life and very little knowledge of it: he was simply impersonating
an ignorant old farmer. The dialect does not ring true. There
never has been a time, for instance, when "ministratin'" for
ministering, "familiously" for familiarly, "resignated" for resigned, and "when the army broke out" for when the war broke
out, have been used in Indiana save by those with whom they are
individual peculiarities. He is simply reporting the ignorance of
one old man in the Artemus Ward fashion. Dialect with him
is the record of a town man's mimicry of country crudeness. It
is conventional rather than realistic. It is a humorous device
like A. Ward's cacography. The first Johnson annotation will
illustrate:

Benj. F. Johnson, of Boone County, who considers the *Journal* a
"very valubul" newspaper, writes to inclose us an original poem, de-
siring that we kindly accept it for publication, as "many neghbors
and friends is astin' him to have the same struck off."

He issued the series at his own expense in 1883 with the title
*The Old Swimmin'-Hole and 'Leven More Poems by Benj. F.
Johnson, of Boone,* and he continued the masquerade until after
the publication of *Afterwhiles* in 1887. After the great vogue of
this later volume he began to publish voluminously until his
final collected edition numbered fourteen volumes.

Riley not only inherited Will Carleton's public entire, but he
added to it very considerably. He too dealt freely in sentiment
and he too wrote always with vocal interpretation in mind. Undoubtedly the wide vogue of his poems has come largely from
this element. People have always enjoyed hearing the poems
read with an appropriate acting out of the part more than they
have enjoyed reading them for themselves. The poems, more
over, appeared in what may be called the old homestead period
in America. Denman Thompson first brought out his *Joshua
Whitcomb* in 1875 and his *The Old Homestead* in 1886. Riley
found a public doubly prepared. He revived old memories—
the word "old" is almost a mannerism with him: "The Old
Swimmin'-Hole," "Old Fashioned Roses," "The Old Hay-Mow,"
"The Old Trundle Bed," "Out to Old Aunt Mary's," "The

Boys of the Old Glee Club," "An Old Sweetheart of Mine," etc.
Especially did he appeal to those whose childhood had been
spent in the country.

Finally, he added to Carleton's devices a metrical facility and
a jigging melody that is perhaps his most original contribution
to the period. More than any one else Riley is responsible for
the modern newspaper type of ballad that is to poetry what rag-
time is to music. There is a fatal facility to such a melody as,

> Old wortermelon time is a-comin' round again,
>   And there ain't no man a-livin' any tickleder 'n me,
>   Fer the way I hanker after wortermelons is a sin—
>   Which is the why and wharefore, as you can plainly see.

Or this,

> I ain't, ner don't p'tend to be,
> Much posted on philosofy;
> But thare is times, when all alone,
> I work out idees of my own.
> And of these same thare is a few
> I'd like to jest refer to you—
> Pervidin' that you don't object
> To listen clos't and rickollect.

In his preference for native themes and homely, unliterary
treatment of seemingly unpoetic material he continued the work
of the Pike County balladists. As the *Nation*, reviewing his *Old
Fashioned Roses*, expressed it, he finds pleasure in "some of the
coarser California flavors." His own standards for poetry he has
given clearly, and they are in full accord with the spirit of the
period:

> The poems here at home!—Who'll write 'em down,
> Jes' as they air—in Country and in Town?—
> Sowed thick as clods is 'crost the fields and lanes,
> Er these-'ere little hop-toads when it rains!—
> Who'll "voice" 'em? as I heerd a feller say
> 'At speechified on Freedom, t' other day,
> And soared the Eagle tel' it 'peared to me,
> She was n't bigger 'n a bumblebee!

> What We want, as I sense it, in the line
> O' poetry is somepin' Yours and Mine—
> Somepin' with live-stock in it, and outdoors,
> And old crick-bottoms, snags, and sycamores:
> Putt weeds in—pizen-vines, and underbresh,

> As well as Johnny-jump-ups, all so fresh
> And sassy-like!—and groun'-squir'ls,—yes, and "We,"
> As sayin' is,—"We, Us and Company!"

But one cannot be sure of him. He is an entertainer, an actor, a mimicker. Does his material really come "from the hart out" or is he giving, what one always suspects, only excellent vaudeville? Even in his most pathetic moments we catch for an instant, or we feel that we do, a glimpse of the suave face of the platform entertainer.

Once in a while his childhood lyrics ring true. A little note of true pathos like this from *Poems Here at Home* is worth a library of *The Flying Islands of the Night* and of his other voluminous echoes of *Alice in Wonderland:*

> Let me come in where you sit weeping,—aye,
> Let me, who have not any child to die,
> Weep with you for the little one whose love
>   I have known nothing of.
>
> The little arms that slowly, slowly loosed
> Their pressure round your neck; the hands you used
> To kiss.—Such arms—such hands I never knew.
>   May I not weep with you?
>
> Fain would I be of service—say some thing,
> Between the tears, that would be comforting,—
> But ah! so sadder than yourselves am I,
>   Who have no child to die.

Despite his enormous vogue, Riley must be dismissed as artificial and, on the whole, insincere. He seems always to be striving for effect—he is an entertainer who knows his audience and who is never for a moment dull. He has little of insight, little knowledge of the deeps of life and the human soul, little of message, and he wrote enormously too much. He must be rated finally as a comedian, a sentimentalist, an entertainer.

His influence has been great. A whole school of imitators has sprung up about him, the most of whom have perished with the papers to which they have contributed. The strongest of them all undoubtedly was Sam Walter Foss (1858–1911) whose *Back Country Poems* were genuine and distinctive. Drummond's *Habitant* ballads, which rank with the strongest dialect poetry of the century, belong to Canadian rather than American literature. Stedman's praise of them is none too high: "Most of us are content if we sing an old thing in a new way, or a new

thing in an old way. Dr. Drummond has achieved the truest
of lyrical successes; that of singing new songs, and in a new
way. His poems are idyls as true as those of Theocritus or
Burns or our own poet of *The Biglow Papers.*" [3]

III

Greatly different from Riley, yet greatly like him in many
ways, was Eugene Field, in whom the lawlessness of the West
and the culture of the East met in strange confusion. Though
of Western origin—he was born at St. Louis in 1850—he spent
the formative years of his life between six and nineteen with
his father's relatives at Amherst, Massachusetts. He completed
a year at Williams College, then, called West by the death of his
father, whose law practice at St. Louis had been distinctive, he
was put by his guardian into Knox College. After a year he
was transferred to the University of Missouri, but coming of
age at the close of his junior year, and his share of his father's
estate becoming available, he decided in the spring of 1872 to
leave college and travel in Europe. Accordingly, to quote his
own words, he spent "six months and [his] patrimony in France,
Italy, Ireland, and England."

As a general rule one should quote the autobiographical statements of Eugene Field with extreme caution, but one can trust
this bit of his "Auto-analysis":

In May, 1873, I became a reporter on the St. Louis *Evening Journal.*
In October of that year I married Miss Julia Sutherland Comstock of
St. Joseph, Mo., at that time a girl of sixteen. We have had eight
children—three daughters and five sons.

My newspaper connections have been as follows: 1875–76, city editor of the St. Joseph (Mo.) *Gazette;* 1876–80, editorial writer on the
St. Louis *Journal* and St. Louis *Times-Journal;* 1880–81, managing
editor of the Kansas City *Times;* 1881–83, managing editor of the Denver *Tribune.* Since 1883 I have been a contributor to the Chicago
Record (formerly *Morning News*).[4]

His success with the Denver *Tribune,* to which he contributed
such widely copied work as that published in his first thin volume, *The Tribune Primer* (1882), attracted attention. He began to receive offers from Eastern papers, one at least from

---

[3] *Life of Stedman,* ii:208.
[4] Thompson's *Eugene Field,* ii:236.

Dana, editor of the New York *Sun,* but it was not until Melville E. Stone offered him the humorous column of his paper, the Chicago *News,* that Field decided to turn eastward. He had begun to dream of a literary career and this dream, always a vague one, for he was chained by poverty to a tyrannical profession, seemed more possible in a less tense atmosphere than that of the Western mining center. Arriving at Chicago in 1883, he set out to make his new column a thing with distinction. *Flats and Sharps* was the name he gave it, and into it he poured a mélange of all things: poetry in every key, paragraphs on all subjects, parodies, hoaxes, mock reviews, pseudo news, personals, jokes—everything. He threw himself completely into the thing: it became his life work; "practically everything he ever wrote appeared at one time or another in that column."

But newspaper humor usually perishes with the flimsy leaves upon which it is recorded. Not until Field had written "Little Boy Blue" in 1887 did he become at all known to the reading public. The publication of the popular editions of *A Little Book of Profitable Tales* and *A Little Book of Western Verse* in 1890, only five years before his death, marks, perhaps, the time of his general acceptation as a writer. Hardly had the public learned to know him before they were called upon to mourn his early death. Indeed, the work by which he is now best known was done almost all of it in the last six or seven years of his life. It was only in this brief later period that he was a "bibliomaniac" or a lover of Horace or a student of the old English ballads.

One must classify Eugene Field first of all as a humorist, one of the leading figures in that nondescript school of newspaper comedians that has played such a part in the history of the period. To a personality as high spirited and as whimsical as Artemus Ward's he added the brilliancy of a Locker-Lampson and the improvidence of a Goldsmith as well as the kindly heart. Seriousness seemed foreign to his nature: his life was a perpetual series of hoaxes and practical jokes and hilarious sallies. No one has surpassed him in the making of parodies, of rollicking paraphrases and adaptations, in skilful blendings of modern and antique, in clever minglings of seriousness and humor. He was a maker of brilliant trifles and sparkling *non sequiturs.* His irreverence is really startling at times. He can make the *Odes*

of Horace seem fit material for the funny column of a Chicago
daily newspaper:

> Boy, I detest the Persian pomp;
>   I hate those linden-bark devices;
> And as for roses, holy Moses!
>   They can't be got at living prices!
> Myrtle is good enough for us,—
>   For *you,* as bearer of my flagon;
> For *me,* supine beneath this vine,
>   Doing my best to get a jag on!

He is boon companion of the old Sabine poet. He slaps him on
the back and invites him to all kinds of costly revelry, assuring
him that Mæcenas will pay the freight. And Horace by no
means takes offense. He is a congenial soul.

> I might discourse
> Till I was hoarse
> Upon the cruelties of Venus;
>   'T were waste of time
>   As well as rime,
> For you 've been there yourself, Mæcenas!

In the presence of such an incorrigible joker the reader feels
always that he must be on his guard. One is never safe. Leaf-
ing the pages of the large collected edition of the poems, glancing over the Bret Harte echoes like "Casey's Table D'Hôte,"
smiling at such outrageous nonsense as "The Little Peach" and
"The Onion Tart," one suddenly draws a sharp breath. At last
the heart of Eugene Field:

> Upon a mountain height, far from the sea,
>   I found a shell,
> And to my listening ear the lonely thing
> Ever a song of ocean seemed to sing,
>   Ever a tale of ocean seemed to tell.
>
> .   .   .   .
>
> Strange, was it not? Far from its native deep,
>   One song it sang,—
> Sang of the awful mysteries of the tide,
> Sang of the misty sea, profound and wide,—
>   Ever with echoes of the ocean rang.
>
> And as the shell upon the mountain height
>   Sings of the sea,
> So do I ever, leagues and leagues away,—
> So do I ever, wandering where I may,—
>   Sing, O my home! sing, O my home! of thee.

A lyric worthy of any anthology. Yet one quickly finds that it is not Eugene Field at all. He wrote it deliberately as a hoax, a practical joke on Modjeska, who all the rest of her life was obliged to deny the authorship which Field had cunningly fastened upon her. The case is typical. Like Riley, the man is making copy. He uses pathos and sentiment and the most sacred things as literary capital. One wonders where one can draw the line. Was he really sincere in his child lyrics and his bibliomaniac writings or was he cleverly playing a part?

In criticizing Field one must remember the essential immaturity of the man. His frequent artificiality and his lack of sincerity came from his boyishness and his high spirits. He looked at life from the angle of mischievous boyhood. Moreover, he wrote always at the high tension of the newspaper office, for a thing that had no memory, a column that had but one demand—*more!* It bred in him what may be denominated, perhaps, the ephemeral habit. He was all his life a man preëminently and predominatingly of the present moment, and thus he stands a type of the literary creator that was to follow him.

For Field more than any other writer of the period illustrates the way the old type of literary scholar was to be modified and changed by the newspaper. Every scrap of Field's voluminous product was written for immediate newspaper consumption. He patronized not at all the literary magazines, he wrote his books not at all with book intent—he made them up from newspaper fragments. He wrote always a timely thing to the people, a thing growing out of the present moment for the people to read, making palatable for them even Horace and the severer classics. He was thus one of the leading forces in what may be called that democratizing of literature for which the period so largely stands.

He has been given a place far beyond his real deserts. The sentiment of "Little Boy Blue" and the other child lyrics, the whimsical fun and high spirits of his comic verse, endeared him to the public that enjoyed Riley. Then his whimsical, Goldsmith-like personality helped his fame, as did also his death, since it followed so quickly his late discovery by the reading public that it gave the impression he had been removed like Keats at the very opening of his career. He must be rated, however, not for what he wrote, though a few pieces, like his

child lyrics and his bibliomaniac ballads, will continue long in
the anthologies, but for the influence he exerted. He was a
pioneer in a peculiar province: he stands for the journalization
of literature, a process that, if carried to its logical extreme, will
make of the man of letters a mere newspaper reporter.

IV

In his own estimation Field was distinctively a Western poet;
he gave to his poetry the name "Western verse"; and he refused
the offers of Dana and others because he was not at all in sympathy with the Eastern ideals. To quote his biographer, he felt
that Chicago "was as far East as he could make his home without coming within the influence of those social and literary
conventions that have squeezed so much of genuine literary
flavor out of our literature." [5]

What New York might have made of Field we may learn, perhaps, from the career of Henry Cuyler Bunner, for nearly twenty
years the most brilliant poetic wit in the East. He, too, had
approached literature from the journalistic entrance. At eighteen he had left school to begin an apprenticeship on the brilliant
but short-lived *Arcadian,* and at twenty-two he was editor of the
newly established *Puck,* a position that he held until his death
at forty-one.

No man ever turned off verse and prose with more facility or
in greater quantity. "The staff of the paper was very small,
and little money could be spent for outside contributions; and
there were many weeks when nearly half the whole number was
written by Bunner." [6] Like Field, he could write a poem while
the office boy, who had brought the order, stood waiting for the
copy to carry back with him. For more than ten years he furnished nearly all the humorous verse for the periodical, besides
numberless paragraphs, short stories, and editorials. But he
was more fastidious than Field, inasmuch as he kept this journalistic material strictly unconnected with his name. It was a
thing alone of the editorial office, no more to be mingled with
his more literary product than Charles Lamb's India office books
were to be brought into his *Elia* essays. The greater number of
those who laughed over the verses of the whimsical "V. Hugo

[5] Thompson, *Eugene Field,* i: 193.
[6] Brander Matthews, *The Historical Novel,* 173.

Dusenberry, professional poet,'' never once dreamed that he was
H. C. Bunner, author of the exquisite lyrics in *Airs from Arcady* and *Rowen,* and the carefully wrought stories—French in
their atmosphere and their artistic finish—*Short Sixes* and *Love
in Old Cloathes.* The skilful parodies and timely renderings, the
quips and puns—all the voluminous mélange, indeed, of the
poetic Yorick—lie buried now in the files of *Puck.* Their creator refused to republish them, and we to-day can but yield to
his wish and judge him only by that which he himself selected
for permanence.

Judged by this, Bunner undoubtedly is our chief writer of
vers de société, our laureate of the trivial. He is restrained,
refined, faultless. He is of the artificial world, where fans flutter and dancers glide and youth is perennial. Triolets penciled
in the program while the orchestra breathed its melody, epigrams
over the tea-cups, conceits for a fan, *amours de voyage,* lines
written on the menu, *amoretti,* valentines—these are his work,
and no one has done them more daintily or with more skill of
touch. Trifles they are, to be sure, yet Bunner, like every master of the form, makes of them more than trifles. A hint of
tears there may be, the faintest breath of irony, the suspicion,
vague as an intuition, of satire or facetiousness or philosophy,
the high spirits and the carelessness of youth, yet a flash here
and there into the deeps of life as, for instance, in ''Betrothed''
and ''A Poem in the Programme,'' and ''She was a Beauty in
the Days when Madison was President.''

The French forms, imported echoes of Dobson and Lang and
Gosse—ballades, rondels, rondeaux, and the like, that so be-
witched the younger poets of the mid-eighties—found in Bunner
perhaps their most skilful American devotee. Perhaps no one
but he has ever succeeded in English with the chant royal, or has
found it possible to throw into that most trivial of all verse
forms, triolets, a throb of life, as in ''A Pitcher of Mignonette'':

> A pitcher of mignonette
> In a tenement's highest casement:
> Queer sort of flower-pot—yet
> That pitcher of mignonette
> Is a garden in heaven set,
>   To the little sick child in the basement—
> The pitcher of mignonette,
>   In the tenement's highest casement.

The period, especially in its later years, has run abundantly
to these trivial, though difficult, forms of verse. As poetry ceased
more and more to be a thing of vision and compelling power,
it became more and more a thing of daintiness and brilliancy.
The American *Lyra Elegantiarum* for the period has been more
sparkling and abundant than the English, more even than the
French. John Godfrey Saxe (1816–1887) belongs almost wholly
to the days of Holmes and Lowell, but the greater number of
our trivial makers fall into the group that was active during the
closing quarter of the century. To mention all of them would
be to call the roll of the younger American poets. Perhaps the
most noteworthy, however, are Mary Mapes Dodge (1838–1905),
whose dainty and tender ''The Minuet'' gives her a place in
the choir; James Jeffrey Roche (1847–1908); Walter Learned
(1847——); Richard Kendall Munkittrick (1853–1911); Samuel Minturn Peck (1854——), in many respects the most
delightful of the group; Clinton Scollard (1860——); John
Kendrick Bangs (1862——), and such modern instances as
Oliver Herford, Gelett Burgess, and Carolyn Wells. One
might, indeed, collect a notable anthology of *vers de société* from
the files of *Life* alone.

V

A large amount of the poetry of the era has been written by
women. After the war their thin volumes, bound in creamy
vellum and daintily tinted cloth, began more and more to fill the
book tables, until reviewers no longer could give separate notice
to them, but must consider the poets of a month in groups of
ten or twelve. The quality of the feminine product was high
enough to find place in the most exclusive monthlies, and the
quantity published was surprising. The *Atlantic Monthly,* for
instance, during the decade from 1870 published 108 poems by
Longfellow, Whittier, Holmes, Lowell, and Aldrich, and 450
other poems, and of the latter 201 were by women. The feminine novelists and short story writers, so conspicuous during all
the period, were, indeed, almost all poets, some of them voluminous. One may note the names not only of the older group—
Mrs. Stuart Phelps Ward, Mrs. Cooke, Mrs. Spofford, Miss
Woolson—but of such later writers as Mrs. Freeman, Alice
Brown, Mrs. Deland, and Mrs. Riggs.

Very little of this mass of poetry has been strong enough to demand republication from the dainty volumes in which it first appeared. It has been smooth and often melodious, but for the most part it has been conventional. Prevailingly it has been short lyric song in minor key, gentle and sentimental—graceful exercises in verse rather than voices from a soul stirred to utterance and caring not. In a sonneteering age this feminine contingent has swelled enormously the volume of sonnets. Helen Hunt Jackson's thin volume contains one hundred, Louise Chandler Moulton's one hundred and thirty-one, yet in both collections occurs no sonnet one would dream of adding to the select few that undoubtedly are worth while. Here and there in Mrs. Jackson a bit of work like "Poppies on the Wheat," "Glimpses," "Vashti," that rises, perhaps, a little above the level monotony of the times, but in the vital seventies in America why should one have published sonnets? Even as she was shaping them, Emma Lazarus (1849–1887) was demanding in major key,

How long, and yet how long,
Our leaders will we hail from over seas,
Masters and kings from feudal monarchies,
    And mock their ancient song
With echoes weak of foreign melodies?

This fresh young world I see,
With heroes, cities, legends of her own;
With a new race of men, and overblown
    By winds from sea to sea,
Decked with the majesty of every zone.

The distant siren-song
Of the green island in the eastern sea,
Is not the lay for this new chivalry.
    It is not free and strong
To chant on prairies 'neath this brilliant sky.

The echo faints and fails;
It suiteth not, upon this western plain,
Our voice or spirit; we should stir again
    The wilderness, and make the vales
Resound unto a yet unheard-of strain.

The life of Emma Lazarus was brief and externally eventless. Born in New York City in a home of refinement and wealth, as a child precocious, inclined to seriousness, intense, she passed her early life among books rather than among companions. At seventeen she had issued a collection of verses, melancholy even above the usual poetry of women, valueless utterly; then at twenty-one she had published again, now a long poem, Greek in its chaste beauty, *Admetus,* inscribed "To My Friend Ralph Waldo Emerson." Two forces were contending, even as they had contended in Heine. In Paris in later years before the Venus of the Louvre she wrote a sonnet, and, miracle among modern sonnets, it is impassioned, unfettered, alive—a woman's soul:

> . . . I saw not her alone,
> Serenely poised on her world-worshiped throne,
> As when she guided once her dove-drawn car,—
> But at her feet a pale, death-stricken Jew,
> Her life adorer, sobbed farewell to love.
> Here *Heine* wept! Here still he weeps anew,
> Nor ever shall his shadow lift or move,
> While mourns one ardent heart, one poet-brain,
> For vanished Hellas and Hebraic pain.

Until 1876 quiet emotion, Hellenic beauty, romance without passion. "Tannhäuser" suggests William Morris and *The Earthly Paradise.* Then came *The Spagnioletto,* a tense drama, which showed for the first time the latent embers in her Hebraic soul. It needed but a breath to kindle them and that breath came with reports of the Jewish massacres of 1879. No more of Hellenism. With Liebhaid in *The Dance of Death,* that most tense drama in American literature, she could cry out:

> No more of that.
> I am all Israel's now—till this cloud pass,
> I have no thought, no passion, no desire,
> Save for my people.

Henceforth fiery lyrics of denunciation, rallying cries, translations of Hebrew prophets, songs of encouragement and cheer, as "The Crowing of the Red Cock," "In Exile," "The New Ezekiel," "The Valley of Baca," and, most Hebraic of all, "The Banner of the Jew," with its ringing lines:

> Oh, for Jerusalem's trumpet now,
> To blow a blast of shattering power,

> To wake the sleepers high and low,
> And rouse them to the urgent hour!
> No hand for vengeance—but to save,
> A million naked swords should wave.

The fire was too intense for the frail, sensitive body. Suddenly, like Heine, she was on a "mattress grave," powerless, though never so eager, never so quivering with burning message. She died at thirty-eight.

No more impetuous and Hebraic lines in the literature of the period than hers. Often she achieved a distinction of phrase and an inevitableness of word and of rhythm denied to all but the truest of poets. No other American woman has surpassed her in passion, in genuineness of emotion, in pure lyric effect.

Other impassioned singers there have been. Ella Wheeler Wilcox (1855——) wrote of love with lyric abandon, but she mingled too much of sentimentality and all too much of posing and of tawdriness. Anne Reeve Aldrich (1866–1892) in *Songs About Life, Love, and Death* struck deeper notes, and Elizabeth Akers Allen (1832–1911), though she wrote exceedingly much in the key of the conventional mid-century sadness and longing, yet now and then sent forth lyrics that laid bare her woman's soul.

One may not dismiss so confidently Celia Thaxter, the poet of the *Isles of Shoals*. She was, to be sure, no dominating voice in the period, no poet with whom distinction of phrase and poetic melody were native and spontaneous. Rather was she of the Jean Ingelow type, feminine, domestic, tremulous with sentiment. In one area, however, she commanded: her poetry of the sea was autochthonic, and it sprang not from books, but from her life. Her childhood she had passed in the seclusion of the lighthouse keeper's home on White Island, a storm-beaten rock off the New Hampshire coast. For months at a time no visitors came save the sea gulls and the migrating birds. Her companion through all her young girlhood was the ocean. She grew to know intimately all its thousand moods, the sea gardens along the rocks at low tide, the ships that hovered like clouds on the horizon, the flowers in the rock crannies, the sandpipers that flitted before her on the beach. The birds that flew against the lantern of the lighthouse on migrating nights furnished the first tragedy of her life:

Many a May morning have I wandered about the rock at the foot of the tower, mourning over a little apron brimful of sparrows, swallows, thrushes, robins, fire-winged blackbirds, many-colored warblers and fly-catchers, beautifully clothed yellow-birds, nuthatches, catbirds, even the purple finch and scarlet tanager and golden oreole, and many more besides—enough to break the heart of a small child to think of! [7]

No ordinary child, this lonely little islander. The lure of the sea possessed her, the terror of its storms, the beauty of its summer moods, the multitudinous variety of its voice. ''Many a summer morning have I crept out of the still house before any one was awake, and, wrapping myself closely from the chill wind of dawn, climbed to the top of the high cliff called the Head to watch the sunrise.'' It was this communion with the sea that awoke the poet soul within her:

Ever I longed to *speak* these things that made life so sweet, to speak the wind, the cloud, the bird's flight, the sea's murmur. A vain longing! I might as well have sighed for the mighty pencil of Michel Angelo to wield in my impotent child's hand. Better to "hush and bless one's self with silence"; but ever the wish grew. Facing the July sunsets, deep red and golden through and through, or watching the summer northern lights—battalions of brilliant streamers, advancing and retreating, shooting upward to the zenith, and glowing like fiery veils before the stars; or when the fog bow spanned the silver mist of morning, or the earth and sea lay shimmering in a golden haze of noon; in storm or calm, by day or night, the manifold aspects of Nature held me and swayed all my thoughts until it was impossible to be silent any longer, and I was fain to mingle my voice with her myriad voices, only aspiring to be in accord with the Infinite harmony, however feeble and broken the notes might be.[8]

The first poem of hers to gain the ear of the public was ''Land-Locked,'' accepted by Lowell and published in the *Atlantic*, March, 1861. Its closing stanzas ring with sincerity. It is the voice of every inland dweller whose youth has been spent by the sea:

> Neither am I ungrateful; but I dream
> Deliciously how twilight falls to-night
> Over the glimmering water, how the light
> Dies blissfully away, until I seem

[7] *Among the Isles of Shoals*, 111.
[8] *Ibid.*, 141.

To feel the wind, sea-scented, on my cheek,
To catch the sound of dusky flapping sail
And dip of oars, and voices on the gale
Afar off, calling low—my name they speak!

O Earth! thy summer song of joy may soar
Ringing to heaven in triumph. I but crave
The sad, caressing murmur of the wave
That breaks in tender music on the shore.

About all her poetry of the sea there are genuineness and truth to experience. All of them are fragments of autobiography: "Off Shore," "The Wreck of the Pocahontas," "The Sandpiper," "Watching," "At the Breakers' Edge," "The Watch of Boon Island," "Leviathan"—all of them have in them the heart of the northern Atlantic. They are not deep like Whitman's mighty voicings, but they are the cry of one who knew and loved the sea better than any other American who has ever written about it.

Her prose study *Among the Isles of Shoals,* overflorid though it may be in places, is nevertheless one of the notable books of the period. Nowhere may one find so complete a picture of the northern ocean in all its moods and aspects. Its pictures of storm and wreck, its glimpses of the tense and hazardous life of dwellers by the ocean, its disclosings of the mystery and the subtle lure of the sea, stir one at times like the deeper notes of poetry.

One of the most perplexing of later poetic problems came in 1890 with the publication by Thomas Wentworth Higginson of the posthumous poetry of Emily Dickinson (1830–1886). The explanation by Higginson that the poet was a daughter of the treasurer of Amherst College, that she was a recluse "literally spending years without setting her foot beyond the doorstep and many more years during which her walks were strictly limited to her father's grounds," and that she had written "verses in great abundance," refusing, however, save in three or four instances, to allow any of them to be published, that she wrote "absolutely without thought of publication, and solely by way of expression of the writer's own mind,"— all this aroused curiosity. At last one might see, perchance, a woman's soul.

The poems are disappointing. Critics have echoed Higginson, until Emily Dickinson has figured, often at length, in all the later histories and anthologies, but it is becoming clear that she was overrated. To compare her eccentric fragments with Blake's elfin wildness is ridiculous. They are mere conceits, vague jottings of a brooding mind; they are crudely wrought, and, like their author's letters, which were given to the public later, they are colorless and for the most part lifeless. They reveal little either of Emily Dickinson or of human life generally. They should have been allowed to perish as their author intended.

Most of the feminine poets of the later generation have been over-literary. There is grace and finish in the work of Louise Imogen Guiney (1861——), but nowhere in all her carefully selected final volume, *Happy Ending*, are there lines that suddenly send the pulses into quicker beat and haunt the memory. It is beautiful, but it is of a piece with ten thousand other beautiful pieces; there is nothing to compel the reader, nothing to lead him into fresh fields. Of all too many of the later feminine poets may we say this: of Ina Donna Coolbrith, for instance, and Helen Gray Cone (1859——), Dora Read Goodale (1866——), Katharine Lee Bates (1859——).

Only one other feminine singer has done work that compels attention, Edith Matilda Thomas (1854——). Only by birth and rearing was she of Ohio. To read her poems is to be transported into that no-man's land which so many poets have called Arcady. She is more Greek than American. She has reacted little upon her time, and she might be dismissed with mere mention were there not in many of her poems a lyric distinction that has been rare in American poetry. A fragment from her work will make this clearer than exposition. Here, for instance, are the opening stanzas of "Syrinx":

Come forth, too timid spirit of the reed!
  Leave thy plashed coverts and elusions shy,
And find delight at large in grove and mead.
  No ambushed harm, no wanton's peering eye,
The shepherd's uncouth god thou needst not fear—
Pan has not passed this way for many a year.

'Tis but the vagrant wind that makes thee start,
  The pleasure-loving south, the freshening west;
The willow's woven veil they softly part,
  To fan the lily on the stream's warm breast:

No ruder stir, no footstep pressing near—
Pan has not passed this way for many a year.

Unlooked-for music indeed from the banks of the Ohio. Her muse was remote, unimpassioned, classical, yet no lyrist of the period has had more of the divine poetic gift of expression. She seems curiously out of place in the headlong West in those stormy closing years of the nineteenth century.

V

Belated singers of the mid-century music were Richard Watson Gilder (1844–1909), Edward Roland Sill (1841–1887), George E. Woodberry (1855———), and Henry Van Dyke (1852———), all of them poets like Miss Thomas, who were remote from their era, workers in art and beauty rather than voices and leaders.

One may pause long with Gilder. No other man of his generation did so much to turn the direction of the period and to determine its nature. As managing editor of *Scribner's Monthly* from the first number to the last, and then after the death of Holland, editor of the *Century Magazine,* he exerted for twenty-eight years an influence upon American letters that cannot be overestimated. In a way he is the central literary figure of the period, even more so than Dr. Holland. More than any one else he was responsible for the revolution in magazine management for which the period stands, and more than any one else he helped to gather the new school of novelists and short story writers and poets that made the era distinctive. He was the James T. Fields of the national period.

He was first of all an editor, then he was a humanitarian, active in all movements for city betterment, then he was a poet. Beginning with *The New Day* in 1875, he issued many small volumes of delicate verse, mystical often in tone, always serious, always artistic. That he knew the divine commission of the poet he revealed in his volume *The Celestial Passion,* 1878:

Dost thou not know this is the poet's lot:
Mid sounds of war—in halcyon times of peace—
To strike the ringing lyre and not to cease;
In hours of general happiness to swell
The common joy; and when the people cry
With piteous voice loud to the pitiless sky,
'Tis his to frame the universal prayer
And breathe the balm of song upon the accursed air?

But he himself seemed not bound by this ideal of the poet. His carefully wrought verses add little that is new, and little that may be understood by those for whom a poet should sing. They lack substance, the *Zeitgeist*, masculinity. Stedman could say that they are "marked by the mystical beauty, intense emotion, and psychological emotion of the elect *illuminati*," but the criticism, even were it true, was condemnatory. Gilder's definition did not mention the "elect *illuminati*."

It is depressing to think that this most virile of men, who was the tireless leader of his generation in so many beneficent fields of activity, must be judged in the coming periods solely by this volume of poems. For classic poetry was not his life-work, not his enthusiasm, not himself—it was a rarely furnished room in the heart of his home, rather, where at times he might retire from the tumult and enjoy the beauty he had gathered in the realms of gold. He was not a poet, singing inevitable lines, spontaneous and inspired. His poems lacked lyric distinction, that compelling quality that sinks a poem into the reader's soul, and, lacking it, they have little hope for permanence. They are finished always and coldly beautiful, but finish and beauty are not enough. So it is with George E. Woodberry's polished work, and Father Tabb's. It is not vital with the life of an epoch, it is not the voice of a soul deeply stirred with a new and compelling message. All too often it has come from deliberate effort; it is a mere performance.

With the work of Edward Rowland Sill one must be less positive. Here we find conflict, reaction, spontaneous expression. He was by no means a voice of his era, a robust shouter like Whitman and Miller: he was a gentle, retiring soul who felt out of place in his generation. Seriousness had come to him as a birthright. Behind him were long lines of Connecticut Puritans. He was frail, moreover, of physique, with a shrinking that was almost feminine from all that was discordant and assertive. After his graduation at Yale, the poet of his class, in 1861, he was unable to settle upon a profession. He attempted theology, and then, disillusioned, for bare support he drifted into teaching. Year after year passed with the problem unsettled, until he awoke to find that teaching was to be his life-work. He had hidden among the children in the schoolroom, and the things he had dreamed over had passed him by. His external biography is largely a list of schools and positions. At forty-six he died.

Poetry to Sill was a peculiarly personal thing, almost as much so as it was to Emily Dickinson. He was not eager to publish, and much that he did send to the magazines bore other names than his own. He wrote, as Thoreau wrote his journal, with simple directness for himself and the gods, and as a result we have in his work the inner history of a human soul. There is no artificiality, no sentimental vaporings, no posing for effect. It is not art; it is life.

Here is poetry of struggle, poetry not of the spirit of an epoch but of the life of an individual at odds with the epoch, introspective, personal. One thinks of Clough, who also was a teacher, a gentle soul oppressed with doubts and fears, a struggler in the darkness of the late nineteenth century. But Sill was less masculine than Clough. His doubtings are gentle and half apologetic. Never is he bitter or excited or impetuous. To such robust climaxes as "Say not the Struggle Naught Availeth" he is incapable of rising: he broods, but he is resigned. He exhorts himself deliberately to cheerfulness and faith and to heights of manhood where all that is low may fall away. Erotic passion has no part in his work. He has deliberately conquered it:

> Is my life but Marguerite's ox-eyed flower,
> That I should stand and pluck and fling away,
> One after one, the petal of each hour,
> Like a love-dreamy girl, and only say,
> "Loves me," and "loves me not," and "loves me"? Nay!
> Let the man's mind awake to manhood's power.

No poet has shrunk more sensitively from the realistic, material age of which he was a part than Sill. His poems deal with the realm of the spirit rather than with the tangible. They are without time and place and material basis. One may illustrate with the poems he wrote for Yale gatherings. They are colorless: change but the name and they would apply as well to Harvard or Princeton. Read in connection with Hovey's dramatic, intensely individual Dartmouth poems and they seem like beautiful clouds. They are serious, often over-serious, they have no trace of humor, they deal with the soul life of one upon whom the darkness threatens constantly to fall.

His claim to remembrance comes not from lyrical inspiration, for he was not lyrically gifted. He lacked what Gilder and Woodberry lacked. Once in a while he made a stanza that approaches lyric distinction, as, perhaps, in this final one of "A Foolish Wish":

'T is a child's longing, on the beach at play:
"Before I go,"
He begs the beckoning mother, "Let me stay
One shell to throw!"
'T is coming night; the great sea climbs the shore—
Ah, let me toss one little pebble more,
Before I go!

But not often lines so inevitable. His power came largely from the beauty and purity of his own personality. His own conception of a poem was, that "coming from a pure and rich nature, it shall leave us purer and richer than it found us." Judged by such a standard, Sill holds a high place among the poets. Nothing that he has written but leaves us purer and richer of soul and more serious before the problems of life. Eight or ten of his lyrics for a long time undoubtedly will hold their place among the very highest pieces of American reflective poetry.

It was the opinion of Edmund Gosse that the period was notably deficient in serious verse.[9] No statement could be more wide of the mark; the period has abounded in serious poetry and its quality has been high. To consider in detail this mass of poetry, however, were to exceed our limits. We can only single out one here and there a little more notable than the others—John Boyle O'Reilly (1844–1890), for instance, with his Celtic fancy and his graphic power to depict life in the Southern Seas; Maurice Francis Egan (1852——) and Lloyd Mifflin (1846–——), makers of beautiful and thoughtful sonnets; S. Weir Mitchell (1829–1914), a poet of rare distinction as well as a novelist; Frank Dempster Sherman (1860–1916), maker of madrigals and joyous lyrics; Charles Warren Stoddard (1825–1903), whose songs have a lyric quality that is distinctive, and Abram Joseph Ryan (1839–1886), a beautiful and heroic soul, who had he written but a single lyric would occupy a high place

9 *The Poems of Madison Cawein.* Vol. I. Introduction.

among American poets. His "The Conquered Banner" was the
voice of a people:

> Furl that Banner, softly, slowly!
> Treat it gently—it is holy—
> For it droops above the dead.
> Touch it not—unfold it never—
> Let it droop there, furled forever,
> For its people's hopes are fled.

VI

The two most prominent younger poets of the South were
Robert Burns Wilson (1850–1916) and Madison Cawein (1865–
1914), both residents of Kentucky, one at Frankfort, the other
at Louisville, and both contemplative Nature poets who voiced
but little the spirit of their period. Of the two, Wilson undoubtedly was the most inspired singer, as Cawein was the most
careful observer of Nature.

Of Wilson we may say that he was a later Thomas Buchanan
Read, a devotee of art, a painter of landscapes and portraits,
whose work was seen in many distinctive galleries, and in addition to this a poet—most pictorial of poets, whose stanzas seem
like inscriptions for his paintings. When the lyrics "When
Evening Cometh On" and "June Days" appeared in *Harper's*
in 1885, it was felt that a new singer had come. There was distinction in the lines, there was restraint, there was more than
promise, there was already fulfilment. One feels a quality in
a stanza like this that he may not explain:

> Though all the birds be silent—though
> The fettered stream's soft voice be still,
> And on the leafless bough the snow
> Be rested, marble-like and chill—
> Yet will the fancy build from these
> The transient but well-pleasing dream
> Of leaf and bloom among the trees,
> And sunlight glancing on the stream.

It has somehow the singing quality that may not be learned,
that may not be taught. Finer still when there is joined with it
graphic power that arrests and pleases the eye, and pathos that
grips hard the heart, as in a lyric like this:

Such is the death the soldier dies:
He falls—the column speeds away;
  Upon the dabbled grass he lies,
His brave heart following, still, the fray.

The smoke-wraiths drift among the trees,
The battle storms along the hill;
  The glint of distant arms he sees;
He hears his comrades shouting still.

A glimpse of far-borne flags, that fade
And vanish in the rolling din:
  He knows the sweeping charge is made,
The cheering lines are closing in.

Unmindful of his mortal wound,
He faintly calls and seeks to rise;
  But weakness drags him to the ground—
Such is the death the soldier dies.

Wilson's poetic product was small, but it stands distinctive.

The work of Cawein has been far more widely trumpeted. He had the good fortune to attract the attention of Howells with his first book and to be commended by him persistently and with no uncertain voice. "There is much that is expressive of the new land," Howells wrote in "The Editor's Study," "as well as of the young life in its richly sensuous, boldly achieved pieces of color. In him one is sensible (or seems so) of something different from the beautiful as literary New England or literary New York conceived it. He is a fresh strain." [10] He deplored the gorgeous excesses of the poems and the touches for merely decorative effect, but he defended them as the natural exuberance of extreme youth. With time they would disappear: undoubtedly a great poet had arisen. Thus encouraged, Cawein began upon a poetic career that in single-hearted devotion to the lyric muse has been equaled only by Clinton Scollard. Before his death he had issued more than twenty volumes of lyrics and his collected work had been published in five thick volumes.

The final estimate of the poet cannot yet be written. It is too soon, but even now one may venture certain predictions. Cawein wrote enormously too much, and he wrote all too often with merely literary intent. He was not a lyrist born: he had

[10] *Harper's Monthly*, May, 1888.

little ear for music, and he blended meters and made rimes seemingly with the eye alone. One can not feel that a passage like this, for instance, sang itself spontaneously:

> Seemed that she
> Led me along a flower-showered lea
> Trammeled with puckered pansy and the pea;
> Where poppies spread great blood-red stain on stain,
> So gorged with sunlight and the honied rain
> Their hearts are weary; roses lavished beams
> Roses, wherein were huddled little dreams
> That laughed coy, sidewise merriment, like dew
> Or from fair fingers fragrant kisses blew.

There is a straining constantly for the unusual in epithet, a seeking for a picturing adjective that shall give verisimilitude in an utterly new way. "The songs have all been sung," he would seem' to argue, "but the picturing adjectives have not all been used and the striking conceits." One might open at random for an illustration:

> Athwart a sky of brass long welts of gold;
> A bullion bulk the wide Ohio lies.

> Up from the glimmering east the full moon swung,
> A golden bubble buoyed zenithward.

> Between the pansy fire of the west,
> And poppy mist of moonrise in the east,
> This heartache will have ceased.

"It is as if we had another Keats," says Howells, and in saying it he touches the fatal weakness of the poet. There is lack of virility in great parts of his work, there is lack of definiteness and of vigor. He tells nothing new and he adds nothing to the old by his telling. Even Baskerville can say, "There is little or no Southern, not to say Kentucky, atmosphere in Mr. Cawein's poetry. His flowers and birds and rocks and trees do not appear to us as objects of the rich, warm Southern nature. He frequently mentions the whole register of flowers and birds in his poetry—almost, we might say, drags them into his descriptions by force—but he has not created a warm, genial, Southern poetic atmosphere in which they may thrive." [11]

[11] *Southern Writers*, Vol. II, p. 355.

Nevertheless, it is only in his Nature poetry that he is at all convincing. He can paint a summer noon, or a summer shower, and he can detail minutely the flowers and the mosses and the birds in an old fence corner or an old garden. Pictures like this have, undoubtedly, a certain kind of value:

> Bubble-like the hollyhocks
> Budded, burst, and flaunted wide
> Gipsy beauty from their stocks;
> Morning-glories, bubble-dyed,
> Swung in honey-hearted flocks.
>
> Tawny tiger-lilies flung
> Doublets slashed with crimson on;
> Graceful girl slaves, fair and young,
> Like Circassians, in the sun
> Alabaster lilies swung.
>
> Ah, the droning of the bee
> In his dusty pantaloons,
> Tumbling in the fleurs-de-lis;
> In the drowsy afternoons
> Dreaming in the pink sweet-pea.

Always is he heavy with adjectives, profuse, gorgeous; always is he dreamy and remote. One turns page after page of the thick volumes of the collected lyrics to find some simple human bit that came hot from the heart of a poet, some stanza that compels quotation, but one gets lost at length in the maze of sweetness. If any of his poems are to outlast their generation it will be some of the Nature pieces, but landscape studies, flower songs, and pretty conceits about bees and birds are thin material of which to make enduring poetry.

VII

With Richard Hovey (1864–1900), representative of the poets of the second generation of the National period, our survey closes. Hovey was a later Lanier, excited, impetuous, possessed by poetry until it ruled all his thinking. Like Lanier, he was Gallic of temperament rather than Teutonic. He read enormously—the Elizabethans, Tennyson, Whitman, the pre-Raphaelites, Dobson, Kipling, and later, in France, Paul Verlaine, Maeterlinck, Stéphane Mallarmé, and all the later symbolists. After his college course at Dartmouth he was, at brief intervals, theological student, newspaper reporter, actor, lecturer in Alcott's Concord school of philosophy, and in his last year, like Lanier, professor of literature in one of the larger universities—Barnard College, New York—yet his one profession all his life long was poetry. His facility was marvelous. He wrote an elegy of purest Greek type and he added a canto to *Don Juan;* he wrote Arthurian masques and dramas and then rollicking Bohemian songs and *vers de société.*

His facility was his weakness. Like Lanier he was too excited, too given to improvisation and the blending of meters. His dramatic interludes like *The Quest of Merlin* and *Taliesin* are marvelous in their workmanship, their mastery of all the intricacies of prosody, but they come near to being void of human interest. Lanier dominated his first poem *The Laurel* and there are echoes of Whitman and others in his later work. He matured slowly. At his death he had arrived at a point where there was promise of creative work of highest distinction. He was breaking from his Bohemianism and his excited Swinburnian music and was touching his time. His definition of poetry makes his early death seem like a tragedy. Of the poet he wrote, "It is not his mission to write elegant canzonettas for the delectation of the Sybaritic dilettanti, but to comfort the sorrowful and hearten the despairing, to champion the oppressed and declare to humanity its inalienable rights, to lay open to the world the heart of man, all its heights and depths, all its glooms and glories, to reveal the beauty in things and breathe into his fellows a love of it and so a love of Him whose manifestation it is. . . . In the appointed work of every people, the poets have been the leaders and pioneers." [12]

His most finished work is his elegy on the death of Thomas William Parsons, *Seaward,* which at times has a lyric quality that brings it into the company even of *Adonais* and *Thyrsis.* One is tempted to quote more than a single stanza:

> Far, far, so far, the crying of the surf!
> Still, still, so still, the water in the grass!
> Here on the knoll the crickets in the turf
> And one bold squirrel barking, seek, alas!
> To bring the swarming summer back to me.
> In vain; my heart is on the salt morass
> Below, that stretches to the sunlit sea.

[12] *Dartmouth Magazine,* Vol. XX, p. 95.

His most spontaneous and original outbursts are doubtless his Dartmouth lyrics—a series distinctive among college poetry, worthy of a place beside Dr. Holmes's Harvard lyrics—and his rollicking convivial songs that have in them the very soul of good fellowship. There is in all he wrote a Whitman-like masculinity. He could make even so conventional a thing as a sonnet a thing to stir the blood with:

> When I am standing on a mountain crest,
>   Or hold the tiller in the dashing spray,
> My love of you leaps foaming in my breast,
>   Shouts with the winds and sweeps to their foray;
> My heart bounds with the horses of the sea,
>   And plunges in the wild ride of the night,
> Flaunts in the teeth of tempest the large glee
>   That rides out Fate and welcomes gods to flight.
> Ho, love! I laugh aloud for love of you,
>   Glad that our love is fellow to rough weather;
> No fretful orchid hot-housed from the dew,
>   But hale and hearty as the highland heather,
>   Rejoicing in the wind that stings and thrills,
>   Comrade of ocean, playmate of the hills.

He is the singer of men—of Western men, red-blooded and free—the very opposite of Cawein. He wrote songs to be sung in barrack rooms and at college reunions—songs of comradeship and masculine joy:

> Give a rouse, then, in the Maytime
>   For a life that knows no fear!
> Turn night-time into daytime
>   With the sunlight of good cheer!
>   For it's always fair weather
>   When good fellows get together
> With a stein on the table and a good song ringing clear.

And again this

> Comrades, give a cheer to-night,
>   For the dying is with dawn!
> Oh, to meet the stars together,
>   With the silence coming on!
>   Greet the end
>   As a friend a friend
> When strong men die together.

His Launcelot and Guenevere cycle, which was to be complete in nine dramas, only four of which he lived to finish, though undoubtedly the best was yet to come, has in it enough of strength to make for itself, fragment as it is, a high place in our literature. The dramas are in different key from Tennyson's. In the *Idyls of the King* the old legend is domesticated and the table round is turned into a tea table. Hovey in his *Marriage of Guenevere* and *The Birth of Galahad* puts virile power into his knights, makes of Launcelot the hero of the cycle, and gives to Guenevere a reality that is Shakespearian. Few indeed have been the poets of the younger school who have dared to plan on so grand a scale or to venture to offer something new in a field that has been so thoroughly exploited.

BIBLIOGRAPHY

WILL CARLETON. (1845–1912.) *Poems*, 1871; *Farm Ballads*, 1873; *Farm Legends*, 1875; *Young Folks' Centennial Rhymes*, 1876; *Farm Festivals*, 1881; *City Ballads*, 1885; *City Legends*, 1889; *City Festivals*, 1892; *Rhymes of Our Planet*, 1895; *The Old Infant, and Similar Stories*, 1896; *Songs of Two Centuries*, 1902; *Poems for Young Americans*, 1906; *In Old School Days*, 1907; *Drifted In*, 1907.

JOHN JAMES PIATT. (1835–1917.) *Poems of Two Friends* [with Howells], 1859; *The Nests at Washington* [with Sarah Morgan Piatt], 1864; *Poems in Sunshine and Firelight*, 1866; *Western Windows and Other Poems*, 1869; *Landmarks and Other Poems*, 1871; *Poems of House and Home*, 1879; *Penciled Fly-Leaves* [prose], 1880; *Idyls and Lyrics of the Ohio Valley*, 1884; *The Children Out of Doors* [with Mrs. Piatt], 1885; *At the Holy World*, 1887; *A Book of Gold*, 1889; *Little New-World Idyls*, 1893; *The Ghost's Entry and Other Poems*, 1895.

JAMES WHITCOMB RILEY. (1849–1916.) *The Old Swimmin'-Hole*, 1883; *The Boss Girl and Other Sketches*, 1886; *Afterwhiles*, 1887; *Pipes o' Pan at Zekesbury*, 1889; *Rhymes of Childhood Days*, 1890; *An Old Sweetheart of Mine*, 1891; *Old Fashioned Roses*, 1891; *Neighborly Poems on Friendship, Grief, and Farm Life*, 1891; *Flying Islands of the Night*, 1892; *Poems Here at Home*, 1893; *Poems and Yarns* [with Edgar Wilson Nye], 1893; *Green Fields and Running Brooks*, 1893; *Armazindy*, 1894; *The Child World*, 1896; *Rubaiyat of Doc Sifers*, 1897; *Poems and Prose Sketches*, Homestead Edition, 10 vols., 1897; *Child Rhymes*, 1898; *Love-Lyrics*, 1899; *Farm Rhymes*, 1901; *Book of Joyous Children*, 1902; *A Defective Santa Claus*, 1904; *His Pa's Romance*, 1904; *Out to Old Aunt Mary's*, 1904; *Songs o' Cheer*, 1905; *While the Heart Beats Young*, 1906; *Morning*, 1907; *The Raggedy Man*, 1907; *The Little Orphant Annie Book*, 1908; *The Boys of the Old Glee Club*, 1908; *Songs of Summer*, 1908; *Old Schoolday Romances*, 1909; *The Girl I Loved*, 1910; *Squire Hawkins's Story*, 1910; *When She Was About Sixteen*, 1911; *The Lockerbie Book*, 1911; *Down Round the River and Other Poems*, 1911; *A Summer's Day and Other Poems*, 1911; *When the Frost Is on the Punkin and Other*

Poems, 1911; *All the Year Round,* 1912; *Knee Deep in June and Other Poems,* 1912; *The Prayer Perfect and Other Poems,* 1912; *Good-bye, Jim,* 1913; *A Song of Long Ago,* 1913; *He and I,* 1913; *When My Dreams Come True,* 1913; *The Rose,* 1913; *Her Beautiful Eyes,* 1913; *Away,* 1913; *Do They Miss Me?* 1913; *The Riley Baby Book,* 1913; *Biographical Edition of the Works of James Whitcomb Riley.* Complete Works. 1913.

EUGENE FIELD. (1850–1896.) *Tribune Primer,* 1882; *Culture's Garland, Being Memoranda of the Gradual Rise of Literature, Art, Music, and Society in Chicago and Other Western Ganglia,* 1887; *A Little Book of Western Verse,* 1889, 1890; *A Little Book of Profitable Tales,* 1889, 1890; *With Trumpet and Drum,* 1892; *Second Book of Verse,* 1893; *Echoes from the Sabine Farm* [with Roswell M. Field], 1893; *The Holy Cross and Other Tales,* 1893; *Love Songs of Childhood,* 1894; *The Love Affairs of a Bibliomaniac, The House, Songs and Other Verse, Second Book of Tales,* published posthumously in the Sabine edition; *The Works of Eugene Field.* Sabine Edition. Ten vols. 1896. The Poems of Eugene Field, Complete Editions. One volume. 1910. *Eugene Field, A Study in Heredity and Contradictions.* Slason Thompson. Two volumes. 1901.

HENRY CUYLER BUNNER. (1855–1896.) *A Woman of Honor,* 1883; *Airs from Arcady, and Elsewhere,* 1884; *In Partnership: Studies in Storytelling* [with James Brander Matthews], 1884; *Midge,* 1886; *Story of a New York House,* 1887; *Short Sixes: Stories to Be Read While the Candle Burns,* 1890; *Zadoc Pine, and Other Stories,* 1891; *Rowen: Second-Crop Songs,* 1892; *Made in France: French Tales Told with a U. S. Twist,* 1893; *More Short Sixes,* 1895; *Love in Old Cloathes, and Other Stories,* 1896.

EMMA LAZARUS. (1849–1887.) *Poems and Translations,* 1866; *Admetus,* 1871; *Alide: a Romance,* 1874; *The Spagnoletto: a Play,* 1876; *Heine's Poems and Ballads* [a translation], 1881; *Songs of a Semite,* 1882; *Poems of Emma Lazarus,* 1888.

CELIA THAXTER. (1836–1894.) *Poems,* 1872; *Among the Isles of Shoals,* 1873; *Drift-weed: Poems,* 1878; *Poems for Children,* 1883; *The Cruise of the Mystery, and Other Poems,* 1886; *An Island Garden,* 1894; *Poems,* Appledore Edition. Edited by Sarah Orne Jewett, 1896; *Letters of Celia Thaxter,* 1895.

EDITH M. THOMAS. (1854———.) *A New Year's Masque,* 1884; *The Round Year,* 1886; *Lyrics and Sonnets,* 1887; *The Inverted Torch,* 1890; *Fair Shadow Land,* 1893; *In Sunshine Land,* 1894; *In the Young World,* 1895; *Winter Swallow; with Other Verse,* 1896; *Dancers and Other Legends and Lyrics,* 1903; *Cassia, and Other Verse,* 1905; *Children of Christmas, and Others,* 1907; *Guest at the Gate,* 1909.

RICHARD WATSON GILDER. (1844–1909.) *The New Day,* 1875; *The Celestial Passion,* 1878; *Lyrics,* 1878; *The Poet and His Master, and Other Poems,* 1878; *Lyrics and Other Poems,* 1885; *Poems,* 1887; *Two Worlds, and Other Poems,* 1891; *Great Remembrance, and Other Poems,* 1893; *Five Books of Song,* 1894; *For the Country,* 1897; *In Palestine and Other Poems,* 1898; *Poems and Inscriptions,* 1901; *A Christmas Wreath,* 1903; *In the Heights,* 1905; *Book of Music,* 1906; *Fire Divine,*

1907; *Poems,* Household Edition, 1908; *Lincoln the Leader,* 1909; *Grover Cleveland,* 1910.

EDWARD ROLAND SILL. (1841–1887.) *The Hermitage and Other Poems,* 1867; *Venus of Milo, and Other Poems,* 1883; *Poems,* 1887; *The Hermitage, and Later Poems,* 1889; *Christmas in California: a Poem,* 1898; *Hermione, and Other Poems,* 1899; *Prose,* 1900; *Poems,* special edition, 1902; *Poems, Household Edition,* 1906; *The Life of Edward Rowland Sill,* by W. B. Parker, 1915.

ROBERT BURNS WILSON. (1850–1916.) *Life and Love,* 1887; *Chant of a Woodland Spirit,* 1894; *The Shadows of the Trees,* 1898; *Until the Day Break* [a novel], 1900.

MADISON JULIUS CAWEIN. (1865–1914.) *Blooms of the Berry,* 1887; *The Triumph of Music and Other Lyrics,* 1888; *Accolon of Gaul and Other Poems,* 1889; *Lyrics and Idyls,* 1890; *Days and Dreams,* 1891; *Poems of Nature and Love,* 1893; *Intuitions of the Beautiful,* 1895; *White Snake and Other Poems,* from the German, 1895; *Garden of Dreams,* 1896; *Undertones,* 1896; *Shapes and Shadows,* 1898; *Myth and Romance, a Book of Verses,* 1899; *One Day and Another,* 1901; *Weeds by the Wall,* 1901; *A Voice on the Wind and Other Poems,* 1902; *Vale of Tempe; Poems,* 1905; *In Prose and Verse,* 1906; *Poems,* 5 volumes, 1908; *Shadow Garden* [a Phantasy] and Other Plays, 1910; *So Many Ways,* 1911.

RICHARD HOVEY. (1864–1900.) *The Laurel: an Ode,* 1889; *Launcelot and Guenevere: a Poem in Dramas,* 1891; *Seaward: an Elegy on the Death of Thomas William Parsons,* 1893; *Songs from Vagabondia* [with Bliss Carman], 1894; *More Songs from Vagabondia* [with Bliss Carman], 1896; *The Quest of Merlin,* 1898; *The Marriage of Guenevere,* 1898; *The Birth of Galahad,* 1898; *Along the Trail: Book of Lyrics,* 1898; *Last Songs from Vagabondia* [with Bliss Carman], 1900; *Taliesin,* 1900; *Along the Trail,* 1907; *Launcelot and Guenevere: a Poem in Dramas,* 5 vols., 1907; *To the End of the Trail,* 1908.

CHAPTER XVI

THE TRIUMPH OF THE SHORT STORY

Voluminous as may seem the poetry of the period when viewed by itself, it sinks into insignificance when viewed against the mass of prose that was contemporaneous with it. Overwhelmingly was it an age of prose fiction. He who explores it emerges with the impression that he has been threading a jungle chaotic and interminable. To chart it, to find law and tendency in it, seems at first impossible. For a generation or more every writer seems to have had laid upon him a necessity for narration. Never before such widespread eagerness to din tales into the ears of a world.

It was an age of brief fiction—this fact impresses one first of all. The jungle growth was short. Not half a dozen writers in the whole enormous group confined themselves to novels of length; the most distinctive fictional volumes of the period: *The Luck of Roaring Camp, Old Creole Days, In the Tennessee Mountains, Nights with Uncle Remus, In Ole Virginia, A New England Nun, Deephaven, Main-Traveled Roads, Flute and Violin,* and the like, were collections of tales. One may venture to call the period the age of the short story, or more accurately, perhaps, the age of short-breathed work. Everywhere literature in small parcels. In January, 1872, the *North American Review,* guardian of the old traditions, thought the conditions serious enough to call for earnest protest:

A new danger has recently shown itself. . . . The great demand on all sides is for *short* books, *short* articles, *short* sketches; no elaborate essays, no complete monographs, are wanted . . . condensed thought, brief expression, the laconian method everywhere. . . . The volume sinks into an article, the article dwindles to an item to conciliate the demands of the public.

That this shortness of unit was a sign of weakness, we to-day by no means concede. It was rather a sign of originality, the symptom of a growing disregard for British methods and British opinion. The English genius always has been inclined to ponderousness—to great, slow-moving novels, to elaborate essays that get leisurely under way, to romances that in parts are treatises and in parts are histories, everywhere to solidity and deliberateness of gait. The *North American Review* protest was a British protest; it was the protest of conservatism against what to-day we can see was the new spirit of America. The American people from the first had been less phlegmatic, less conservative, than the English. There were climatic influences, it may be; there was surely a spirit of intensity everywhere that made for short efforts. The task of subduing in a single century a raw continent produced a people intolerant of the leisurely and the long drawn out. Poe perceived the tendency early. In a letter to Professor Charles Anthon he wrote:

Before quitting the *Messenger* I saw, or fancied I saw, through a long and dim vista the brilliant field for ambition which a magazine of bold and noble aims presented to him who should successfully establish it in America. I perceived that the country, from its very constitution, could not fail of affording in a few years a larger proportionate amount of readers than any upon earth. I perceived that the whole energetic, busy spirit of the age tended wholly to magazine literature—to the curt, the terse, the well timed and the readily diffused, in preference to the old forms of verbose and ponderous and inaccessible.

This far-sightedness made of Poe the father of the American type of short story. Irving undoubtedly had sown the earliest seeds, but Irving was an essayist and a sketch-writer rather than a maker of short stories in the modern sense. It was Poe's work to add art to the sketch—plot structure, unity of impression, verisimilitude of details, matter-of-factness, *finesse*—and, like Hawthorne, to throw over it the atmosphere of his own peculiar personality. That he evolved the form deliberately can not be doubted. In his oft-quoted review of Hawthorne's tales he laid down what may be considered as the first rules for short story writing ever formulated. His theories that all art is short-breathed, that a long poem is a *tour de force* against nature, and that the unit of measure in fiction is the amount that may be read with undiminished pleasure at a single sitting, are too well known to dwell upon.

But the short story of the mid-century, even in its best specimens, was an imperfect thing. In Hawthorne's tales the quality
of the sketch or the essay is always discernible. All of Poe's
tales, and Hawthorne's as well, lack vigor of characterization,
sharpness of outline, swiftness of movement. "The Gold Bug,"
for instance, has its climax in the middle, is faulty in dialect, is
utterly deficient in local color, and is worked out with characters as lifeless as mere symbols.

The vogue of the form was increased enormously by the an-
nuals which figured so largely in the literary history of the mid-
century, by the increasing numbers of literary pages in weekly
newspapers, and by the growing influence of the magazines.
The first volume of the *Atlantic Monthly* (1857) had an average of three stories in each number. But increase in quantity
increased but little the quality. The short story of the annual
was, for the most part, sentimental and over-romantic. Even
the best work of the magazines is colorless and ineffective when
judged by modern standards. Undoubtedly the best stories
after Poe and Hawthorne and before Harte are Fitz-James
O'Brien's "Diamond Lens," 1858, and "What Was It?" 1859,
Edward Everett Hale's "The Man Without a Country," 1863,
and "The Brick Moon," 1869, and Thomas Wentworth Higginson's "The Haunted Window," 1867. Well wrought they
are for the most part, unusual in theme, and telling in effect,
yet are they open nevertheless to the same criticisms which we
have passed upon Poe.

The short story in its later form dates from Harte's "The Luck
of Roaring Camp." Harte added reality, sharpness of outline,
vividness of setting, vigor of characterization. The new period
demanded actuality. The writer must speak with authority; he
must have been a part of what he describes; he must have seen
with his own eyes and he must reproduce with a verisimilitude
that grips the reader and hastens him on as if he himself were
a participant in the action. There must be at every point sense
of actuality, and, moreover, strangeness—new and unheard-of
types of humanity, uncouth dialects, peculiar environments. It
was far more concentrated than the mid-century work, but it
was much more given to general description and background effects and impressionistic characterization.

In the mid-eighties came the perfecting of the form, the molding of the short story into a finished work of art. Now was demanded compression, nervous rapidity of movement, sharpness of characterization, singleness of impression, culmination, *finesse*—a studied artistry that may be compared with even the best work of the French school of the same period. Stories like those of Aldrich, Stockton, Bunner, Garland, Allen, Bierce, Grace King, Mrs. Chopin, Stephen Crane, and Frank Norris, from the standpoint of mere art at least, come near to perfection.

The decline of the short story, its degeneration into a journalistic form, the substitution all too often of smartness, paradox, sensation, for truth—all this is a modern instance outside the limits prescribed for our study.

I

After Harte and the early local-colorists the next to develop the short story was Frank R. Stockton. No writer of the period has been more variously estimated and labeled. By some critics he has been rated as a mere humorist, by others as a novelist, by still others as a writer of whimsicalities in a class by himself.

It is undoubtedly true that his personality was so interfused with his writings that the generation who knew and loved him were too kind in their judgments. Behind his every story they saw the genial, whimsical creator and they laughed even before they began to read. But a new generation has arrived to whom Stockton is but a name and a set of books, and it is becoming more and more evident now that very much that he wrote was ephemeral. To this generation he is known as the author of a single short story, or perhaps three or four short stories, of a type that has its own peculiar flavor.

Stockton was born in Philadelphia in 1834, was educated in the high school there, and then, at the request of his father, learned the trade of wood engraving. But his inclinations were literary, and he was soon an editorial worker on his brother's newspaper. Later he joined the staff of *Hearth and Home* in New York, then became connected with the new *Scribner's Monthly*, and finally became assistant editor of *St. Nicholas*. The wide popularity of his stories induced him at length to withdraw from editorial work to devote his whole time to his writings. He became exceedingly productive: after his fiftieth year he published no fewer than thirty volumes.

To understand Stockton's contribution to the period one must bear in mind that he adopted early the juvenile story as his form of expression, and that his first book, *Ting-a-ling Stories,* appeared four years after *Alice in Wonderland.* When, at the age of forty-eight he gained general recognition with his *The Lady, or the Tiger?* he had published nine books, eight of them juveniles. The fact is important. He approached literature by the Wonderland gate and he never wandered far from that magic entrance. After his short stories had made him famous he continued to write juveniles, adapting them, however, to his new audience of adult readers. He may be summed up as a maker of grown-up juveniles, a teller, as it were, of the adventures of an adult Alice in Wonderland.

All of his distinctive work was short. *Rudder Grange,* which first made him at all known, was a series of sketches, the humorous adventures of a newly married couple, the humor consisting largely of incongruous situations. Even his so-called novels, like *The Casting Away of Mrs. Lecks and Mrs. Aleshine* and its sequel *The Dusantes,* are but a series of episodes joined together as loosely as Alice's well-known adventures. Plot there is really none. Characterization, however, there is to a degree: the two women do carry their provincial Yankee personalities and the atmosphere of their little home village into whatever amazing environment they may find themselves, but one can not say more.

There seems on the author's part a constant endeavor in all of his work to invent incongruous situation and preposterous suggestion, and a determination to present this topsy-turvy world gravely and seriously as if it were the most commonplace thing in the world. He makes it plausible by the Defoe method of multiplying minor details and little realistic touches until the reader is thrown completely off his guard. For instance, in the novel *The Dusantes* the coach in which the party is traveling is overtaken by night in the high mountains and before morning is completely buried by a great snow storm. The following day, after they had hollowed out a room for themselves in the snow, this adventure befalls them:

I heard a low crunching sound on one side of me, and, turning my head, I saw in the wall of my excavation opposite to the stage coach and at a distance of four or five feet from the ground an irregular hole in the snow, about a foot in diameter, from which protruded the head of a man. This head was wrapped, with the exception of the face, in a brown woolen comforter. The features were those of a man of about fifty, a little sallow and thin, without beard, whiskers, or mustache, although the cheeks and chin were darkened with a recent growth.

The astounding apparition of this head projecting itself from the snow wall of my cabin utterly paralyzed me, so that I neither moved nor spoke, but remained crouching by the fire, my eyes fixed upon the head. It smiled a little, and then spoke.

"Could you lend me a small iron pot?" it said.

Another coach, it seems, had likewise been snowed under, and the chief occupant had tried to tunnel his way out for help, with the result as recorded. The passage is typical. It illustrates a mannerism that mars all his work. He is not telling a culminating story: he is adding incongruity to incongruity for merely humorous effect, and after a time the reader tires. It seems at length as if he were straining at every point to bring in something totally unexpected and preposterous. In short compass the device succeeded, but incongruity may not rule longer than the moment.

It is to Stockton's short stories, then, that we are to look for his distinctive work. Of one story we need say little. The sensation it made has few parallels in the history of the period and the influence it excited was undoubtedly great. Aldrich several years earlier had told a story which depended for its effect upon a startling closing sentence, but *Marjorie Daw* attracted little attention as compared with the tremendous vogue of *The Lady, or the Tiger?* It was a step in the direction of more elaborate art. It began to be realized that the short story writer had the reader at his mercy. It was recognized that it was a part of his art to startle, to perplex, to tantalize, to lead into hidden pitfalls, yet always in a way to please and to stimulate. From *Marjorie Daw* and *The Lady, or the Tiger?* it was but a step to the jugglery of O. Henry.

None of Stockton's other short stories ever reached the vogue of this lucky hit, but many of them surpass it in all the requisites of art. "Negative Gravity," "The Transferred Ghost," "The Remarkable Wreck of the Thomas Hyke," and "The Late Mrs.

Null'' may be cited as examples. In all of them the art consists in perfect naturalness, in an exquisite simplicity of style, and in topsy-turvyness made within short compass completely plausible. We are led into a world of negative gravity where everything goes completely by opposites. In ''The Transferred Ghost'' we are gravely assured that Mr. Hinckman, at the point of death, has a ghost appointed to haunt his late residence. He does not die, however, and as a result the poor ghost is haunted by the living Mr. Hinckman until it is nearly frightened out of its existence. And so skilful is the author that the story becomes convincing.

Very much of the success of the work depends upon the element that we call style. Stockton indeed is one of the half dozen prose writers of the period to whom may be applied the now old-fashioned term stylist. There is grace and character in his every sentence, a dignity despite the whimsical content that never descends to vulgarity or to what James has termed ''newspaperese.'' Always is he clear, always is he simple—his early experience with juveniles taught him that—and always is he perfectly natural. Moreover, to all this he adds a delightfully colloquial attitude toward his reader—a familiar personal tone at times that is like nothing so much as Charles Lamb.

He was an anomaly in the period. In an age of localized fiction he produced work as unlocalized as is Carroll's *Through the Looking Glass;* instead of using dialect and curious provincial types, he dealt always with refined gentle folk amid surroundings that seem to have little to do with the actual solid earth; in a period that demanded reality and fullness of life he wrote little that touches any of the real problems of his time or that has in it anything to grip or even to move the reader: even his murders are gentle affairs. There are no moments of real emotion: all is *opéra bouffe;* all is cheery and whimsically conceived.

That there was knowledge of the human heart behind his quaint creations undoubtedly is true. *The Lady, or the Tiger?* is founded on a subtle study of humanity, yet even as one says it he is forced to admit that it added little to the real substance of the period. He was content to be a mere entertainer, aware undoubtedly that the entertainment that delights one generation all too often is obsolete in the next.

II

The appearance of "Monsieur Motte" in the *New Princeton Review* of January, 1886, marks another step in the development of the short story. It was as distinctively French in its atmosphere and its art as if it had been a translation from Maupassant, yet it was as originally and peculiarly American as even *Madame Delphine,* which in so many ways it resembles. Its English, which is Gallic in idiom and in incisive brevity; its atmosphere quivering with passion; its characters whimsical, impulsive, exquisite of manners; its dainty suggestions of femininity, as in the case of the little Creole maiden Marie Modeste or the stately Madame Lareveillère; its hints of a rich and tragic background, and its startling "Marjorie Daw" culmination—there is no Monsieur Motte; Monsieur Motte is only the pathetic *négresse* Marcélite—all this was French, but the background was old Creole New Orleans, and it was drawn by one who professed herself a severe realist, or, to quote her own words, "I am not a romanticist, I am a realist *à la mode de la Nouvelle-Orleans.* I have never written a line that was not realistic, but our life, our circumstances, the heroism of the men and women that surrounded my early horizon—all that was romantic. I had a mind very sensitive to romantic impressions, but critical as to their expression."

The writer was Grace Elizabeth King, daughter of a prominent barrister of New Orleans, herself with a strain of Creole blood, educated at the fashionable Creole *pension* of the Mesdames Cenas—the Institute St. Denis of "Monsieur Motte" and "Pupasse"—bilingual like all the circle in which she moved, and later a resident for some two years in France—no wonder that from her stories breathes a Gallic atmosphere such as we find in no other work of the period. Three more episodes, each a complete short story—"On the Plantation," "The Drama of an Evening," and "The Marriage of Marie Modeste"—she added to her first story, bits of art that Flaubert would have delighted in, and issued them in 1888 under the title *Monsieur Motte.* She followed it with *Earthlings,* which she has never republished, from *Lippincott's Magazine,* and with other stories and sketches contributed to *Harper's* and the *Century* that later appeared as *Tales of a Time and Place* and *Balcony Stories.*

The impulse to write fiction came to Miss King from a conviction that Cable had done scant justice to the real Creoles of Louisiana. She would depict those exclusive circles of old Creole life that she herself had known in her early childhood, circles almost exclusively French with just a touch, perhaps, of Spanish. She would differ from Cable as Sarah Orne Jewett differs from Mary E. Wilkins Freeman in her pictures of New England life. Her sketches, therefore, are more minutely drawn, more gentle, more suggestive of the richness and beauty of a vanished age that was Parisian and Bourbon in its brilliancy. She excels in her pictures of old Mesdames, relics of the old régime, drawn by the lightest of touches and suggestions until they are intensely alive, like Bon Maman or like Madame Josephine in "A Delicate Affair." A hint or a suggestion is made to do the work of a page of analysis. Note a passage like this:

She played her game of solitaire rapidly, impatiently, and always won; for she never hesitated to cheat and get out of a tight place, or into a favorable one, cheating with the quickness of a flash, and forgetting it the moment afterward.

Mr. Horace was as old as she, but he looked much younger, although his dress and appearance betrayed no evidence of an effort in that direction. Whenever his friend cheated, he would invariably call her attention to it; and as usual she would shrug her shoulders and say, "Bah! Lose a game for a card!" and pursue the conversation.

All her feminine creations are Gallic, like Marie Modeste, or, better still, the vividly drawn Misette in *Earthlings,* volatile, lovable—impossible. She is always at her best while depicting these whimsical, impracticable, tropic femininites; she makes them not so bewitching as does Cable, but she makes them more real and more intensely alive.

Her earlier stories are the best, judged merely as short stories. As she continued her work she discovered more and more the wealth of romantic material in the annals of the old city, especially in the studies of Charles Gayarré (1805–1895), greatest of Southern historians. The influence of his work upon her becomes increasingly evident. Her stories grew into sketches. *Balcony Stories* are not so much stories as they are realistic sketches of social conditions in New Orleans after the Reconstruction. More and more she wrote studies in Creole atmospheres, impressions of picturesque places and persons after the

manner of Hearn, until at length she abandoned fiction altogether to devote herself to history. In the period when historical fiction for a time ruled everything, she wrote history itself
in a manner that was as graphic and as picturesque as fiction.
Perhaps nothing that she has written has in it more of vitality
than her history of New Orleans and its people. It is possible
that her final place is to be with the historians rather than with
the makers of fiction.

In the technique of the short story she was surpassed by a
later worker in Louisiana materials, Kate Chopin (1851–1904),
some of whose work is equal to the best that has been produced
in France or even in America. She wrote but little, two volumes of stories, notably *Bayou Folks,* containing all that is now
accessible of her shorter work. Many of her sketches and stories
have never been republished from the magazines.

The strength of Mrs. Chopin's work came partly from the
strangeness of her material—she told of the Grand Pré Acadians
in the canebrakes of central Louisiana—and from her intimate
knowledge of her field, but it came more from what may be
described as a native aptitude for narration amounting almost to
genius. She was of Celtic temperament—her father was a Gal-
way County Irishman and her mother was of mingled French
and old Virginian stock. Educated in the Convent of the Sacred Heart at St. Louis, married at nineteen to a New Orleans
cotton factor, spending fourteen years in Louisiana, the last four
of them in the remote hamlet of Cloutiersville in Natchitoches
Parish, "a rambling little French village of one street, with the
Catholic church at one end, and our plantation at the other, and
the Red River flowing through everybody's backyard," left a
widow at thirty-five with six children—all this had little to do
with the making of literature. Indeed, until her return to St.
Louis a year after her bereavement, she had never even thought
of writing. She began almost by chance, and, succeeding from
the first, she wrote story after story almost without effort and
wholly without study of narrative art. For a decade her work
was in all of the Northern magazines, then five years before her
death, discouraged by the reception of her novel *The Awakening,*
she became silent.

No writer of the period was more spontaneously and inevitably a story teller. There is an ease and a naturalness about

her work that comes from more than mere art. She seldom gave to a story more than a single sitting, and she rarely revised her work, yet in compression of style, in forbearance, in the massing of materials, and in artistry she ranks with even the masters of the period. A story like "Desireé's Baby," with its inevitableness and its culminating sentence that stops for an instant the reader's heart, is well-nigh perfect. She was emotional, she was minutely realistic, and, unlike Grace King, used dialect sometimes in profusion; she was dramatic and even at times melodramatic, yet never was she commonplace or ineffective. She had command at times of a pervasive humor and a pathos that gripped the reader before he was aware, for behind all was the woman herself. She wrote as Dickens wrote, with abandonment, with her whole self. There is art in her work, but there is more than art. One may read again and again such bits of human life as "Madame Celestin's Divorce": it is the art that is independent of time and place, the art indeed that is universal.

III

Of a type the direct opposite was James Lane Allen, who was not inspired and who was not an improvisatore. To Allen fiction was an art learned with infinite patience. He was years in the mastering of it, years in which he studied literature with the abandonment of a Maupassant. He approached it deliberately; he made himself the most scholarly of the novelists of the period—graduate and graduate student of Transylvania University, first applicant for the degree of doctor of philosophy at Johns Hopkins, though he never found opportunity for residence, teacher for years of languages, and then professor of Latin and higher English at Bethany College, West Virginia.

The circumstances of his early life made a literary career difficult. He had been born on a small Kentucky plantation a few miles out of Lexington, miles that he walked daily while gaining his education. A college course for him meant toil and sacrifice. The war had brought poverty, and the death of the father imposed new burdens. Like Lanier, he was forced to teach schools when he would have studied at German universities, but, like Lanier, he somehow had caught a vision of literature that dominated him even through decades of seeming hopelessness. Few have had to fight longer for recognition and few

have ever worked harder to master the art with which they were
to make their appeal. Like Howells, he studied masters and
read interminably, pursuing his work into the German and the
French, writing constantly and rewriting and destroying. And
the result, as with Howells, was no immaturities. His first book,
Flute and Violin, published when he was forty-two, is by many
regarded as his best work. To his earliest readers it seemed as
if a new young writer had arrived to whom art was a spontaneous thing mastered without effort.

A study of the available fragments of Allen's work written
earlier than the stories in this first volume reveals much. He
began as a critic. In Northern journals after 1883 one may find
many articles signed with his name: sharp criticisms of Henry
James, appreciations of Heine and Keats, studies of the art of
Balzac and his circle, letters on timely subjects which show the
wideness of his reading and the gradual shaping of his art. He
evolved his method deliberately after consideration of all that
had been done in England and America and France. By no
other writer of the period was the short story worked out with
more care or with more knowledge of requirements.

Especially significant is an article entitled "Local Color" in
the *Critic* of 1886. The time has come, he contended, when the
writer of fiction must broaden the old conceptions of art. Now
the novelist must be "in some measure a scientist; he must comprehend the natural pictorial environment of humanity in its
manifold effects upon humanity, and he must make this knowledge available for literary presentation." Other requirements
had become imperative:

> From an artistic point of view, the aim of local color should be
> to make the picture of human life natural and beautiful, or dreary, or
> somber, or terrific, as the special character of the theme may demand;
> from a scientific point of view, the aim of local color is to make the
> picture of human life natural and—intelligible, by portraying those
> picturable potencies in nature that made it what it was and must go
> along with it to explain what it is. The novelist must encompass both
> aims.

He must also be a stylist. "The happiest use of local color,"
he declares, "will test to the uttermost one's taste and attain-
ments as a language colorist." And again, "The utmost in the
use of local color should result, when the writer chooses the

most suitable of all colors that are characteristic; when he makes these available in the highest degree for artistic presentation; and when he attains and uses the perfection of coloring in style."

One makes another discovery as one works among these earlier fragments: Allen, like Howells, was a poet. His first contributions to the larger magazines—*Harper's* and the *Atlantic*—were poems, beautiful, serious, colorful.

After these preliminaries one is prepared to find work done with excess of care, with precision and balance, and, moreover, to find color in its literal sense, poetic atmosphere and poetic phrasing, scientific truth too, nature studied as Thoreau studied it, and Burroughs. The six stories in *Flute and Violin* stand by themselves in American literature. They are not perfect examples of the short story judged by the latest canons. They make often too much of the natural background, they lack in swiftness, and they do not culminate with dramatic force. They are poetic, at times almost lyrical. Open, for instance, *A Kentucky Cardinal:*

March has gone like its winds. The other night as I lay awake with that yearning which often beats within, there fell from the upper air the notes of the wild gander as he wedged his way onward by faith, not by sight, towards his distant bourn. I rose and, throwing open the shutters, strained eyes toward the unseen and unseeing explorer, startled, as a half-asleep soldier might be startled by the faint bugle-call of his commander, blown to him from the clouds. ·What far-off lands, streaked with mortal dawn, does he believe in? In what soft sylvan waters will he bury his tired breast? Always when I hear his voice, often when not, I too desire to be up and gone out of these earthly marshes where hunts the dark Fowler—gone to some vast, pure, open sea, where, one by one, my scattered kind, those whom I love and those who love me, will arrive in safety, there to be together.

One thinks of Thoreau—one thinks of him often as one reads Allen. Everywhere Nature, and Nature with the metaphysical light upon it. And connected with Nature always the tragedy of human life—beauty of landscape expressed in perfect beauty of language, but under it and behind it struggle and passion and pain. Nowhere else in the period such distinction of expression, such charm of literary atmosphere, combined with such deep soundings into the heart of human life. "The White Cowl" which appeared in the *Century* of 1888 and later "Sister

Dolorosa'' may be compared with no other American work later than "Ethan Brand.''

In his first period Allen was distinctively a writer of short stories and sketches. His canvas was small, his plots single and uncomplicated, his backgrounds over-elaborate, impeding the movement of the plot and overshadowing the characters. His art began with landscape—his second book, much of the matter of which was written before the contents of the first, was wholly landscape, landscape idealized and made lyric. Then came *John Gray,* a preliminary sketch, and *A Kentucky Cardinal* and its sequel *Aftermath,* long and short stories, parables, humanity beginning to emerge from the vast cosmic nature spectacle and to dominate. Over everything beauty, yet through it all a strain of sadness, the sadness of youth repressed, of tragedy too soon.

The second period began in 1896 with the publication of *Summer in Arcady.* The novelist had moved permanently to New York City. He had gained a broader outlook; he had felt the new forces that were moving Thomas Hardy and the French novelists. His early work seemed to him now narrow and weak, mere exercises of a prentice hand. He would work with the novel now rather than with the short story; he would deal with broad canvas, with the great fundamental problems that complicate human life. His essay in the *Atlantic* of October, 1897, explains the new period in his work. Literature even into the mid-nineties had been feminine rather than masculine, he averred. The American novelists had aimed too much at refinement.

They sought the coverts where some of the more delicate elements of our national life escaped the lidless eye of publicity, and paid their delicate tributes to these; on the clumsy canvases of our tumultuous democracy they watched to see where some solitary being or group of beings described lines of living grace, and with grace they detached these and transferred them to the enduring canvases of letters; they found themselves impelled to look for the minute things of our humanity, and having gathered these, to polish them, carve them, compose them into minute structures with minutest elaboration . . . polishing and adornment of the little things of life—little ideas, little emotions, little states of mind and shades of feeling, climaxes and dénouements, little comedies and tragedies played quite through or not quite played through by little men and women on the little stage of little playhouses.

So much for the past, for the feminine age to which his own earlier work had belonged. A new age had arisen; a masculine age, less delicate, less refined, less heedful of little things, a strenuous age, more passionate and virile, less shrinking and squeamish.

It is striking out boldly for larger things—larger areas of adventure, larger spaces of history, with freer movements through both: it would have the wings of a bird in the air, and not the wings of a bird on a woman's hat. It reveals a disposition to place its scenery, its companies of players, and the logic of its dramas, not in rare, pale, half-lighted, dimly beheld backgrounds, but nearer to the footlights of the obvious. And if, finally, it has any one characteristic more discernible than another, it is the movement away from the summits of life downward towards the bases of life; from the heights of civilization to the primitive springs of action; from the thin-aired regions of consciousness which are ruled over by Tact to the underworld of consciousness where are situated the mighty workshops, and where toils on forever the cyclopean youth, Instinct.

It was more than the analysis of a far-seeing critic: it was the call of a novelist to himself to abandon the small ideals and narrow field of his early art, and strike out into the main currents of the age.

Let us try for a while the literary virtues and the literary materials of less self-consciousness, of larger self-abandonment, and thus impart to our fiction the free, the uncaring, the tremendous fling and swing that are the very genius of our time and spirit.

Following this declaration came the three major novels, *The Choir Invisible,* which was his old short story *John Gray* enlarged and given "fling and swing," *The Reign of Law,* and *The Mettle of the Pasture,* novels of the type which he had denominated masculine, American, yet to be grouped with nothing else in American literature, their only analogues being found in England or France.

In all his work he had been, as he had promised in his essay on "Local Color," essentially scientific in spirit, but now he became direct, fearless, fundamental. Nature he made central now. The older art had made of it a background, a thing apart from humanity, sometimes sympathetic, sometimes indifferent, but Allen, like Hardy and his school, made of it now a ruling force, a dominating personality in the tragedy. The first title

of *Summer in Arcady* as it ran serially in the *Cosmopolitan* was
Butterflies: a Tale of Nature. Its theme was the compelling
laws within human life: instincts, inheritances, physical forces
that bind beyond power to escape. Man is not to be treated as
apart from Nature but as inseparably a part of Nature, hurled
on by forces that he does not understand, ruled all unknowingly
by heredity, fighting senseless battles that, could he but know
all, would reduce life to a succession of ironies: "If Daphne
had but known, hidden away on one of those yellow sheets [on
which her own runaway marriage had just been recorded, the
last of a long series of such marriages] were the names of her
own father and mother."

In these later novels one finds now fully developed an element
that had been latent in all of his early work—a mystic symbolism
that in many ways is peculiar to Allen. *Summer in Arcady* is
built up around a parallelism that extends into every part of
the story:

Can you consider a field of butterflies and not think of the blindly
wandering, blindly loving, quickly passing human race? Can you
observe two young people at play on the meadows of Life and Love
without seeing in them a pair of these brief moths of the sun?

And *The Reign of Law* is a parable from beginning to end,
a linking of man to Nature, a parallelism between human life
and the life of the hemp of the Kentucky fields:

Ah! type, too, of our life, which also is earth-sown, earth-rooted;
which must struggle upward, be cut down, rooted and broken, ere the
separation take place between our dross and our worth—poor perish-
able shard and immortal fiber. Oh, the mystery, the mystery of that
growth from the casting of the soul as a seed into the dark earth,
until the time when, led through all natural changes and cleansed of
weakness, it is borne from the field of its nativity for the long service.

All of his work is essentially timeless and placeless. He
had had from the first little in common with the other short
story writers of locality. Of dialect he has almost none; of
the negro who so dominates Southern literature he shows only
a glimpse in one or two of his earlier sketches. His background,
to be sure, is always Kentucky and this background he describes
with minuteness, but there is no attempt to portray personalities or types peculiar to the State. He is working rather in the

realm of human life. Always is he tremendously serious. A lambent humor may play here and there over the tales, but everywhere is there the feeling of coming tragedy. Too much concerned he is, perhaps, with the conception of sex as the central problem of life—*Summer in Arcady* and *The Mettle of the Pasture* were greeted with storms of disapproval—but one feels that he is sincere, that he stands always on scientific grounds, and that he is telling what he conceives to be the undiminished truth about modern life.

And his solution, so far as he offers a solution, is free from bitterness or pessimism. He is superior to Hardy inasmuch as he is able to rise above the pagan standpoint and see the end of the suffering and the irony crowned with ultimate good. John Gray in *The Choir Invisible* summed up the philosophy of the author in sentences like these: "To lose faith in men, not in humanity; to see justice go down and not to believe in the triumph of injustice; for every wrong that you weakly deal another or another deals you to love more and more the fairness and beauty of what is right, and so to turn the ever-increasing love from the imperfection that is in us all to the Perfection that is above us all—the perfection that is God: this is one of the ideals of actual duty that you once said were to be as candles in my hand. Many a time this candle has gone out; but as quickly as I could snatch any torch—with your sacred name on my lips—it has been relighted."

The volume of his writings is small. He has worked always slowly, revising, rewriting, never satisfied. His earlier short stories are perhaps his most perfect work; his longer short stories, like *A Kentucky Cardinal,* his most charming; and his later novels like *The Mettle of the Pasture,* his most enduring, inasmuch as they contain the chief substance of what he had to say to his generation. His weakness has been a fondness for elaboration: in *The Reign of Law* a chapter is given to the life history of the hemp plant and to a parallelism between it and human life. The movement of his stories is constantly impeded by what is really extraneous material, endless descriptions of landscape, beautiful in itself but needless, and unnecessary episodes: a cougar "gaunt with famine and come for its kill" is creeping up to John Gray, who is weaponless, but before the final spring four pages about the habits of the animal—a chapter altogether for the adventure, and after it is all told it is "lumber" so far as the needs of the novel are concerned.

But there is a more fundamental weakness: his work on the whole is the product of a follower rather than a leader. He learned his art deliberately impelled not by a voice within which demanded expression but by a love for beautiful things and a dogged determination to win in the field that he had chosen for his life work. By interminable toil and patience, and by alertness to seize upon every new development in his art, he made himself at last a craftsman of marvelous skill, even of brilliancy. He was not a voice in the period; rather was he an artisan with a sure hand, a craftsman with exquisite skill.

IV

The triumph of the short story came in the early nineties. In the September, 1891, issue of *Harper's Monthly* Mr. Howells, reviewing Garland's *Main-Traveled Roads,* commented on the fact that collections of stories from the magazines were competing on even terms with the novels:

We do not know how it has happened; we should not at all undertake to say; but it is probably attributable to a number of causes. It may be the prodigious popularity of Mr. Kipling which has broken down all prejudices against the form of his success. The vogue that Maupassant's tales in the original or in versions have enjoyed may have had something to do with it. Possibly the critical recognition of the American supremacy in this sort has helped. But however it has come about, it is certain that the result has come, and the publishers are fearlessly venturing volumes of short stories on every hand; and not only short stories by authors of established repute, but by new writers who would certainly not have found this way to the public some time ago.

During this decade the short story reached its highest level. In February, 1892, the *Atlantic Monthly* in a review of current collections of short stories by Thomas Nelson Page, Joel Chandler Harris, James Lane Allen, Octave Thanet, Hamlin Garland, Richard Harding Davis, Elizabeth Stuart Phelps, Rose Terry Cooke, George A. Hibbard, William Douglas O'Connor, Clinton Ross, Thomas A. Janvier, H. C. Bunner, Brander Matthews, and Frank R. Stockton, remarked of the form that "in America it is the most vital as well as the most distinctive part of literature. In fact, it flourishes so amply that this very prosperity nullifies most of the apologies for the American novel." But even within the limits of the decade of its fullest success came the decline. The enormous vogue of the form resulted in the journalization of it. O. Henry with his methods helped greatly to devitalize and cheapen it. With him the short story became fictional vaudeville. Everywhere a straining for effect, a search for the piquant and the startling. He is theatric, stagy, smart, ultra modern. Instead of attempts at truth a succession of smart hits: "The wind out of the mountains was singing like a jew's-harp in a pile of old tomato-cans by the railroad track"; "A bullet-headed man Smith was, with an oblique, dead eye and the mustache of a cocktail mixer," etc. He is flippant, insincere, with an eye to the last sentence which must startle the reader until he gasps. After O. Henry the swift decline of the short story, the inclusion of it in correspondence courses, and the reign of machine-made art.

V

But during the decade of the high tide came some of the strongest work in American literature. It was the period of the earlier and better work of Hamlin Garland and Alice French, of Richard Harding Davis and Ambrose Bierce, of Mrs. Deland and F. H. Smith, with Garland, perhaps, the most distinctive worker. Garland began as an iconoclast, a leader of the later phase of realism—depressed realism after the Russian and the French types. His little book of essays, *Crumbling Idols,* breezy and irreverent, with its cry for a new Americanism in our literature, new truth, new realism, was the voice of the new generation after Harte and Howells, the school inspired by Ibsen, Hardy, Tolstoy, Maupassant. The Middle West was his background and he knew it with completeness. He had been born in a Wisconsin "coulé" on a ragged, half-broken farm, and before he was eleven he had migrated with his parents westward, three different times. His boyhood had followed the middle western border. The father was of Maine Yankee stock, full of the restlessness and eagerness of his generation. In his son's record he stands out in almost epic proportions.

Hour after hour we pushed westward, the heads of our tired horses hanging ever lower, and on my mother's face the shadow deepened, but my father's voice calling to his team lost nothing of its edge. He was in his element. He loved this shelterless sweep of sod. This westward march delighted him. I think he would have gladly kept on until he reached the Rocky Mountains.[1]

He had stopped this time in Iowa and had begun once again the tremendous task of making a farm out of the virgin prairie. The boy took his full share of work. Speaking of himself in the third person, he says: "In the autumn that followed his eleventh birthday he plowed for seventy days, overturning nearly one hundred and fifty acres of stubble." At fifteen he was head farmer and took a man's place on the reaper, at the threshing, and in all of the farm work. Education came to him as he could get it. He attended the winter sessions of the district school and he read all the books that the neighborhood afforded. By rarest good fortune his father subscribed for the new *Hearth and Home* in which the serial *The Hoosier Schoolmaster* was running, and in the boy's own words in later years the story was a "milestone in his literary progress as it was in the development of distinctive Western fiction."

His later struggles toward culture, his graduation in 1881 from Cedar Valley Seminary, Osage, Iowa, his school teaching in Illinois and Dakota, his experience as a settler during the Dakota land "boom" of 1883, his Howells-like journey to Boston the following year, and his years of life there as teacher and eager student, must be passed over swiftly. He haunted the Boston public library and read enormously, he became impressed with the theories of the new French school of "Veritists," and he soon began to write, first photographic sketches of Middle-Western life—corn and wheat raising, rural customs, and the like—then after a long period he returned West for his first vacation. At Chicago he visited Joseph Kirkland (1830–1894), author of *Zury: the Meanest Man in Spring County* (1887), a book of crude yet strong pictures of Western life, and the call was another milestone in his literary life.

The result of that vacation was three books of short stories, their author's most distinctive work, *Main-Traveled Roads, Prairie Folks,* and *Other Main-Traveled Roads.* His own account of the matter is worthy of quotation:

[1] *Collier's,* May 9, 1914.

The entire series was the result of a summer-vacation visit to my old home in Iowa, to my father's farm in Dakota, and, last of all, to my birthplace in Wisconsin. This happened in 1887. I was living at the time in Boston, and had not seen the West for several years, and my return to the scenes of my boyhood started me upon a series of stories delineative of farm and village life as I knew it and had lived it. I wrote busily during the two years that followed, and in this revised definitive edition of *Main-Traveled Roads* and its companion volume, *Other Main-Traveled Roads* (compiled from other volumes which now go out of print), the reader will find all of the short stories which came from my pen between 1887 and 1889.

It remains to say that, though conditions have changed somewhat since that time, yet for the hired man and the renter farm life in the West is still a stern round of drudgery. My pages present it—not as the summer boarder or the young lady novelist sees it—but as the working farmer endures it.

After the years at Boston the life of his native region had taken on for him a totally new aspect. He saw it now as Howard saw it in "Up the Coulé," the grinding toil of it, the brutality and hopelessness and horror of it, and it filled him with fierce anger. He wrote with full heart and with an earnestness that was terrible, and he had the courage of his convictions. Will Hannan takes Agnes from the hell into which she has married and bears her into his own new home of love and helpfulness and there is no apology, and again the same theme in later tales. There is the grimness and harshness and unsparing fidelity to fact, however unpleasant, that one finds in the Russian realists, but there is another element added to it: the fervor and faith of the reformer. Such a story as "Under the Lion's Paw," for instance, does not leave one, like Ibsen and Hardy, in despair and darkness; it arouses rather to anger and the desire to take action harsh and immediate. There is no dodging of facts. All the dirt and coarseness of farm life come into the picture and often dominate it. The author is not writing poetry; despite his *Prairie Songs* he is no poet. Howard is visiting home after a long absence:

It was humble enough—a small white story-and-a-half structure, with a wing set in the midst of a few locust trees; a small drab-colored barn with a sagging ridge-pole; a barnyard full of mud, in which a few cows were standing, fighting the flies and waiting to be milked. An old man was pumping water at the well; the pigs were squealing from a pen near by; a child was crying. . . .

As he waited, he could hear a woman's fretful voice, and the impatient jerk and jar of kitchen things, indicative of ill-temper or worry. The longer he stood absorbing this farm-scene, with all its sordidness, dullness, triviality, and its endless drudgeries, the lower his heart sank. All the joy of the home-coming was gone, when the figure arose from the cow and approached the gate, and put the pail of milk down on the platform by the pump.

"Good-evening," said Howard, out of the dusk.

Grant stared a moment. "Good-evening."

Howard knew the voice, though it was older and deeper and more sullen. "Don't you know me, Grant? I am Howard."

The man approached him, gazing intently at his face. "You are?" after a pause. "Well, I'm glad to see you, but I can't shake hands. That damned cow has laid down in the mud."

But the most pitiful pictures are those of the women. Lucretia Burns is a type:

She had no shawl or hat and no shoes, for it was still muddy in the little yard, where the cattle stood patiently fighting the flies and mosquitoes swarming into their skins, already wet with blood. The evening was oppressive with its heat, and a ring of just-seen thunder-heads gave premonitions of an approaching storm.

She arose from the cow's side at last, and, taking her pails of foaming milk, staggered toward the gate. The two pails hung from her lean arms, her bare feet slipped on the filthy ground, her greasy and faded calico dress showed her tired and swollen ankles, and the mosquitoes swarmed mercilessly on her neck and bedded themselves in her colorless hair.

The children were quarreling at the well, and the sound of blows could be heard. Calves were querulously calling for their milk, and little turkeys, lost in a tangle of grass, were piping plaintively.

It was a pitifully worn, almost tragic face—long, thin, sallow, hollow-eyed. The mouth had long since lost the power to shape itself into a kiss, and had a droop at the corners which seemed to announce a breaking-down at any moment into a despairing wail. The collarless neck and sharp shoulders showed painfully.

It is the tragic world of Mary E. Wilkins—her obstinate, elemental, undemonstrative rustics moved into a new setting. As in her work, simplicity, crude force, the power of one who for a moment has forgotten art and gives the feeling of actual life, verisimilitude that convinces and compels. The little group of stories is work sent hot from a man's heart, and they are alive as are few other stories of the period, and they will live. They are part of the deeper history of a section and an era.

This element of purpose is found in all of Garland's work. Nowhere is he a mere teller of tales. The Scotch and Yankee elements within him made of him a preacher, a man with a message. The narrow field of his first success could not long be worked, and, like the true son of a pioneer, he began to follow his old neighbors in their further migrations westward. His later work took the form of novels, many of them dealing with the extreme West and all of them saturated with purpose. His *Captain of the Gray Horse Troop,* for instance, attempted for the Indian what *Ramona* tried to do. It is a powerful study of the wrongs done a race, and, moreover, it is a novel. Still later the native mysticism of his race showed itself in such novels as *The Tyranny of the Dark, The Shadow World, Victor Ollnee's Discipline*—spiritualistic propaganda.

With the novel he has not fully succeeded. He lacks power of construction and ability for extended effort. The short story "A Branch Road" in *Main-Traveled Roads* has a gripping power, but the same theme treated at novel length in *Moccasin Ranch* becomes too much an exploiting of background. There is a sense of dilution, a loss of effect. The author's first fine edge of anger, of conviction, of complete possession by his material, is gone, and we have the feeling that he has become a professional man of letters, an exploiter of what he considers to be salable material. His best long novel is *Rose of Dutcher's Coolly. Money Magic* has a certain sense of power connected with it, but it lacks the final touch of actual life. Unlike *The Rise of Silas Lapham,* with which it may be compared, it leaves us unsatisfied. The quivering sense of reality that one finds in *Main-Traveled Roads* is not there. It is a performance, a brilliant picture made deliberately and coldly by a man in his study, whereas a story like "Among the Corn Rows" reads as if it had taken possession of its author, and had been written with a burst of creative enthusiasm. One late fragment of Garland's must not be overlooked, his *A Son of the Middle Border,* a part of which has appeared in serial form. It is an autobiography, and it is more: it is a document in the history of the Middle West. It has a value above all his novels, above all else that he has written, saving always those tense short stories of his first inspiration.

VI

The Western stories of Alice French antedated by several years Garland's first work and perhaps had an influence upon it. Her strong story "The Bishop's Vagabond" appeared in the *Atlantic* as early as 1884 and her collection *Knitters in the Sun* by Octave Thanet came out in 1887. Her work, however, has not the originality and the sharpness of outline of Garland's and it has failed to hold the high place that was at first assigned to it. She is to be classed with Miss Woolson rather than with Mrs. Wilkins Freeman, with Miss Murfree rather than with Harris. She was not a native of the regions she chose as her literary field, but she entered them with curiosity and studied their peculiarities carefully with open note-book for Northern readers.

Her father and her brothers were extensive manufacturers, and contact with their work gave her a knowledge of labor conditions and of economic problems that enabled her in the early eighties to contribute to the *Atlantic* and other magazines able papers, such as "The Indoor Pauper" and "Contented Masses," papers widely commented upon for their brilliancy and breadth of view. But the success won everywhere by the feminine short story writers tempted her from these economic studies, and for a time she wrote local color tales with variety of background— Canada, Florida, Iowa. Then, with ample means at her disposal, she built at Clover Bend, Arkansas, a summer home on the banks of the Black River, and, like Miss Murfree, became interested in the crude social conditions about her, so different from those of her native New England or her adopted Iowa city of Davenport. Stories like "Whitsun Harp, Regulator" and "Ma' Bowlin'" followed, then the fine studies entitled "Plantation Life in Arkansas" and "Town Life in Arkansas."

These earlier stories are often dramatic, even melodramatic, and they abound in sentiment. Sometimes a character stands out with sharpness, but more often the tale impresses one as a performance rather than a bit of actual life. The intense feeling that Garland, who wrote as if his material came from out his own bitter heart, throws into his stories she does not have. She stands as an outsider and looks on with interest and takes notes, often graphic notes, then displays her material as an exhibitor sets forth his curious collection.

More and more the sociological specialist and the reformer took control of her pen. Even her short stories are not free from special pleading: "Convict Number 49," for instance, is not so much a story as a tract for the times. In her novels the problem dominates. *The Man of the Hour* and *The Lion's Share* treat phases of the labor problem, and *By Inheritance* is a study of the negro question with an attempted solution. The story, despite dramatic intensity at times and lavish sentiment, fails often to interest the reader unless he be a sociologist or a reformer. Already she holds her place by reason of a few of her earlier short stories, and it would seem that even these are now losing the place that once undoubtedly was theirs.

More convincing, though perhaps ᵗhey have had smaller influence upon their time, have been the Vermont stories of Rowland E. Robinson, which are genuine at every point and full of subtle humor, and the Adirondack stories of Philander Deming, which began to appear in the *Atlantic* in the mid-seventies. Both men have written out of their own lives with full hearts, and both have added to their material a touch of originality that has made it distinctive.

VII

In tracing the development of the short story to the end of the century one must pause at the exquisite work of H. C. Bunner, who undoubtedly did much toward bringing the form to mechanical perfection. His volume entitled *Made in France: French Tales with a U. S. Twist,* suggests one secret of his art. He had a conciseness, a brilliancy of effect, an epigrammatic touch, that suggest the best qualities of French style. In his volumes *Short Sixes* and *More Short Sixes* he is at his best— humorous, artistic, effective, and in addition he touches at times the deeper strata of human life and becomes an interpreter and a leader.

French in effect also is Ambrose Bierce, who in his earlier work displayed a power to move his readers that is little found outside of Poe. Reserve he has, a directness that at times is disconcerting, originality of a peculiar type, and a command of many of the subtlest elements of the story-telling art, but lacking sincerity, he fails of permanent appeal. He writes for effect, for startling climax, for an insidious attack upon his reader's nerves, and often, as in his collection entitled *In the Midst of Life,* he works his will. But he is not true, he works not in human life as it is actually lived, but in a Poe-like life that exists only in his own imaginings. In his later years journalism took the fine edge from his art and adverse criticism of his work turned him into something like a literary anarchist who criticized with bitterness all things established. A few of his novels may be studied with profit as models of their kind, but the greater part of his writings despite their brilliancy can not hope for permanence.

One may close the survey with Richard Harding Davis, who may be taken as the typical figure of the last years of the century. Davis was a journalist, peculiarly and essentially a journalist. He began his career in a newspaper office and all that he did was colored by the newspaper atmosphere. Literature to him was a thing to be dashed off with facility, to be read with excitement, and to be thrown aside. The art of making it he learned as one learns any other profession, by careful study and painstaking thoroughness, and having mastered it he became a literary practitioner, expert in all branches.

"Gallagher" was his first story, and it was a brilliant production, undoubtedly his best. Then followed the Van Bibber stories, facile studies of the idle rich area of New York life of which the author was a mere spectator, remarkable only for the influence they exerted on younger writers. Of the rest of his voluminous output little need be said. It is ephemeral, it was made to supply the demand of the time for amusement. With O. Henry, Edward W. Townsend of the "Chimmie Fadden" stories, and others, its author debauched the short story and made it the mere thing of a day, a bit of journalism to be thrown aside with the paper that contained it. On the mechanical side one may find but little fault. As a performance it is often brilliant, full of dash and spirit and excessive modernness, but it lacks all the elements that make for permanence—beauty of style, distinction of phrase, and, most of all, fidelity to the deeper truths of life. It imparts to its reader little save a momentary titillation and the demand for more. It deals only with the superficial and the coarsely attractive, and we feel it is so because of its author's limitations, because he knows little of the deeps of character, of sacrifice, of love in the genuine sense, of the fundamental stuff of which all great literature has been woven. He is the maker of extravaganzas, of Zenda romances, of preposterous combinations like *A Soldier of Fortune*, which is true neither to human nature nor to any possibility of

terrestrial geography; he is a special correspondent with facile
pen who tells nothing new and nothing authoritative—a man
of the mere to-day, and with the mere to-day he will be forgotten. Were he but an isolated case such criticism were unnecessary; he might be omitted from our study; but he is the
type of a whole school, a school indeed that bids fair to exert
enormous influence upon the literature, especially upon the fiction, of the period that is to come.

VIII

Thus the fiction of the period has expressed itself prevailingly
in short-breathed work. Compared with the fiction of France
or England or Russia, with the major work of Balzac or Thackeray or Tolstoy, it has been a thing of seeming fragments. Instead of writing "the great American novel," which was so
eagerly looked for during all the period, its novelists have preferred to cultivate small social areas and to treat even these by
means of brief sketches.

The reasons are obvious. American life during the period
was so heterogeneous, so scattered, that it has been impossible
to comprehend any large part of it in a single study. The novelist who would express himself prevailingly in the larger units
of fiction, like Henry James, for instance, or F. Marion Crawford, has been forced to take his topics from European life. The
result has been narrowness, cameos instead of canvases, short
stories rather than novels. In a period that over enormous
areas was transforming thousands of discordant elements into
what was ultimately to be a unity, nothing else was possible.
Short stories were almost imperative. He who would deal with
crude characters in a bare environment can not prolong his story
without danger of attenuation. The failure of Miss Murfree,
and indeed of nearly all of the short story writers when they
attempted to expand their compressed and carefully wrought
tales into novels, has already been dwelt upon.

But shortness of unit is not a fault. The brevity of the form,
revealing as it does with painful conspicuousness all inferior
elements, has resulted in an excellence of workmanship that has
made the American short story the best art form of its kind to
be found in any literature. The richness of the materials used
has also raised the quality of the output. The picturesqueness

of American life during the period has made possible themes of absorbing interest and unusual vividness of picturing, and the elemental men and passions found in new and isolated areas have furnished abundance of material for characterization. Until the vast field of American life becomes more unified and American society becomes less a matter of provincial varieties, the short story will continue to be the unit of American fiction.

BIBLIOGRAPHY

FRANK RICHARD STOCKTON. (1834–1902.) *Ting-a-ling Stories,* 1869; *Roundabout Papers,* 1872; *The Home,* 1872; *What Might Have Been Expected,* 1874; *Tales Out of School,* 1875; *Rudder Grange,* 1879; *A Jolly Fellowship,* 1880; *The Floating Prince,* 1881; *The Story of Viteau,* 1884; *The Lady, or the Tiger? and Other Stories,* 1884; *The Casting Away of Mrs. Lecks and Mrs. Aleshine,* 1886; *A Christmas Wreck and Other Stories,* 1886; *The Late Mrs. Null,* 1886; *The Hundredth Man,* 1887; *The Bee Man of Orne,* 1887; *The Dusantes,* 1888; *Amos Kilbright,* 1888; *Personally Conducted,* 1889; *The Great War Syndicate,* 1889; *Ardis Claverden,* 1890; *Stories of Three Burglars,* 1890; *The Merry Chanter,* 1890; *The Squirrel Inn,* 1891; *The House of Martha,* 1891; *Rudder Grangers Abroad,* 1891; *The Clocks of Rondaine,* 1892; *The Watch-Maker's Wife,* 1893; *Pomona's Travels,* 1894; *The Adventures of Captain Horn,* 1895; *Mrs. Cliff's Yacht,* 1896; *Stories of New Jersey,* 1896; *A Story-Teller's Pack,* 1897; *The Great Stone of Sardis,* 1898; *The Girl at Cobhurst,* 1898; *Buccaneers and Pirates of Our Coast,* 1898; *The Vizier of the Two-Horned Alexander,* 1899; *The Associate Hermits,* 1899; *A Bicycle of Cathay,* 1900; *Afield and Afloat,* 1900; *The Novels and Stories of Frank R. Stockton,* Shenandoah Edition, 18 vols., 1900; *Kate Bonnet,* 1902.

GRACE KING. (1852——.) *Monsieur Motte,* 1888; *Earthlings* [in *Lippincott's Magazine*]; *Tales of a Time and Place,* 1892; *Jean Baptiste Le Moyne, 'Sieur de Bienville* [Makers of American Series], 1892; *Balcony Stories,* 1893; *History of Louisiana* [with J. R. Ficklen], 1894; *New Orleans, the Place and the People,* 1895; *De Soto and His Men in the Land of Florida,* 1898; *Stories from Louisiana History* [with J. R. Ficklen], 1905.

KATE CHOPIN. (1851–1904.) *At Fault, a Novel,* 1890; *Bayou Folk,* 1894; *A Night in Acadie and Other Stories,* 1897; *The Awakening, a Novel,* 1899.

JAMES LANE ALLEN. (1849——.) *Flute and Violin, and Other Kentucky Tales and Romances,* 1891; *The Blue-Grass Region of Kentucky,* 1892; *John Gray: a Kentucky Tale of the Olden Time,* 1893; *A Kentucky Cardinal: a Story,* 1894; *Aftermath: Part Two of a Kentucky Cardinal,* 1895; *Summer in Arcady: a Tale of Nature,* 1896; *The Choir Invisible,* 1897; *The Reign of Law: a Tale of the Kentucky Hemp Fields,* 1900; *The Mettle of the Pasture,* 1903; *The Bride of the Mistletoe,* 1909; *The Doctor's Christmas Eve,* 1910; *A Heroine in Bronze,* 1912.

HAMLIN GARLAND. (1860——.) *Main-Traveled Roads: Six Mississippi Valley Stories,* 1891; *Jason Edwards: an Average Man,* 1892; *Little Norsk; or, Ol' Pap's Flaxen,* 1892; *Member of the Third House: a Dramatic Story,* 1892; *A Spoil of Office: a Story of the Modern West,* 1892; *Prairie Folks: or, Pioneer Life on the Western Prairies, in Nine Stories,* 1893; *Prairie Songs,* 1893; *Crumbling Idols: Essays on Art, Dealing Chiefly with Literature, Painting, and the Drama,* 1894; *Rose of Dutcher's Coolly,* 1895; *Wayside Courtships,* 1897; *Ulysses S. Grant, His Life and Character,* 1898; *The Spirit of Sweetwater,* 1898; *Boy Life on the Prairie,* 1899; *The Trail of the Gold-Seekers: Record of Travel in Prose and Verse,* 1899; *The Eagle's Heart,* 1900; *Her Mountain Lover,* 1901; *The Captain of the Grayhorse Troop,* 1902; *Hesper,* 1903; *The Light of the Star,* 1904; *The Tyranny of the Dark,* 1905; *Witch's Gold: New Version of the Spirit of Stillwater,* 1906; *Money Magic,* 1907; *The Long Trail,* 1907; *The Shadow World,* 1908; *Moccasin Ranch, a Story of Dakota,* 1909; collected edition, ten volumes, 1909; *Cavanagh, Forest Ranger,* 1910; *Other Main-Traveled Roads,* 1910; *Victor Ollnee's Discipline,* 1911.

ALICE FRENCH, "OCTAVE THANET." (1850——.) *Knitters in the Sun,* 1887; *Expiation,* 1890; *We All,* 1891; *Otto the Knight and Other Trans-Mississippi Stories,* 1891; *Stories of a Western Town,* 1892; *Adventures in Photography,* 1893; *The Missionary Sheriff: Incidents in the Life of a Plain Man Who Tried to Do His Duty,* 1897; *The Book of True Lovers,* 1897; *The Heart of Toil,* 1898; *A Slave to Duty and Other Women,* 1898; *A Captured Dream and Other Stories,* 1899; *The Man of the Hour,* 1905; *The Lion's Share,* 1907; *By Inheritance,* 1910; *Stories That End Well,* 1911; *A Step on the Stair,* 1913.

ROWLAND EVANS ROBINSON. (1833–1900.) *Uncle Lisha's Shop: Life in a Corner of Yankeeland,* 1887; *Sam Lovel's Camp: Uncle Lisha's Friends Under Bark and Canvas,* 1889; *Vermont: a Study in Independence,* 1892; *Danvis Folks,* 1894; *In New England Woods and Fields,* 1896; *Uncle Lisha's Outing,* 1897; *Hero of Ticonderoga,* 1898; *A Danvis Pioneer,* 1900; *Sam Lovel's Boy,* 1901; *In the Greenwood,* 1904; *Hunting Without a Gun and Other Papers,* 1905; *Out of Bondage and Other Stories,* 1905.

PHILANDER DEMING. (1829——.) *Adirondack Stories,* 1880, 1886; *Tompkins and Other Folks: Stories of the Hudson and the Adirondacks,* 1885.

AMBROSE BIERCE. (1842–1914.) *Cobwebs from an Empty Skull,* 1874; *The Monk and the Hangman's Daughter* [with Gustav Adolph Danzinger], 1892; *Tales of Soldiers and Civilians* [later changed to *In the Midst of Life*], 1892; *Black Beetles in Amber,* 1895; *Can Such Things Be?* 1894; *Fantastic Fables,* 1899; *Shapes of Clay,* 1903; *The Cynic's Word Book,* 1906; *Son of the Gods and a Horseman in the Sky,* 1907; *The Shadow on the Dial and Other Essays,* 1909; *Write It Right: Little Blacklist of Literary Faults,* 1909; Collected Works. Twelve Volumes. 1909–12.

RICHARD HARDING DAVIS. (1864–1916.) *Gallagher and Other Stories,* 1891; *Stories for Boys,* 1891; *Van Bibber and Others,* 1892; *The West from a Car Window,* 1892; *Rulers of the Mediterranean,* 1894; *Exiles and Other Stories,* 1894; *Our English Cousins,* 1894; *Princess Aline,* 1895;

About Paris, 1895; *Cinderella and Other Stories*, 1896; *Three Gringos in Venezuela and Central America*, 1896; *Cuba in War Time*, 1897; *Soldiers of Fortune*, 1897; *A Year from a Reporter's Notebook*, 1898; *The King's Jackal*, 1898; *The Lion and the Unicorn*, 1899; *Novels and Stories*, six volumes, 1899; *With Both Armies in South Africa*, 1900; *In the Fog*, 1901; *Captain Macklin*, 1902; *Ranson's Folly*, 1902; *The Bar Sinister*, 1904; *Miss Civilization: a Comedy*, 1905; *Real Soldiers of Fortune*, 1906; *Farces*, 1906; *The Scarlet Car*, 1907; *The Congo and Coasts of Africa*, 1907; *Vera, the Medium*, 1908; *White Mice*, 1909; *Once upon a Time*, 1910; *The Dictator, a Farce*, 1910; *Galloper, a Comedy*, 1910; *The Consul*, 1911; *The Man Who Could not Lose*, 1911; *The Red Cross Girl*, 1912; *The Lost Road*, 1913; *With the Allies*, 1914.

CHAPTER XVII

I

In 1870 American fiction ran in two currents: fiction of the *Atlantic* type, read by the cultivated few, and fiction of Bonner's *New York Ledger* type, read openly by the literate masses and surreptitiously by many others. There was also a very large class of readers that read no novels at all. Puritanism had frowned upon fiction, the church generally discountenanced it, and in many places prejudice ran deep. George Cary Eggleston in the biography of his brother has recorded his own experience:

It will scarcely be believed by many in the early years of the twentieth century, that as late as the end of the third quarter of the nineteenth, there still survived a bitter prejudice against novels as demoralizing literature, and that even short stories were looked upon with doubt and suspicion. . . . When *The Hoosier Schoolmaster* began to appear, a member of the publishing house was sorely troubled. He had been a bitter and vehement opponent of novels and novel reading. He had published articles of his own in denunciation of fiction and in rebuke of his friends in a great publishing house for putting forth literature of that character. He now began to suspect that *The Hoosier Schoolmaster* was in fact a novel, and he was shocked at the thought that it was appearing in a periodical published by himself. . . . When the story was about to appear in book form Edward wrote "A Novel" as a sub-title, and the publisher referred to was again in a state of nervous agitation. He could in no wise consent to proclaim himself as a publisher of novels. In view of the large advance orders for the book he was eager to publish the novel, but he could not reconcile himself to the open admission that it was a novel.[1]

While *The Bread-Winners* was running its anonymous course in the *Century* in 1884, its author, now known to have been John Hay, felt called upon to issue an explanatory note:

[1] *The First of the Hoosiers*, 343. See also the editorial on novel-reading *Scribner's Mo.*, 4:493.

I am engaged in business in which my standing would be seriously compromised if it were known I had written a novel. I am sure that my practical efficiency is not lessened by this act, but I am equally sure that I could never recover from the injury it would occasion me if known among my own colleagues. For that positive reason, and for the negative one that I do not care for publicity, I resolved to keep the knowledge of my little venture in authorship restricted to as small a circle as possible. Only two persons besides myself know who wrote *The Bread-Winners*.

The final breaking down of this prejudice and the building up of the new clientele of readers that at length gave prose fiction its later enormous vogue is one of the most interesting phenomena of the period. The novel gained its present respectability as a literary form by what may be called an artifice. It came in disguised as moral instruction, as character-building studies of life, as historical narrative, as reform propaganda. *Uncle Tom's Cabin*, which had been read by thousands who had never opened a novel before, had begun the work. *The Hoosier Schoolmaster* was allowed to appear in the columns of *Hearth and Home* because it was a moral tale for children and because it was written by a minister whose motives no one could question. So with the works of the Rev. E. P. Roe, and the stories of Dr. J. G. Holland, who had gained an enormous following with his series of lay sermons published under the name of Timothy Titcomb.

Perhaps Dr. Holland, more than any other writer of the time, is responsible for this rehabilitation of the novel. He understood the common people. His own origin had been humble— the son of a mechanic of western Massachusetts, blessed with poverty, educated through his own efforts, enabled after a long struggle to take a medical diploma—educator, school teacher, superintendent of schools in Vicksburg, Mississippi, and finally, under Samuel Bowles, assistant editor of the Springfield, Massachusetts, *Republican*, which, largely through his efforts, arose to national importance. He was forty when the Timothy Titcomb letters entered upon their enormous popularity—it is estimated that nearly half a million copies of the series were sold first and last; he was fifty when he established *Scribner's Monthly* and assumed its editorship.

Scribner's under his direction became for the new period what the *Atlantic Monthly* had been for the period before. He was a moralist, a plain man of the people, and he knew his clientele; he knew the average American reader that makes up the great democratic mass, the reader who had bought *The Wide, Wide World*, and *Uncle Tom's Cabin*, and the *Titcomb Letters*. He gave them first of all a serial novel by the Rev. George Mac-Donald, and he printed at the close of the first volume of the *Monthly* a letter from a reader, sample of thousands which had filled his mail. Here is an extract:

> I know of no writings better calculated than his [MacDonald's] to draw out what is noble and true in the reader, or call forth fine feelings and high resolves. They give impulse to life. We come away from reading one of his books stronger and better prepared for our life-work. Is not this the surest test of excellence in a book?

It was this purpose that inspired his own fiction, *Arthur Bonnicastle, Nicholas Minturn,* and the others, earnest, moral tales sprinkled freely with sentiment, wholesome, but not high in literary merit. No other man did so much to direct the period into the well-known channels which it took. His whole influence was democratic. He would publish literature for the people, and to him literature was a serious thing, the voice of life. The group of new authors which he gathered about him is comparable only with the group that James T. Fields gathered about himself in the earlier golden days of the *Atlantic*.

II

The period of moralizing fiction culminated with the work of the Rev. Edward Payson Roe, whose first novel, *Barriers Burned Away* (1872), with its background of the great Chicago fire, and its tense moral atmosphere which skilfully concealed its sensationalism and its plentiful sentiment, became enormously popular. When its author died in 1888 his publishers estimated that 1,400,000 copies of all his novels had been sold, not counting pirated editions in many foreign languages, and the sale of the books has been steady up to the present time.

Roe, like Holland, had sprung from the common people and had been largely self-educated. For a time he had attended Williams College, Massachusetts, he had enlisted for the war as the chaplain of a regiment, and after the war had settled down as pastor of the First Church at Highland Falls, New York.

After nine years his health failed him and he betook himself to an out-of-doors life, fruit raising at Cornwall-on-Hudson, and his experience he embodied in several practical handbooks like *Success with Small Fruits*, first published serially in *Scribner's*. The last years of his life he gave to fiction, turning it out with facility and in quantity and always with the theory that he was thereby continuing his work as a pastor. "My books," he wrote, "are read by thousands; my voice reached at most but a few hundred. My object in writing, as in preaching, is to do good; and the question is, Which can I do best? I think with the pen, and I shall go on writing no matter what the critics say."[2]

That his novels are lacking in the higher elements of literary art, in structure and style and creative imagination, is apparent even to the uncritical, but that they are lacking in truth to life and power to move the reader no one can declare. At every point they are wholesome and manly. Roe's assertion that he worked with reverence in the fundamental stuff of life one must admit or else deny his contention that, "The chief evidence of life in a novel is the fact that it lives."[3] Surely it must be admitted that few novels of the period have shown more vitality.

His influence has been considerable. With Holland and his school he helped greatly in the building up of that mass of novel readers, mostly women it must be said, which by the middle of the eighties had reached such enormous proportions. He led readers on to Lew Wallace's *The Fair God* and *Ben Hur*, and to the novels of Frances Hodgson Burnett, who added to the conventional devices of Holland and Roe—sentiment, sensation, love-centered interest culminating inevitably in marriage at the close of the story—literary art and a certain dramatic power. She was realistic in method,—her *That Lass o' Lowrie's* (1877) reproduced the Lancashire dialect in all its uncouthness—but the atmosphere of her work was romantic. Her *Little Lord Fauntleroy* (1886), unquestionably the most successful juvenile of the period, has been described as "a fairy tale of real life." All of her books, indeed, have this fairy tale basis. She has been exceedingly popular, but she cannot be counted among the original forces of the period. From her the current of popularity flowed

[2] Roe's *E. P. Roe. Reminiscences of His Life*, 127.
[3] See E. P. Roe's "The Element of Life in Fiction." *Forum*, 5: 226.

on to F. Marion Crawford's cosmospolitan work, to Margaret
Deland's strong problem novel *John Ward, Preacher;* then it
swelled into a flood with *David Harum* and the historical novels
that made notable the nineties. At the close of the century fiction was read by all and in quantities that seem incredible.

III

In a chapter which traces the growth of the novel, in distinction from the growth of the sketch or the short story, F.
Marion Crawford must be given a leading place. Of all American writers he devoted himself most fully to the major form of
fiction. He wrote forty-five novels, and few sketches and short
stories: he was a novelist and only a novelist. He appeared at
the one moment when the type of fiction which he represented
was most certain of wide recognition. His earliest book, *Mr.
Isaacs* (1882), dealt with a new, strange environment—India,
five years before Kipling made it his background; it had a religious atmosphere—the mystic beliefs of the Orient; and it told
a story with sentiment and with dramatic movement. *Zoroaster,* with its opening sentence, ''The hall of the banquets was
made ready for the feast in the palace of Babylon,'' appealed
to an audience that had rated *Ben Hur* among the greatest of
novels.

But the earliest books of Crawford showed little of the main
current of his work. No two novelists could differ more radically than he and Roe. To him the purpose-novel was a bastard
thing unworthy the powers of a true artist.

Lessons, lectures, discussions, sermons, and didactics generally belong
to institutions set apart for especial purposes and carefully avoided,
after a certain age, by the majority of those who wish to be amused.
The purpose-novel is an odious attempt to lecture people who hate lectures, to preach to people who prefer their own church, and to
teach people who think they know enough already. It is an ambush,
a lying-in-wait for the unsuspecting public, a violation of the social
contract—and as such it ought to be either mercilessly crushed or
forced by law to bind itself in black and label itself "Purpose" in very
big letters.[4]

The office of the novel was, therefore, entertainment and only
entertainment. He has been the chief exponent in America of

[4] *The Novel: What It Is.*   17.

art for art's sake. A novel, he maintained, is a little "pocket-stage" whose only office is to please.

The life and the training of Crawford gave him a viewpoint which was singularly different from that held by the short story writers who were so busily exploiting provincial little neighborhoods in all the remote nooks and corners of the land. His training had given him an outlook more cosmopolitan than even that of Henry James. He had been born at Bagni-di-Lucca, in Tuscany, son of Thomas Crawford the sculptor, and he had spent the first eleven years of his life in Rome. Later he had studied at Concord, New Hampshire; at Trinity College, Cambridge; at Karlsruhe, at Heidelberg; and finally at Rome, where he had specialized in the classics. In 1873 he was at Allahabad, India, connected with the *Indian Herald*, and later on, his health failing, he visited his uncle in New York, Samuel Ward, brother of Julia Ward Howe, and at his advice threw some of his Indian experiences into the form of fiction. The instant success of *Mr. Isaacs* determined his career. After extensive travels in Turkey and elsewhere, he settled down in Italy in a picturesque villa overlooking the Bay of Naples, and there he spent the remaining years of his life, years of enormous literary productivity, and of growing popularity with readers both in America and in Europe.

No other American novelist has ever covered so much of territory. He wrote with first-hand knowledge of life in America, in England, in Germany, in Italy, in Constantinople, and India, and he wrote with scholarly accuracy historical novels dealing with times and places as diverse as Persia in the times of Zoroaster; as the second crusade—*Via Crucis;* as the era of Philip II in Spain—*In the Palace of the King;* as Venice in the Middle Ages—*Marietta, a Maid of Venice;* as early Arabia—*Kahled;* and as early Constantinople—*Arethusa.*

The heart of his work undoubtedly is made up of the fifteen novels that deal with life in Rome and its environs: *Saracinesca, Sant' Ilario, Don Orsino, Taquisara, Corleone, Casa Braccio, A Roman Singer, Marzio's Crucifix, Heart of Rome, Cecilia, Whosoever Shall Offend, Pietro Ghisleri, To Leeward, A Lady of Rome,* and *The White Sister.* The novels deal almost exclusively with the middle and higher classes of Rome, classes

of which most Americans know nothing at all, for, to quote from
the opening chapter of *To Leeward:*

There are two Romes. There is the Rome of the intelligent foreigner, consisting of excavations, monuments, tramways, hotels, typhoid
fever, incense, and wax candles; and there is the Rome within, a city
of antique customs, good and bad, a town full of aristocratic prejudices, of intrigues, of religion, of old-fashioned honor and new-fash-
ioned scandal, of happiness and unhappiness, of just people and
unjust.

It is this other half Rome, unknown to the casual tourist,
unknown to any not native born and Romanist in faith, that he
has shown us, as Howells attempted to show the social life of
Boston and New England, and as Cable sought to enter the heart
of Creole New Orleans. With what success? Those who know
most of Roman life have spoken with praise. He has given to
his aristocracy perhaps too much of charm, they say; too much
of inflexible will, it may be; too much of fire and fury; yet on
the whole he has been true to the complex life he has sought
to reproduce, truer, perhaps, than Howells has been to Boston
or Cable to New Orleans, for he has worked from the inside
as one native born, as one reared in the society he describes, even
to the detail of accepting its religious belief. One may well
believe it, for everywhere in the novels is the perfection of naturalness, the atmosphere of reality.

With his seven stories of American life, *An American Politician* and the others, he is less convincing. He wrote as a
foreigner, as an observer of the outward with no fullness of
sympathy, no depth of knowledge. He was European in viewpoint and in experience, and he knew better the European background—Germany as in *Greifenstein* and *The Cigarette-Maker's
Romance,* or England as in *The Tale of a Lonely Parish,* or even
Constantinople as in *Paul Patoff.*

He wins us first with his worldliness, his vast knowledge of
the surfaces of life in all lands. He is full of cosmopolitan
comparisons, wisdom from everywhere, modern instances from
Stamboul and Allahabad and Rome. To read him is like walking through foreign scenes with a fully informed guide, a mar
velous guide, indeed, a patrician, a polished man of the world.
Everywhere in his work an atmosphere of good breeding—

charming people of culture and wideness of experience: diplomats, artists, statesmen, noblemen, gentlemen of the world and ladies indeed. There is no coarseness, no dialect, no uncouth characters. We are in the world of wealth, of old-established institutions, of traditions and social laws that are inflexible. In the telling of the tale he has but a single purpose:

> We are not poets, because we can not be. We are not genuine playwriters for many reasons; chiefly, perhaps, because we are not clever enough, since a successful play is incomparably more lucrative than a successful novel. We are not preachers, and few of us would be admitted to the pulpit. We are not, as a class, teachers or professors, nor lawyers, nor men of business. We are nothing more than public amusers. Unless we choose we need not be anything less. Let us, then, accept our position cheerfully, and do the best we can to fulfil our mission, without attempting to dignify it with titles too imposing for it to bear, and without degrading it by bringing its productions down even a little way, from the lowest level of high comedy to the highest level of buffoonery.[5]

From this standpoint he has succeeded to the full. He has told his stories well; he holds his reader's interest to the end. Slight though his stories may often be in development, they are ingenious always in construction and they are cumulative in interest. He has undoubted dramatic power, sparkling dialogue, thrust and parry, whole novels like *Saracinesca*, for instance, that might be transferred to the stage with scarcely an alteration. His characters and episodes appeal to him always from the dramatic side. The novel, indeed as he defines it is a species of drama:

> It may fairly be claimed that humanity has, within the past hundred years, found the way of carrying a theater in its pocket; and so long as humanity remains what it is, it will delight in taking out its pocket-stage and watching the antics of the actors, who are so like itself and yet so much more interesting. Perhaps that is, after all, the best answer to the question, "What is a novel?" It is, or ought to be, a pocket-stage. Scenery, light, shade, the actors themselves, are made of words, and nothing but words, more or less cleverly put together. A play is good in proportion as it represents the more dramatic, passionate, romantic, or humorous sides of real life. A novel is excellent according to the degree in which it produces the illusions of a good play—but it must not be forgotten that the play is the thing, and that illusion is eminently necessary to success.[5]

[5] *The Novel: What It Is.* 22, 49.

Often he overdoes this dramatic element and becomes melodramatic; we lose the impression of real life and feel an atmosphere of staginess, that exaggeration of effect which thrills for a moment and then disgusts.

And right here comes the chief indictment against him: he works without deep emotion, without tenderness, without altruism, without the higher reaches of imagination. He has no social or moral purpose, as Howells had. He sees the body but not the soul, society rather than life in its deeper currents, a society marvelously complex in its requirements and its accouterments, its conventions and traditions, but he looks little below the superficial, the temporal, the merely worldly. He is inferior to Howells inasmuch as he lacks poetry, he lacks humor, he lacks heart. He is inferior to James and George Meredith inasmuch as he had no power of introspection and no distinctive style. He had no passion—he never becomes enthusiastic even about his native Italy; he had little love for nature —the city engrosses him, not trees and mountains and lakes. He writes of the human spectacle and is content if he bring amusement for the present moment.

He was, therefore, one more influence in the journalization of the novel. He wrote rapidly and easily, and his style is clear and natural, but it is also without distinction. His pictures are vividly drawn and his stories are exceedingly readable —journalistic excellences, but there is nothing of inspiration about them, no breath of genius, no touch of literature in the stricter sense of that word. Like every skilful journalistic writer, he has the power to visualize his scene, to paint characters with vividness, and to make essentials stand out. Notably was this true of his historical fiction. Characters like Philip II. and Eleanor, Queen of France, he can make real men and women that move and convince. He has created a marvelous gallery of characters, taking his forty-five novels together, complex and varied beyond that produced by any other American novelist, and there are surprisingly few repetitions. He stands undoubtedly as the most brilliant of the American writers of fiction, the most cosmopolitan, the most entertaining. His galaxy of Roman novels, especially the *Saracinesca* group, bids fair to outlive many novels that contain deeper studies of human life and that are more inspired products of literary art.

IV

The direct opposite of F. Marion Crawford, in literary belief, as in background and object, was Margaretta Wade Deland, who came into literary prominence at the close of the eighties. Unlike Crawford, she was a poet, a realist, a depicter of life within a narrow provincial area, and, moreover, a worker in the finer materials of life, the problems of the soul.

The essentials of her biography are few. She was born and reared at Manchester, a little Pennsylvania village, now swallowed up by the great manufacturing city of Allegheny; she went at sixteen to New York to study drawing and design at Cooper Institute; and after her graduation she became instructor in design at the Girls' Normal College, New York City. In 1880 she was married to Lorin F. Deland and removed to Boston, where she has since resided. In 1886 she issued her first book—a collection of poems entitled *An Old Garden,* and two years later *John Ward, Preacher,* a novel that attracted instant and widespread attention because of its likeness in theme to *Robert Elsmere,* then at the height of its enormous vogue. Since that time she has published four other major novels: *Sidney, Philip and His Wife, The Awakening of Helena Richie,* and *The Iron Woman,* and many short stories, notably the collections entitled *The Wisdom of Fools, Old Chester Tales,* and *Dr. Lavendar's People.*

By nature and early environment Mrs. Deland was serious and contemplative. The little Pennsylvania town, later to be immortalized as Old Chester, during her childhood was a place of traditions, a bit of antiquity amid the newness about it, of well-bred old English and Scotch and Irish families with deep religious prejudices and with narrow yet wholesome and kindly ideals. She was reared in a religious atmosphere—her father was a Presbyterian and her mother an Episcopalian, the combination so disastrous in *John Ward, Preacher.* She lived amid books, all of which she might read save only the novels, a prohibition that proved to be a good one, for when at last she was led to write fiction of her own, she went about it with no conventional preconceptions. It made for freshness, for originality, of concentration upon life rather than upon form and the tradition of the elders. It was an environment that cultivated the poet as well as the Puritan within her, the sensitiveness for

Nature, the deeps of love and life that were to find expression
in a note like this, recorded in her first volume:

> O distant Christ, the crowded, darkening years
> Drift slow between thy gracious face and me:
> My hungry heart leans back to look for thee,
> But finds the way set thick with doubts and fears.
>
> My groping hands would touch thy garment's hem,
> Would find some token thou art walking near;
> Instead, they clasp but empty darkness drear,
> And no diviner hands reach out to them.
>
> My straining eyes, O Christ, but long to mark
> A shadow of thy presence, dim and sweet,
> Or far-off light to guide my wandering feet,
> Or hope for hands prayer-beating 'gainst the dark.

It was, therefore, but natural that her work should be both
serious and ethical and that it should be touched with beauty.
In *John Ward, Preacher,* she took as her theme the revolt of a
soul against the infallibilities of a system of belief. It is not
necessarily a religious novel or yet a purpose novel. The primary *motif* of *Robert Elsmere* is theological and doctrinal discussion. It is religious polemic made attractive by being cast
into story form and as such it deserves the anathema of Crawford, but in Mrs. Deland's novel the human interest is para-
mount. Religion is the force that acts upon two lives, just as
jealousy might have been taken or misdirected love or any other
human dynamic, and the novel is the record of the reactions
under the stress.

So with all her novels. The theme is the destruction or the
redemption of a soul, the abasement or the rehabilitation of a
character through some immaterial force applied from within.
She deals with great ethical and sociological forces: heredity,
as in her novelette *The Hands of Esau;* divorce, as in *The Iron
Woman;* the compelling power of love, as in *Sidney.* Her
primary aim is not, as with Crawford and Harte, simply to
entertain; it is rather to expose the human soul to its own view,
to show it its limitations and its dangers, that the soul may be
purged through fear of what may be—the aim indeed of the
Greek drama. Her equipment for the work was complete. To
feminine tenderness and insight she added a depth of view and

an analysis that is masculine. She was a poet too, but a poet with the severity of form and the moving realism of the short story writer. Two of her novels, *The Awakening of Helena Richie* and *The Iron Woman*, have not been surpassed in construction and in moving power by any other writer of the period.

Her *Old Chester Tales* also, with their central figure Dr. Lavendar, have the elements that make for permanence. They are really without time or place. Old Chester undoubtedly is in western Pennsylvania, the author's native town, but it might be New England as well. The tales deal with universal types and with universal *motifs* with a broadness and a sympathy and a literary art that raises them into the realm of the rarer classics. From them emerges the figure of Dr. Lavendar to place beside even Adams and Primrose. Place is not dwelt upon; humanity is all. They are not so much stories as fragments of actual life touched with the magic of poetry and of ethic vision. From that worldly social area of life presented to us by such latter-day novelists as Crawford and Edith Wharton and Robert Chambers they are as far removed as is a fashionable Newport yacht, with its club-centered men and cigarette-smoking women, from the simple little hamlet among the hills.

V

During the closing years of the century there came into American literature, suddenly and unheralded, a group of young men, journalists for the most part, who for a time seemed to promise revolution. They brought in with a rush enthusiasm, vigor, vitality; they had no reverence for old forms or old ideals; they wrote with fierceness and cocksureness books like Garland's *Crumbling Idols* and Norris's *The Responsibilities of the Novelist*, which called shrilly for Truth, TRUTH: ''Is it not, in Heaven's name, essential that the people hear not a lie, but the Truth? If the novel were not one of the most important factors of life; if it were not the completest expression of our civilization; if its influence were not greater than all the pulpits, than all the newspapers between the oceans, it would not be so important that its message should be true.'' They would produce a new American literature, one stripped of prudishness and convention; they would go down among the

People and tell them the plain God's Truth as Zola defined Truth, for the People were hungry for it. "In the larger view, in the last analysis, the People pronounce the final judgment. The People, despised of the artist, hooted, caricatured, and vilified, are, after all, and in the main, the real seekers after Truth." The group was a passing phenomenon. Many of its members were dead before they had done more than outline their work: Wolcott Balestier and Stephen Crane at thirty, Frank Norris at thirty-two, Henry Harland and Harold Frederic in the early forties, and the others, like R. H. Davis, for instance, turned at length to historical romance and other conventional fields.

The impetus undoubtedly came from the enormous and sudden vogue of Kipling. Balestier was his brother-in-law and had collaborated with him in writing *The Naulahka*. Then he had written the novel *Benefits Forgot*, a work of remarkable promise, but remarkable only for its promise. The vigor and directness and picturing power of the young Kipling were qualities that appealed strongly to young men of journalistic training. Like him, they were cosmopolitans and had seen unusual areas of life. Crane had represented his paper in the Greco-Turkish War and in the Cuban campaign, Norris had been in the South African War, Richard Harding Davis had been at all the storm centers of his time, Frederic was the European correspondent of the New York *Times,* and Harland became at length editor of the London *Yellow Book.*

The genius of the group undoubtedly was Stephen Crane (1871–1900). He was frail of physique, neurotic, intense, full of a vibrant energy that drove him too fiercely. He was naturally lyrical, romantic, impulsively creative, but his training made him, as it made most of the group, a realist—a depressed realist after Zola. His earliest work was his best, *Maggie, a Girl of the Streets*, a grim and brutal picture of the darker strata of New York City—his most distinctive creation. But he had no patience, no time, for collecting material. He was too eager, too much under the dominance of moods, to investigate, and his later novel, *The Red Badge of Courage,* which purports to be a realistic story of army life in the Civil War, is based upon a kind of manufactured realism that is the product not of observation or of gathered data, but of an excessively active imagination. When he died, though he was but thirty, he had done his work. Despite his lyrical power and his undoubted imagination, his place is not large.

For Frank Norris (1870–1902) more may be said, though undoubtedly he has been judged by his contemporaries more by what he dreamed or doing and what, perhaps, he might have done had he lived than by his actual accomplishment. He had had unusual training for the epic task he set himself. He had been born in Chicago and had spent there the first fifteen years of his life, he had been educated in the San Francisco high school, at the University of California, and at Harvard, then for a year or two he had studied art in Paris. Later he was war correspondent of the San Francisco *Chronicle,* then editor of the San Francisco *Wave,* then special war correspondent for *McClure's Magazine* during the Spanish War.

When he began to write fiction, and he began early, he was an ardent disciple of Zola, a realist of the latter-day type, a teller of the Truth as Zola conceived of the Truth. "Mere literature" was a thing outworn, graces of style and gentleness of theme belonged to the effeminate past. A masculine age had come to which nothing was common or unclean provided it were but the Truth. Like Crane, he was eager, excited, dominated by his theme until it became his whole life. He could work only in major key, in *fortissimo,* with themes continent-wide presented with the Kipling vigor and swing.

In his earlier work, *Vandover and the Brute, McTeague,* and the like, he swung to the extreme of his theory. To tell the truth was to tell with microscopic detail the repulsive things of physical life. There are stories of his that reek with foul odors and jangle repulsively upon the eye and the ear. The short fiction "A Man's Woman" is an advance even upon Zola. It is Truth, but it is the truth about the processes of the sewer and the physiological facts about starvation:

The tent was full of foul smells: the smell of drugs and of moldy gunpowder, the smell of dirty rags, of unwashed bodies, the smell of stale smoke, of scorching sealskin, of soaked and rotting canvas that exhaled from the tent cover—every smell but that of food.

McTeague is a brutal book: it gets hold of one's imagination and haunts it like an odor from a morgue. So with certain scenes from *Vandover and the Brute.* One sees for weeks the

ghastly face of that drowning Jew who, after the wreck of the
steamer, was beaten off again and again until his mashed fingers
could no longer gain a hold. True to life it undoubtedly is, but
to what end?

Norris's master work was to be his trilogy, the epic of the
wheat, the allegory of financial and industrial America. He explained his purpose in the preface to *The Pit:*

> These novels, while forming a series, will be in no way connected
> with each other save by their relation to (1) the production, (2) the
> distribution, (3) the consumption of American wheat. When com-
> plete they will form the story of a crop of wheat from the time of
> its sowing as seed in California to the time of its consumption as
> bread in a village of Western Europe.
>
> The first novel, *The Octopus,* deals with the war between the wheat
> grower and the Railroad Trust; the second, *The Pit,* is the fictitious
> narrative of a "deal" in the Chicago wheat pit; while the third, *The
> Wolf,* will probably have for its pivotal episode the relieving of a
> famine in an old world community.

He lived to complete only the first two, and it is upon these
two that his place as a novelist must depend. They represent
his maturer work, his final manner, and they undoubtedly show
what would have been his product had he been spared to complete his work.

The two books impress one first with their vastness of theme.
The whole continent seems to be in them. They have an un-
tamed power, an elemental quality, an unconfined sweep that is
Russian in its quality. They are epics, epics of a new continent
with its untold richness in corn and wheat, its enmeshing railroads, its teeming cities of the plain, its restless human types—
new birth of our new soil. The excitement and the enthusiasm
of the novelist flow from every page. To read long is to be
filled with the trembling eagerness of the wheat pit and the
railroad yard. The style is headlong, excited, illuminated hotly
with Hugo-like adjectives. Through it all runs a symbolism
that at times takes full control. The railroad dominates *The
Octopus,* the wheat *The Pit* as fully as the hemp dominates
Allen's *Reign of Law.* The books are allegories. The Western
farmer is in the grip of an octopus-like monster, the railroad,
that is strangling him. The ghastly horror of the locomotive
that plows at full speed through a flock of sheep is symbolic of
his helplessness.

To the right and left, all the width of the right of way, the little bodies had been flung; backs were snapped against the fence-posts; brains knocked out. Caught in the barbs of the wire, wedged in, the bodies hung suspended. Under foot it was terrible; the black blood, winking in the starlight, seeped down into the clay between the ties with a long sucking murmur. . . . Abruptly, Presley saw again in his imagination the galloping monster, the terror of steel and steam, with its single eye, cyclopean, red, shooting from horizon to horizon; but saw it now as the symbol of a vast power, huge, terrible, flinging the echo of its thunder over all the reaches of the valley, leaving blood and destruction in its path; the leviathan, with tentacles of steel clutching into the soil, the soulless Force, the iron-hearted Power, the Monster, the Colossus, the Octopus.

Garland in such pictures as "Under the Lion's Paw" tends to arouse his reader to mutiny, to the cry "This thing must stop!" Norris fills him with shuddering horror and leaves him unnerved.

Tremendous energy the novels undoubtedly have and truth too, so far as it goes. They have imaginative power of no inferior type and an ardor that is contagious. It was worth while to have written them: they picture for all time a unique phase of American life, but it is no great loss to our literature that the two were not expanded into a long series. In the higher sense of the word they are not literature; they are remarkably well done newspaper "stories." Like most of the work of his group of writers, they are journalistic in pitch and in intent: stirring narratives, picturesque presentings of unusual material, timely studies in dynamic style. But literary art is founded upon restraint, reserve, poise. These stories lack finish, concentration, and even, at times, good taste. Everywhere full organ, everywhere tenseness, everywhere excitement. A terrible directness there is, but it tends no whither and it comes to no terminus of conclusion.

Norris unquestionably lacked knowledge of many of the most fundamental areas of human life. He was too insistently modern. Like the mere journalist, he was obsessed with but a single thought: the value of the present moment. He lacked a sense of the past, personal background, inner life, power to weigh and balance and compare, and, lacking these, he lacked the elements that make for the literature of permanence.

Henry Harland's (1861–1905) earliest work, *As It Was Written* (1885), *Mrs. Peixada,* and *The Yoke of the Thora* (1887), written under the pen name "Sidney Luska," presented certain phases of Jewish life and character in New York with a grim power that seemed promising, but his later work was decadent. Harold Frederic was a more substantial figure. A typical American, self-made and self-educated, climbing by rapid stages from the positions of farm hand, photographer, and proof-reader to the editorship of influential papers like the Albany *Journal,* at twenty-eight he was the European representative of the New York *Times* and an international correspondent of rare power. Novel-writing he took up as a recreation. His earliest work, which appeared in *Scribner's Magazine, Seth's Brother's Wife* (1887), was a novel of New York farm life, Garland-like in its depressing realism. Later stories like *In the Valley* and *The Copperhead* dealt with a background of the Civil War. His greatest success came with *The Damnation of Theron Ware,* published in England with the title *Illumination,* a remarkable book especially in its earlier chapters, full of vigor and truth. Undoubtedly he possessed the rare gift of story-telling, and had he, like Crawford, devoted himself wholly to the art, he might have done work to compare with any other written during the period. But he was a journalist with newspaper standards, he worked in haste, he lacked repose and the sense of values, and as a result a republication of his novels has not been called for. He is to be ranked with Crane and Norris as a meteor of brilliance rather than a fixed light.

VI

The new realism was short lived. Even while its propaganda like *Crumbling Idols* and *The Responsibilities of the Novelist* were spreading the news that Walter Scott was dead and that the god of things as they are had come in his power, a new romantic period already had begun. Maurice Thompson, one of the most clear-eyed critics of the period, wrote in May, 1900:

Just how deep and powerful the present distinct movement toward a romantic revival may be no one can tell. Many facts, however, point to a veering of popular interest from the fiction of character analysis and social problems to the historical novel and the romance of heroic adventure. We have had a period of intense, not to say morbid, introversion directed mainly upon diseases of the social, domestic, political, and religious life of the world. It may be that, like all other currents of interest when turned upon insoluble problems, this rush of inquiry, this strain of exploitation, has about run its course. . . . Great commercial interest seems to be turned or turning from the world of commonplace life and the story of the analysis of crime and filth to the historical romance, the story of heroism, and the tale of adventure. People seem to be interested as never before in the interpretation of history. It may be that signs in the air of great world changes have set all minds more or less to feeling out for precedents and examples by which to measure the future's probabilities.[6]

The causes of this later wave of romanticism, a wave that was wider than America, have been variously estimated. Harold Frederic suggested Blackmore as the possible fountain head. "Was it *Lorna Doone*, I wonder, that changed the drift in historical fiction? The book, after it was once introduced to public attention by that comic accident which no one can blame Mr. Blackmore for grinding his teeth over, achieved, as it deserved, one of the great successes of our time—and great successes set men thinking." [7] Paul Leicester Ford, himself an historian and a notable producer of historical romance, was inclined to another explanation: "At the present moment [1897] there seems a revival of interest in American history, and the novelist has been quickly responsive to it." [8] The English critic E. A. Bennett offered still another solution: "America is a land of crazes. In other words, it is simple: no derision is implied. . . . And America is also a land of sentimentalism. It is this deep-seated quality which, perhaps, accounts for the vogue of history in American fiction. The themes of the historical novel are so remote, ideas about them exist so nebulously in the mind, that a writer may safely use the most bare-faced distortions to pamper the fancy without offending that natural and racial shrewdness which would bestir itself if a means of verification were at hand. The extraordinary notion still obtains that human nature was different 'in those days'; that the good old times were, somehow, 'pretty,' and governed by fates poetically just." [9]

Ford undoubtedly was right in assigning the immediate outburst at the close of the century to a new interest in American

6 The *Independent*, 52:1182.
7 The *Bookman*, 8:330.
8 The *Atlantic*, 80:720.
9 E. A. Bennett, *Fame and Fiction*, page 163.

history. The war with Spain brought about a burst of patriotism and of martial feeling that made the swashbuckling romance and the episode from the American Revolution seem peculiarly appropriate. But the war was by no means the only cause. The reaction had come earlier, a reaction from the excess of reality that had come with the eighties. The influence of Stevenson must not be overlooked, Stevenson who, type of his age, had sickened early of the realistic, the analytic, the problematic.

"I do desire a book of adventure," Stevenson had written to Henley as early as 1884, "a romance—and no man will get or write me one. Dumas I have read and re-read too often; Scott, too, and I am short. I want to hear swords clash. I want a book to begin in a good way; a book, I guess, like *Treasure Island*. . . . Oh, my sighings after romance, or even Skeltery, and O! the weary age which will produce me neither!

" 'CHAPTER I

" 'The night was damp and cloudy, the ways foul. The single horseman, cloaked and booted, who pursued his way across Willesden Common, had not met a traveler, when the sound of wheels. . . .'

" 'CHAPTER II

" ' "Yes, sir," said the old pilot, "she must have dropped into the bay a little afore dawn. A queer craft she looks."

" ' "She shows no colors," returned the young gentleman, musingly.

" ' "They're a-lowering of a quarter-boat, Mr. Mark," resumed the old salt. "We shall soon know more of her."

" ' "Aye," replied the young gentleman called Mark, "and here, Mr. Seadrift, comes your sweet daughter Nancy tripping down the cliff."

" ' "God bless her kind heart, sir," ejaculated old Seadrift.' "

Be the cause what it may, for a time historical romance was the dominant literary form in America. In 1902, Bliss Perry, editor of the *Atlantic,* could write of "the present passion for historical novels." To what extent they were a passion may be learned from the records of publishers. By the summer of 1901, Ford's *Janice Meredith* had sold 275,000 copies, Mary Johnston's *To Have and to Hold,* 285,000, and Churchill's *The Crisis,* 320,000, and his *Richard Carvel,* 420,000. [10] One might give equally large figures for such favorites as Charles Major's *When Knighthood Was in Flower,* Tarkington's *Monsieur Beaucaire,* Mitchell's *Hugh Wynne, Free Quaker,* Thompson's

[10] Halsey, *Our Literary Deluge,* page 24.

Alice of Old Vincennes, and very many others, foreign as well as American.

The novels fall into two classes: those in which the historical element is made emphatic and those which are pure romances. Of the former class Paul Leicester Ford's *Janice Meredith* is, perhaps, the best type; of the latter, Mitchell's *Hugh Wynne.* Ford was first of all a historian, a bibliographer, a tireless delver among historical sources. He had been educated in his father's library, which contained the finest collection of Americana in the world, and at twelve we find him publishing on his own press a genealogy of Webster of his own compilation. His later bibliographical and historical work centered about the American Revolution. When he turned to fiction it was as a historian, a specialist who would exploit real historical characters and real areas of American life. *The Honorable Peter Stirling* was a study of ward politics with the young Grover Cleveland as the central figure. It was an accurate picture, vigorous and truthful, and even though a fiction it is a valuable historical document. So it was with *Janice Meredith,* a historian's daydream over his Americana. It presents an accurate picture of the social conditions of its time. Many of its characters are revolutionary leaders: Washington is a central figure—"The true George Washington," presented with all his failings as well as with all his excellences.

It was natural that Ford should make much of the material that he knew so thoroughly: he brought it in sometimes for its own sake rather than for the sake of the story. Undoubtedly he falsified history by making his real personages, like Washington and Franklin, take part in conversations that never occurred and do things that strictly never were done, but it is equally true that he has given us the best conception that is now possible of how it must have felt to live in the days of the Revolution. His chief excellences were his vigor and vivacity, and his Norris-like mastery of details. He was a realist enamoured of truth who extended his realism into the domain of romance. His faults all centered about his undoubted deficiency in literary art: he lacked constructive power and distinction of style. His stories are the diversions of a professional historian, brilliant but without promise of permanence.

Typical of the second variety of historical romance is the work

of Silas Weir Mitchell, poet, romancer, artist, and historian.
Dr. Mitchell was of Philadelphia as Dr. Holmes was of Boston,
and like Dr. Holmes he gave his most vigorous years completely
to his profession. He was fifty-three and one of the leading
world specialists on nervous diseases when he wrote his first
full novel, *In War Time*. His own explanation, given in later
years to a gathering of University of Pennsylvania men, has
often been quoted:

When success in my profession gave me the freedom of long summer
holidays, the despotism of my habits of work would have made entire
idleness mere *ennui*. I turned to what, except for stern need, would
have been my lifelong work from youth—literature—bored by idleness,
wrote my first novel.

The confession in the latter sentence is significant. Poetry
all his life was to him an exalted thing, as it was, indeed, to
Stoddard and the other poets of beauty. In later years he published many volumes of it and contributed it to the magazines,
but never for money. It explains much in his work. No other
novelist of the period has so filled his fiction with quoted lyrics
and with lyrical prose. It is here that he differs from writers
like Ford and Norris: he would produce literature.

His list of work is a varied one. His first long novel and
also his last dealt with the Civil War, in which he had served
three years as a surgeon. Then, like Dr. Holmes, he wrote
pathological studies on which he brought to bear his vast medical knowledge, novels like *Dr. North and His Friends* and *Constance Trescott;* he wrote brilliant tales of French life, like *The
Adventures of François,* Dr. Mitchell's favorite among his
novels, and *A Diplomatic Adventure;* he wrote idyllic studies
of Nature like *When All the Woods Are Green,* and *Far in the
Forest,* and, best of all, the historical romances *Hugh Wynne,
Free Quaker,* and *The Red City.*

These novels more than any others written during the period
are products of an exact and extensive knowledge of the materials of which they are woven. We feel at every point that
we are in the hands of an expert, the ablest neurologist of his
generation, who has seen intimately vast areas of life of which
the average reader knows nothing. His analysis of a character
has the exactness of a clinic and he adds to it, moreover, an

imaginative power that makes us see as well as know and feel.
He is skilful in characterization. "Character," he once wrote,
"is best delineated by occasional broad touches, without much
explanatory comment, without excess of minute description. If
I fail to characterize, I fail in novel writing." He has not
failed. Octavia Blake in the novel *Roland Blake* is drawn with
peculiar skill; so is Lucretia Hunter in *Circumstance,* so is Constance Trescott, that study of over-devotion. Always is he best
in his studies of femininity, doubtless because women had played
so large a part in his medical practice.

With few exceptions his characters are from the higher
classes, "gentlefolk," he has called them in his novel *Dr. North,*
and he has made them alive, as Howells was unable to do, and
even James. He has discussed the point himself: "Nor can I
tell why some men can not create gentlefolk. It is not knowledge, nor is it the being in or of their world that gives this
power. Thackeray had it; so had Trollope; Dickens never; nor,
in my mind, was George Eliot always happy in this respect;
and of the living I shall say nothing." [11] We feel this quality
most strongly in his historical novels. He knew intimately his
background, Old Philadelphia with its exclusive aristocracy,
and he has been able to transport his reader into the very atmosphere of old Second Street, in the days when it contained the
most distinctive social set in America. He was a part of it;
he wrote as if he were writing his own family history, lovingly,
reverently. He was writing romance, but he was writing it as
one who is on sacred historical ground where error of fact or of
inference is unpardonable. He has himself outlined the work
of the historical romancer:

Suppose I have a story to tell and wish to evolve character amid
the scenery and events of an historical episode. Suppose, for instance, the story to lie largely in a great city. For years I must study
the topography, dress, manners, and family histories; must be able in
mind to visit this or that house; know where to call, whom I shall see,
the hours of meals, the diet, games, etc. I must know what people
say on meeting and parting. Then I must read letters, diaries, and so
on, to get the speech forms and to enable me, if it be autobiography,
to command the written style of the day. Most men who write thus
of another time try to give the effect of actuality by an excessive use
of archaic forms. Only enough should be used to keep from time
to time some touch of this past, and not so much as to distract inces-

santly by needless reminders. It is an art, and, like all good art effects, it escapes complete analysis.

Then as to the use of historical characters. These must naturally
influence the fate of your puppets; they must never be themselves the
most prominent personages of your story.[11]

He presents his material with skill: he is a story-teller; his
plots move strongly and always by means not of explanations
but of the self-development of his characters. Even his most
minor figures form a distinct part of the movement. His style
has more of distinction than has any other of the later romancers. He brought to his work the older ideals of literary
form and expression, and he wrought not with the haste of the
journalist and special correspondent, but with the leisure of
the deliberate man of letters. Without question he is as large
a figure in his period as Dr. Holmes was in his, and there are
those who would rank him as the greater of the two. That he
has not been given a more commanding place is due undoubtedly
to his great fame as a medical expert. The physician has over-
shadowed the author.

VII

The enormous quantity and richness of the fiction of the
period make impossible extended criticism of any save those
who were leaders or innovators. Many did most excellent work,
work indeed in some cases that seems to point to permanence,
yet since they brought nothing new either in material or in
method we need not dwell long upon them.

No type of fiction, for instance, was more abundant all
through the period than that which we have called the E. P.
Roe type, and the most voluminous producer of it undoubtedly
was Captain, later General, Charles King, who created no fewer
than fifty-five novels of the half-sensational, half-sentimental
type which we associate with the name of Roe. With his wide
knowledge of army life, especially as lived in the frontier camps
of the West after the Civil War, he was able to give his work
a verisimilitude that added greatly to their popularity. The
love story was skilfully blended with what seemed to be real
history. The frontier stories of Mary Hallock Foote, wife of
a civil engineer whose work called him into the mining camps

11 *Dr. North and His Friends.* Chapter 16.

of Colorado and Idaho, have the same characteristics. Their
author, a clever illustrator, was able to extend her art to her
descriptions of the primitive regions and savage humanity of
the frontier, and for a time she was compared even with Bret
Harte. But not for long. Her books, save for their novelty
of setting, have no characteristics that are not conventional.
Better is the work of Clara Louise Burnham. There is in her
fiction more of imaginative power and more command of the
subtleties of style, but even her best efforts fall far short of
distinction.

Of the romancers of the period the leader for a time unquestionably was Julian Hawthorne, only son of the greatest of
American romancers. In his earlier days he devoted himself
to themes worthy of the Hawthorne name and treated them in
what fairly may be called the Hawthorne manner. His novels,
like *Bressant* and *Archibald Malmaison,* were hailed everywhere
as remarkably promising work and there were many who pre-
dicted for him a place second only to his father's. But the man
lacked seriousness, conscience, depth of life, knowledge of the
human heart. After a short period of worthy endeavor he
turned to the sensational and the trivial, and became a yellow
journalist. No literary career seemingly so promising has ever
failed more dismally.

Stronger romancers by far have been Blanche Willis Howard,
Frederick J. Stimson, and Arthur Sherburne Hardy. Few
American women have been more brilliant than Miss Howard.
Her *One Summer* has a sprightliness and a humor about it that
are perennial, and her Breton romance *Guenn* is among the
greatest romances of the period in either England or America.
The spirit of true romance breathes from it; and it came alive
from its creator's heart and life. So far does it surpass all her
other work that she is rated more and more now as a single-
work artist. She passed her last years away from America in
Stuttgart, where her husband, Herr von Teuffel, was acting as
court physician to the king of Würtemberg. Hardy also was a
romancer, a stylist of the French type, brilliant, finished. Few
have ever brought to fiction a mind more keenly alert and more
analytical. He was a mathematician of note, a writer of
treatises on least squares and quaternions. · But he was a poet
as well and a romancer. His *But yet a Woman* has an atmos-

phere about it that is rarely found in literature in English. His *Passe Rose* is the most idealistic of all the historical romances: it moves like a prose poem. Stimson too had artistic imagination, grace of style of the old type joined to the freshness and vigor of the new period. It is to be regretted that he chose to devote himself to the law and write legal treatises that are everywhere recognized as authoritative rather than to do highly distinctive work in the more creative field of prose romance. None of these writers may be said to have added anything really new to the province in which they worked and so may be dismissed with a brief comment. They worked in old material with old methods and largely with old ideals, and though they worked often with surpassing skill, they were followers rather than leaders.

Several novels made much stir in the day of their first appearance, Bellamy's *Looking Backward,* for instance, John Hay's *The Bread-Winners* (1884), and Fuller's *The Cliff Dwellers,* that picture of Chicago life that for a time was thought to be as promising as Frank Norris's realistic work. Robert Grant's humorous and sprightly studies of society and life were also at various times much discussed, but all of them are seen now to have been written for their own generation alone. With every decade almost there comes a newness that for a time is supposed to put into eclipse even the fixed stars. A quarter of a century, however, tells the story. The Norwegian scholar and poet and novelist Boyesen, who did what Howells really did not do, take Tolstoy as his master, was thought for two decades to be of highest rank, but to-day his work, save for certain sections of his critical studies, is no longer read.

Even F. Hopkinson Smith is too near just at present for us to prophesy with confidence, yet it is hard to believe that his Colonel Carter is to be forgotten, and there are other parts of his work, like *Tom Grogan* and *Caleb West,* books that centered about his profession of lighthouse architect, that seem now like permanent additions to American fiction. There was a breeziness about his style, a cosmopolitanism, a sense of knowledge and authority that is most convincing. Some of his short stories, like those for instance in *At Close Range*—"A Night Out," to be still more specific—have a picturing power, a perfect naturalness, an accuracy of diction, that mark them as

triumphs of realism in its best sense. Like Dr. Mitchell, he came
late to literature, but when he did come he came strongly, laden
with a wealth of materials, and he has left behind him a handful at least of novels and studies that bid fair to endure long.

VIII

Of the younger group of novelists, those writers born in the
sixties and early seventies and publishing their first novels during the first decade of the new century, we shall say little. The
new spirit of nationality that came in the seventies did not furnish the impulse that produced the work of this second generation of the period. It is a school of novelists distinct and by
itself. We may only call the roll of its leaders, arranging it,
perhaps, in the order of seniority: Gertrude Franklin Ather-
ton (1859——), Bliss Perry (1860——), Owen Wister
(1860——), John Fox, Jr. (1863——), Holman F. Day
(1865——), Robert W. Chambers (1865——), Meredith
Nicholson (1866——), David Graham Philips (1867–1911),
Robert Herrick (1868——), Newton Booth Tarkington
(1869——), Mary Johnston (1870——), Edith Wharton (——),
Alice Hegan Rice (1870——), Winston Churchill (1871——),
Stewart Edward White (1873——), Ellen Anderson Glasgow
(1874——), Jack London (1876–1916). The earlier work of
some of these writers falls under classifications which we have
already discussed, as for instance Churchill's *Richard Carvel,*
Mary Johnston's *Prisoners of Hope,* Chambers's *Cardigan,* and
Wister's *The Virginian.* Of the great mass of the fiction of the
group, however, and of a still younger group we shall say nothing. It was not inspired by the impulse that in the sixties and
the seventies produced the National Period.

BIBLIOGRAPHY

JOSIAH GILBERT HOLLAND. (1819–1881.) *History of Western Massa-
chusetts,* 1855; *The Bay Path,* 1857; *Bitter-Sweet* [a poem], 1858; *Let-
ters to Young People,* 1858; *Gold Foil,* 1859; *Miss Gilbert's Career,* 1860;
Lessons in Life, 1861; *Letter to the Joneses,* 1863; *Plain Talks on Familiar
Subjects,* 1865; *Life of Lincoln,* 1865; *Kathrina* [a poem], 1867; *The
Marble Prophecy,* 1872; *Arthur Bonnicastle,* 1873; *Garnered Sheaves,* 1873;
Mistress of the Manse, 1874; *Seven Oaks,* 1875; *Nicholas Minturn,* 1877;
Every-Day Topics (two series), 1876, 1882.
    EDWARD PAYSON ROE. (1838–1888.) *Barriers Burned Away,* 1872;

What Can She Do? 1873; *The Opening of a Chestnut Burr*, 1874; *From Jest to Earnest*, 1875; *Near to Nature's Heart*, 1876; *A Knight of the Nineteenth Century*, 1877; *A Face Illumined*, 1878; *A Day of Fate*, 1880; *Without a Home*, 1881; *His Somber Rivals*, 1883; *An Unexpected Result*, 1883; *Nature's Serial Story*, 1884; *A Young Girl's Wooing*, 1884; *Driven Back to Eden*, 1885; *An Original Belle*, 1885; *He Fell in Love with His Wife*, 1886; *The Earth Trembled*, 1887; *Found, yet Lost*, 1888; *Miss Lou*, 1888; *E. P. Roe: Reminiscences of His Life*. By his sister, Mary A. Roe, 1899.

FRANCIS ELIZA HODGSON BURNETT. (1849——.) *That Lass o' Lowrie's*, 1877; *Surly Tim*, 1877; *Haworth's*, 1879; *Louisiana*, 1880; *A Fair Barbarian*, 1881; *Through One Administration*, 1883; *Little Lord Fauntleroy*, 1886; *Editha's Burglar*, 1888; *Sara Crewe*, 1888; *The Pretty Sister of José*, 1889; *Little Saint Elizabeth*, 1890; *Giovanni and the Other*, 1892; *The One I Knew Best of All* [autobiography], 1893; *Two Little Pilgrims' Progress*, 1895; *A Lady of Quality*, 1896; *His Grace of Osmonde*, 1897; *In Connection with the De-Willoughby Claim*, 1899; *The Making of a Marchioness*, 1901; *The Methods of Lady Walderhurst*, 1902; *In the Closed Room*, 1904; *A Little Princess: Being the Whole Story of Sara Crewe*, 1905; *Dawn of a To-morrow*, 1906; *Earlier Stories*, first and second series, 1906; *Queen Silver-Bell*, 1906; *Racketty-Packetty House*, 1906; *The Shuttle*, 1907; *Cozy Lion*, 1907; *Good Wolf*, 1908; *Spring Cleaning; as Told by Queen Crosspatch*, 1908; *Land of the Blue Flower*, 1909; *Baby Crusoe and His Man Saturday*, 1909; *Secret Garden*, 1911; *My Robin*, 1912; *T. Tembaron*, 1913.

FRANCIS MARION CRAWFORD. (1854–1909.) *Mr. Isaacs*, 1882; *Doctor Claudius*, 1883; *A Roman Singer*, *To Leeward*, and *An American Politician*, 1884; *Zoroaster*, 1885; *A Tale of a Lonely Parish*, 1886; *Marzio's Crucifix*, *Paul Patoff*, and *Saracinesca*, 1887; *With the Immortals*, 1888; *Greifenstein* and *Sant' Ilario*, 1889; *The Cigarette-maker's Romance*, 1890; *Kahled* and *The Witch of Prague*, 1891; *The Three Fates*, *The Children of the King*, and *Don Orsino*, 1892; *Marion Darche*, *Pietro Ghisleri*, and *The Novel: What It Is*, 1893; *Katherine Lauderdale*, *Love in Idleness*, *The Ralstons*, *Casa Braccio*, and *Adam Johnstone's Son*, 1894; *Taquisara*, and *Corleone*, 1896; *Ave Roma Immortalis*, 1898; *Via Crucis*, 1899; *In the Palace of the King*, *Southern Italy and Sicily*, and *The Rulers of the South*, 1900; *Marietta, a Maid of Venice*, 1901; *Cecilia, A Story of Modern Rome*, 1902; *The Heart of Rome*, and *Man Overboard*, 1903; *Whosoever Shall Offend*, 1904; *Fair Margaret and Salve Venetia*, 1905; *A Lady of Rome*, 1906; *Arethusa and The Little City of Hope*, 1907; *The Primadonna* and *The Diva's Ruby*, 1908; *The White Sister*, 1909.

MARGARETTA WADE DELAND. (1857——.) *The Old Garden and Other Verses*, 1886; *John Ward, Preacher*, 1888; *Florida Days*, 1889; *Sidney*, 1890; *Story of a Child*, 1892; *Mr. Tommy Dove, and Other Stories*, 1893; *Philip and His Wife*, 1894; *The Wisdom of Fools*, 1897; *Old Chester Tales*, 1898; *Dr. Lavendar's People*, 1903; *The Common Way*, 1904; *The Awakening of Helena Ritchie*, 1906; *An Encore*, 1907; *R. J. Mother and Some Other People*, 1908; *Where the Laborers Are Few*, 1909; *The Way of Peace*, 1910;

The Iron Woman, 1911; *The Voice*, 1912; *Partners*, 1913; *The Hands of Esau*, 1914.

STEPHEN CRANE. (1871–1900.) *The Black Riders and Other Lines*, 1895; *The Red Badge of Courage: Episode of the American Civil War*, 1895; *Maggie: a Girl of the Streets*, 1896; *George's Mother*, 1896; *The Little Regiment, and Other Episodes of the American Civil War*, 1896; *The Third Violet*, 1897; *The Open Boat, and Other Tales of Adventure*, 1898; *The Monster and Other Stories*, 1899; *Active Service: a Novel*, 1899; *War Is Kind*, 1899; *Whilomville Stories*, 1900; *Great Battles of the World*, 1900; *Wounds in the Rain: War Stories*, 1900.

FRANK NORRIS. (1870–1902.) *Moran of "The Lady Letty,"* 1898; *Blix*, 1899; *McTeague: a Story of San Francisco*, 1899; *A Man's Woman*, 1900; *The Octopus: a Story of California*, 1901; *The Pit: a Story of Chicago*, 1902; *A Deal in Wheat, and Other Stories*, 1903; Complete Works. Golden Gate Edition. Seven Volumes, 1903; *Responsibilities of the Novelist and Other Literary Essays*, 1903; *Vandover and the Brute*.

HAROLD FREDERIC. (1856–1898.) *Seth's Brother's Wife: a Study of Life in the Greater New York*, 1887; *The Lawton Girl*, 1890; *In the Valley*, 1891; *Young Emperor William II. of Germany*, 1891; *The New Exodus: a Study of Israel in Russia*, 1892; *The Return of O'Mahony*, 1892; *The Copperhead*, 1893; *Marsena, and Other Stories of the War Time*, 1894; *Mrs. Albert Grundy: Observations in Philistia*, 1896; *The Damnation of Theron Ware*, 1896; *March Hares*, 1896; *The Deserter and Other Stories: a Book of Two Wars*, 1898; *Gloria Mundi*, 1899; *The Market-Place*, 1899.

PAUL LEICESTER FORD. (1865–1902.) *Who Was the Mother of Franklin's Son?* 1889; *The Honorable Peter Stirling and What People Thought of Him*, 1894; *The True George Washington*, 1896; *The Great K. and A. Robbery*, 1897; *The Story of an Untold Love*, 1897; *Tattle Tales of Cupid*, 1898; *Janice Meredith: a Story of the American Revolution*, 1899; *The Many-sided Franklin*, 1899; *Wanted: a Match-maker*, 1900; *A House Party*, 1901; *Wanted: a Chaperon*, 1902; *A Checked Love Affair; and the Cortelyou Feud*, 1903; *Love Finds a Way*, 1904; *Thomas Jefferson*, 1904. His bibliographies and edited work not listed.

SILAS WEIR MITCHELL. (1829–1914.) *Hephzibah Guiness*, 1880; *Thee and You*, 1880; *A Draft on the Bank of Spain*, 1880; *In War Time*, 1882; *The Hill of Stones and Other Poems*, 1883; *Roland Blake*, 1886; *Far in the Forest*, 1889; *The Cup of Youth and Other Poems*, 1889; *The Psalm of Death and Other Poems*, 1890; *Characteristics*, 1892; *Francis Blake: a Tragedy of the Sea*, 1892; *The Mother and Other Poems*, 1892; *Mr. Kris Kringle: a Christmas Tale*, 1893; *Philip Vernon: a Tale in Prose and Verse*, 1895; *When All the Woods Are Green: a Novel*, 1894; *Madeira's Party*, 1895; *Hugh Wynne, Free Quaker*, 1897; *Adventures of Francois, Foundling, Thief, Juggler, and Fencing Master, During the French Revolution*, 1898; *Autobiography of a Quack*, 1900; *Dr. North and His Friends*, 1900; *The Wager and Other Poems*, 1900; *Circumstance*, 1901; *A Comedy of Conscience*, 1903; *Little Stories*, 1903; *New Samaria* and *The Summer of St. Martin*, 1904; *The Youth of Washington*, 1904; *Constance Trescott*, 1905; *A Diplomatic Adventure*, 1905; *The Red City: a Novel of the Second*

Administration of President Washington, 1907; *John Sherwood, Ironmaster,* 1910; *The Guillotine Club and Other Stories,* 1910; *Westways,* 1913. His many medical works not listed.

CHARLES KING. (1844———.) *The Colonel's Daughter; or, Winning His Spurs,* 1883; *Marion's Faith,* 1886; *The Deserter,* 1887; *From the Ranks,* 1887; *A War-Time Wooing,* 1888; *Between the Lines,* 1889; *Sunset Pass,* 1889; *Laramie; or, the Queen of Bedlam: a Story of the Sioux War of 1876,* 1889; *Starlight Ranch, and Other Stories of Army Life on the Frontier,* 1890; *The Colonel's Christmas Dinner,* 1890; *Campaigning with Crook and Stories of Army Life,* 1890; *Trials of a Staff Officer,* 1891; *Two Soldiers,* 1891; *Dunraven Ranch,* 1891; *Captain Blake,* 1891; *Foes in Ambush,* 1893; *A Soldier's Secret: a Story of the Sioux War of 1890,* 1893; *Waring's Peril,* 1894; *Initial Experience and Other Stories,* 1894; *Cadet Days: a Story of West Point,* 1894; *Under Fire,* 1895; *Story of Fort Frayne,* 1895; *Rancho del Muerlo,* 1895; *Captain Close,* 1895; *Sergeant Croesus,* 1895; *An Army Wife,* 1896; *A Garrison Tangle,* 1896; *A Tame Surrender: a Story of the Chicago Strike,* 1896; *Trooper Ross,* 1896; *Trumpeter Fred: a Story of the Plains,* 1896; *Warrior Gap: a Story of the Sioux Outbreak of 1868,* 1897; *Ray's Recruit,* 1898; *The General's Double: a Story of the Army of the Potomac,* 1898; *A Wounded Name,* 1898; *Trooper Galahad,* 1899; *From School to Battlefield,* 1899; *In Spite of Foes,* 1901; *From the Ranks,* 1901; *Norman Holt: a Story of the Army of the Cumberland,* 1901; *Ray's Daughter: a Story of Manila,* 1901; *Conquering Corps Badge and Other Stories of the Philippines,* 1902; *The Iron Brigade,* 1902; *Way Out West,* 1902; *An Apache Princess,* 1903; *A Daughter of the Sioux,* 1903; *Comrades in Arms,* 1904; *A Knight of Columbia,* 1904; *A Medal of Honor,* 1905; *Famous and Decisive Battles of the World,* 1905; *A Soldier's Trial: an Episode of the Canteen Crusade,* 1905; *Farther Story of Lieutenant Sandy Ray,* 1906; *Tonio, Son of the Sierras,* 1906; *Captured: a Story of Sandy Bay,* 1907; *The Rock of Chicamauga,* 1907; *To the Front,* 1908; *Lanier of the Cavalry,* 1909; *The True Ulysses S. Grant,* 1914.

MARY HALLOCK FOOTE. (1847———.) *The Led-Horse Claim: Romance of a Mining Camp,* 1883; *John Bodewin's Testimony,* 1885; *The Last Assembly Ball,* 1886; *The Chosen Valley,* 1892; *Cœur d'Alene,* 1894; *In Exile and Other Stories,* 1894; *The Cup of Trembling and Other Stories,* 1895; *Little Fig-tree Stories,* 1899; *The Prodigal,* 1900; *The Desert* and *The Sown,* 1902; *A Touch of Sin and Other Stories,* 1903; *Royal Americans,* 1910; *Picked Company: a Novel,* 1912.

CLARA LOUISE BURNHAM. (1854———.) *No Gentleman,* 1881; *A Sane Lunatic,* 1882; *Dearly Bought,* 1884; *Next Door,* 1886; *Young Maids and Old,* 1888; *The Mistress of Beech Knoll,* 1890; *Miss Bragg's Secretary,* 1892; *Dr. Latimer,* 1893; *Sweet Clover,* 1894; *The Wise Woman,* 1895; *Miss Archer Archer,* 1897; *A Great Love,* 1898; *A West Point Wooing,* 1899; *Miss Prichard's Wedding Trip,* 1901; *The Right Princess,* 1902; *Jewel,* 1903; *Jewel's Story Book,* 1904; *The Opened Shutters,* 1906; *The Leaven of Love,* 1908; *Clever Betsey,* 1910; *The Inner Flame,* 1912.

JULIAN HAWTHORNE. (1846———.) *Bressant,* 1873; *Idolatry,* 1874; *Saxon Studies,* 1875; *Garth,* 1877; *Mrs. Gainsborough's Diamonds,* 1878;

Archibald Malmaison, 1879; *Sebastian Strome*, 1880; *Fortune's Fool*, 1883; *Dust: a Novel*, 1883; *Beatrix Randolph*, 1883; *Prince Saroni's Wife*, 1884; *Noble Blood*, 1884; *Nathaniel Hawthorne and His Wife: a Biography*, 1885; *Love—or a Name*, 1885; *Sinfire*, 1886; *The Trial of Gideon*, 1886; *John Parmelee's Curse*, 1886; *Confessions and Criticisms*, 1887; five novels from the Diary of Inspector Byrnes: *The Tragic Mystery*, *The Great Bank Robbery*, *An American Penman*, *Section 558*, 1887, and *Another's Crime*, 1888; *The Professor's Sister: a Romance; A Miser of Second Avenue*, 1888; *A Dream and a Forgetting*, 1888; *David Poindexter's Disappearance*, 1888; *Kildhurin's Oak*, 1889; *Constance*, 1889; *Pauline*, 1890; *A Stage Friend*, 1890; *American Literature: an Elementary Textbook* [with Leonard Lemmon], 1891; *Humors of the Fair*, 1893; *Six Cent Sam's*, 1893; *The Golden Fleece: a Romance*, 1896; *A Fool of Nature*, 1896; *Love Is a Spirit*, 1896; *A History of the United States*, 1898; *Hawthorne and His Circle*, 1903; *The Secret of Solomon*, 1909; *Lovers in Heaven*, 1910; *The Subterranean Brotherhood*, 1914.

BLANCHE WILLIS HOWARD, Mrs. von Teuffel. (1847–1898.) *One Summer*, 1877; *One Year Abroad*, 1877; *Aunt Serena*, 1881; *Guenn: a Wave of the Breton Coast*, 1884; *The Open Door*, 1891; *A Fellowe and His Wife* [with W. Sharp], 1892; *A Battle and a Boy*, 1892; *No Heroes*, 1893; *Seven on the Highways*, 1897; *Dionysius, the Weaver's Heart's Dearest*, 1899; *The Garden of Eden*, 1900.

EDWARD BELLAMY. (1850–1898.) *Six to One: a Nantucket Idyl*, 1878; *Dr. Heidenhoff's Process*, 1880; *Miss Luddington's Sister: a Romance of Immortality*, 1884; *Looking Backward, 2000–1887*, 1888; *Equality*, 1897; *A Blindman's World, and Other Stories*, 1898; *The Duke of Stockbridge: a Romance of Shay's Rebellion*, 1900.

HJALMAR HJORTH BOYESEN. (1848–1895.) *Gunnar*, 1874; *A Norseman's Pilgrimage*, 1875; *Tales from Two Hemispheres*, 1876; *Falconberg*, 1879; *Goethe and Schiller: Their Lives and Works*, 1879; *Queen Titania*, 1881; *Ilka on the Hill-Top*, 1881; *Idyls of Norway and Other Poems*, 1882; *A Daughter of the Philistines*, 1883; *The Story of Norway*, 1886; *The Modern Vikings*, 1887; *Vagabond Tales*, 1889; *The Light of Her Countenance*, 1889; *The Mammon of Unrighteousness*, 1891; *Essays on German Literature*, 1892; *Boyhood in Norway*, 1892; *The Golden Calf: a Novel*, 1892; *Social Strugglers*, 1893; *Commentary on the Writings of Henrik Ibsen*, 1894; *Literary and Social Silhouettes*, 1894; *Essays on Scandinavian Literature*, 1895.

ARTHUR SHERBURNE HARDY. (1847——.) *Francesca of Rimini: a Poem*, 1878; *But Yet a Woman*, 1883; *The Wind of Destiny*, 1886; *Passe Rose*, 1889; *Life and Letters of Joseph Hardy Neesima*, 1891; *Songs of Two*, 1900; *His Daughter First*, 1903; *Aurélie*, 1912; *Diane and Her Friends*, 1914. His mathematical works not listed.

ROBERT GRANT. (1852——.) *The Little Tin Gods-on-Wheels; or, Society in Our Modern Athens*, 1879; *The Confessions of a Frivolous Girl*, 1880; *The Lambs: a Tragedy*, 1882; *An Average Man*, 1884; *Face to Face*, 1886; *The Knave of Hearts: a Fairy Story*, 1886; *A Romantic Young Lady*, 1886; *Jack Hall*, 1887; *Jack in the Bush; or, a Summer on a Sal-*

mon River, 1888; *The Carletons*, 1891; *Mrs. Harold Stagg*, 1891; *The Reflections of a Married Man*, 1892; *The Opinions of a Philosopher*, 1893; *The Art of Living*, 1895; *A Bachelor's Christmas*, 1895; *The North Shore of Massachusetts*, 1896; *Search-Light Letters*, 1899; *Unleavened Bread*, 1900; *The Undercurrent*, 1904; *The Orchid*, 1905; *Law-breakers and Other Stories*, 1906; *The Chiffendales*, 1909; *Confessions of a Grandfather*, 1912.

FREDERICK JESUP STIMSON, "J. S. of Dale." (1855——.) *Rollo's Journey to Cambridge*, 1879; *Guerndale, an Old Story*, 1882; *The Crime of Henry Vane*, 1884; *The Sentimental Calendar*, 1886; *First Harvests*, 1888; *Mrs. Knollys and Other Stories*, 1894; *Pirate Gold*, 1896; *King Noanett: a Story of Old Virginia and Massachusetts Bay*, 1896; *Jethro Bacon of Sandwich*, 1902; *In Cure of Her Soul*, 1906. His law publications not listed.

HENRY BLAKE FULLER. (1857——.) *The Chevalier of Pensieri-Vani*, 1891; *The Chatelaine of La Trinité*, 1892; *The Cliff-Dwellers*, 1893; *With the Procession*, 1895; *The Puppet-Booth: Twelve Plays*, 1896; *From the Other Side: Stories of Transatlantic Travel*, 1898; *The Last Refuge: a Sicilian Romance*, 1900; *Under the Skylights*, 1901; *Waldo Trench and Others: Stories of Americans in Italy*, 1908.

FRANCIS HOPKINSON SMITH. (1838–1915.) *Old Lines in New Black and White*, 1885; *Well-Worn Roads*, 1886; *A White Umbrella in Mexico*, 1889; *A Book of the Tile Club*, 1890; *Col. Carter of Cartersville*, 1891; *A Day at Laguerre's*, 1892; *American Illustrators*, 1892; *A Gentleman Vagabond and Some Others*, 1895; *Tom Grogan*, 1896; *Gondola Days*, 1897; *Venice of To-day*, 1897; *Caleb West*, 1898; *The Other Fellow*, 1899; *The Fortunes of Oliver Horn*, 1902; *The Under Dog*, 1903; *Col. Carter's Christmas*, 1904; *At Close Range*, 1905; *The Wood Fire in Number 3*, 1905; *The Tides of Barnegat*, 1906; *The Veiled Lady*, 1907; *The Romance of an Old-Fashioned Gentleman*, 1907; *Peter*, 1908; *Forty Minutes Late*, 1909; *Kennedy Square*, 1911; *The Arm-Chair at the Inn*, 1912; *In Thackeray's London*, 1913; *In Dickens's London*, 1914.

CHAPTER XVIII

In forms other than fiction and poetry the period was also voluminous. The greater part of our historical writings has been produced since 1870 and the same is true of our biography. Literary quality, however, has suffered. Emphasis has been placed upon material rather than upon graces of style; upon matter, but little upon manner. Never before have historian and biographer been so tireless in their search for sources: the *Battles and Leaders of the Civil War* is a veritable library of materials; the Life of Lincoln by Nicolay and Hay contains one million five hundred thousand words. It is as long as Bancroft's whole history of the United States, it is twice as long as Green's *History of the English People,* and it contains three hundred thousand words more than Gibbon's *Decline and Fall of the Roman Empire.* It has been a development from the spirit of the era: the demand for actuality. Never before such eagerness to uncover new facts, to present documents, to be realistically true, but it has been at the expense of literary style. A few books, like General Grant's *Memoirs* and Captain Mahan's *The Influence of Sea Power upon History,* have had the power of simplicity, the impelling force that comes from consciousness only of the message to be delivered. But all too often the material has been presented in a colorless, journalistic form that bars it forever from consideration as literature in the higher sense of that term. The most of it, even the life of Lincoln, is to be placed in the same category as scientific writings and all those other prose forms that are concerned only with the presenting of positive knowledge. Parkman seems to have been the last historian who was able to present his material with literary distinction.

The essay has been voluminous all through the period, but it too has changed its tone. More than any other literary form it has been the medium through which we may trace the transition from the old period to the new. American literature had begun with the essay, and we have seen how the form, designated by the name of sketch, grew in the hands of Irving and Hawthorne and Poe into what in the period of the seventies became recognized as a distinct literary form with the name of short story.

The literary essay is a classical form: to flourish, it needs the atmosphere of old culture and established social traditions; it must work in the materials of classic literature; it is leisurely in method, discursive, gently sentimental. It was the dominating form, it will be remembered, in the classical age of Addison, the age of manners and mind. It was peculiarly fitted, too, to be the literary vehicle of the later classical age in America, the Europe-centered period of Irving and Emerson and Willis and Holmes. The early pilgrims to the holy land of the Old World sent back their impressions and dreamings in the form of essays: Longfellow's *Outre-Mer*, for example, and Willis's *Pencillings by the Way*. On the same shelf with *The Sketch Book* belong Willis's *Letters from Under a Bridge*, Dana's *The Idle Man*, Donald G. Mitchell's *Reveries of a Bachelor*, Curtis's *Prue and I*, and a great mass of similar work, enough indeed to give color and even name to its period. This shelf more than any other marks the extent of England's dominion over the literature of the first three quarters of the nineteenth century: it was the most distinctive product of our classical age. Until America has a rich background of her own with old culture and traditions, with venerable native classics from which to quote, and a long vista of romantic history down which to look, her contemplative and strictly literary essays must necessarily be redolent of the atmosphere of other lands.

I

The National Period, with its new breath of all-Americanism, its new romantic spirit, its youthful exuberance, and its self-realization, has been, therefore, not a period in which the essay of the old type could find congenial soil. Instead of the Irving sketch there has been the vivid, sharply cut short story; instead of the contemplative, dreamy study of personalities and institutions—Irving's "The Broken Heart," Longfellow's "Père la Chaise"—there has been incisive, analytical, clearly cut special studies, like Woodrow Wilson's *Mere Literature and Other Essays;* instead of the delightful, discursive personal tattle of a Charles Lamb and a Dr. Holmes there has been the colorless editorial essay, all force and facts, or the undistinctive, business-like special article, prosiest of all prose.

The transition figure in the history of the American essay was Charles Dudley Warner, the last of the contemplative *Sketch Book* essayists, and, with Higginson, Burroughs, Maurice Thompson, and others, a leading influence in the bringing in of the new freshness and naturalness and journalistic abandon that gave character to the prose of the later period. He was a New Englander, one of that small belated group born in the twenties—Mitchell, Hale, Higginson, Norton, for example—that found itself in a Janus-like position between the old school of Emerson and Longfellow and the new school of non-New Englanders—Harte, Hay, Howells, Mark Twain. Warner was peculiarly a transition figure. He could collaborate with Mark Twain on that most distinctively latter-day novel *The Gilded Age,* and be classed by his generation with the humorists of the Burdette, Josh Billings group, yet at the death of George William Curtis he could be chosen as without question the only logical heir to the Editor's Easy Chair department of *Harper's Magazine.*

Warner was born in 1829, the birth year of Dr. S. Weir Mitchell, and his birthplace was a farm in western Massachusetts, where his ancestors for generations had been sturdy Puritan yeomen. The atmosphere of this home and the round of its life he has described with autobiographic pen in *Being a Boy,* the most valuable of all his studies. Concerning the rest of his life one needs only to record that he was graduated from Hamilton College in 1851 and from the law department of the University of Pennsylvania in 1857, and that after four years of legal practice in Chicago he was invited by his classmate, Senator J. R. Hawley, to remove to Hartford, Connecticut, to become associate editor of the paper that was soon merged with the Hartford *Courant.* To this paper either as its editor or as a contributor he gave the best years of his life. He used his vacations for foreign travel, at one time spending a year and a half abroad, and in his later years he saw much of his own land, but always he traveled pen in hand, ready to embody every observation and sentiment in a letter for the readers at home. Travel letters of the older type they were, such as Taylor wrote home from Germany and Curtis sent from the Nile and the Levant, gently sentimental, humorous in a pervasive way, perfectly natural, unconscious of style.

Warner was forty and a confirmed journalist before he published anything in book form, and even this first volume was not written with book intent. He had contributed a rambling series of papers to the *Courant*, a sort of humorous echo of Greeley's *What I Know about Farming*, careless, newspapery, funny in a chuckling sort of way, and perfectly unconventional and free from effort. Naturalness was its main charm. The period was ready for out-of-doors themes simply presented, and it found an enthusiastic circle of readers who demanded its publication in book form. Henry Ward Beecher was among them and as an inducement he promised an introductory letter. The result was *My Summer in a Garden*, 1870, a book that sprang into wide popularity and that undoubtedly was one of the formative influences of the new period. He followed it with *Backlog Studies*, a series of sketches of the Donald G. Mitchell variety, and then with various travel books like *Saunterings* and *My Winter on the Nile*. Late in life he published novels, *A Little Journey in the World, The Golden House*, and others dealing with phases of life in New York City, and he served as editor of several important series of books, notably The American Men of Letters Series of biographies, to which he himself contributed the life of Irving.

Time enough has elapsed to enable us to consider the work of Warner apart from the charm of his personal presence, and it is seen now that his generation overestimated his work. He was in no sense an inspired soul; he had little to offer that was really new. He wrote like the practical editor of a daily paper, fluently, copiously, unhesitatingly. The style is that of the practised worker who dictates to his stenographer. There is lack of incisiveness, sharpness of outline, cohesion of thought. He lacks revision, flashes of insight, creative moments when the pen is forgotten. He wrote on many topics, but there are no passages that one is compelled to quote. He was a classicist who wrote with perfect coolness, just as others had written before him. His gentle spirit, his sentiment, his Puritan conscience, and a certain serenity of view that whispered of high character and perfect breeding, endeared him to his first readers. But his style of humor belonged only to his own generation— it was not embodied at all in a humorous character; and his ethical teachings seem trite now and conventional. His influence at a critical period of American literature entitles him to serious consideration, but he won for himself no permanent place. He will live longest, perhaps, in a few of his shorter pieces: *Being a Boy,* "How Spring Came in New England," "A-Hunting the Deer," and "Old Mountain Phelps."

There are those who would rate his novels above his essays, those indeed who would rate them even with the work of Howells. Not many, however. That his fiction has about it a certain power can not be denied. Its author had the journalistic sense of the value of contemporary events, as well as the journalistic faculty for gathering interesting facts. He had, too, what so many novelists lack, the power to trace by almost imperceptible processes the gradual growth of a character. *A Little Journey in the World,* for instance, is a study of degeneration, skilfully done. A woman who has been reared among humble yet ennobling surroundings removes to New York and marries a very rich man and we are shown how little by little all that is really fine at the heart of her life is eaten away though the surface remains as beautiful as ever. There is a naturalness about it that is charming, and there is evident everywhere an honesty of purpose and a depth of experience that are unusual, but one may not say more. The novels came from the critical impulse rather than from the creative. They are humanitarian documents rather than creations breathing the breath of life. They do not move us. To realize where they fail one has but to compare his chapters in *The Gilded Age* with Mark Twain's. It is like looking from a still-life picture on a parlor wall out upon an actual steamboat pulling showily up to a Mississippi wharf.

II

The opposite of Warner in every respect was Lafcadio Hearn, a figure more picturesque even than Joaquin Miller and more puzzling than Whitman. Instead of serene classicism, genius; instead of Puritan inflexibility and reverence for the respectable, tumultuous wanderings—a man without a country, without a

religion, without anything fixed save a restless love of the beautiful—emotional, a bundle of nerves, moody, sudden, the gorgeous Gallic at eternal odds with the florid, beauty-loving
Hellenic; a man forever homeless, yet forever pathetic with a
nostalgia that finally broke his heart. His personality was a
strangely elusive one, and his biography, especially in its earlier
years, is as full of romantic conjecture as De Quincey's early
life or Byron's. His very name was romantic. His father,
member of an ancient Irish family, had accompanied his regiment as surgeon-major into the East, and while stationed at
Corfu had become infatuated with a beautiful Grecian girl,
Rosa Cerigote, and had married her. Lafcadio they named their
son from the island where he was born, his mother's home,
Leucadia, in modern Greek Lefcadia, the Ionian island of
Sappho. Here he spent his babyhood, how much of it we do
not know. Of his father, he has said nothing, and of his mother,
only this hint in a later bit of impressionism—elusive, suggestive, characteristic:

> I have memory of a place and a magical time, in which the sun and
> the moon were larger and brighter than now. Whether it was of this
> life or of some life before, I can not tell, but I know the sky was very
> much more blue, and nearer to the world—almost as it seems to be-
> come above the masts of a steamer steaming into the equatorial sum-
> mer. . . . Each day there were new wonders and new pleasures for
> me, and all that country and time were softly ruled by one who
> thought only of ways to make me happy. . . . When day was done
> and there fell the great hush of the light before moonrise, she would
> tell me stories that made me tingle from head to foot with pleasure.
> I have never heard any other stories half so beautiful. And when the
> pleasure became too great, she would sing a weird little song which
> always brought sleep. At last there came a parting day; and she wept
> and told me of a charm she had given that I must never, never lose,
> because it would keep me young, and give me power to return. But I
> never returned. And the years went; and one day I knew I had
> lost the charm, and had become ridiculously old.

Was it the Ægean island of his birth or was it the West Indian
island to which his father later was ordered with his regiment?
We do not know. We know, however, that the mother lived for
a time in Ireland, that another son was born, and then when
the elder boy was seven she went away to Smyrna never to
return. The rest is conjecture, save for the significant fact
that both parents soon afterward married again.

The boy, unwelcome, forlorn, out of sympathy with his surroundings, was sent to live with his aunt in Ireland, then later was put to school in France in preparation for the priesthood. Two years in France, formative years in which he learned among a myriad of other things the fluent use of French, then in 1865 we find him in the Roman Catholic college at Durham, England, where came to him the first great tragedy of his life: an accident at play that left him blinded in one eye and partly blinded in the other. Soon afterwards came the break with his aunt—father and mother had passed out of his life—he refused to become a priest, refused to live longer in any paths save his own, and for the rest of his life he was a wanderer.

There is much in his life and temperament to suggest De Quincey. Hearn, too, for a vague period—two or three years it may have been—wandered in the lower strata of London, half dead with hunger and sickness, aflame with imagination, restless, ambitious. At nineteen we find him in New York, reading in the public library, eagerly, omnivorously, despite his feeble vision, then suddenly, how we do not know, he is in Cincinnati, Ohio, where he makes the whole city gasp with horror at the story he writes of a murder in one of their narrow streets, and secures a position on the *Enquirer*. In 1877 he has wandered as far south as New Orleans, where for the first time in his life he finds congenial atmosphere and where he supports himself by reporting for the *Times-Democrat*.

Now it was that his French schooling had its effect. The Creole *patois* delighted him; he compiled a book of Creole proverbs, *Gombo Zhèbes* he fantastically called it; and he fed his imagination with the old French past of the city, wandering as Cable had done among its ancient buildings, and, like Cable again, devouring its romantic old chronicles. French novels he read interminably, eagerly, especially the romantics—Hugo, Gautier, Baudelaire. How richly he read them we learn from his letters, most of all from those written in his later life to Professor Basil Hall Chamberlain and preserved in Elizabeth Bisland's third volume. Few have read more discerningly or have voiced their findings more brilliantly. This of Loti:

There is not much heart in Loti, but there is a fine brain.—To me Loti seems for a space to have looked into Nature's whole splendid burning fulgurant soul, and to have written under her very deepest and strongest inspiration. He was young. Then the color and the light faded, and only the worn-out blasé nerves remained; and the poet became—a little morbid modern affected Frenchman.

Strange self-revealment. It was of himself he was speaking, had he but realized it. He too began with power under the deepest and strongest inspiration; he too had caught a vision, splendid, burning, fulgurant. If there was an undoubted genius in our national period it was Hearn. He poured his eager dreamings at first into the New Orleans papers: "Fantastics," they have been called, by the editor who of late has hunted them from their forgotten columns. Then came *Chita*, written after a visit to Grande Isle in the Gulf of Mexico and published first in the *Times-Democrat* with the title *Torn Letters*, and then in *Harper's Magazine*, April, 1888.

Here for the first time we get the measure of the man, his Celtic imagination, fervor and intensity, his Greek passion for beauty. It is not English at all: it is the dream of a Celtic Greek, who has saturated himself with the French romantics and the color and the profusion of the tropic gulf lands. It is not, as the magazine termed it, a novelette; it is a loosely gathered bundle of fictional sketches, lurid patches, "torn letters," indeed, written with torrential power and blazing with color. Everywhere landscapes intense, drawn with fewest strokes, impressions, suggestions. He would make you feel the desolate shore on the gulf side of the island, but he selects only a single detail:

> The trees—where there are any trees—all bend away from the sea; and even of bright hot days when the wind sleeps, there is something grotesquely pathetic in their look of agonized terror. A group of oaks at Grande Isle I remember as especially suggestive: five stooping silhouettes in line against the horizon, like fleeing women with streaming garments and wind-blown hair—bowing grievously and thrusting out arms desperately northward as to save themselves from falling. And they are being pursued indeed—for the sea is devouring the land. Many and many a mile of ground has yielded to the tireless charging of Ocean's cavalry.

Always is he a colorist, and always does he use his colors daintily, effectively, distinctively—one feels rather than sees:

> The charm of a single summer day on these island shores is something impossible to express, never to be forgotten. Rarely, in the

paler zones, do earth and heaven take such luminosity: those will best understand me who have seen the splendor of a West Indian sky. And yet there is a tenderness of tint, a caress of color in these Gulf-days which is not of the Antilles—a spirituality, as of eternal tropical spring.

It describes his own style; one need say no more.

When he would describe action there is in him a Byronic power that lays hold on one and chokes and stifles. Who outside of *Don Juan* has made us feel so fearfully a tropic hurricane?

Then arose a frightful cry—the hoarse, hideous, indescribable cry of hopeless fear—the despairing animal-cry man utters when suddenly brought face to face with Nothingness, without preparation, without consolation, without possibility of respite. *Sauve qui peut!* Some wrenched down the doors; some clung to the heavy banquet tables, to the sofas, to the billiard tables—during one terrible instant—against fruitless heroisms, against futile generosities—raged all the frenzy of selfishness, all the brutalities of panic. And then—then came, thundering through the blackness, the giant swells, boom on boom!—One crash!—the huge frame building rocks like a cradle, seesaws, crackles. What are human shrieks now?—the tornado is shrieking! Another!—chandeliers splinter; lights are dashed out; a sweeping cataract hurls in: the immense hall rises—oscillates—twirls as upon a pivot—crepitates—crumbles into ruin. Crash again!—the swirling wreck dissolves into the wallowing of another monster billow; and a hundred cottages overturn, spin on sudden eddies, quiver, disjoint, and melt into the seething.

So the Hurricane passed.

Chita, like all the rest of Hearn's work, is a thing of fragments. It leaps and bounds, it chokes with tropic heat, it blazes with the sunsets of the Mexican gulf, it stagnates with torrid siestas, it is raucous with the voices of tropic insects and birds. It is incoherent, rhapsodic, half picture, half suggestion—materials rather than final structure. The style is wholly Gallic, like Cable's early style—sudden breaks—dashes—sentences stripped to the bare nouns and adjectives, swift shiftings of scenes, interjected exclamations, prayers:

Thou primordial Sea, the awfulness of whose antiquity hath stricken all mythology dumb—thou most wrinkled living Sea, etc.

Then swiftly following:

Eighteen hundred and sixty-seven;—midsummer in the pest-smitten city of New Orleans.

Heat motionless and ponderous. The steel-blue of the sky bleached from the furnace-circle of the horizon;—the lukewarm river yellow and noiseless as a torrent of fluid wax. The nights began with a black heat;—there were hours when the acrid air seemed to ferment for stagnation, and to burn the bronchial tubing;—then, toward morning it would grow chill with venomous vapors, with morbific dews—till the sun came up to lift the torpid moisture, and to fill the buildings with oven-heat. And the interminable procession of mourners and hearses and carriages again began to circulate between the centers of life and death;—and long trains of steamships rushed from the port with heavy burden of fugitives.

Then terror that lays cold hands on the heart: Julian dying of fever.

From New Orleans he went in 1887 to the Windward Islands for new sensation, new color, new barbaric areas of human life. *Two Years in the French West Indies* is the literary result of it, a chaotic book, flashlights, impressions, but no single completed impression, no totality, but the soul of the West Indies none the less, revealed with a rare, queer art that was individual. But no place, not even those Circe islands which he paints as the dream and the ultimate of human desire, could detain him long. Fickleness was in his blood, wandering was his birthright. Again he is in New York, and then with a commission from the Harpers he sails to Japan, where, in the rush and tumult of new sensation, he forgets his commission and loses himself completely in the new delicious world of impression.

For Hearn was as unpractical as Shelley and he was without Shelley's ideals and altruistic dreams. He lived in a vague world of vision, of sensation, of intangible beauty. He could say of himself:

Always having lived in hopes and imaginations, the smallest practical matters that everybody should know, I don't know anything about. Nothing, for example, about a boat, a horse, a farm, an orchard, a watch, a garden. Nothing about what a man ought to do under any possible circumstances. I know nothing but sensation and books.

Though he was now forty, he entered this new world as one new born into it. He adopted its costume, he slept with his head on a wooden pillow, he acquired citizenship, he married a Japanese wife and established a Japanese home, and he even went over completely to the Buddhist religion.

The book *Glimpses of Unfamiliar Japan,* 1894, marks the beginning of his second literary period. Henceforth his writings center about Japan. He wrote no treatise, no serious study of actual conditions; he wrote impressions, fragmentary suggestions of the Japan that was passing away, the romantic Japan of the ideal old régime, survivals of which he found everywhere. Japanese art and Japanese romance found in him a curious affinity. They mellowed and soothed the tumultuous spirit of his first art period. His impressionism became more subtly suggestive, more magically vague, more daintily colored. There had always been within him a strong element of mysticism, legacy of his Irish ancestry, and the subtly mystical side of Buddhism appealed to it strongly. He was able to interpret it for occidental comprehension, and he was able to make more comprehensible the subtle connotation of Japanese art, and to catch the subtler inner consciousness of Japan as no other of the Western world has ever caught it. In his first enthusiasm he wrote:

This is a land where one can really enjoy the Inner Life. Every one has an inner life of his own—which no other life can see, and the great secrets of which are never revealed, though occasionally when we create something beautiful we betray a faint glimpse of it.

But the newness of this new world he had entered wore away at length. He was a creature of enthusiastic moments and he needed swift changes of sensation. He had reveled in the old, ideal Japan, but he found himself unable to live in it. A new régime had begun. He was filled with contempt at what he called "the frank selfishness, the apathetic vanity, the shallow, vulgar skepticism of the new Japan that prates its contempt about Tempo times, and ridicules the dear old men of the premeiji era." His last years were bitter with financial embarrassment, and full of feverish literary creation for the sake of his growing family. The glow and fervor and genius of his first period faded more and more from his work;—he himself faded out. He felt the gulf that he had erected between himself and his race. To his sister he wrote: "I feel myself in exile; and your letters and photographs only make me homesick for English life." He died of his own vehemence, worn out by oversensation, unnerved by restlessness and nostalgia and longing for he knew not what.

The likeness of Hearn to De Quincey is almost complete. He

had De Quincey's irresoluteness, his jangling nerves, his dominating fancy, his discursiveness, his gorgeous imagination, his oriental soul hampered with the fetters of occidental science. He too was essentially fragmentary in his literary output, a man of intense moods intensely painted, a man of books but of no single, unified, compelling book. One may not read essays like "Gothic Horror" or "The Nightmare Touch," or a passage like this from "Vespertina Cognitio," and not think of the great English opium-eater:

It must have been well after midnight when I felt the first vague uneasiness—*the suspicion*—that precedes a nightmare. I was half-conscious, dream-conscious of the actual—knew myself in that very room—wanted to get up. Immediately the uneasiness grew into terror, because I found that I could not move. Something unutterable in the air was mastering will. I tried to cry out, and my utmost effort resulted only in a whisper too low for any one to hear. Simultaneously I became aware of a Step ascending the stair—a muffled heaviness; and the real nightmare began—the horror of the ghastly magnetism that held voice and limb—the hopeless will-struggle against dumbness and impotence. The stealthy Step approached—but with lentor malevolently measured—slowly, slowly, as if the stairs were miles deep. It gained the threshold—waited. Gradually then, and without sound, the locked door opened; and the Thing entered, bending as it came—a thing robed—feminine—reaching to the roof, not to be looked at! A floor-plank creaked as It neared the bed;—and then—with a frantic effort—I woke, bathed in sweat; my heart beating as if it were going to burst. The shrine-light had died: in the blackness I could see nothing; but I thought I heard that Step retreating. I certainly heard the plank creak again. With the panic still upon me, I was actually unable to stir. The wisdom of striking a match occurred to me, but I dared not yet rise. Presently, as I held my breath to listen, a new wave of black fear passed through me; for I heard moanings—long nightmare moanings—moanings that seemed to be answering each other from two different rooms below. And then close to me my guide began to moan—hoarsely, hideously. I cried to him:—
"Louis!—Louis!"
We both sat up at once.

Like De Quincey, he lingers over the flavor of words, gathering them everywhere he may and gloating over them, tasting them with half-closed eyes like an epicure, and using them ever delicately, suggestively, inevitably.

For me words have color, form, character: they have faces, ports, manners, gesticulations; they have moods, humors, eccentricities;—they have tints, tones, personalities. . . . Surely I have never yet made and never expect to make any money. Neither do I expect to write ever for the multitude. I write for beloved friends who can see color in words, can smell the perfume of syllables in blossom, can be shocked with the fine elfish electricity of words. And in the eternal order of things, words will eventually have their rights recognized by the people.

His essays, therefore, even as he has intimated, are for the few who are attuned to them, who have sense for delicate suggestion, for ''the phosphorescing of words, the fragrance of words, the noisomeness of words, the tenderness, the hardness, the dryness or juiciness of words.'' Aside from his vision of beauty, his intensity, his suggestiveness of style, he has brought not much. The romancers of the period, a few of them, like Grace King, for example, have felt his influence, but it has not been a large one. He stands almost an isolated figure in his period, an intensely individual soul, a solitary genius like Poe. His place is a secure one. His circle of readers will never be large, but it will always be constant.

III

Another phase of French influence one finds in the work of Agnes Repplier, perhaps the leading writer of ''the light essay'' —the term is her own—in the later years of the period. Born of French parentage in Philadelphia, educated at a convent where prevailed French language and ideals, she was Gallic both by temperament and training. She was not influenced as Cable undoubtedly was influenced and Hearn: there is small trace in her essays of French style echoed consciously or unconsciously. The influence was deeper, it was temperamental and racial, manifesting itself spontaneously in the display of those literary qualities that we associate with the word ''French.'' Her favorite reading was largely in the English. She read enormously and she read note-book in hand. She added, moreover, culture and impressions by much residence abroad, and when she began to write it was with rich store of material. She began deliberately and she worked like a true classicist, leisurely, with no genius, and no message to urge her on. Her delight it was to talk about her reading, to add entertaining episodes, to embroider with witty observation and pithy quotation or epigram. Save for the autobiographical study ''In Our Convent Days,'' her writings mostly deal with the world of books.

Miss Repplier first came into notice in 1886 when one of her essays came to Aldrich, who was delighted with it and who made haste to introduce her to the *Atlantic* circle. Two years later came her first book, *Books and Men,* and since that time her essays, goodly in number and scattered through many magazines, have become a well-known feature of the times. Themes she takes to suit her fancy, apparently at random, though more often phases of her beloved "happy half century": "A Short Defense of Villains," "Benefits of Superstition," "The Deathless Diary," "The Accursed Annual," "Marriage in Fiction," and all other topics pertinent to Dr. Johnson's little world. She adds not much to our knowledge, and she comes not often to any new conclusions, but she is so companionable, so sparkling and witty, that we can but read on with delight to the end. We are in an atmosphere somehow of old culture and patrician grace, of courtliness and charm:

> Thou mindest me of gentle folks—
> Old gentlefolks are they—
> Thou sayst an undisputed thing
> In such a solemn way.

A little of feminine contrariness there may be, perhaps, at times. A thing has been generally disparaged: she will defend it. Richardson's Sir Charles Grandison may be mentioned: "I think, myself, that poor Sir Charles has been unfairly handled," she will retort. "He is not half such a prig as Daniel Deronda; but he develops his priggishness with such ample detail through so many leisurely volumes." And her protest becomes almost acrimonious if anything of the new be flippantly boasted of as superior to the old:

"We have long ago ceased to be either surprised, grieved, or indignant at anything the English say of us," writes Mr. Charles Dudley Warner. "We have recovered our balance. We know that since *Gulliver* there has been no piece of original humor produced in England equal to Knickerbocker's *New York;* that not in this century has any English writer equaled the wit and satire of the *Biglow Papers.*"

Does this mean that Mr. Warner considers Washington Irving to be the equal of Jonathan Swift; that he places the gentle satire of the American alongside of those trenchant and masterly pages which constitute the landmarks of literature? "Swift," says Dr. Johnson, with. reluctant truthfulness, "must be allowed for a time to have dictated the

political opinions of the English nation." He is a writer whom we
may be permitted to detest, but not to undervalue. His star, red as
Mars, still flames fiercely in the horizon, while the genial luster of
Washington Irving grows dimmer year by year. We can never hope
to "recover our balance" by confounding values, a process of self-
deception which misleads no one but ourselves.

Realism, the new smartness of Western veritism, the cry that
romance is dead, and that Walter Scott is outworn, found in her
no sympathy. Her heart was in the eighteenth century rather
than in what she has called "this overestimated century of prog·
ress." And so thoroughly convinced is she, it is impossible not
to agree with her:

> Lord Holland, when asked by Murray for his opinion of *Old Mor-
> tality,* answered indignantly: "Opinion? We did not one of us go to
> bed last night! Nothing slept but my gout." Yet *Rokeby* and *Childe
> Harold* are both in sad disgrace with modern critics and *Old Mortality*
> stands gathering dust on our book-shelves. . . . We read *The Bos-
> tonians* and *The Rise of Silas Lapham* with a due appreciation of their
> minute perfections; but we go to bed quite cheerfully at our usual
> hour, and are content to wait an interval of leisure to resume them.
> Could *Daisy Miller* charm a gouty leg, or *Lemuel Barker* keep us awake
> till morning?

A paragraph like this may be said to contain all the various
elements of her style:

> There are few things more wearisome in a fairly fatiguing life than
> the monotonous repetition of a phrase which catches and holds the
> public fancy by virtue of its total lack of significance. Such a phrase
> —employed with tireless irrelevance in journalism, and creeping into
> the pages of what is, by courtesy, called literature—is the "new
> woman." It has furnished inexhaustible jests to *Life* and *Punch,* and
> it has been received with all seriousness by those who read the present
> with no light from the past, and so fail to perceive that all femininity
> is as old as Lilith, and that the variations of the type began when Eve
> arrived in the Garden of Paradise to dispute the claims of her prede-
> cessor. "If the fifteenth century discovered America," says a vehement
> advocate of female progress, "it was reserved for the nineteenth cen-
> tury to discover woman"; and this remarkable statement has been
> gratefully applauded by people who have apparently forgotten all
> about Judith and Zenobia, Cleopatra and Catherine de Medici, Saint
> Theresa and Jeanne d'Arc, Catherine of Russia and Elizabeth of Eng-
> land, who played parts of some importance, for good and ill, in the
> fortunes of the world.

Here is the note of dissent from the widely accepted; the appeal to antiquity; the pithy quotation; the allusion that takes for granted a cultivated reader; the sprightly tripping of sentences; the witty turn; and the atmosphere of feminine vivacity and brilliance. Apt quotations sparkle from every paragraph. Often she opens breezily with a quotation; she illustrates at every point with epigrams and witty sayings from all known and unknown sources; and she ends smartly by snapping the whip of a quotation in the final sentence or paragraph.

The bent of her work, taking it all in all, is critical, and often in her criticism, especially her criticism of literature, she rises to the point of distinction. One may quote paragraphs here and there that are as illuminating as anything in American criticism. She is quick to see fallacies and to press an absurd deduction to its ridiculous end. She illumines a whole subject with a paragraph. This for example on Hamlin Garland:

Mr. Hamlin Garland, whose leaden-hued sketches called—I think unfairly—*Main-Traveled Roads* have deprived most of us of some cheerful hours, paints with an unfaltering hand a life in which ennui sits enthroned. It is not the poverty of his Western farmers that oppresses us. Real biting poverty, which withers lesser evils with its deadly breath, is not known to these people at all. They have roofs, fire, food, and clothing. It is not the ceaseless labor, the rough fare, the gray skies, the muddy barn-yards, which stand for the trouble in their lives. It is the dreadful weariness of living. It is the burden of a dull existence, clogged at every pore, and the hopeless melancholy of which they have sufficient intelligence to understand. Theirs is the ennui of emptiness, and the implied reproach on every page is that a portion, and only a portion, of mankind is doomed to walk along these shaded paths; while happier mortals who abide in New York, or perhaps in Paris, spend their days in a pleasant tumult of intellectual and artistic excitation.

And few have put their criticism into more attractive form. It is penetrating and true and in addition it has a sparkle and wit about it that makes it anything but dry reading. Who has written more sympathetically, more understandingly, more delightfully about Charles Lamb than she if one takes her work all together. Here is a glimpse, yet how illuminating:

Truest of all, is Charles Lamb who, more than any other humorist, more than any other man of letters, belongs exclusively to his own land, and is without trace or echo of foreign influence. France was to Lamb, not a place where the finest prose is written, but a place where he ate frogs—"the nicest little delicate things—rabbity-flavored.

Imagine a Lilliputian rabbit." Germany was little or nothing, and America was less. The child of London streets,

"Mother of mightier, nurse of none more dear,"

rich in the splendid literature of England, and faithful lover both of the teeming city and the ripe old books, Lamb speaks to English hearts in a language they can understand. And we, his neighbors, whom he recked not of, hold him just as dear; for his spleenless humor is an inheritance of our mother tongue, one of the munificent gifts which England shares with us, and for which no payment is possible save the frank and generous recognition of a pleasure that is without a peer.

But critic in the sense that Paul Elmer More is a critic, she certainly is not. She is temperamental rather than scientific. She makes brilliant observations, but she has no system, no patient analytical processes. She is, like Henry James, a critic by flashes, but those flashes often illuminate the whole landscape.

She is a suggestive writer, a writer who makes her reader think, who restores him as the dynamo restores the battery. Her world is a small one and it is not necessarily American, but it is intensely alive. In her own "happy half century," quoting Dr. Johnson, discoursing of Fanny Burney or Hannah More, or when telling of her cat or of the mystic lore of cats quoting Montaigne and Loti, or of those still more feminine topics: mirrors, spinsters, letters, the eternal feminine, she induces "electrical tingles of hit after hit." Her work must be classed with that of Lamb, of Loti, of Hearn, as work peculiarly personal, work that makes its appeal largely on account of the surcharged individuality behind it.

With Miss Repplier's essays may be classed those of Samuel McChord Crothers (1857——), Edward S. Martin (1856——) and Louise Imogen Guiney, who wrote for cultured people on topics for the most part drawn from the world of books. The work of Dr. Crothers is the most distinctive of the three. His wisdom, his delicate humor, his unfailing sense of values have made his papers, the most of them published in the *Atlantic,* a source of real delight and profit to an increasing circle. His books, like those of Miss Repplier, may be safely placed in the trunk when one starts on his summer's vacation and can take but few. They are wise, still books that one may live with.

IV

The period has abounded in critics from the first. The best of Lowell's prose came in the years following the war, and all of Stedman's was written after 1870. The great multiplication of newspapers and the increasing number of magazines led more and more to the production of book reviews. The *North American Review* no longer said the last word about a book or an author. In 1865 Edwin L. Godkin (1831–1902) founded the New York *Nation* and contributed to it some of the most fearless and discriminating work of the period; in 1880 Francis F. Browne (1843–1913) founded the Chicago *Dial* and made its reviews among the best in America; and in 1881 Jeannette L. Gilder (1849–1916) and her brother, Joseph B. Gilder (1858——), established the New York *Critic*, a journal that for two decades exerted a formative influence upon the period.

A few of the great numbers of book reviewers have done worthy work, some of them even distinctive work, though most of it lies buried now in the great ephemeral mass. Howells and Aldrich, Horace E. Scudder (1838–1902) and Bliss Perry (1860——) in the *Atlantic,* Henry M. Alden (1836——) in *Harper's,* Maurice Thompson (1844–1901) in the *Independent,* and Hamilton W. Mabie (1846–1916) in the *Outlook,* all did work that undoubtedly helped to shape the period, but not much of it may rank as permanent literature. It has been too often journalistic: hastily prepared, a thing of the day's work.

Much fine criticism has come sporadically from pens consecrated to other literary tasks. Nearly all of the major poets of the period as well as the novelists and essayists have at one time or another made excursions into the field, sometimes producing only a brilliant bit of temperamental impressionism, sometimes working out studies that are systematic and complete. James, Howells, Whitman, Burroughs, Lanier, Crawford, Torrey, John Fiske, Maurice F. Egan, Henry Van Dyke, George E. Woodberry, James Brander Matthews have all added brilliant chapters to the sum of American criticism, but none may be called a critic in the sense Sainte-Beuve was a critic. Their work has been avocational, fitful excursions rather than systematic exploration.

During the later years of the period there has been but one who may be called a critic in the broader sense of the term—

scholarly, leisurely of method, systematic, detached, literary in style and finish—a critic and only a critic, Paul Elmer More, whose *Shelburne Essays* are our nearest approach to those *Causeries du Lundi* of an earlier age. His birth and education in the West, in St. Louis, was an advantage at the start: it took from his later criticism that New England-centered point of view that is so evident in the work of critics like Richardson and Barrett Wendell. The New England culture he got in due time at Harvard, where he took two advanced degrees, and he broadened his outlook still further by pursuing his studies in European universities, returning at length to teach Sanscrit at Harvard and later at Bryn Mawr. Oriental language was his specialty. One catches the spirit of his earlier period by examining his first publications, among them *A Century of Indian Epigram,* "Translations or paraphrases in English verse of a hundred epigrams and precepts ascribed to a Hindu sage." This early enthusiasm for things oriental gave him a singularly valuable equipment for criticism. It broadened his view: it put into his hands the two opposite poles of human thought. His essay on Lafcadio Hearn is illuminating, not only of Hearn but of More himself. We can illustrate only lamely with fragments:

> Into the study of these by-ways of Oriental literature he has carried a third element, the dominant idea of Occidental science; and this element he has blended with Hindu religion and Japanese æstheticism in a combination as bewildering as it is voluptuous. In this triple union lies his real claim to high originality. . . .
>
> Beauty itself, which forms the essence of Mr. Hearn's art, receives a new content from this union of the East and the West. . . .
>
> Is it not proper to say, after reading such passages as these, that Mr. Hearn has introduced a new element of psychology into literature? We are indeed living in the past, we who foolishly cry out that the past is dead. In one remarkable study of the emotions awakened by the baying of a gaunt white hound, Mr. Hearn shows how even the very beasts whom we despise as unreasoning and unremembering are filled with an articulate sense of this dark backward and abysm of time, whose shadow falls on their sensitive souls with the chill of a vague dread—dread, I say, for it must begin to be evident that this new psychology is fraught with meanings that may well trouble and awe the student.
>
> In the ghostly residuum of these psychological meditations we may perceive a vision dimly foreshadowing itself which mankind for centuries, nay, for thousands of years, has striven half unwittingly to

keep veiled. I do not know, but it seems to me that the foreboding of this dreaded disclosure may account for many things in the obscure history of the race, for the long struggle of religion against the observations of science which to-day we are wont to slur over as only a superficial struggle after all. In the haunting fear of this disclosure I seem to see an explanation, if not a justification, of the obscurantism of the early church, of the bitter feud of Galileo and the burning of Giordano Bruno, of the recent hostility to Darwinism, and even of the present-day attempt to invalidate the significance of this long contest.[1]

In another and a far more unusual way he qualified himself for his high office of critic: he immured himself for two years in solitude, with books as his chief companions, and it was in this wilderness that the *Shelburne Essays*—Shelburne was the name of the town of his hermitage—were born. His own account is illuminating:

In a secluded spot in the peaceful valley of the Androscoggin I took upon myself to live two years as a hermit, after a mild Epicurean fashion of my own. Three maiden aunts wagged their heads ominously; my nearest friend inquired cautiously whether there was any taint of insanity in the family; an old gray-haired lady, a veritable saint, who had not been soured by her many deeds of charity, admonished me on the utter selfishness and godlessness of such a proceeding. . . . As for the hermit . . . having found it impossible to educe any meaning from the tangled habits of mankind while he himself was whirled about in the imbroglio, he had determined to try the efficiency of undisturbed meditation at a distance. So deficient had been his education that he was actually better acquainted with the aspirations and emotions of the old dwellers on the Ganges than with those of the modern toilers by the Hudson or the Potomac. He had been deafened by the "Indistinguishable roar" of the streets, and could make no sense of the noisy jargon of the market place.[2]

The period gave him time to read, leisurely, thoughtfully, with no nervous subconsciousness that the product of that reading was to be marketable. When he wrote his first papers he wrote with no press of need upon him. He had evolved his own notion of the function of literature and of the critic. This was what he evolved: and it is worthy of study:

There is a kind of criticism that limits itself to looking at the thing in itself, or at the parts of a thing as they successively strike the mind.

[1] *Shelburne Essays*, Second Series.
[2] "A Hermit's Note on Thoreau." *Shelburne Essays*, First Series.

This is properly the way of sympathy, and those who choose this way are right in saying that it is absurd or merely ill-tempered to dwell on what is ugly in a work of art, or false, or incomplete. But there is a place, also for another kind of criticism, which is not so much directed to the individual thing as to its relation with other things, and to its place as cause or effect in a whole group of tendencies. No criticism, to be sure, can follow one or the other of these methods exclusively, as no product of art can ever be entirely isolated in its genesis or altogether merged in the current of the day. The highest criticism would contrive to balance these methods in such manner that neither the occasional merits of a work nor its general influence would be unduly subordinated, and in so far as these essays fail to strike such a balance—I wish this were their only failure—they err sadly from the best model.[3]

In the eight volumes now issued there are eighty-five essays on topics as varied as George Crabbe, Hawthorne, Swinburne, Walt Whitman, The Bhagavad Gita, Pascal, Plato, Nietzsche. Nearly two-thirds of them all deal with representative English writers; some fifteen have to do with Americans. In the criticizing of them he has held steadfastly to the contention that men of letters are to be viewed not alone as individuals but as voices and as spiritual leaders in their generations. The soul of literature is not art and it is not alone beauty. For decadents like Swinburne he has small sympathy and he can even rebuke Charles Lamb for "his persistent refusal to face, in words at least, the graver issues of life." He takes his stand at a point so elevated that only the great masters who have been the original voices of the race are audible. He dares even to speak of "the jaunty optimism of Emerson," and to suggest that his confidence and serenity were all too often taken by his generation for original wisdom.

The foundation of his work is religious—religious in the fundamental, the oriental, sense of the word. He has been consistent and he has been courageous. That America has a critic with standards of criticism, an official critic in the sense that Sainte-Beuve was official, and that as editor of the leading critical review of America this critic has a dominating clientele and a leader's authority, is one of the most promising signs for that new literary era which already is overdue.

[3] *Shelburne Essays,* Eighth Series. Preface.

BIBLIOGRAPHY

CHARLES DUDLEY WARNER. (1829–1900.) *My Summer in a Garden,*
1870; *Saunterings,* 1872; *Backlog Studies,* 1872; *The Gilded Age* [with
Mark Twain], 1873; *Baddeck, and That Sort of Thing,* 1874; *My Winter
on the Nile Among the Mummies and Moslems,* 1876; *In the Levant,* 1877;
Being a Boy, 1877; *In the Wilderness,* 1878; *Washington Irving,* 1881;
Captain John Smith, 1881; *A Roundabout Journey,* 1884; *Their Pilgrimage,* 1887; *On Horseback: a Tour in Virginia, North Carolina, and Tennessee, with Notes on Travel in Mexico and California,* 1888; *Studies in the
South and West, with Comments on Canada,* 1889; *A Little Journey in
the World: a Novel,* 1889; *Our Italy,* 1891; *As We Were Saying,* 1891;
As We Go, 1894; *The Golden House,* 1895; *The People for Whom Shakespeare Wrote,* 1897; *The Relation of Literature to Life,* 1897; *That Fortune: a Novel,* 1899; *Fashions in Literature and Other Essays,* 1902; Complete works, 15 vols. Edited by T. R. Lounsbury, 1904; *Charles Dudley
Warner,* by Mrs. James T. Fields, 1904.

LAFCADIO HEARN. (1850–1904.) *Stray Leaves from Strange Literatures:
Stories from the Anvari-Soheili, Baitál-Packisi, Mahabharata, etc.,* 1884;
Gombo Zhèbes, 1885; *Some Chinese Ghosts,* 1887; *Chita: a Memory of Last
Island,* 1889; *Two Years in the French West Indies,* 1890; *Youma: the
Story of a West Indian Slave,* 1890; *Glimpses of Unfamiliar Japan,* 1894;
Out of the East: Reveries and Studies in New Japan, 1895; *Kokoro: Hints
and Echoes of Japanese Inner Life,* 1896; *Gleanings in Buddha-fields:
Studies of Hand and Soul in the Far East,* 1897; *Exotics and Retro-
spectives,* 1899; *In Ghostly Japan,* 1899; *Shadowings,* 1900; *Japanese
Miscellany,* 1901; *Kotto: Being Japanese Curios with Sundry Cobwebs,*
1902; *Japanese Fairy Tales,* 1903; *Kwaidan,* 1904; *Japan: an Attempt at
Interpretation,* 1904; *The Romance of the Milky Way and Other Studies,*
1905; *Letters from the Raven: the Correspondence of Lafcadio Hearn
with Henry Watkin,* 1905, 1907; *Life and Letters of Lafcadio Hearn,* 2
vols., by Elizabeth Bisland, 1906; *Concerning Lafcadio Hearn,* with a Bib-
liography by Laura Stedman, by G. M. Gould, 1908; *Japanese Letters of
Lafcadio Hearn,* edited by Elizabeth Bisland, 1910; *Leaves from the Diary
of an Impressionist: Early Writings;* with an Introduction by Ferris
Greenslet, 1911; *Lafcadio Hearn in Japan,* by Y. Noguchi, 1911; *Lafcadio
Hearn,* by N. H. Kennard, 1912; *Lafcadio Hearn,* by E. Thomas, 1912;
Fantastics and Other Fancies, with an Introduction by Dr. Charles W.
Hutson, 1914.

AGNES REPPLIER. (1857———.) *Books and Men,* 1888; *Points of View,*
1891; *Essays in Miniature,* 1892; *Essays in Idleness,* 1893; *In the Dozy
Hours and Other Papers,* 1894; *Varia,* 1897; *Philadelphia, the Place and
the People,* 1898; *The Fireside Sphinx,* 1901; *Compromises,* 1904; *In Our
Convent Days,* 1905; *A Happy Half Century,* 1908; *Americans and Others,*
1912; *The Cat,* 1912.

PAUL ELMER MORE. (1864———.) *Helena, and Occasional Poems,* 1890;
The Great Refusal: Letters of a Dreamer in Gotham, 1894; *A Century of*

Indian Epigrams; Chiefly from the Sanscrit of Bhartrihari, 1898; *Shelburne Essays*, First series, 1904; Second and Third series, 1905; Fourth series, 1906; Fifth series, 1908; Sixth series, 1909; Seventh series, 1910; Eighth series, 1913; *Nietzsche*, 1912.

INDEX